The darker side of Restoration politics is the subject of this book, which provides the first history and analysis of the intelligence and espionage activities of the regime of Charles II (1660–85). It is concerned with the mechanics, activities and philosophy of the intelligence system which developed under the auspices of the office of the Secretary of State and which emerged in the face of the problems of conspiracy as well as international politics. It aims to show how the Restoration regime operated in this covert world through the development of intelligence networks on a local and international level, the use made of the Post Office, as well as codes and ciphers, and the employment of spies, informers and assassins. The careers of a number of spies employed by the regime are examined through a series of detailed case studies. The book takes a revisionist stance, providing a balanced and objective portrait of the dark byways of the Restoration politics particularly in the 1660s and 1670s and seeks to fill the gap in the current historical literature.

Cambridge Studies in Early Modern British History

INTELLIGENCE AND ESPIONAGE IN THE REIGN OF CHARLES II, 1660–1685

Cambridge Studies in Early Modern British History

This is a series of monographs and studies covering many aspects of the history of the British Isles between the late fifteenth century and the early eighteenth century. It includes the work of established scholars and pioneering work by a new generation of scholars. It includes both reviews and revisions of major topics and books, which open up new historical terrain or which reveal startling new perspectives on familiar subjects. All the volumes set detailed research into our broader perspectives and the books are intended for the use of students as well as of their teachers.

For a list of titles in the series, see end of book.

INTELLIGENCE AND ESPIONAGE IN THE REIGN OF CHARLES II, 1660–1685

ALAN MARSHALL

Department of History,
Bath College of Higher Education

Published by the Press Syndicate of the University of Cambridge
The Pitt Building, Trumpington Street, Cambridge CB2 1RP
40 West 20th Street, New York, NY 10011–4211, USA
10 Stamford Road, Oakleigh, Melbourne, 3166, Australia

First published 1994

Printed in Great Britain at the University Press, Cambridge

A catalogue record for this book is available from the British Library

Library of Congress cataloguing in publication data

Marshall, Alan, 1957–
Intelligence and espionage in the reign of Charles II,
1660–1685 / Alan Marshall.
p. cm. – (Cambridge studies in early modern British history)
Based on the author's thesis (Ph.D, University of Lancaster, 1991).
Includes bibliographical references and index.
ISBN 0 521 43180 8
1. Great Britain – History – Charles II, 1660–1685. 2. Intelligence service – Great Britain – History – 17th century. 3. Espionage – Great Britain – History – 17th century.
I. Title. II. Series.
DA448.M37 1994 93–44477
363.2'83'094109032 – dc20 CIP

ISBN 0 521 43180 8 hardback

CE

For my parents and my sister

'Mix with hired slaves, bravos, and common stabbers,
Nose-slitters, alley-lurking villains ... join
With such a crew and take a ruffian's wages
To cut the throats of wretches as they sleep.'

Thomas Otway, *Venice Preserved* (1682), Act III

Bring not every man into thine house; for many are the plots of the deceitful man ... and as one that is a spy, he looketh upon thy falling. For he lieth in wait to turn things that are good into evil; and in things that are praiseworthy he will lay blame ... Receive [such] a stranger into thine house and he will distract thee with brawls, and estrange thee from thine own.

Ecclesiasticus, xi, verses 32–4

CONTENTS

ACKNOWLEDGEMENTS

The production of historical monographs being something which is invariably a combined effort, there are a number of people and institutions to thank for helping this particular project reach fruition. The original research work was funded partly by a British Academy grant as well as a Scoluoudi History Research Fellowship at the Institute of Historical Research. I am grateful to both of these institutions for their assistance. I should also like to thank the Twenty-Seven Foundation for providing a grant to finance some further research for the book. Equally I must also thank my history colleagues at Bath College of Higher Education who tried hard to make the teaching load lighter. I also wish to thank the staff of the following libraries and record offices which I visited during the course of the research for this book who were most helpful in answering enquiries and providing access to the relevant manuscript material as well as books: the Bodleian Library in Oxford; the British Library; Codrington Library, All Souls College, Oxford; Cumbria Record Office (Carlisle); Cumbria Record Office (Kendal); Downing College Library, Cambridge; Durham University Library and Archives; Edinburgh University Library; the Greater London Record Office; the House of Lords Record Office; the Institute of Historical Research Library; Kent Record Office; Lancaster University Library; the Newcastle Literary and Philosophical Society Library (a never failing source for books otherwise unobtainable elsewhere); Newcastle University Library; the Public Records Office in Chancery Lane, where the documents in their care were always produced with promptness; Queens College Library, Oxford, as well as Westminster City Archives.

On a personal level there are many people who assisted in seeing this project through to completion from its first inception as an original Ph.D thesis submitted to the University of Lancaster in 1991. Above all are the late Professor Geoffrey Holmes and Dr John Morrill who jointly supervised the original thesis and whose help, friendship and advice I have greatly valued. Special thanks to John Morrill who read the complete manuscript and whose advice and comments were unfailingly helpful. As this book was reaching its final stages I learned sadly of the death of Geoff Holmes after a long illness. I was especially grateful to Geoff Holmes whose pupil I was, and it can be truthfully said that if this book has some merits then Geoff's teaching and friendship will invariably have been responsible for them. He will be sorely missed.

A number of people have also given of their time and interest to provide comments, assistance or merely listen to various sections of this book in draft form. In particular I should like to thank Ian Roy, John Miller, Stuart Handley, Mark Knights, David Hayton, Ella Holmes, David Davies, Graham Ford, Nick Drew, Paul Hyland, Shiela Smith, Janet Clare, Paul Hopkins, Maggie Collins (for all those Inter-Library loans at Bath), Tania Hajjar, Dorothy Gardner; Professor Eric Evans and Professor J. R. Jones examined the original Ph.D thesis and their comments were also very helpful. Last, but by no means least, I am eternally grateful for the advice, help, encouragement and support of Claire Tylee who made it all worthwhile.

ABBREVIATIONS

Abbott, 'English Conspiracy'	W. C. Abbott, 'English Conspiracy and Dissent, 1660–1674', *American Historical Review*, 14, 1909, pp. 503–38, 696–722
Add.	Additional Manuscripts
Ashcraft, *Revolutionary Politics*	R. Ashcraft, *Revolutionary Politics and Locke's 'Two Treatises of Government'* (Princeton, 1986)
Barbour, *Arlington*	V. Barbour, *Henry Bennet Earl of Arlington Secretary of State to Charles II* (Washington D.C., 1914)
Arlington's Letters	T. Bebington, *The Right Honourable the Earl of Arlington's Letters to Sir William Temple and to the Several Ambassadors to Spain* (1701)
BDBR	*Biographical Dictionary of British Radicals of the Seventeenth Century*, edited by R. Greaves and R. Zaller (3 vols., Brighton, 1982–4)
Bod. Lib.	Bodleian Library, Oxford
BL	British Library, London
Browning, *Danby*	A. Browning, *Thomas Osborne Earl of Danby and Duke of Leeds, 1632–1712* (3 vols., Glasgow, 1951)
Burnet, *History*	G. Burnet, *History of My Own Time*, edited by O. Airy (2 vols., Oxford, 1897–1900)
CCLSP	*Calendar of the Clarendon State Papers Preserved in the Bodleian Library*, edited by O. Ogle, W. H. Bliss, W. D. Macray and F. J. Routledge (5 vols., Oxford, 1869–1970)

Clarendon, *Life*	Clarendon, *The History of the Rebellion and Civil Wars in England also His Life Written by Himself in which is included a Continuation of his History of the Grand Rebellion* (Oxford, 1843)
CSPCol.	*Calendar of State Papers Colonial Series: America and the West Indies*, edited by N. Sainsbury (1860–)
CSPD	*Calendar of State Papers, Domestic Series of the Reign of Charles II*, edited by M. A. E. Green, F. H. Blackburne-Daniel and F. Bickely (28 vols., 1860–1939)
CSPV	*Calendar of State Papers and Manuscripts Relating to English Affairs, Existing in the Archives and Collections of Venice*, edited by R. Brown (1884–)
CT Bks	*Calendar of Treasury Books, 1660– Preserved in the Public Record Office*, edited by W. A. Shaw (1904–)
DNB	*The Dictionary of National Biography*, edited by L. Stephen and S. Lee (63 vols., 1885–1900)
EHR	*English Historical Review*
Essex Papers	*Essex Papers, 1672–1679*, edited by O. Airy, Camden Society (2 vols., 1890–1913)
Evans, *Principal Secretary*	F. M. G. Evans (Higham), *The Principal Secretary of State: A Survey of the Office from 1558 to 1680* (Manchester, 1923)
Evelyn, *Diary*	*The Diary of John Evelyn*, edited by E. S. Beer (6 vols., Oxford, 1955)
Flemings in Oxford	*The Flemings in Oxford Being Documents Selected from the Rydal Papers in Illustration of the Lives and Ways of Oxford Men, 1650–1700*, edited by J. R. Magrath (3 vols., Oxford, 1904–24)
Greaves, *Deliver Us From Evil*	R. L. Greaves, *Deliver Us From Evil: The Radical Underground in Britain, 1660–1663* (Oxford, 1986)
Greaves, *Enemies Under His Feet*	R. L. Greaves, *Enemies Under His Feet: Radicals and Nonconformists in Britain 1664–1667* (Stanford, 1990)

Greaves, *Secrets of the Kingdom*	R. L. Greaves, *Secrets of the Kingdom: British Radicals from the Popish Plot to the Glorious Revolution of 1688–89* (Stanford, 1992)
Grey, *Debates*	A. Grey, *Debates of the House of Commons* (10 vols., 1769)
Haley, *William of Orange*	K. H. D. Haley, *William of Orange and the English Opposition 1672–4* (Oxford, 1953)
Haley, *Shaftesbury*	K. H. D. Haley, *The First Earl of Shaftesbury* (Oxford, 1968)
HJ	*Historical Journal*
HLQ	*Huntington Library Quarterly*
HMC	*Historical Manuscript Commission, 1st–12th Reports*; Buccleuch MSS; Downshire MSS; Earl of Westmorland; Finch MSS; Heathcote MSS; House of Lords MSS; Le Fleming MSS; Ormonde MSS; Various Collections
H of P	*The History of Parliament: The House of Commons, 1660–1690*, edited by B. D. Henning (3 vols., 1983)
Hutton, *Charles II*	R. Hutton, *Charles II King of England, Scotland and Ireland* (1989)
Hutton, *Restoration*	R. Hutton, *The Restoration: A Political and Religious History of England and Wales* (Oxford, 1985)
Lister, *Clarendon*	T. H. Lister, *The Life and Administration of Edward, First Earl of Clarendon* (3 vols., 1837–8)
Ludlow, *Memoirs*	*The Memoirs of Edmund Ludlow, Lieutenant-General of the Horse in the Army of the Commonwealth of England 1625–1672*, edited by C. H. Firth (2 vols., 1894)
Ludlow, *Voyce*	*Edmund Ludlow 'A Voyce From the Watch Tower Part Five: 1660–1662'*, edited by A. B. Worden, Camden Fourth Series, 21 (1978), pp. 721–934. Any references thereafter are from Bod. Lib. MSS Eng. Hist. c.487, 'Edmund Ludlow, A Voyce From the Watchtower'

Machiavelli, *Discourses*	N. Machiavelli, *The Discourses on Government*, edited by B. Crick (Harmondsworth, 1979)
Magalotti, *Relazione*	*Lorenzo Magalotti At the Court of Charles II: His Relazione d'Inghilterre of 1668–9*, edited and translated by W. E. Knowles-Middleton (Ontario, 1980)
Marshall, 'Blood'	A. Marshall, 'Colonel Thomas Blood and the Restoration Political Scene', *HJ* 32, 3, 1989, pp. 561–82
Miscellanea Aulica	*Miscellanea Aulica: Or a Collection of State Treatises Never Before Published*, edited by T. Brown (1702)
Nicholas Papers	*The Nicholas Papers: The Correspondence of Sir Edward Nicholas*, edited by G. E. Warner, Camden Society (4 vols., 1887–1920)
Pepys, *Diary*	*The Diary of Samuel Pepys*, edited by R. Latham and W. Matthews (11 vols., 1970–83)
PP	*Past and Present*
PRO	Public Record Office, London
Remarks	R. H., 'Remarks on the Life and Death of the Famed Mr Blood' (1680), printed in *The Somers Tracts* (2nd collection, 1748–52), iii, pp. 219–35
RO	Record Office
Rowen, *De Witt*	H. H. Rowen, *John de Witt, Grand Pensionary of Holland, 1625–1672* (Princeton, 1978)
Sainty, *Secretaries of State*	J. C. Sainty, *Officials of the Secretaries of State 1660–1782*, Office Holders in Modern Britain Series (1973)
Sprunger, *Dutch Puritanism*	K. L. Sprunger, *Dutch Puritanism: A History of the English and Scottish Churches in the Netherlands in the 16th and 17th Centuries* (Leiden, 1982)
SP	State Papers

State Trials	T. B. Howell, *State Trials* (21 vols., 1816)
Swart, *Netherland-Historian*	S. Swart, *The Netherland-Historian, A True and Exact Relation of the Late Warrs [1672] to the End of the Year 1674* (Amsterdam, 1675)
Thurloe State Papers	*The State Papers of John Thurloe*, edited by T. Birch (7 vols., 1742)
TRHS	*Transactions of the Royal Historical Society*
Underdown, *Royalist Conspiracy*	D. Underdown, *Royalist Conspiracy in England 1649–1660* (New Haven, 1960)
Williamson Correspondence	*Letters Addressed to Sir Joseph Williamson While Plenipotentiary at the Congress of Cologne in the Years 1672–1674*, edited by W. D. Christie, Camden Society (2 vols., 1874)

Place of publication is London, unless otherwise stated.

Introduction

I

In his secret paper, 'A Brief Discourse Concerning the Nature and Reason of Intelligence', written during the course of the reign of William III, Sir Samuel Morland, who had served the regimes of both Oliver Cromwell and Charles II in the secret dealings of government, attempted to capture the rationale and philosophy behind the Restoration regime's intelligence system. The foundation of the philosophy which Morland outlined was clarity itself. His view was that all mankind possessed a fallen nature and thus was unable to be held to anything in political life if his vital interests, his survival and need for power, were threatened, Morland's political man was 'governed wholly by politick maxims'[1] and while this was most visible in the relations between nation-states such tendencies were equally visible in the relationship between government and people. In such relationships the sanctions laid down by religion had little effect, for men merely paid lip service to keeping the 'most sacred promise[s] & solemn agreements', which were as 'easily broke[n] as Sampson's cords'.[2] In such a philosophy nothing could be ruled out that gave an advantage to 'political man'. As the ruler mistrusted his neighbour in international politics so he should also mistrust his own people. Given this situation it was beholden upon the ruler to discover and assess the 'tempers of his own subjects' as well as 'the first ferments of all factions; in order to manage the 'lopping men of so many different parties & the Heroes of the populace'.[3] This was particularly true of England, for the English, according to Morland, were an especially difficult people, being 'untam'd horses [who] have thrown their unskilful riders many times within these fifty years'.[4] The key to controlling and governing an essentially anarchical world, or so Morland

[1] BL Add. MSS 47133, fos. 8–13. Compare these views with those of Dudley Bradstreet in Chapter 5.

[2] BL Add. MSS 47133, fos. 8–13. Morland's view of mankind is similar to that expressed by Machiavelli. See N. Machievelli, *The Prince* (Oxford, 1984), p. 56.

[3] BL Add. MSS 47133, fos. 8–13. [4] *ibid.*

believed, lay in intelligence and espionage activities directed so as to prevent any problems. Good intelligence, as another contemporary put it, was often 'the mother of prevention'.[5] The unsavoury activities intelligence work involved on the early modern scene were thus seen as vital to the arts of government. A neglect of them could lead 'a Prince [to] lose his Crown or life'.[6] In spite of the obvious importance Morland laid upon them the intelligence and espionage activities of the Caroline regime during the period 1660–85 have been somewhat neglected by most historians and it is the purpose of the present work to examine in detail the mechanics of the Restoration regime's intelligence system, its concerns, both domestic and foreign, as well as the philosophy which lay behind it. In short this book is an attempt to throw some light on the darker areas of Restoration politics.[7]

Until comparatively recently the subject of intelligence itself had undoubtedly suffered from neglect by academic historians. In the political history of most periods it has usually been the 'missing dimension'.[8] It was missing because of the alleged difficulties imposed by the sources, or the claim that such secret activities lacked a real historical record. The non-availability of a historical record was thought only to be matched by the large degree of myth-making which went on in the popular historical works on the subject. And indeed the popular history of intelligence has had a strong tendency to regurgitate old myths, invariably ignoring the more interesting reality which lies beyond them, and in so doing has done the subject something of a disservice.[9] In the early modern period at least, the archives can produce a wealth of illuminating evidence about the dark underbelly of the politics of the period. Moreover the historian does not suffer from the same restrictions which are forced upon his colleagues studying in the modern era.[10] Naturally enough these documents, as with

[5] Durham University Library MSS, Cosin Letter Books, 1 (b), 132, I. Basire to Sir P. Musgrave, 17 May 1665. See also D. Defoe, *A Dialogue Betwixt Whig and Tory, alias Williamite and Jacobite* (1693), p. xi; G. Monck, *Observations on Military and Political Affairs* (1796), p. 61.

[6] BL Add. MSS 47133, fos. 8–13.

[7] Previous work on this subject is now rather dated; see P. M. Fraser, *The Intelligence of the Secretaries of State 1660–1688* (Cambridge, 1956), which is mainly concerned with the newsletter system and was in any case never intended to be comprehensive. See also J. Walker, 'The Secret Service Under Charles II and James II', *TRHS*, 4th series, 15, 1932, pp. 211–35, an article derived from his original Ph.D thesis 'The Republican Party in England From the Restoration to the Revolution (1660–1688)' University of Manchester, 1930–1.

[8] C. Andrew and D. Dilks, eds., *The Missing Dimension: Governments and Intelligence Communities in the Twentieth Century* (1985), p. 2.

[9] Examples of this abound; see R. Deacon, *A History of the British Secret Service* (1982) as one example.

[10] Restrictions on access to documents are the major problem here. Of the plethora of works on the modern period few can be highly recommended, one of the exceptions being C. Andrew, *Secret Service: The Making of the British Intelligence Community* (1986).

all historical records, have their problems. There are many of what S. R. Gardiner once labelled the 'ragged ends'[11] of history in the stories which emerge from the archives, but once the popular misconceptions have been scraped away, this area of government can provide a valuable insight into both the psychology as well as some of the methods of early modern government. At the least it provides an understanding of the means by which the regime of Charles II operated in the murky underworld of the political history of the period.

Intelligence, of course, can simply mean 'evaluated information' and in our period this use of the term was common enough, but it also denoted a wide variety of covert government activities related to the security of the Stuart regime. In essence there were, and still are to some extent, two sides to this aspect of intelligence. The first of these related to the gathering of information by a variety of means, some legal, others less so. The second was what we might term a 'police and security' dimension which could have either defensive or offensive capacities. In order to function as a government the Stuart regime needed to gather information which enabled it to take the actual decisions of government at its highest levels. From this basic requirement it logically followed that information not easily obtainable had to be obtained covertly. Hence the development of the regime's espionage activities. It was a development common to most governments of the period.

In the case of England such activities had and always have lacked a certain degree of continuity. In the English nation-state much seems to have depended upon the presence of the dynamic individual in government who came to see it as his duty to provide such services. This was true from the sixteenth century and was to remain so until at least the beginning of the twentieth century. The role of the individual in such obscure and often inglorious areas of government was therefore a significant one and it will be seen most obviously in the prominent figure of Sir Joseph Williamson. Having said this it is also possible to perceive from the late sixteenth century onwards a bureaucracy growing up to deal with the problem in the shadows of the nation-state. Intelligence work was always linked to diplomacy and this as well as the problem of domestic dissent came under the auspices of the office of the Secretary of State. This office in particular took a leading role in intelligence work. The reasoning behind this is dealt with

One of the most disappointing is B. Porter, *Plots and Paranoia: A History of Political Espionage in Britain, 1790–1988* (1989). While Porter has interesting and important things to say, the numerous attempts to be 'amusing', whether deliberate or not, ultimately tend to become merely irritating and to devalue the book as a whole.

[11] See S. R. Gardiner, *What the Gunpowder Plot Was* (1897) for more on this.

more fully below,[12] but the major figures in the English intelligence world of the early modern period, including Francis Walsingham, Robert Cecil, John Thurloe, Sir Henry Bennet, Earl of Arlington, Joseph Williamson, and Robert Harley, invariably seem to have held this office or to have been associated with it. Yet as has already been noted there was never a great deal of continuity in intelligence and espionage matters from one reign to another and lessons learned in one reign frequently had to be relearned at a later date.[13] Only in the 1660s with the establishment of the English Republic did espionage begin to be taken more seriously by the state. It became regarded as something not merely to be provided only by the personally inspired minister, but as an accepted part of state business. That this should take place in the somewhat innovative 1650s is natural enough perhaps, for the main factor which led to this development was a growing concern over security and, as fear of domestic dissent and internal rebellion were to plague the majority of the post-Civil War regimes until well into the early nineteenth century, there was a corresponding growth in covert intelligence gathering. Information and security became the mainsprings during the 1650s in pushing forward the development of intelligence activities in an English context and this was carried forward into the reign of Charles II.

The tools used by the government in either of these capacities will become clear as the present work unfolds. On the espionage front, however, it might be said that six main sources of gathering covert information existed in this period. The first, and most notorious, of these was the spy. The spy was an individual who was recruited, authorised, or instructed to obtain information for intelligence purposes, or to act against the regime's enemies. An informer on the other hand could be distinguished from a spy by the fact that he or she was normally connected with the legal system and had personally initiated his or her investigations and accusations, usually for financial gain. Informers might later come under

[12] See Chapter 1.

[13] The exception, as always, remained English activities in Ireland. Anglo-Irish relations in this area are, as yet, only unevenly covered by historians and concentration has remained largely in the late eighteenth and early nineteenth centuries. Hardly anything at all has been undertaken on this subject by historians of the Stuart period. Indeed little is said on the Irish side of such affairs in what follows. It remains a large task and would necessitate another equally large book. An interesting comparison with the period with which this book deals is the England of the 1790s. See H. T. Dickinson, *British Radicalism and the French Revolution 1789–1815* (1985); R. Wells, *Insurrection: The British Experience, 1795–1803* (Gloucester, 1973); W. J. Fitzpatrick, *Secret Service Under Pitt* (1892); C. Emsley, 'The Home Office and Its Sources of Information and Investigation, 1791–1801', *EHR*, 94, 1979, pp. 532–61; M. Hutt, 'Spies in France, 1793–1808', *History Today*, 12, 1962, pp. 158–67; J. L. Baxter and F. K. Donnelly, 'The Revolutionary "Underground" in the West Riding: Myth or Reality?', *PP* 64, pp. 124–32.

the control of the government but invariably initiated their careers by themselves. Hence the regime usually acted in a passive rather than active capacity in the case of such people. A further source was that of unsolicited information. This emerged from a general pool of undirected or casual sources. Many old scores were paid off by this means and such information was more often than not untrustworthy, but still taken seriously. On the local level the newly installed regime had access to the work of the county and parish officers. These ranged from Lords Lieutenant, to militia officers, justices of the peace and down to the humble parish constable. To supplement this there was the interception of correspondence through the Post Office; a longstanding means by which early modern governments could gather information and keep a wary eye on the opinions of their people. Finally the diplomatic corps provided an international dimension to the Stuart regime's intelligence activities. Diplomacy and war brought with them endless opportunities for gathering illicit information. In the seventeenth century in particular diplomacy was merely warfare by other means and espionage remained its cutting edge.

This book therefore examines not only the inheritance left to the Caroline regime in this area by the Republic, but the work of the regime through the use of such sources. The first chapter deals with the central control and development of the English intelligence system from 1660 to 1685, especially the major role played by the office of the Secretary of State. Chapter 2 examines the use made by the Caroline regime of the Post Office for intelligence purposes as well as the use of codes and ciphers. In Chapter 3 there is an examination of intelligence activities on the local scene, particularly in the north of England during the early 1660s. Chapters 4, 5 and 6 examine the world of the spies on the ground, their recruitment, numbers and instructions, as well as individual case studies of some of the spies who found themselves employed by the Stuart regime. Chapter 7 examines English 'secret services' in the context of the foreign and diplomatic scene, while the final chapter deals with the problem of assassination in an English context.

II

John Morrill has noted that the 'Revolution proved [to be] a curious kind of Cheshire cat, it vanished leaving only a scowl behind.'[14] How significant, frightening, or dangerous this scowl was is a contentious element in Restoration historiography and historians of the period have usually

[14] J. Morrill, Introduction to *Revolution and Restoration, England in the 1650s* (1992), p. 14.

divided into two camps over this question. There are those who believe that the threat from conspiracy and plots was in reality negligible and has been overrated, and there are those who claim the restored regime faced a very serious threat from day one of its existence. Understanding the reality of the threat the regime faced is crucial in many respects, as part of the justification for the creation of the regime's intelligence system in the 1660s was to counter this threat and to maintain the Stuart regime's security against its radical enemies. Clearly then this problem of the 'radical underground', as one historian has labelled part of the opposition to the regime, is an important one.[15]

Even by European standards early modern England had a notorious reputation for violence, instability and rebellion. In 1660 foreign observers of the English scene were quickly assessing the chances of the new royal regime surviving on the 'merry-go-round' of English politics. Two decades of political instability and the effects of civil war could not be lightly shaken off. While the return of the king in May 1660 was greeted with noisy and drunken protestations of loyalty, the celebrations of May 1660 concealed a troubled nation, uncertain and traumatised by its experiences. The continuity of the 1650s with the post-1660 situation has until recently been underestimated. There were many political, religious and social problems to deal with and clearly not everyone could be satisfied. Many were soon to feel as alienated from the untrustworthy group of politicians who now ran the country as they had once been from the generals of the 1650s. For amongst certain elements of the population Charles II and his new regime were also unpopular. Benefit of hindsight has tended to obscure this point. The king himself did not help his cause. He was a man who had spent most of his adult life in foreign parts, to whom English ways were somewhat alien, and who was rumoured to be a Roman Catholic, or at least of doubtful religious persuasion. Charles, it should be recalled, was also the king who had been stigmatised by republican propagandists as a 'young Tarquin' and with his somewhat chaotic lifestyle and cynical personality the new king certainly tried to live up to that character's vices. Moreover the complex and secretive nature of his character set the tone for the regime. Morally bankrupt himself, Charles II had a talent for obscuring his motives which was matched only by his servants' greed for power and position. Indeed the king's ministers themselves were men of contradictory loyalties. While some had served him in exile, others had served the Lord Protector, but for the most part after 1660 they worked hard at serving themselves. To add to this impression there remained deep-rooted political and religious problems in the country. The arrival of the monarchy had

[15] So labelled by Richard Greaves; for more on his work see below.

certainly not solved these and Restoration England therefore was a country living under the shadow of the past. While the newly launched ship of state might look secure on the surface, underneath it was threatened with the barnacles of the previous twenty years and, some thought, with a crew who were soon navigating it towards the rocks.

The undercurrent of criticism of the restored monarchy came to the ears of the new regime in a number of ways. One of the means by which the regime gained a first impression of its relationship with the people was through the numbers of prosecutions for seditious words.[16] It is clear that indictments for seditious words can be variously read; they tell us as much about those who brought the prosecutions to show their loyalty as those who expressed the opinions which got them into trouble. Indictments invariably rose and fell with the political circumstances, the level of interest and the concern over security on a national and local level. In any case by 1660 political comments had become commonplace in English alehouses and taverns and such comments could not be easily suppressed. The failure of censorship during the wars, as well as the freedom of speech that had so characterised the previous eleven years, left as a legacy at the Restoration the view that it was part of the Englishman's birthright to grumble about the times. Certainly in the Restoration period there were at least two major phases of hostility which can be traced in such indictments; 1660–5 and 1679–85.[17] In the first phase those who were self-conscious supporters of the collapsed republican regime became mixed with those who related salacious gossip about the new king and his family. It has reasonably been argued that the latter elements sprang from a long tradition of anti-popery and xenophobia which were in part a critique of the failure of reform of both the church and state. They were linked to the longstanding fear of the subversion of the protestant state by a pro-Catholic monarch and his 'corrupt' court. As the various political and diplomatic crises broke over the state these were also added to the mix, with more general complaints about government policy and even some nostalgia for the past strengths of the Cromwellian regime, which with its demise began to take on the usual mythological overtones of a 'golden age' and not just amongst its previous supporters.[18] There were also tinges of millennarianism in this period, indeed the millennarian element tended to take comfort from the disasters

[16] For some work on seditious words see P. K. Monod, *Jacobitism and the English People, 1688–1788* (Cambridge, 1993), pp. 233–66.

[17] Much of the following is based on B. Sharp, 'Popular Political Opinion in England 1660–1685', *History of European Ideas*, 10, 1989, pp. 13–29; also T. Harris, *London Crowds in the Reign of Charles II: Propaganda and Politics from the Restoration until the Exclusion Crisis* (Cambridge, 1987), pp. 50–1 *et passim*.

[18] See the comments of Pepys, *Diary*, IV, p. 367; VIII, pp. 249, 322.

of the early 1660s, contemplating them with some satisfaction. Many of the complaints about the king reflected not only a suspicion of his religion, but also his sexuality, his unfathomable motivation and the corrupt nature of the court he ruled. The latter was a recurrent problem of the Stuart dynasty's occupation of the throne and stemmed from underlying fears of popery and arbitrary government. One individual, for example, expressed the view that Charles II would undoubtedly bring in 'superstition and popery and that we must fall down againe [to] worshipp stocks and images' while another hoped 'before ... three years goe about [to] see [further] alteration in government'.[19] Fears of popery and, by implication, arbitrary government, were thus deeply embedded in the English psyche and, as the Venetian ambassador noted, there was no lack of 'evil humours' in the nation to 'rekindle civil strife'.[20] While most of what we may term the 'good old cause' critique had begun to fade by the 1670s, only to be adopted in some later Whig propaganda, the anti-popish rhetoric swiftly replaced it and was to find another target in the converted Catholic James, Duke of York.

What is clear is that viewing the Restoration from the back alleyways of its political life provides further evidence that 1660 was never such a watershed as was once claimed. The state lived under the shadow of the events of the 1640s and 1650s and the politicians within it were operating with all the mental baggage of that period. This undoubtedly shaped their responses to criticism, as well as to the practical problems of government. The fear of the 'fanaticks' return was initially strong upon them and mixed with the problems of the church settlement and dissent. They were a generation of politicians who were riven with faction, hostility, the rhetoric of anti-popery and hatred of the 'fanaticks' and who worked in a morally bankrupt court. They came to expect hostility from their political rivals and naturally expected it from their old enemies. The exiles amongst them also had first-hand experience of attempting to overthrow governments through conspiracy and rebellion. They had suffered, fought and plotted their way through the 1650s and Charles and his key ministers brought all of these experiences into government with them. In any case the royalists and Cromwellians who made up the government were used to plots as a part of political life. They expected trouble and were not about to be caught out, by rebels, dissenters or 'fanaticks'.

One of the most crucial questions faced by the regime, of course, was the form a religious settlement should take, and on the religious problems of

[19] J. Raine, *Depositions From the Castle of York Relating to Offences Committed in the Northern Counties in the Seventeenth Century*, Surtees Society, 40 (1861), pp. 83, 93.
[20] *CSPV*, 1661–4, p. 40.

the country much has been written.[21] In many senses the religious problem began with Charles himself who, for a variety of motives, favoured toleration.[22] Liberty of conscience, however, was not something sought by others, particularly the newly restored Anglican bishops, and it was a concept cluttered with the burden of the past, as well as the practicalities of government in both church and state. In short it would be difficult to achieve. The re-emergence of the Anglican church and the loyalty in parliament which it invoked, the fear that liberal ideas in religion could bring only trouble in their wake and the belief that every dissenter was a potential regicide was matched with a singular inability, common in the seventeenth century as a whole, to see the other person's point of view. The result was the imposition of strict penal laws and the view that a nation weighed under the sins of the 1640s and 1650s should be purged of dissent. Persecution and repression naturally followed in the early 1660s. It was the insurrection of January 1661 by the Fifth Monarchists which provided another impetus to this. Again the impact of this event has often been underestimated. Thomas Venner and his men disrupted the streets of London for three days and created a situation in which all dissenters were linked to insurrection and plotting whether they liked it or not. In the aftermath of the rising the regime was flooded with accusations and rumours of plots. This general fear of dissent was something no amount of mutilation to the corpses of Cromwell, Ireton and Bradshaw on 30 January 1661, a mere twenty-four days after Venner's rising, could calm. As Pepys saw it, and his opinion was not uncommon in the government, it appeared that 'their work will be carried on, though they do die'.[23] One result of the rising was the creation of a new army; another effect was the stimulus it gave to the emergence of an effective intelligence system.

Venner's rising also increased the persecution of religious dissenters. A royal proclamation of 10 January 1661 banned all meetings of Baptists, Quakers and Fifth Monarchists in the wake of the rising and within weeks some 4,230 Quakers alone were languishing in gaol; other dissenters were harried and often incarcerated in vile conditions.[24] This persecution was not continuous and often hampered by the reluctance of local authorities to persecute neighbours, but it could be severe. The dissenters' response could take a number of forms including either continuing in their beliefs,

[21] See J. Spurr, *The Restoration Church of England, 1646–1689* (New Haven, 1991); I. M. Green, *The Re-Establishment of the Church of England 1660–1663* (Oxford, 1978); M. Watts, *The Dissenters From the Restoration to the French Revolution* (Oxford, 1985).

[22] Hutton, *Charles II*, pp. 182–4; J. Miller, *Charles II* (1991) p. 54.

[23] For the rising and a contemporary opinion see Pepys, *Diary*, II, pp. 7–8, 11; also C. Burrage, 'The Fifth Monarchy Insurrections', *EHR* 25, 1910, pp. 722–47.

[24] See G. R. Cragg, *Puritanism in The Period of the Great Persecution 1660–1688* (Cambridge, 1957), pp. 38–43.

as did the Quakers, and remaining defiant in the face of persecution or, they could compromise. The first choice meant persecution and hardship, while the second a sense of betrayal.[25] Another alternative was to take their religion underground, which is what occurred in many cases.[26] Dissent often entered a semi-twilight world of private meetings, in private houses or secret meetings in secluded places. Some Presbyterians even concealed their services under the guise of feasts, while other nonconformists took to holding services in places obscure enough to elude discovery. Meetings could be held at night, in concealed rooms or in the countryside. In the face of penal laws such as the Five Mile Act of 1665 some ministers were forced into using disguises, or into seeking protection from their congregations. Many historians of the period have seen such actions as unheroic, but effective in that religious dissent survived. But in contemporary terms these actions could also be taken another way. Such secret meetings could only mean one thing to a worried government and its supporters: treason and rebellion. In fact such secretive activities often rebounded on the religious dissenters, as they showed all the traditional signs of the plot. The problem for the dissenters was further compounded by an active hard core of troublemakers in whom the Stuart regime was particularly interested. It was these men, ex-soldiers, ex-ministers and ex-politicians, true rebels in word and deed, who were the real problem for the regime and, it might be said, for their fellow co-religionists, for the regime was consistently unable to distinguish between the vast majority of nonconformists who wanted freedom from persecution and a quiet life and the more dangerous radical element. These rebels were difficult to track down as they inhabited the twilight and shadows of London's meanest streets and alleys, or moved further afield in Ireland, the north of England and the Low Countries. These were the men who lived in the dark underbelly of Restoration politics, haunting coffee houses and taverns, scheming and plotting their days away. Despite their lack of numbers some of them were actually very dangerous and did represent a threat to the regime.

Within this context therefore we can now examine the problem of how far the plots faced by the regime were real or merely products of the Caroline regime's overheated imagination. It is of course essential to note that the mid-to-late seventeenth century was the era *par excellence* of plots, whether real or imagined, and some of the evidence of the many schemes which emerged into the public world was tainted not only by lies, but also

[25] See C. Hill, *A Turbulent, Seditious, and Factious People: John Bunyan and His Church* (Oxford, 1989), p. 119.
[26] Cragg, *Puritanism*, pp. 42–3.

malice and paranoia. Given the circumstances, the nation expected plots and as a result plots were uncovered. Furthermore the plots of the early 1660s should also be seen in the context of the wealth of lies which successfully struck at English political life in the period 1678–83. In this light the reality of the earlier conspiracies becomes an even more pertinent question. An examination of the period 1678–83 teaches above all that not all plots were real, nor all plotters genuine and a nation which was to credulously believe the lies of a Titus Oates would be more than willing to accept the lies of many of his lesser precursors during the troubled and equally unstable 1660s.

Hence the historical arguments over whether the plots of the 1660s were real or feigned has been a long-running and occasionally contentious one. To the politically prejudiced Whig and Tory historians of the later seventeenth and eighteenth centuries such issues were often matters of simple black and white. Most Whig historians were positive that these plots were mere shams, designed mainly to persecute the politically unorthodox, whom a vicious government wished to destroy, or at least stifle. Thus the men caught up in them were no real threat, merely pawns in the 'real' plot of the period: the Caroline regime's attempt to stifle English liberties and establish popery and arbitrary government. Amongst the nonconformist community the 'plots' were similarly seen as schemes to persecute the righteous; or if they did exist, the righteous were not really involved, only reluctantly caught up in their wake. Tory historians obviously took a different viewpoint. They never really doubted the reality of the plots, but claimed that behind the lesser fry whom the government so often arrested were men who had been intent on destroying the monarchy since at least May 1660 if not before. They were the same radical, fanatic individuals who had executed the 'martyr king' Charles I, and were also intent upon murdering his son and heir in order to turn the country over to republicanism or anarchy; which to some amounted to the same thing. At the least they would have brought renewed civil war. It was thus beholden on the regime to use all the tools at its disposal to uncover their 'foul and secretive' dealings. In Bishop Parker's *History, or the Tories Chronicle*, a classic example of this view, it was claimed that there were four factions of opposition after the Restoration: the broken officers of Cromwell's army, the 'fighting little preachers' of the Gospel, the parliamentmen of the late republican state and all sacrilegious persons who had allowed the Restoration to occur and then resented it. Having included in his scheme just about everyone who could oppose the regime, Parker then went on to claim that they were allies in a widespread conspiracy and had possessed a secret general assembly of representatives, alongside a smaller council of six, drawn from the Presbyterians, the Independents, the Anabaptists, the Fifth Monarchists, as well as the Levellers.[27] To hunt such men down and execute justice upon them was therefore a legitimate act of government for they posed a terrible threat to the state itself. At the opposite extreme of the political perspective a republican radical such as Edmund Ludlow saw most of the plots of the 1660s as bogus, for according to him such schemes were part of the time of trial for the saints, who were suffering under a tyrannical and bloodthirsty regime for the sins of the 1650s. To Ludlow and his compatriots the Caroline regime was capable of anything, from torture to coercion, in order to achieve its aims.[28]

A division existed therefore between the believers and the non-believers and modern historians faced with this problem have also divided amongst themselves.[29] The most prominent historian on this question has been Richard L. Greaves. His trilogy on radicalism underground spans the years 1660–89 and performs a sterling service in detailing the various plots, real or imagined, in this period.[30] There are, however, some flaws in his work. The first two volumes with their largely narrative structure certainly left little time for reflection, and a useful dose of scepticism on occasion would have been helpful. To answer this criticism Greaves did produce a rather limited and somewhat tetchy footnote in his third volume. In this he claimed that he had attempted in the first two volumes to 'provide the reader with a clear sense of the extent to which the government faced an incessant stream of allegations . . . [and] Any suggestion that my discussion of such reports automatically attributes validity to the charges they encompassed is, of course, absurd'.[31] But this was never explicitly stated in the first two works and readers were left, if they could do so, to draw such a conclusion themselves. Some of the factual errors in the three works are

[27] *Bishop Parker's History, or The Tories Chronicle, from the Restauration of King Charles II 1660, to the year 1680* (1730), p. 37 *et passim*. See also Clarendon, *Life*, I, 285–6; II, pp. 42–3.

[28] Ludlow, *Voyce*, pp. 279, 291. As a Whig view see T. Rapin de Thoyras, *The History of England, Written in French by M. Rapin de Thoyras* (2 vols., 1732–3), I, p. 627; also L. Echard, *The History of England* (3 vols., 1718), II, p. 65.

[29] See as a starting point Walker, 'The Republican Party in England'; J. Walker, 'The Yorkshire Plot', *Yorkshire Archaeological Journal*, 31, 1934, pp. 348–59; Abbott, 'English Conspiracy'; W. G. Johnson, 'Post Restoration Non-Conformity and Plotting, 1660–1675', unpublished MA thesis, University of Manchester, 1967; M. Goldie, 'Danby, the Bishops and the Whigs', in T. Harris, *et al.*, eds., *The Politics of Religion in Restoration England* (1990), pp. 75–105; N. H. Keeble, Rewriting the Restoration, *HJ*, 35, 1992, pp. 233–5. Ashcraft, *Revolutionary Politics*.

[30] See Greaves, *Deliver Us From Evil*; *Enemies Under His Feet*; *Secrets of the Kingdom*. Of the trilogy the last work is undoubtedly the best. It provides, for example, a generally sober and judicious view of the Rye House Plot schemes, although the section on the death of the Earl of Essex seems a rather dubious tale. As a counter to this see M. Macdonald, 'The Death of the Earl of Essex, 1683', *History Today*, 41, November 1991, pp. 13–18.

[31] See Greaves, *Secrets of the Kingdom*, p. 427.

noted below, but the general theme also bears examination. Greaves' main thesis revolves around the question of the radical nature of the men whose activities he is describing and how widespread the threat was to the regime. While one cannot help feeling that in his view the agenda was already set and that it all must inevitably end in 1776 and another, but more long-lasting, 'glorious revolution', this discussion must be seen in light of the major debate over the concept of radicalism in the period as a whole.[32] In some instances Greaves' presentation of the radicals *is* sustained by a reading of the evidence and there were undoubted continuities between the radical ideas of the 1640s and 1650s and those from 1660 to 1689, although I am more inclined to think that on the ground, as opposed to the intellectuals, these links were neither as sustained or as unbroken as both he and Christopher Hill on occasion have attempted to make out, Greaves' concept of a 'radical underground' in particular appears to imply much more unity amongst these people than there was in reality. While it seems to him at least that the broad spectrum of overall dissent is not in doubt, stretching from republican assassins at one extreme to religious pacifists at the other, such a view must be qualified for there are considerable doubts not only over the actual numbers of individuals involved in conspiracy but also as to whether their political philosophy, at least until the 1680s, was as developed as he makes out. We may also argue that their efforts in the 1660s were not as widely supported as both he and Christopher Hill have suggested.[33] It is clear that there was a considerable amount of grumbling, but it is also possible to argue that the actual numbers involved in plotting may well have been much smaller and more atypical in their viewpoint than has been previously suggested. It is equally likely that the frequent claims by the dissenters that the majority of nonconformists were not involved in such violent schemes were indeed true. In fact the term 'radical' in both Greaves' work and elsewhere, often becomes so broad as to make it more than a little dubious as a label, or even as a self-consciously anachronistic term, for it not only seems to include the majority of dissenters of all types but becomes, as Jonathan Clark puts it, a 'holdall for ... ahistorical assumptions' as well as a rather romanticised refusal to understand the period in its own terms. Indeed there are some implicitly 'Whiggish' views

[32] In particular the shrewd comments made on this subject by J. C. D. Clark, *Revolution and Rebellion, State and Society in England in the Seventeenth and Eighteenth Centuries* (Cambridge, 1987), pp. 97–103.

[33] Hill suggests this in *Bunyan* pp. 115–16. The obvious exception to this lies in Ireland. Inevitably different conditions prevailed in that country and there was a clear threat to the regime at various times. In particular the Dublin Plot of 1663 represented a real danger which could have gained widespread support from the disaffected elements in Ireland. For a discussion of this plot see S. J. Connolly, *Religion, Law and Power. The Making of Protestant Ireland 1660–1760* (Oxford, 1992), pp. 24–32.

in Greaves' work.[34] Clearly then, although his three volumes have proved valuable in setting a framework, for the opposition in the period a more subtle portrait is necessary. It is argued in the following pages that it is more practical to see the underground opposition to the Stuart regime in much more fluid terms than has been previously suggested. Rather than simple black or white we have many subtle shades of grey.

The men who were involved in actual plotting in the 1660s then, I will argue, were a relatively small group. The hard-core rebels may well have been drawn from a wide spectrum of society and dissent, but they had a diversity of beliefs which were not always complementary to each other. However it is occasionally possible to detect three broad militant groupings in the early 1660s which we can label as rebels in opposition to the regime, who were active in plotting and who represented a real threat to the Stuart regime's security. The first group was the Fifth Monarchists and other millennarians, whose belief in the coming of a new era survived May 1660. The violence inherent in their language was sometimes carried through into militant action. Although he was not a Fifth Monarchist, Thomas Blood often fell in with such men and was said to have described them as 'a bold and daring sort of people like himself ... [judging] them very proper for his management'.[35] The second group involved in plotting was the hard-core of military conspirators in the 1660s: men such as the ex-officers Captain John Mason, John Atkinson, the Stockinger, Robert Atkinson whom we meet below, Captain Lockyer, the one-handed Major Lee, Nathaniel Strange, Captain Roger Jones, who was the author of the notorious underground pamphlet *Mene Tekel: Or the Downfall of Tyranny*[36] and a man 'not heard of formerly' one Mr Allen whom someone, seeing the name in the document written by Leving, wrote above it 'his true name is Bludd'.[37] These men lurked in London for the most part, moving from place to place as soon as the regime picked up their trail. If their safe lodgings were found or suspected they sent messages to their comrades to 'forewarne them lest they should be snapt'. If any of the rebels were arrested the rest 'dislodge and so [it is] hard to find any of them'.[38] As has been noted the real threat came from these disgruntled ex-military men and a few radical ministers of the gathered churches. This group also moved swiftly into the edges of criminality and operated on both sides of the

[34] Clark, *Revolution and Rebellion*, p. 103. For Greaves' rather 'Whiggish' views see as examples Greaves, *Deliver Us From Evil*, pp. 6, 15, 229; *Secrets of the Kingdom*, p. 344.

[35] *Remarks*, III, p. 222.

[36] R. Jones, *Mene Tekel: Or the Downfall of Tyranny* (1663).

[37] PRO SP 29/102, fos. 48–9.

[38] PRO SP 102, fo. 175, and PRO SP 29/115, fo. 72v. R. H., the author of the earliest biography of Thomas Blood, also describes the rebel's security system and it confirms Leving and Atkinson's revelations to some extent. See *Remarks*, p. 222; and below, Chapter 5.

political line, in which casual brutality, betrayal and trepanning were all too common. Their plotting was endless and their planning usually far too ambitious in design to be executed, but the government never underestimated them and nor should historians. The last group was that often articulate group of radicals, some commonwealthsmen and Levellers, who during the mid-1660s became linked to aristocrats such as the Duke of Buckingham. The most notable of them was the ex-Leveller John Wildman who was to move in and out of conspiracy for most of his life. He also frequented the circles of Buckingham in the 1660s and then found himself in the Whig faction in the 1670s.[39] To some extent all of these men later joined with the more moderate Whigs in the 1670s and early 1680s and used them as stalking horses. They still retained their identity as extremists in that party and came to enjoy greater strength as the crisis of the early 1680s intensified.[40] However, in many instances the men involved on the ground in opposing the regime in the 1660s had not time to be philosophers, for they were rebels caught up in the day-to-day action of rebellion and in a world where there was little time for sustained reflection.[41] We can be assured that their ideology was invariably drawn from a religious background. It involved ideas of liberty of conscience for their fellows, as well as a dislike of arbitrary government and popery, but was not necessarily republican in nature.

Given the fluidity of the Restoration period it should be expected that it has always proved rather difficult to group such people into a coherent whole. In the early 1660s a far more realistic portrait of these men than Greaves' rather uniform 'radical underground' is of an increasingly small group of desperadoes and adventurers on the fringes of or sometimes directly involved with the criminal underground, who lacked coordination, were often deeply divided, whether in exile or in London, and more often than not inhabited a tavern culture where imagined realities could be played out in varying degrees of intoxication in deep, but essentially meaningless, plans. For them the 'experience of defeat' was indeed an embittering experience of unfocused anger and despair as one plan after another failed. When they did get a rebellion off the ground in the north of England, as opposed to Scotland or Ireland where the conditions were

39 For Wildman see M. Ashley, *John Wildman, Plotter and Postmaster: A Study of the English Republican Movement in the Seventeenth Century* (1947). See also M. Goldie, 'The Roots of True Whiggism, 1688–94', *History of Political Thought*, 1, 1980, pp. 195–236.

40 To some extent therefore I follow the line originally laid down by the work of J. R. Jones, *The First Whigs: The Politics of the Exclusion Crisis, 1678–1683* (Oxford, 1961), pp. 15–16.

41 There are exceptions, see for instance A. Marshall, 'Notes From Thomas Blood's Pocket Book' (unpublished paper); also Jones, *Mene Tekel.*

slightly more propitious, it was also destined to fail, penetrated by government agents, betrayed by their own comrades, and launched into the wilderness of the north with little thought of what was going to happen next. It is also clear that these men were still riven with the factionalism that had damaged their cause and lost them power in the 1650s. Moreover until the 1670s there was no powerful figure or institutional focus to unite them. The re-emergence of such radicals in the mid-1670s occurred because of the increasing possibilities of using parliament and the City of London as vehicles for the growing Country and Whig interest and because they found a leadership once again in ex-ministers, MPs and aristocrats such as Buckingham, Shaftesbury and Monmouth who led the opposition. They followed such men not because they shared the values of a group of essentially greedy politicians, but because they offered a way out of endless plotting. They followed Monmouth to disaster in 1685 because he offered them a chance of power. Thus the survivors of the small group of men who engaged in serious plotting in the 1660s and frequently dragged others into their schemes were to emerge as the extremists of the Whig party: inheritors of radical viewpoints, supporters of exclusion and occasionally closet republicans. Even then the divisions amongst them remained, which often makes the idea of an all-encompassing label a rather dubious concept. How far men such as John Wildman, Robert Ferguson or Richard Rumbold and the others who involved themselves in renewed plotting after 1681 were typical 'Whigs' is debatable. It is the very fluidity of the late 1670s and early 1680s which forces us to reject the idea of a coherent body of underground opposition or a party. There were various factions and the extremists faced with political failure again and again returned to the failed tactics, plotting and conspiracy which was to end in the Rye House Plot of 1683.

Given then that the numbers of dedicated activists were small, their influence often negligible, their schemes failures and occasionally downright foolish, given that they also often existed in a form of chronic distrust and disarray, why study them at all, for surely they really were negligible in all senses of that word? This however is to force the argument too far. Loosely linked, clumsy and semi-criminal though they were, they did succeed in frightening the authorities on more than one occasion. Part of the interest in such men lies in the fluidity of their schemes and ideas, part in the rough politics of violence many of them favoured, but the major part of the interest lies in the fact that the Stuart regime spent so much time and resources in dealing with the threat they were thought to pose. The official line on the conspiracies of such men is not that hard to uncover. The king himself gave the government's view in 1664 in a speech to parliament. It was classic Tory conspiracy theory, tailored to suit Charles II's occasionally gullible, but almost always volatile, parliamentary audience. Certainly, said Charles, there were plots, but the regime had timely notice of such designs. Nevertheless it was obviously always going to be a near-run thing, for even now such desperate villains were still attempting to fulfil their plans and thus the danger was not yet past. According to the king a standing council of the rebels was resident in London itself, but the government was on its trail. Thus the king ended his speech with the view that it was necessary to be 'watchful to prevent [such] as they are continu[ing] their mischief'.[42] This shrewd mixture of truth and exaggeration raised both fear and hope in one breath, alongside the hint that only monarchical government stood between the nation and republican anarchy. In addition, and to titillate his audience, there were the hints of secret knowledge and secret designs in the political shadows to deal with the threat. It was a calculated official line for credulous parliamentary consumption. But the government did actually believe there was a danger and that it was necessary to take action to curb the threat. Hence its moves to tighten penal laws, to arrest suspects and use spies and informers to hunt down actual or potential rebels. It was not that the regime believed everything it heard from such sources, indeed it was often more moderate in its actions than one might have expected, but occasionally it was necessary to believe in these schemes in order to gain certain political advantages. Moreover as Clarendon pointed out, 'it was not wisdome [for any government] to neglect small beginnings'.[43] In any case more often than not proof was difficult to come by and even harder to sustain. As Arlington put it, however morally certain of the dangers the regime was, it might not be able to 'produce such convincing proofs as will come home to the enquiry of the law', but what 'can be made clear, may be so'.[44] Such an attitude allowed the regime to at least try to convince the country of the reality of the danger it believed was facing it and the benefits of monarchical government. In any case many historians are apt to forget that plots were taken as part and parcel of political life. The period's political life was one in which the idea of legitimate opposition was very slow to emerge. It naturally looked upon the alternative ideas to those of the government as illegitimate designs. As John Dryden was to point out,

> Plots, true or false are necessary things,
> To raise up commonwealths and ruin kings.[45]

[42] BL Add. MSS 23,904, fos. 105v–106.
[43] Clarendon quoted in Ludlow, *Voyce*, p. 276.
[44] *Miscellanea Aulica*, pp. 307–9.
[45] John Dryden, *Absalom and Achitophel*, in J. Dryden, *Poems*, ed. K. Walker (Oxford, 1987), lines 83–4.

III

During the course of the English Civil Wars espionage had come into its own as a means of gaining intelligence on both sides of the political divide, whether parliamentarian or royalist. The type of intelligence in which both sides were interested was as much military as political. During the first years of the conflict Clarendon for one was scornful of such work claiming that, before Edgehill for example, intelligence activities, or a lack of them, had led to 'neither army ... [knowing] where the other was'.[46] In fact it was clear that intelligence activities were on a primitive level and that most civil war battles were more often the result of armies meeting accidentally rather than as any intelligence coup. The responsibility for gathering military intelligence fell upon the holders of the post of scoutmaster. This title, apparently peculiar to the English military world, had originally had a purely military function. The scoutmaster had sent out his scouts in advance of the army in order to reconnoitre the ground ahead. This original function however had soon expanded into more general espionage activities. It meant the scoutmaster became familiar with employing and dealing with spies who were used for gathering all types of intelligence. It also meant that they were forced into assessing the information when it actually came in.[47] One example of a wartime scoutmaster at work was Sir Samuel Luke who was based at Newport Pagnell and acted as the scoutmaster to the army of the Earl of Essex. Luke was praised both for his efficiency and means of gathering knowledge of royalist intentions.[48] In addition to his scouts, who also acted as message carriers, Luke drew his casual informers from various backgrounds, whether occupied townsfolk with parliamentary sympathies, such as Joel Stevenson, a grocer from Reading, or military men on secret missions.[49] Luke was also able to place agents in the court at Oxford. Sir George Downing had also acted as Scoutmaster-General to the army and, as will be seen below, was able to pick up many of the tricks of the trade which he was to use in his diplomatic career.[50]

The spies located in Oxford were doubtless useful to parliament. There was an unsuspected spy, for example, in the service of Sir Edward Nicho-

[46] Clarendon quoted in I. G. Philip, ed., *The Journal of Sir Samuel Luke*, Oxfordshire Record Society, 29 (1947), pp. ix–x.

[47] See C. H. Firth, *Cromwell's Army: A History of the English Soldier During the Civil Wars, the Commonwealth and the Protectorate* (1967), pp. 63–6; R. E. Scouller, *The Armies of Queen Anne* (Oxford, 1966), pp. 62, 65; PRO SP 77/35, fo. 91v.

[48] *Journal of Sir Samuel Luke*, p. vi; H. G. Tibbutt, ed., *The Letter Book of Sir Samuel Luke, 1644–45*, Bedfordshire Record Society, 42 (1963); *DNB*, Sir Samuel Luke.

[49] *Journal of Sir Samuel Luke*, pp. 6–7, 10, 11–12, 25–6.

[50] For Downing see below, pp. 263–70.

las, the royal Secretary of State. Prince Rupert's secretary accepted £200 a month from the parliamentarians for his intelligence, but this excessively high salary came to an abrupt halt when he was caught and executed. As a military base and the royalist headquarters wartime Oxford was the focus of endless opportunities for parliamentary spies to gather intelligence.[51] The metropolis of London offered equally rich pickings for those spies employed by Charles I. Some of these royalist agents were run by John Barwick who was the staunch Anglican royalist whom Charles had sent to London for this very purpose. Barwick had been installed as chaplain to the Bishop of Durham's family in order to provide him with a reason for being in London. The bishop's house was fortunately a spacious mansion which proved ideal for concealing the tools of the espionage trade such as cipher keys and so on and in spite of the 'sagacious and quick-witted' parliamentary counter-intelligence network Barwick was able to organise a reliable royalist spy network in the capital. It enabled him to convey intelligence from London to Oxford as well as relay the king's orders from Oxford to London. A man of courage and presence of mind, his prudence in this work was only matched by a complete disregard for the dangers involved. Unfortunately his health gave way under the strain and he was forced to call upon the assistance of his brothers. The Barwicks were then betrayed and John was placed in the Tower of London. Despite threats of torture and bribes he remained loyal until his release in 1652, whereupon he began his work all over again, but this time for the exiled King Charles II.[52]

Imprisonment was merely one of the hazards for the spy in wartime England. Sometimes capture meant death. The lynchings were made into public lessons in order to make it clear that there were dangers in following such a trade.[53] Both sides resorted to hanging in order to discourage others who might be considering the trade. Prior to execution some captured spies were also tortured in order to extract information. A royalist spy taken at Reading, for example, had lighted matches put under his fingers to make him talk, while a woman caught spying at Latham House lost three fingers in this way.[54] This did not prevent the trade continuing with increasing ingenuity. Sir Samuel Luke caught one man who had gone through the lines disguised as a fiddler,[55] yet another was caught with messages con-

[51] See J. Webb, ed., *Military Memoirs of Colonel John Birch*, Camden Society (1873), pp. 167–8. See also the case of Francis Cole who was engaged by Sir Samuel Luke and captured in Oxford, *Mercurius Aulicus*, 13 January 1643–4, pp. 771–2. I am indebted to Dr Ian Roy for this reference.

[52] P. Barwick, *The Life of John Barwick* (1728), pp. 45–6; *DNB*, John Barwick.

[53] C. Carlton, *Going to the Wars: The Experience of the British Civil Wars, 1638–1652* (1992), pp. 263–4; Birch, *Memoirs*, p. 168.

[54] *ibid.* [55] Luke, *Letter Book*, pp. 21–2.

cealed in his wooden leg. A number of women were also caught up in the wartime espionage trade and all too often took graver risks than the men by passing through enemy lines. They sometimes concealed information about their persons in the, possibly vain, hopes that the licentious soldiery would not molest them. An early addition to the espionage world was doctors and surgeons. The medical world might profess a studied neutrality, but quite frequently it was not solely interested in medical matters and used its trade to spy. Medics were viewed with suspicion by both sides. With the Civil Wars at an end new opportunities opened up in the 1650s for espionage activities. One might assume that the Restoration regime of 1660, with ten or eleven years of conspiracy and secret dealings behind it, would be well versed in the techniques and methods of intelligence work. In the main however the inheritance which Joseph Williamson and the Restoration regime were to draw upon came from two sources. The royalists' own secret activities during the 1650s provided one of these, while the other was the experience of the English republican regimes of that decade.

On the whole royalist dealings with the areas of espionage and intelligence in the aftermath of the Civil Wars must be said to have been somewhat ineffective. It was to be George Monck and his allies rather than any secret schemes the royalists laid which were ultimately to engineer the Restoration. Aside from conspiracies, actual intelligence gathering in England by the royalists proved to be a difficult undertaking. Sir Edward Nicholas, who as Secretary of State to the exiled king had co-ordinated such official activities, had done his best in rather trying circumstances. Nicholas was hampered by various factors which lay beyond his control. One of these was the intense factionalism and feuding of the royalist exiles, which in turn led to their laxity in security and thus damaged the royal cause. It was a great asset to the Republic that some royalists talked in their cups in dubious company.[56] Much more significant than these lapses perhaps was the basic lack of funds for intelligence gathering by the royalist camp. Without sufficient funds little could be achieved. There were a few notable agents of the crown, such as Major (later Sir) Nicholas Armorer, Daniel O'Neill, or John Barwick, but their influence upon such matters after 1660 appears to have been rather negligible. As to Sir Edward Nicholas himself, his role in this world after 1660 remained a prominent but not entirely successful one. Perhaps of more importance to the returning royalists of 1660 was the experience of being on the receiving end of the activities of the English Republic in such affairs.

Many of the methods and techniques which found their way into the

[56] See C. H. Firth, *The Last Years of the Protectorate, 1656–1658* (2 vols., 1909), I, p. 29.

Restoration regime's work in this area of government appear to have been drawn from the experience of its former enemies. The new regime had the advantage of being able to pluck from the ruins of the Republic some of the more choice pieces of debris from its intelligence system. There was much to learn from this, experience having taught them that the Republic's intelligence activities had usually been fairly effective. Not only the methods but most of its highest officials, as well as some of its agents, were available for close study after May 1660. The former Secretary of State John Thurloe was apparently quite willing to talk freely with the new regime. Indeed he was to have 'free liberty to attend the secretary of state at such times as they shall appoint and for so long a time as they shall own his attendance for the service of the state'.[57] Joseph Williamson, for one, knew exactly where to contact Thurloe, 'at Dr Clerkes in Green Lane where he lodges', for the 'under-secretary' noted this address in his address book.[58] The exact relationship between the pair is teasingly obscure but, as will be seen, Williamson was ever eager to obtain information and was to have the assistance of two of Thurloe's former associates, Morland and Dorislaus, in the Post Office. It is possible therefore that he may well have taken the opportunity to probe the former secretary on his methods. Thurloe was to supply other members of the new regime with information when he was asked.[59] On the other hand Thurloe's somewhat underrated predecessor, Thomas Scot, who had been the Republic's intelligence chief from 1649 to 1653 and again in late 1659 and early 1660, was more harshly treated.[60] He was interrogated shortly after his capture in 1660 and proceeded to tell his questioners all he knew of the Republic's espionage activities in the vain hope that his life would be spared. As a regicide this could not happen, but the information he gave was valuable. Many of the names of the former agents of the regime also came to light. Indeed some of them were incarcerated in the Tower, where they were persuaded to give further evidence of the English Republic's secret dealings.

The Stuart regime would have found some interesting techniques and methods from all of these sources. Both Scot and Thurloe had been efficient protectors of the republican regime. Although neither could have pre-

[57] *Thurloe State Papers*, I, p. xix.

[58] PRO SP 9/32, fo. 212; *Thurloe State Papers*, I, p. xix.

[59] See C. H. Firth, 'Secretary Thurloe on the Relations of England and Holland', *EHR*, 21, 1906, pp. 319–27; PRO SP 18/220, fo. 114; BL Stowe MSS 185, fo. 183. See also C.H. Firth, 'Thurloe and the Post Office', *EHR*, 13, 1898, pp. 527–33. Thurloe's infamous 'black book' replete with the names of traitorous royalists, does not appear to have ever existed, nor did he appear to need such a thing. See K. Feiling, *A History of the Tory Party, 1640–1714*, (1965), p. 182.

[60] For which see C. H. Firth, 'Thomas Scot's Account of his Actions as Intelligencer During the Commonwealth', *EHR*, 12, 1897, pp. 116–26.

vented the English Republic from imploding, both went some way to preventing its many enemies damaging the infant state. The figure of John Thurloe, so beloved of many popular historians, has somewhat overshadowed his equally capable predecessor in this field, Thomas Scot. Scot was a zealous advocate of both the regicide and the Rump Parliament in which he was an MP.[61] It was he, as much as anyone, who had laid the foundations of any success which later came to Thurloe. Alongside Haselrige, Vane and Cromwell, Scot had been a guiding force in the Republic's affairs.[62] In 1649 responsibility for intelligence activities had been largely unfixed, but in July of that year Scot had been appointed to the 'trust of Manngeing ye Intelligence both forraine & domestick'.[63] In spite of his lack of experience in such matters and his complete ignorance of foreign languages, Scot was given the post because of his loyalty and diligence to the regime. It was a fortunate choice for he performed creditably whilst in office. Initially Scot seems to have had little enough to guide him in his task. Those previously involved in such affairs evidently kept their experience to themselves. Scot did gain the assistance of Major George Bishop as well as a small, later a larger, standing committee on examinations, whose chairman was John Bradshaw. This busied itself in hearing, as well as examining witnesses and suspects.[64]

The royalists claimed that soon after Scot's appointment his informers and spies were 'swarming over all England as Lice and Frogs did in Egypt'.[65] The reality was somewhat different. Although Scot did well he was, as he himself admitted, always faced with a shortage of funds. This meant that he could not 'dive very deepe' as a rule.[66] The system which he created also lacked the comprehensive nature later seen in Restoration England which was able to draw not only upon the reports of spies but also supplement this by information gathered from the loyal local gentry and officers. Scot's informants remained a mixture of military men, untrustworthy professionals, such as Joseph Bamfield,[67] and royalists whose loyalty was often dubious to say the least. One of his best agents appears to have been an Irish abbot called Father Creely. Creely also went under the name of Captain Holland. He was located in the Queen Mother's court in Paris but also worked in Flanders and had men in Vienna, as well as some intelligence interests in the Vatican amongst the cardinals. In addition Scot

61 For Scot see *BDBR*, III, pp. 149–50.
62 See B. Worden, *The Rump Parliament 1648–1653* (Cambridge, 1974), pp. 35–6.
63 Firth, 'Thomas Scot's Account', p. 118.
64 See G. E. Aylmer, *The State's Servants: The Civil Service of the English Republic, 1649–1660* (1973), p. 21.
65 Clement Walker quoted in D. Underdown, *Royalist Conspiracy*, p. 20.
66 Firth, 'Thomas Scot's Account', p. 124.
67 For this gentleman's career see pp. 168–75.

gained control of Colonel Robert Werden in the Duke of York's entourage, although it is possible that Werden played a double game with Scot by joining the intelligence system either to mislead him or as a form of personal insurance for the future.[68] As well as these sources Scot gathered information from many of his fellow Rump MPs who were usually given it as a first line of enquiry by informants. It is somewhat redolent of Scot's hazy approach to such dealings that he wasn't particularly interested in controlling these sources, so such information was invariably second-hand. However, he did try to cross-check their intelligence with sources of his own.[69]

For foreign affairs there were other routes to use. Scot sent out one of his servants, Louis de Bourgoigne, who had originally assisted him in learning French, to tour the coast of France from Calais to Boulogne.[70] There he contacted groups who favoured the Prince de Condé, then a prominent member of the Fronde. Scot sought to forge a relationship with Cardinal de Retz, Mazarin's rival. Of course most of the schemes fell through in 1653 when the Rump itself was dissolved by Cromwell. How effective Scot's intelligence work was remains a debatable point. During the Anglo-Dutch War Scot was to claim that he had been able to obtain 'the minutes or heads of every nights debate in the Closet Councils and whole Resolutions [of the Dutch] as often as was possible'.[71] One of his sources in the Netherlands was Mr Cheshire, an Englishman who had lived there for some time. Unfortunately for him, Cheshire was 'forc'd to run for it [on] being discovered'.[72] Other agents were sent into Denmark and based in cities across Europe, but it was never a system which covered the whole of the continent. One final source of information, which proved valuable to successive governments, came through the interception of letters in the Post Office. For letters in cipher Scot called on Dr John Wallis of Oxford University to decipher them. Wallis was described as a 'jewell for a Prince[']s use & service in that kind'. Thus it comes as no surprise that Wallis also served Thurloe and the restored monarchy.[73]

Scot was, of course, replaced by John Thurloe in this field. To label Thurloe's work in this area as the replacement of mere competence by 'genius' as David Underdown has, is to somewhat overstate the case.[74] Thurloe had many successes and failures during his time in office and part

[68] See Underdown, *Royalist Conspiracy*, pp. 148, 288–9, 319.
[69] Firth, 'Thomas Scot's Account', p. 119.
[70] *ibid.*, p. 119.
[71] *ibid.*, pp. 119–21. This was hardly a difficult task with a government notorious for its leaks of political information.
[72] *ibid.*, p. 121.
[73] Firth, 'Thomas Scot's Account', p. 121. For more on Wallis see pp. 93–5.
[74] Underdown, *Royalist Conspiracy*, p. 61.

of his good fortune lay in his ability to stress the former over the latter. The creation of the 'all seeing little secretary' was a myth which in itself played a useful part in preventing conspiracies and plots. The myth, which survived into the 1660s, was often enough to spread dissension amongst the Lord Protector's enemies. However, there is little doubt that Thurloe built upon the solid foundations which Scot had laid down. As Thurloe's intelligence system has still not been examined in the detail it deserves,[75] it is difficult to say with any exactness how effective and just how well informed the regime remained. The general impression is of an efficient intelligence system, but as Andrew Coleby has rightly argued in many areas, especially in the localities, the regime was *not* as well informed as the Caroline government.[76] Though it worked hard to gain acceptance on the level of local government, it never fully succeeded in doing so. At least for some of the time part of the problem may have been the system of major-generals. Security under the major-generals became much tighter and as part of their policing function the occupants of the posts undoubtedly used espionage as a device to control political subversives. One major-general claimed that there was 'hardly a meeting of three cavaliers together on any account, but I am suddenly acquainted with it'.[77] However, their methods often alienated the people in the localities. There was a system of local informers, occasionally brutal interrogations and examinations, in addition to the heavy taxation that was laid upon the royalists. Cromwell also praised the activities of John Barkstead the lieutenant of the Tower. The Lord Protector claimed that 'there never was any design on foot, but we could hear of it out of the Tower'.[78] Barkstead obtained his information from the numbers of visitors who came to see his prisoners, as well as from the prisoners' spirits, which were often raised when there were rumours of a design in the offing. Interrogations and examinations were also supplemented by spontaneous communications from individuals with a gripe or grudge or those who were merely suspicious of their neighbours' activities, as well as the more mercenary domestic and foreign spies.

Another individual who made a contribution both to the republican as well as the newly restored regime of 1660 was George Monck. Monck had

[75] The latest work on Thurloe is disappointing in this respect. See P. Aubrey, *Mr Secretary Thurloe: Cromwell's Secretary of State 1652–1660* (1990). It replaces the very poor biography by D. L. Hobman, *Cromwell's Master Spy: A Study of John Thurloe* (1961) which had few merits; even its title is wrong as Thurloe was, of course, a 'spymaster'. The best examination of Thurloe's character remains Aylmer *State's Servants*, pp. 258–60. See also *BDBR*, III, pp. 237–8.

[76] A. M. Coleby, *Central Government and the Localities: Hampshire 1649–1689* (Cambridge, 1987), p. 33.

[77] D. W. Rannie, 'Cromwell's Major-Generals', *EHR*, 10, 1895, pp. 489, 490–1, 500–1.

[78] Cromwell in C. H. Firth, 'Cromwell and the Insurrection of 1655', *EHR*, 4, 1888, pp. 340–3.

presided over a more than capable espionage system in Scotland during the 1650s.[79] With the assistance of Roger Boyle, Lord Broghill, from 1655 to 1656, he had created the system to guard against trouble from the exiled king's supporters in Scotland, as well as troublesome highlanders at home. In the process Monck dealt with various agents, spies and more casual informers, as well as intercepting the post to uncover the subversive elements in his territory. Once they were identified, Monck was not slow to treat them with his well-known, and calculated, brutality. Periods in gaol, as well as a harsh system of pecuniary fines for future security were his usual tactics. Monck considered spies as men who were easily bought, but useful. His methods were also often brutal, but his experiences were at the service of his new master in 1660 and there is little doubt that he continued to have an interest in this world. Monck's opinion of spies was not high, although he regarded them as essential to government. He was to claim that the spymaster must always 'be suspicious' of his spies.[80] Monck was well aware that espionage was a dangerous trade for both parties and that espionage needed the lubrication of money to work effectively. Monck also believed that plentiful supplies of cash made the unfaithful spy work harder.

If Thurloe's activities were not the only source of intelligence, various case studies of the secretary at work have also uncovered just how effective, and ineffective, his operations could sometimes be. The port of Dover, for example, was never fully closed to the operations of royalist agents.[81] To weigh against this there was the skilfully handled infiltration of the Sealed Knot (a secret group of royalists allegedly planning the overthrow of the Cromwellian regime), as well as the use of the royalist Henry Manning at the centre of the exiled Stuart court, although Manning was caught and shot in 1655.[82] The affair of Sir Richard Willys, however, shows Thurloe's skill as an intelligencer. Even where the information gathered may not have been that vital the very fact that such disloyalty could be found at the heart of royalist plans created distrust amongst them.[83] But as Underdown has pointed out, the fact that almost all of these 'traitors' were uncovered

[79] For the system in the 1650s see F. D. Dow, *Cromwellian Scotland, 1651–1660* (Edinburgh, 1979), pp. 189–90.

[80] Monck, *Observations*, pp. 59–60.

[81] G. R. Smith, 'Royalist Secret Agents at Dover During the Commonwealth', *Historical Studies of Australia and New Zealand*, 12, 1967, pp. 477–90. Also Underdown, *Royalist Conspiracy*, pp. 134–5.

[82] For this see S. R. Gardiner, *History of the Commonwealth and Protectorate* (4 vols., 1989), IV, p. 227.

[83] For Willys see D. Underdown, 'Sir Richard Willys and Secretary Thurloe', *EHR*, 69, 1954, pp. 373–87; M. Hollings, 'Thomas Barret: A Study in the Secret History of the Interregnum', *EHR*, 43, 1928, pp. 33–65.

before the Restoration is revealing in itself.[84] Added to these operations there were the full gamut of secret activities, many of which were to be taken over by the new regime in 1660. In fact so close are many of the Restoration regime's techniques to those of the 1650s that it soon becomes obvious that the Stuart government had first-hand knowledge of them from 1660. They ranged from 'safe houses' in the City of London, where Thurloe or his minions could meet agents, to false addresses. The residences of ambassadors were also closely watched and their letters were 'constantly opened', while Thurloe made sure that he placed men 'in their houses'. These were usually 'some trusty persons, who might be entertained as their domestique servants'.[85] To take care of the various factions and the more dangerous sects, such as the Fifth Monarchists, Thurloe appears to have tried to 'gain over some two or three of the principall members of every such reigning faction'.[86] These would be highly placed individuals deep in the counsels of such people. Moreover they would never know of each other's game. In this way the Cromwellian regime could cross-check the information received and those telling unreliable tales could be threatened. These plotter's designs were crushed in the 'egge and hinder[ed] ... from ever coming to any maturity'.[87] This could often be a demoralising process. If the regime desired it the plans would be allowed to grow, merely in order to crush them more effectively when the time came.

According to John Oldmixon, Thurloe was a 'very dextrous man at getting intelligence'. It was claimed that he had even surpassed Sir Francis Walsingham with his subtlety, precision and success.[88] The elements of timidity in the secretary's character, however, could often lead him to delay decision. Christer Bonde, a Swedish diplomat, pointed out that Thurloe had a tendency to monopolise business in his own hands, invariably a good thing in intelligence work, but he was so 'excessively slow in everything that he has to despatch' that lengthy delays were commonplace.[89] Having said this, in many ways Thurloe was modest enough to be the perfect foil for the Lord Protector and some might rightly argue that it was Oliver rather than John who was the real head of the intelligence system.[90] Under Oliver's guiding hand Thurloe could be a hard taskmaster

[84] Underdown, *Royalist Conspiracy*, p. 319.
[85] Firth, 'Thurloe and the Post Office', p. 533.
[86] *ibid.*, p. 530. [87] *ibid.*, p. 530.
[88] Oldmixon quoted in E. Baker, 'John Thurloe Secretary of State 1652–1660', *History Today*, 8, 1958, p. 550.
[89] M. Roberts, *Swedish Diplomats at Cromwell's Court, 1656–1656; The Missions of Peter Julius Coyet and Christer Bonde*, Camden Society, 36 (1988), p. 289.
[90] See Burnet, *History*, I, p. 127. See also D. Hirst, 'The Lord Protector, 1653–1658', in J. Morrill, ed., *Oliver Cromwell and the English Revolution* (1990), p. 141.

and not someone to be lightly crossed. As he noted in one letter, a 'slight doing of [any of] this business will be of no use to me nor can it be expected to be of any great profit to you'.[91] The good and ill effects of centralisation upon the Cromwellian regime's intelligence system was a pointer for things to come. In some ways this was a shrewd move for it meant that the secretary controlled all the threads of intelligence in his own hands. It had its faults and delays but if nothing else John Thurloe had shown the way in intelligence matters to the new government of 1660. And it is to this new government's intelligence system that we should now turn.

[91] *Thurloe State Papers*, VI, p. 546.

1

The Restoration secretariat and intelligence, 1660–1685

The heart of the Restoration regime's intelligence system from 1660 to 1685 lay within the office of the Secretaries of State. In particular from 1662 to 1674 the most significant work in this area was undertaken within the office of Sir Henry Bennet, Earl of Arlington, where the control of intelligence fell to Sir Joseph Williamson. In a period of great turmoil the Secretary of State's office concerned itself with the Stuart regime's security. Many of the precedents taken from the former republican regimes were re-established under Williamson's control and in turn they passed to his successors in the secretaryship, the Earl of Sunderland, Sir Leoline Jenkins and Charles Middleton. In the context of the threats which faced the regime intelligence and espionage work was an important area for the secretariat as we shall see. As the office developed, the general trend was for increasing centralisation and the creation of a government system of intelligence and espionage activities.

I

The development of the office of Secretary of State within the administration surrounding the monarch was a slow process.[1] The office emerged from the shadow of the post of personal secretary to the king, but by the mid seventeenth century it had become established as a high office of state; although in political terms it still fluctuated in power. To a great degree it was the man who made the office rather than the office the man. The secretaryship undoubtedly found difficulty in divorcing itself from its roots and its relationship to the monarch was both its potential strength and its weakness. One result of this was the dependence of the occupants upon the whim of the king. Charles II employed eleven Secretaries of State in all and of these only the Earl of Arlington might be said to have combined a high degree of royal favour with security of tenure.

[1] See for the background to the office, Evans, *Principal Secretary*; M. A. Thomson, *The Secretaries of State, 1681–1782* (Oxford, 1932; 1968); D. Kynaston, *The Secretary of State* (Lavenham, 1978).

It is possible to perceive four types of secretary in office during the period which is our concern. All had some effect upon the standard of the government's intelligence system. In the first category stand Sir Henry Bennet, Earl of Arlington and Robert Spencer, Earl of Sunderland. These men were front rank ministers of the king, at times, perhaps, 'first ministers'; although Arlington himself was prudent enough not to claim that title, preferring instead the comparative safety of the crowd at court.[2] In their roles as political power brokers, they were men who made and influenced major policy decisions. The second type of secretary was of more practical value in the fields of administration and intelligence. These men were basically 'civil servants', willing, or only allowed perhaps, to achieve the status of an administrator. They were personified by Sir Joseph Williamson and Sir Leoline Jenkins. The third category of secretary fell somewhere between these two. It comprised men who can really be regarded as lightweight political appointees, such as Sir William Morrice, or Sir John Trevor; the latter indeed was Arlington's own nominee and possessed little influence. Alternatively, and lastly, there were slightly weightier figures such as Sir Edward Nicholas or Henry Coventry. Neither of these was a minister of the first rank, but neither was totally negligible politically; on the other hand they cannot be said to have been administrators of the rank of Williamson and Jenkins.

On the practical side, the responsibilities of the secretaries had always been great and were steadily increasing throughout the period. During the Restoration period there were two secretaries at any one time and the business of the office was split between them. In practice, however, one or the other invariably came to dominate the scene and from 1662 to 1674, a crucial period in the development of intelligence work, the first secretary was undoubtedly Arlington.[3] At one level the secretary was to act as the main avenue of communication between the monarch and his subjects as well as with European states. Communications from the king also passed from the secretaries' office to the local authorities and to the church on the domestic scene, while in the realm of foreign affairs the secretaries had to maintain a constant stream of communication with ambassadors, envoys and consuls abroad. Part of the reasoning behind all of this foreign correspondence was clearly related to the world of intelligence. Sir Samuel Morland was later to note that 'all Sovereign Princes & States ought like Cunning Gamesters to use all Endeavours ... to know what Cards are in their neighbours hands, that so they may play their own to the best

[2] See Barbour, *Arlington*, p. 77.

[3] See for example the partition lists of the countries of Europe between the two secretaries in 1662, PRO SP 29/61, fos. 273–7.

advantage'.[4] The intelligence and security functions of the office were, of course, an important area of control. In general Restoration statesmen had a practical attitude to espionage activities, and morality was of little consideration, for after all what was done was done in the name of a king who himself hardly stood for the moral line in political life. In any case, Sir Robert Southwell, in a memorial written for the Earl of Nottingham in 1689, noted that it was certainly the duty of any secretary to quickly 'think ... of spys and Intelligence where needfull Abroad, and the like more especially at Home'.[5] In fact, as will be seen, the secretaries' concern with security could take a variety of forms in addition to the employment of spies to gather intelligence. They were also concerned with the interception of mail at the Post Office, the seizure of papers or individuals by warrant, the suppression of the printing and distribution of 'seditious' material and the interrogation of suspects. Furthermore their concerns also took them into some even less savoury activities. They used informers, double agents and, on occasion, they even countenanced the assassination or kidnapping of those regarded as hostile to the regime. In this respect, a key figure in the early years of the regime was Sir Joseph Williamson. It was Williamson's work and involvement in this aspect of the secretary's office that was crucial to the development of intelligence and espionage in the period. He became, under Arlington, the *de facto* head of a government intelligence system and, moreover, he possessed many of the qualities needed to make him a superior director of such activities.

The collection of intelligence and espionage activities were, of course, only two, though arguably the most significant, aspects of the secretaries' duties. They had other tasks, for their position gave them access to a wide range of administrative and political responsibilities. They were members of the various committees emanating from the Privy Council and both secretaries sat on forty-three out of the fifty-four committees established between 1660 and 1664. By 1668 they had seats on all four of the newly established standing committees. Increasingly in the 1670s and 1680s the duties of the secretaries also took them into parliament as government spokesmen. This work also began to include parliamentary management and tended in the later years of the reign to dominate their office. It illustrates the continuing development of the office into a broader field of administration. The further responsibilities of the secretaries need only be briefly outlined here. They were responsible for the dissemination of official information, in particular via the *London Gazette*. Joseph Williamson also made a significant contribution to the manuscript newsletter

[4] BL Add. MSS 47133, fos. 8–13. [5] BL Add. MSS 38861, fo. 48.

system.[6] The secretariat was involved in the work of the signet office and had links with the naval and military forces of the crown.[7] In short, as H. C. Tomlinson has aptly phrased it, the Secretaries of State were positioned at the 'central station on the crossroads of the administrative plain'.[8]

II

At the Restoration the office of Secretary of State, previously held by John Thurloe alone under the Cromwellian regime, reverted to its old pre-war division. The two men occupying the office after May 1660 were rather different in background and, as it turned out, unwilling, or unable, to use this potentially powerful position to gain political power. One of the posts went to a client of George Monck, Sir William Morrice, while the other was given to the ever faithful royalist Sir Edward Nicholas, who had served the king in his exile. It was soon clear that as the occupant of the southern office, Nicholas, was going to be of far more significance than Morrice. Largely this was due to their backgrounds, Morrice was never really at home in the court and in the new regime. He was faithful enough, but remained something of a background figure and this industrious administrator had fame thrust upon him rather than going out of his way to seize it. As Secretary of State Morrice was involved in some intelligence work, but tended to complain that Nicholas kept him in the dark on such matters. Upon Arlington's arrival in office any light Morrice could shed on intelligence affairs grew ever dimmer. Clarendon's claim that during the Anglo-Dutch War Morrice 'had always better intelligence from Holland' was a statement written with mischief in mind and was simply untrue.[9] Of far more significance than Morrice to the regime's intelligence-gathering activities was a man whom we have met already valiantly attempting to master the world of intelligence for his exiled king, Sir Edward Nicholas.

As it turned out, Sir Edward Nicholas' greatest character trait was his loyalty. In 1660 he was sixty-seven years of age and had served the house of Stuart in times of peace and prosperity as well as war and dearth. Nicholas was well past his prime by 1660 and, perhaps more importantly, he was wholly subservient to the whim of the Lord Chancellor Sir Edward Hyde, Earl of Clarendon. Clarendon approved of Nicholas, as indeed the secre-

[6] See P. M. Handover, *A History of the London Gazette, 1665–1965* (HMSO, 1965), p. 4; also P. M. Fraser, *The Intelligence of the Secretary of State* (Cambridge, 1956).
[7] Evans, *Principal Secretary*, pp. 194, 320–8.
[8] H. C. Tomlinson, *Guns and Government: The Ordnance Office under the Later Stuarts* (1979), p. 29.
[9] For Morrice see *DNB*, William Morrice; Clarendon, *Life*, II, p. 269.

tary did of him. They both shared much of the same outlook on life. To Clarendon, Nicholas was a man of 'good reputation ... great gravity' and 'without any ambitions or designs'.[10] Given such an attitude Nicholas was never going to create a court faction and become a rival to the Chancellor or a really significant figure in the new regime. His influence remained negligible and the unselfish, honest and faithful servant was well aware of it. He grew increasingly ill at ease in the boisterous court and came to fear a revival of the 'Good Old Cause'. His experience in dealing with the intelligence aspects of the secretary's tasks, however, stood him in good stead for there is no doubt that he had a wealth of techniques and practices in this field. His eventual replacement by a younger and certainly more able man, however, came as something of a relief to many in the regime. Indeed it is possible that one of the main reasons why Nicholas was replaced was his lack of efficiency in security matters. The Earl of Inchiquin wrote that the secretary was told by the king that the 'practices of ill spirits throughout the kingdom did require [much] more labour and activity ... [than Nicholas'] years and infirmities could under go'.[11]

By 1662, therefore, Sir Edward Nicholas had lost much of his skill in office and moreover his potentially very powerful office as Secretary of State became enmeshed in the serious clashes of court politics. The general background to the replacement of Sir Edward Nicholas by Sir Henry Bennet in October 1662 is an oft-told tale and one of the most important reasons for it has already been touched on. Of the two Secretaries of State at this period Nicholas was the easier to manoeuvre out of office. Sir William Morrice, by now seen as a 'decrepit old man' by the wits at court, was retained for the moment at the request of George Monck, Duke of Albermarle, rather than for his usefulness.[12] Morrice was being left with less and less to do and was seldom seen at Whitehall. Nicholas, as the client of Clarendon,[13] was chosen to be the sacrificial lamb in order to

[10] Clarendon, *The History of the Rebellion [and] Continuation of the Life* (Oxford, 1843), p. 933, see also *DNB*, Edward Nicholas; D. Nicholas, *Mr Secretary Nicholas, (1593–1669): His Life and Letters* (1955); also G. E. Warner, ed., *The Nicholas Papers: The Correspondence of Sir Edward Nicholas*, Camden Society (4 vols., 1887–1920), I, pp. xii–xvii.

[11] *HMC*, Heathcote MSS, pp. 54–5. See P. Seaward, *The Cavalier Parliament and the Reconstruction of the Old Regime, 1661–1667* (Cambridge, 1989), p. 15 n. 19 for a similar view about Nicholas' place in the regime.

[12] There is no doubt that Morrice was somewhat at sea both in foreign affairs and at court, whose activities and inhabitants he is said to have viewed with some distaste. See *DNB*, William Morrice; Magalotti, *Relazione*, p. 58; Barbour, *Arlington*, p. 56; Burnet, *History*, I, p. 179.

[13] The dismissal of Nicholas represented another political defeat for the minister. On Clarendon's attitudes and problems at this time see R. Ollard, *Clarendon and His Friends* (Oxford, 1988), pp. 240–1.

further the career of Sir Henry Bennet, the king's current favourite.[14] One significant inheritance which Nicholas had left to his successor in office was the tall, well-set, somewhat punctilious Cumbrian scholar who had for the most part run the office, as well as a growing intelligence system, for him: Joseph Williamson.

III

There is little doubt that Joseph Williamson's part in the establishment of an efficient intelligence and espionage system was an important one. For some nineteen years he was to have a major influence on the secretariat's involvement in this covert world. He was a man upon whom his political masters could rely for prompt, effective and usually reliable intelligence and who came to shoulder the bulk of the administration of the office. Indeed his involvement in the work of the secretariat was such that, to many, Williamson, with all his knowledge and files, was the secretariat. Moreover at the same time in which he was involved in the day-to-day routine, an effective means of gathering intelligence came into being. The running of agents, their instruction, wages and the policy towards them came through Williamson. He also initiated a newsletter system, kept himself informed of the business of local government, supervised a 'cabinet noir' within the Post Office, remained in touch with the diplomatic world and attempted to keep his political masters sweet. His reward for all of this was increasing wealth, respect within government circles, as well as a certain degree of personal satisfaction. His role in the Restoration world of intelligence was a crucial one and therefore calls for some detailed examination.

Joseph Williamson was born on 25 July 1633, and was baptised in the parish church of Bridekirk, Cumberland on 4 August 1633.[15] He was the second surviving son of Joseph Williamson the elder, who had been appointed vicar to the parish in 1625; his family was native to Cumberland and had connections with Millbeck Hall which lay two miles north of Keswick.[16] In 1671 Sir Daniel Fleming noted that this was the 'ancient seat

[14] See BL Sloane MSS 856, fo. 456 for Nicholas' resignation and BL Egerton MSS 2538, fo. 186. In the latter it is recorded that common gossip believed a 'popish faction brought [Arlington] in'. Even at this early stage doubts were expressed about Arlington's religion. See also Barbour, *Arlington*, pp. 56–7; Hutton, *The Restoration*, p. 193.

[15] *Williamson Correspondence*, I, p. 132; *The Registers of Bridekirk, 1584–1812*, transcribed by J. F. Haswell (Penrith, 1927), p. 37. Joseph's elder brother George was coroner for Cumberland until 1662 and afterwards Comptroller of Customs in the county. His mother's second marriage produced at least one son and two daughters.

[16] M. W. Taylor, *The Old Manorial Halls of Westmorland and Cumberland* (Kendal, 1892), pp. 320–3.

of the Williamsons'.[17] Williamson himself later owned this property but it is clear that both his father and family were relatively poor, and the word 'hall' was really too grandiose for such a simple structure. From this 'lean, hungry and desolate sort of country'[18] Williamson was clearly going to be forced to move south to make any sort of career. Fortunately he had been well educated at the grammar school founded by Archbishop Grindal at St Bees[19] and this school also had strong links with the Oxford college that, in one way or another, was to dominate Williamson's adult life, Queen's College. Williamson was also bright and reliable enough to secure the patronage of the local MP Richard Tolson, who took him to London in the late 1640s as his clerk and part-time amanuensis. It was through Tolson's interest that the young Williamson was admitted to Westminster School in 1648. Under the formidable Dr Richard Busby, Williamson learnt the formula of hard work and hard living.[20] The ideals of discipline and hard work which were so prominent in Williamson's later character were partly inculcated under this regime. It was said that part of Busby's method was also to teach his students how to collect useful material and to encourage them to keep notebooks as well as the habit of note taking. Williamson's methods in administration later reflected this teaching. Westminster School 'was geared to success' and its pupils had a reputation for 'poise, self-confidence and sophistication' as well as 'stylish classical learning'[21] and

[17] E. Hughes, ed., *Sir Daniel Fleming's Description of Cumberland 1671*, Fleming–Senhouse Papers, Cumberland Record Series, 2 (Newcastle, 1961), p. 48; also F J. Field, *An Amorial For Cumberland* (Kendal, 1937), pp. 266–7. For Cumberland in the Civil Wars and Republic see J. Wilson, ed., *Victoria County History, Cumberland* (2 vols., Westminster, 1901), I, pp. 286–92.

[18] Quoted in J. V. Beckett, *Coal and Tobacco: The Lowthers and the Economic Development of Cumberland, 1660–1760* (Cambridge, 1981), p. 1. For the clergy of the area see E. J. Evans, 'The Anglican Clergy of Northern England', in C. Jones, ed., *Britain in the Age of Party 1680–1750: Essays Presented to Geoffrey Holmes* (1987), pp. 221–40. See also J. Thirsk, ed., *The Agrarian History of England and Wales* (18 vols., 1956–84), I, pp. 3–29; W. Hutchinson, *The History of Cumberland* (2 vols., 1794–7, reprint, Wakefield, 1974), II, p. 244; BL Add. MSS 28945, fo. 198. See also *CSPD*, 1676–77, p. 281.

[19] W. Jackson, *Papers and Pedigrees* (3 vols., 1892), II, pp. 186–255; G. Holmes, *Augustan England: Profession, State and Society, 1680–1730* (1982), p. 60. Also PRO SP 18/205, fo. 61; for Williamson's gifts to the church at Bridekirk in 1678 see Hutchinson, *Cumberland*, II, p. 603. D. Cressy, *Education in Tudor and Stuart England* (1975), p. 83; also E. Hughes, *North Country Life in the Eighteenth Century* (2 vols., Oxford, 1965), II, pp. 293–333.

[20] For Tolson, see *H of P*, III, p. 577; for Busby see *DNB*, Richard Busby; M. Cranston, *John Locke: A Biography* (1985); G. W. Keeton, *Lord Chancellor Jeffreys and the Stuart Cause* (1965), p. 54; J. L. Axtell, ed., *The Educational Writings of John Locke* (Cambridge, 1968). J. Sargeaunt, *Annals of Westminster School* (1898), pp. 79–134. Williamson's contemporaries at Westminster School included John Locke and George Jeffreys as well as the poet John Dryden. See also J. A. Winn, *John Dryden and His World* (New Haven, 1987), pp. 36–57 and pp. 521–24 which gives the curriculum of the school under Busby's regime.

[21] G. V. Bennett, *The Tory Crisis in Church and State* (Oxford, 1975), pp. 26–7 and G. V. Bennett, 'University, Society and Church, 1688–1714', in L. S. Sutherland and L. G.

these were also elements in Williamson's character which others noted in him. In the event he evidently did well enough for Busby to recommend him to Gerard Langbaine the elder, provost of Queen's and one of the board of the governors of St Bees Grammar School and as a 'deserving' youth from the north country Williamson, in September 1650, entered Queen's college as a 'battellor' or 'servitor' to the provost. Williamson's time at Queen's College, if we are to judge from his later life and actions, made a great impact upon him.[22] He was always loyal both to the college and its members, however lowly the latter may have been, and when he did reach a position of power and influence he took a more than ordinary interest in the college's affairs, proving himself to be one of its most generous benefactors.[23] It became, perhaps, more of a home to him than Bridekirk, or Westminster School, had been. Despite this, during his early years there Williamson seems to have lived in some poverty.[24] These factors might well account for his driving ambition, his greed for tangible financial rewards, as well as his penchant for gathering useful information; servants traditionally keep their eyes and ears open and blend into the background – which would have been eminently useful qualities for a future 'spymaster'. Matriculating as Bachelor of Arts in February 1654 he was later to take a Masters degree by diploma in 1657, and serve in France from 1655 to 1658 as a tutor to some young men of quality.[25] By June 1658 Williamson was on his way back to Oxford to take up his fellowship at Queen's College and, perhaps, deacon's orders,[26] and at this stage in Williamson's life an academic career at Oxford seemed the most likely prospect before him.[27] It was events on the wide political stage which were now to change his fortunes. For in May 1660 the Restoration of King Charles II and the Stuart regime took place and Joseph Williamson was one of its more

Mitchell, eds., *The History of the University of Oxford* (4 vols. so far, Oxford, 1986), IV: *The Eighteenth Century*, pp. 359–400. J. R. Magrath, *The Queen's College* (2 vols., Oxford, 1921), II, p. 44.

22 For life at Oxford in the later seventeenth century see Bennett 'University, Society and Church', pp. 359–400. See also R. Trappes-Lomax, ed., *The Diary and Letter Book of Rev. Thomas Brockbank, 1671–1709*, Chetham Society NS, 81 (1930). Brockbank was the son of a poor Westmorland parson and was at Queen's College from 1687 to 1695.

23 See BL Add. MSS 28945, fos. 197–98, for Williamson's legacies to the college; and also C. E. Mallet, *A History of the University of Oxford* (3 vols., Oxford, 1924), I, pp. 286–7; Magrath, *Queen's College*. See also A. Clark, ed., *The Life and Times of Anthony Wood, Antiquary, of Oxford, 1632–95, Described by Himself* (4 vols., Oxford, 1891–5), II, p. 438. Wood notes that at least two bishops and one archdeacon, all Queen's men, owed their position to Williamson's patronage.

24 Magalotti, *Relazione*, p. 44.

25 We can trace Williamson's travels with some accuracy: 1655–6, Saumur, Angers; 1656–7, Saumur; 1657–8, Angers, Saumur, Perpignan, Lyons, Toulon, Moulins, Nevers, Paris, Frankfurt. The Hague, Oxford. Nicholas, with the exiled court of Charles II, was in Flanders or Germany throughout this period.

26 Hutchinson, *Cumberland*, II, p. 245.

27 *CSPD* Commonwealth, 1658–9, p. 82.

immediate beneficiaries. He was able to move from the academic cloisters of Oxford to the palace of Whitehall, 'ill built and nothing but a heap of houses'[28] maybe, but nevertheless the new centre of power and government. Lorenzo Magalotti, who first met Williamson on a visit to England in 1668, noted that Williamson obtained, through the assistance of Gilbert Sheldon, Bishop of London, a post in the office of the Secretary of State Sir Edward Nicholas.[29]

Williamson always retained a sense of obligation to Nicholas for the favour shown to him by bringing him from Oxford to the centre of power, and he later wrote that he was ever 'sensible ... of [the Secretary of State's] goodness to me when I was yet young and low in ... service'.[30] Some of Williamson's Oxford compatriots were no doubt sorry to see him leave Oxford, but for Williamson himself, then twenty-seven, it was an opportunity to be seized and a sign of divine favour, for 'God' as he pointed out, was the 'real author of every good and perfect gift'.[31] The motives of a man such as Williamson taking service in government in this period could often be complex, but in his case it was undoubtedly a mixture of shrewd personal ambition, the prestige the post could bring, as well as the opportunities for advancement and assisting his Oxford college. He also shared the more practical financial motives visible in every Restoration politician or civil servant. There were undoubtedly opportunities for making money in the service of the government and Williamson was to prove that he would never be slow in taking any financial opportunities which presented themselves. This was so much so that by 1668 he was rumoured to be worth 'forty thousand pounds in ready money', although in fact this was an exaggeration.[32]

In July 1660 therefore Williamson entered the office of the southern

[28] Samuel de Sorbiere, *A Voyage to England* (1709), p. 16. The first French edition of this work was published in 1664.

[29] For Sheldon, see H. Craik, *The Life of Edward, Earl of Clarendon* (2 vols., 1911), I, p. 31; Magalotti, *Relazione*, p. 44. For Magalotti in England see R. D. Waller, 'Lorenzo Magalotti in England, 1668–9', *Italian Studies*, 1, no. 2, 1937, pp. 49–66. Also W. E. Knowles-Middleton, 'Some Italian Visitors to the Early Royal Society', *Notes and Records of the Royal Society of London*, 33 (1978–9), pp. 157–74.

[30] BL Egerton MSS 2539, fos. 42–3. [31] *ibid.*

[32] So at least Lorenzo Magalotti claimed; Magalotti, *Relazione*, p. 44. But see PRO SP 105/224, fos. 207–8 on Williamson's negotiations for the post of Secretary of State; although he did end up wealthy enough to be able to lend his friends Lord and Lady O'Brien £6,000 in 1675. See Kent RO 4565, addnl/T212 (3 documents). Later still he was able to buy his wife's Cobham estate outright for £45,000. See E. Wingfield-Stratford, *The Lords of Cobham Hall* (1959), p. 137. He was also owed £6,151. 4s. 4d. in 1680 by Charles II from his time as Secretary of State, Kent RO 4565, E211, fo. 1. That Williamson was interested in money, and correct accounts, is proven by *Correspondence of Henry Hyde, Earl of Clarendon and his Brother Lawrence Hyde, Earl of Rochester* (2 vols., 1828), I, p. 301. Having said this his bequests in his will were generous, for example: Queen's College: £6,000; the creation of a free school in Thetford: £5,000.

secretary as a clerk to Nicholas, but because of his 'knowledge of worldly affairs' and because his patron was 'less and less able to perform his duties of office', his rise was rapid and the burden of work, including that of the gathering of intelligence, began to fall upon him.[33] As well as an eagerness for money Williamson also possessed an eagerness for power and took the opportunities presented to him to widen both his position and his duties in the office, however, much administrative drudgery this entailed. Initially his junior position was not very lucrative, but this improved in time and in December 1661 he was also appointed Keeper of the King's Library at Whitehall and of the State Paper Office with a salary of £160 per annum. For the most part, however, Williamson was kept busy by his clerical duties. The competition for places at all levels of government service was high and at no time more so than in the 1660s. To retain a grip on major office required a great deal more political skill than mere 'clerking', as Williamson's own career in the 1670s was to prove. With Nicholas' retirement however the main problem for the enterprising clerk, widely regarded as the 'intimate favourite' of the secretary, was where the appointment of the new secretary left him, for according to the knowledgable Magalotti, the 'first thing Lord Arlington did was to dismiss Williamson at once from the secretariat'.[34] The prospect of a return to Oxford loomed, but he was almost immediately reinstated because Arlington realised that it was already impossible to run the office without Williamson who had so integrated himself in its work that he proved essential to its running. From that point on he gained the closest ties of 'principle and confidence' of the new secretary. There is unfortunately no corroborative evidence for this story, but that does not make it unlikely.[35] Whatever the truth behind its beginnings in 1662, the partnership between Arlington and Williamson was to have great consequences for the government and the intelligence system of the regime.

IV

Intelligence work in the Restoration period was heavily dependent upon what happened at the centre of government. The methods used in the Secretary of State's office were therefore highly significant to the success or failure of the Restoration system. As he made himself essential to its effectiveness, Sir Joseph Williamson's methods of work in the office need

[33] Magalotti, *Relazione*, p. 44; see also *CSPD*, 1660–1, p. 145; Evelyn, *Diary*, IV, p. 38. Also in the office as a clerk at this period was Charles Whittaker who served Nicholas from May 1660 to October 1662. See Sainty, *Secretaries of State*, pp. 27, 116.

[34] Magalotti, *Relazione*, p. 44.

[35] See for example J. P. Kenyon, *Robert Spencer, Earl of Sunderland* (1958), p. 73.

to be understood as part of the broader schema which went to make up the intelligence system. These methods developed in Williamson's period of office and certain common characteristics can be seen. We can also itemise distinctive traits which led, consciously or unconsciously, to the promotion of reform and efficient working practice in matters of administration and intelligence gathering. These traits are shown in Williamson's attitude towards his work, his use of and willingness to gain knowledge of precedents, the strict discipline in office practice he ensured, which led to a division of labour and a systematic order. He also possessed a methodical nature with an eye for detail, which in some cases degenerated into sheer pedantry, as well as an ability to foresee administrative problems and adapt accordingly, to respond with clarity and learn from errors. In matters of delegation he always showed some reluctance, Williamson's trust was something given only grudgingly to his clerks. All in all Williamson's method was important to the development of the Stuart regime's intelligence system at the centre.

Method can be defined as the rules and practices proper to a particular art. In the wide sense it is a scheme or plan of action intended to produce systematic arrangement or order. As regards Williamson's own administrative method there is little actually written down. Much of it must be interpreted and gleaned from the actual results of his activities and the day-to-day running of the office. Administrators themselves, while in an ideal position to comment upon the methods they use, rarely do so. This is mainly because they tend not to dwell on the problems facing them, much less set them down on paper, but as practical men solve the immediate problems in front of them. In doing so they may thus create a precedent and use that precedent for future action. This, of course, begs the question asked by Professor Aylmer as to whether by our very study of the subject we are reflecting *our* interests rather than theirs and in so doing distorting the actual administrative activities of the time.[36] It is a fine historical line to draw, for as Aylmer has pointed out 'we need to know what they thought important and how they spent their time; not necessarily the same thing'.[37] It is at least fortunate that in the Restoration period there is considerably more evidence available than for the years before 1642 to enable certain aspects of the administrative method used by Williamson and others to be pieced together.

It is again fortunate that Williamson in his few direct references to his ideas on administrative method set out some of his ideals in working practice. These are usually scribbled and often fairly illegible notes in journals

[36] G. E. Aylmer, *The King's Servants: The Civil Service of Charles I* (1961), pp. 155–6.
[37] *ibid.*

or in other obscure documents. In one instance, in an early notebook, there is a note to himself to 'read all my letters of all heads myselfe ... [and] ... ty up all Advisos of one month ... [and to] ... have a memorandum book lye by for notes to be received each night'.[38] Further evidence on his ideal method is forthcoming from other sources. He noted in a letter to Daniel Fleming, a life-long friend, that 'I hope to watch all the Parts of the Businesse of my Trade with greater punctuality.'[39] A more useful measure of his methods is the advice contained within a letter to Robert Yard in 1673 where Williamson noted that it was always best to 'First ... inform yourself, next to be able to give a reasonable account to my Lord Arlington on any occasion where papers are & lastly, as you have time, to take ... short notes on things, to lye by for ... use.'[40] He also stressed the fact that Yard must 'above all be busy at the Deske, working at the Correspondents business, acknowledgeing, encouraging & pressing our Correspondents every where to be diligent'.[41] It is very likely in the years 1662–74 at least that the ideals recommended to Yard were followed by Williamson himself.

In a letter to William Bridgeman from Antwerp in 1673 Williamson also asked to hear from Bridgeman as often

> as the Crowd of the Office Businesse will allow ... You will see a thousand things passe on that side that may be of great use to me to know and if they were not the satisfaction and entertainment the knowledge they would give me is an obligation I shall most particularly owe to you.[42]

This eagerness for knowledge of all sorts, some of it quite esoteric, was also a key to his attitude in matters of intelligence. It can be illustrated by a variety of examples. There is, for instance, the case of William Nicolson, student at Queen's, future Bishop of Carlisle and in 1678 very much one of Williamson's protégés.[43] In 1678 Williamson paid for Nicolson to travel abroad to study at the University of Leipzig.[44] Before he undertook this journey however, Williamson forwarded to Nicolson a three-page body of instructions on what he should see on the road to Leipzig.[45] In these instructions Williamson did not miss the opportunity to gather all the

38 PRO SP 29/87 (notebook, c.1662–3).
39 *Flemings in Oxford*, I, p. 199.
40 PRO SP 81/60/61, fos. 138–9.
41 *ibid.*
42 PRO SP 105/224, fo. 38.
43 For William Nicolson see C. Jones and G. S. Holmes, eds., *The London Diaries of William Nicolson, Bishop of Carlisle, 1702–1718*, (Oxford, 1985); also G. Sutherland and L. G. Mitchell, eds., *History of the University of Oxford* (4 vols. so far, Oxford, 1986), IV, pp. 809–10.
44 *ibid.*
45 BL Add. MSS 41803, fos. 9–10v; also J. W. Stoye, *English Travellers Abroad, 1604–1667: Their Influence in English Society and Politics* (revised edn, 1989), pp. 184–6.

intelligence he possibly could. Far from being a simple 'grand tour' Nicolson was informed that he should arm himself with maps, 'a table book ... in which to note down all that's memorable as you pass up and down',[46] a journal to write all his observations in each night, and he was to obtain further printed commentaries on the places visited. Nicolson was also to gather political and military intelligence concerning fortifications, governors, garrisons and make an assessment of the local political and economic situation.[47] The instructions themselves are unusually detailed in comparison with the more generalised ones given to diplomats, and resemble in many ways the instructions Williamson gave to spies.[48]

Another aspect to this eagerness for knowledge was Williamson's ideas on precedents. During his time in office he gathered together a large collection of precedents used by former Secretaries of State.[49] An example of his enthusiasm for correct precedent is the protracted negotiation with the former Secretary of State Sir Edward Nicholas and the borrowing by Williamson, in Arlington's name, of Nicholas' 'Bookes of Entryes'.[50] They were of use, Williamson informed the ex-Secretary of State, 'many times to witnesse & resolve what hath passed the Office, & to guide in many occasions what or is not to passe'.[51] Indeed so useful were they that Williamson continued to hold onto the entry books 'to take copyes of them to remaine in the office'.[52] Nicholas, while agreeing that the books would be useful to the office, also wished for them back as soon as possible;[53] but it is not clear if Williamson ever returned them. Finally we may cite Matthew Prior as a witness to one further aspect of the Williamson method. Reminiscing in September 1699 he noted that on certain subjects 'there is a great deal to be said, and a great deal to be thought (as Sir Joseph [Williamson] ... used to tell us).'[54]

Certain definite priorities can thus be delineated in Williamson's method and these had a direct effect upon the development of the intelligence system. Firstly there was the need to supervise or oversee work for himself, or where he could not do so in person to have a detailed body of instructions written out to guide his subordinates. There was also the need to record items in accessible form for future reference. There was the compulsion to gather knowledge of all kinds in a systematic manner: knowledge

46 BL Add. MSS 41803, fo. 10. 47 *ibid.*
48 Compare with PRO SP 29/187, fo. 148, and see below, Chapter 4.
49 The remnants of this collection can be found in PRO SP 9.
50 BL Eg. MSS 2539, fos. 42–3.
51 *ibid.* 52 *ibid.* 53 PRO SP 29/163, fo. 132.
54 Matthew Prior quoted by L. G. W. Legg, *Matthew Prior: A Study of his Public Career and Correspondence* (Cambridge, 1921), pp. 44–5.

which might not have been of any immediate value but may have been useful for decision making at some future point.[55] Williamson quickly seems to have realised how true was the old adage that in government knowledge is power, and he acted accordingly. Equally distinctive was the strict reliance upon precedent and thus the priority given to continuity and stability in the administrative process. From the stress on precedent also derives a penchant for problem-solving through a historical perspective. Finally the Williamson of Prior's statement, and of other evidence too, is revealed as a man who is able to tackle problems using a critical ability – an ability to think processes through to their ultimate goal and make a critical judgement.

The secretary's tasks were wide-ranging, but how were they organised in practice? It is possible to gain some idea of the organisation from Williamson's journals of the way in which he at least was able to organise the office and his personal work load. These examples are taken from the periods when he was 'under secretary' and Secretary of State respectively and they show how an efficient administrator could impose his own system upon the office and bring order into what otherwise could have been a chaotic situation. They also show clearly how much the efficiency of the office owed to the methodical mind and effective organising abilities of the man. In 1672–3 for example we find the following classification of the subjects of business in the office outlined and cross-indexed in one of Williamson's journals.

Drawers

1. Plantations Trade
2. Foreign Committee
3. Ceremonials
   Ambassadors
   Heraldry
4. Collection
5. Treaties
   Cuts &c
6. Souveranty
   Precedents
   Stiles

[55] See for an example *CSPD*, 1676–77, pp. 59–60. For a parallel to this attitude, especially useful in the field of intelligence, see J. C. Rule, 'Colbert de Torcy, an Emergent Bureaucracy, and the Formulation of French Foreign Policy, 1698–1715', in R. Hatton, ed., *Louis XIV and Europe* (1976), pp. 276–77. In particular Torcy's 'collector's mania to purchase manuscripts'.

7. Treatyes
   Instruments
   Negotiations
8. Instruments
   Commissions
   Powers
9. Secretary
   Paper Office

The Chimney

The Councell Prizes
Ireland
Military
Navy
The warre with Holland
Min[utes]
Papers of State . . .[56]

There is a certain logic about such organisation and an air of having everything in its place and a place for everything. This is seen with even greater effect by 1675. By 1675, and after Williamson's appointment to the position of northern secretary, the following index was set up to cover the organisation of his work load.

Julius Caesar	I	Military Admiralty Publica Philosophica . . .	Soverainty
Augustus	II	Parliament	
Tiberius	III	Domestic	Collectana Ang[lia] Ecc[lesias]tica Offices London Household Revenue Secretarys Office
Caligula	IV	Ireland Scotland Wales Jersey Guernsey Exam[inations] Inform[ers]	

[56] PRO SP 29/319A (1672–3 journal).

Claudius	V	Trade Plantation Tangier
Nero	VI	Warre between France and Spaine
Galba	VII	Warre between England, France and Holland 1672 & Italy
Otho	VIII	France
Vitellius	VIIII	Spaine Flanders Portugal
Vespasian	X	Germany Turkey, Algiers, Barbary, Tunis &c Tripoli
Titus	XI	Holland Foreign Commitee
Domitian	XII	Sweden Denmark Poland Russia Meditation[57]

In fact these lists can be added to by the inclusion of such diverse items as petitions, domestic and foreign outgoing correspondence, entry books, the *Gazette*, the manuscript newsletter system, translations, numerous other journals dealing with precedents, the king's letters and a variety of other miscellaneous papers. Taken *en masse* they provide a formidable body of work for a relatively small staff of two or three under-secretaries and three or four clerks. That Williamson took on and successfully organised the office into a smooth-running system is a tribute in itself to his energy, ability and ambition. Taken together these lists reveal an exceptionally methodical mind at work.

The increasing work load in the secretaries' offices did of course necessitate the organisation of duties for the staff. In the 1660s and 1670s this organisation in the southern office came under the hand of Williamson and we may take the central years 1672–3 as the example of the way in which the office was organised. It is clear that Williamson was the prime mover in the office and took upon himself the day-to-day running of business. This left William Bridgeman and John Richards to function as Arlington's personal secretaries. Richards was given all Arlington's personal correspondence or despatches to handle. The common orders, business warrants, petitions and other work were divided between Richards, Bridgeman and Williamson. This was partly due to the fact that there were fees to be made

[57] PRO SP 9/157 (1673–5 notebook). Roman numerals refer to cupboards topped by busts of relevant Roman emperors.

out of these particular items. Indeed as J. C. Sainty has pointed out, for the greater part of the period the officers derived their remuneration from official fees.[58] John Cooke, who served in the northern secretary's office from the 1660s to the 1680s, is clearly stated to have received 'fees out of all businesses which pass the kings or the secretary's signature'.[59] He obtained the fee of £1. 0s. 0d. for each warrant, bill or commission and £0. 10s. 0d. for each petition referred, Owen Wynne worked under Jenkins and Middleton as a private or personal secretary in the same office. He was paid by the secretary himself, between £140. 0s. 0d. to £200. 0s. 0d. per annum.[60] Similar proceedings no doubt operated in the southern office.[61]

The open ordinary correspondence, whether domestic or foreign, came directly to Williamson and his clerks. When Williamson left for Cologne in 1673 this task passed to Robert Yard. The control of the bulk of the office correspondence gave Williamson a firm grip on the events occurring outside Whitehall and made him the mainstay of intelligence within, as well as outside, the office. Correspondence would enter the office from the Post Office. Firm directions were laid down by Williamson in 1674 on his appointment as Secretary of State regarding post coming to and going from the office.[62] On receipt the clerks would sometimes prepare it by writing a short summary of all the contents of the letter on the reverse side. These précis dealt with every item in the letter and were a time-saving device to be read by Williamson and Arlington in order that a quick assessment as to whether any action was necessary could be taken. The king himself, of course, when he condescended to read correspondence, or had it read to him, needed a short précis rather than bulky letter. It has already been noted above how it was Williamson's ideal practice to read all the 'heads' of his letters himself.

Letters in cipher which might be coming from diplomats abroad were also given to the clerks to decipher. This was an invariably long and somewhat tedious process over which great care had to be taken. Southwell in his memorial on this matter argued that one of the clerks should be specifically delegated for 'cyphering and uncyphering'. In fact such a post did become permanent in later reigns.[63] The clerk in charge of this task had to be reliable, for ciphers were a complex part of the secretary's business and problems could occur. Too complex a cipher could lead to more errors than were usual and render it unintelligible to the recipient. Conversely too

[58] Sainty, *Secretaries of State*, p. 9.
[59] All Souls College MSS 204, fo. 19 also printed in Evans, *Principal Secretary*, pp. 192–3.
[60] *ibid.* [61] For some of these figures see *CSPD*, 1672–5, pp. 505–13.
[62] PRO SP 29/362, fo. 31.
[63] BL Add. MSS 38861, fo. 46. See also Sainty, *Secretaries of State*, pp. 51–2. For more on ciphers and codes see below, Chapter 2.

simple a cipher was all too easily broken. Sir William Temple in 1668, complaining of a cipher that had gone wrong, noted to Arlington, 'I am apt to imagine the exactness required to this cypher is more than can agree with the haste often necessary in your lordship's office.'[64] Correspondence coming from agents using cover names and addresses in the 1660s appears to have gone by another route. Williamson, for example, is known to have had a list or a book sent to the Post Office containing the names and addresses of those involved in the correspondence which was meant for his eyes only.[65] Very few officials knew of this book and its whereabouts are now lost. Some idea of what might have been contained in it can be found in Williamson's own address book in the state papers where the agents' cover names are written next to their real names.[66] Obviously only the code names and addresses would have been held at the Post Office. Sunderland, when he became Secretary of State, was given a cipher upon which the cover names and addresses to be used for that correspondent were written.[67]

The duties concerned with the Foreign Committee of the Privy Council in the 1660s and 1670s were handled by Arlington himself with the assistance of the ubiquitous Joseph Williamson. It was he who acted as the secretary to the Foreign Committee. This fact negates the French ambassador's view that Williamson was thought a man 'd'espirit [and] est estimé habile n'ayant pas neántmoins cognoissance des secrets desseins du Roy'.[68] As secretary to the Foreign Committee he took down the minutes for all the discussions which took place in that committee and it is his pen upon which we rely for our knowledge of its work.[69] Yard, Swaddell and Benson were the clerks delegated with the task of keeping the entry books and their indexes up to date and drafting correspondence.[70] After the dismissal of Henry Muddiman, responsibility for editing the *Gazette* rested with Robert Perrot and later this passed to Yard.[71] Henry Ball was placed with his four under-clerks in Scotland Yard. Their concern was with the manuscript newsletter service. This produced 'extracts of such common

[64] Sir William Temple, *Works* (4 vols., 1754), I, pp. 410–11.
[65] PRO SP 29/209, fo. 18; and *CSPD*, 1668–9, p. 483.
[66] PRO SP 9/32, fos. 211–30 (Williamson's address book).
[67] BL Add. MSS 40677, fo. 296. For more on this subject see below, Chapter 2.
[68] PRO 31/3/128: 3 April 1673, Colbert to the king.
[69] See PRO SP 104/177 (Committee of Foreign Affairs Journal 1672–3) for an example.
[70] PRO SP 29/441, fos. 126–7.
[71] See Handover, *London Gazette*, pp. 15–16; also J. Sutherland, *The Restoration Newspaper and its Development* (Cambridge, 1986). Yard was to be briefly dismissed in 1676 for allowing information to be sent out in a newsletter which was not only wrong, but should not have gone beyond the Privy Council and then escaped to the coffee-house politicians. Williamson, and more importantly the king, were furious. See PRO SP 44/43, p. 119; *CSPD*, 1676–7, pp. 356–7, 360, 363–4, 368.

news as is fit to be communicated to the king's ministers abroad and to some country friends ... at home'.[72] In return both domestic correspondents and diplomats overseas wrote back to Williamson direct with their local news. The receivers of such newsletters were a very select group. Ball was warned by Williamson in 1673 to 'continue carefull in the regulation & punctual management of the matter of correspondents, giving copies to no other then who now have [the] papers unlesse first ordered by ... Lord [Arlington]'.[73]

In practice the office system as it developed in the 1660s and 1670s appears to have worked rather well. Williamson's vigorous style of management kept the clerks in order and everyone very busy. Occasionally there were lapses, as when Bridgeman and Williamson's two clerks, Swaddell and Yard, fell out and this caused delays in the business of the office.[74] Again, if Pepys is to be believed, the enormous amounts of work which passed through the office occasionally proved too much even for Williamson himself.[75] Attempting to get some business passed through the office in July 1668 Pepys noted that it was 'pretty to see how Mr Williamson did altogether excuse himself that my business was not done'.[76] Coming before Arlington, however, Pepys and Williamson uncovered the fact that the business had been done and moreover the document was written out in Williamson's own hand.[77] Generally such lapses appear to have been rare and standards were kept high. Any comparisons with the procedure in other ministers' offices are difficult to make as there were no set rules and each office handled differing material. Most officials, however, worked according to a set pattern. Some comparisons may be made with the pattern of work in Secretary of State Middleton's office in 1684. Indeed it is possible, as Sainty has argued, that this organisation was more typical in many ways of the procedures in the secretariat than the office Williamson controlled.[78] Be that as it may, and it must be stressed that Williamson's position was in some respects a unique one, there are some similarities. John Cooke as under-secretary to Middleton organised the office in much the same manner as Williamson, and indeed depended on the latter's knowledge on occasion.[79] Owen Wynne took on the role of personal secretary. The clerks appear to have had no particular duties assigned to them and worked under Cooke's orders. He drew up drafts of warrants, letters and handled the correspondence both domestic and foreign. He also adjudicated in precedent and style.[80] Perhaps this office did have one extra

72 PRO SP 29/441, fos. 126–7. 73 PRO SP 81/60/61, fos. 138–9.
74 *Williamson Correspondence*, I, p. 44.
75 This was especially true after 1676. See Grey, *Debates*, VI, pp. 216–40.
76 Pepys, *Diary*, VIII, p. 318.
77 *ibid.* 78 Sainty, *Secretaries of State*, pp. 7–8. 79 *CSPD*, 1668–9, p. 47.
80 Evans, *Principal Secretary*, p. 192.

item which Williamson's did not, for in February 1688 it was discovered that one of the clerks, Samuel De Paz, had been in Dutch pay and had been passing information to them since at least July 1685.[81]

'He is', noted the Italian visitor, Lorenzo Magalotti, on meeting Williamson in 1668, 'a tall man, of very good appearance, clever, diligent, courteous ... not presumptuous ... and he is very inquisitive in getting information'.[82] The latter quality, needless to say, was a very important qualification in the field of intelligence. Some of the elements of character which drove Williamson into becoming a central-administrative cog in the office have already been noted above. The ideals of discipline and hard work were doubtless partly responsible; Oxford and travel abroad during the late 1650s no doubt reinforced them. It may be that as with Pepys in the same period he had felt the frustrations of under-employment.[83] It is certain that he was something of a studious and sober young man when a tutor to his pupils, one of whom subscribed his letter to his 'father' Williamson; the latter was twenty-three at the time.[84] Certainly the strictures heaped upon young Richard Lowther's addiction to tennis in Saumur in 1656 lead one to this impression; 'unless he wholly leaves it I assure you I will leave him' was Williamson's indignant response to the situation.[85] Just as revealing is Williamson's view that characters ruled by their passions were not for him: 'I will never undertake the breeding of any person that shall have his passions for a rule of his actions & not my reason'.[86] It was an ideal Williamson kept to, although he was not entirely free of all passion himself.

Magalotti, whose interest in Williamson is in itself a commentary upon the significance of a man whose post in 1668 was still, officially at any rate, a relatively minor one in government, gives some contemporary opinions of the man. Magalotti noted that 'Many people praise [Williamson] ... others complain about him; some say he counterfeits his good qualities and some maintain that they are rested in his nature.'[87] A more judicious assessment came from that other eminent administrator of the period, Samuel Pepys. On his first encounter with Williamson Pepys thought that Williamson was a 'pretty knowing man and a scholar but it may be thinks himself to be too much so'.[88] Eventually Pepys did come to warm to the Cumbrian and noted that 'the more I [see and] ... know [him] ... the more

[81] J. Childs, *The Army, James II and the Glorious Revolution* (Manchester 1980), p. 141. But see below, Chapter 6.
[82] Magalotti, *Relazione*, pp. 44–5.
[83] R. Ollard, *Pepys: A Biography* (Oxford, 1985), p. 37.
[84] *CSPD*, 1656–7, p. 144.
[85] Cumbria RO (Carlisle), Lowther MSS D/Lons./L1/1/n. 11: 6 September 1656, Saumur, Joseph Williamson to Geoffrey Northleigh.
[86] *ibid.* [87] Magalotti, *Relazione*, p. 46. [88] Pepys, *Diary*, IV, p. 35.

I honour [him]'.[89] Williamson's view of his own position, implicit and frequently explicit in his papers, is not in doubt: he believed himself to be the central hub around which everything else, including my lord Arlington, revolved. He often gave the distinct impression of a man who when away from the office is certain that the place will rapidly run down without his commanding presence. In some senses he was correct, for having created a unique position for himself, when absent there were substantial areas of office work which he alone could attend to adequately and which would face delay until he returned. There was also incessant correspondence back to the clerks in the office during these fairly infrequent periods of absence. By turns the correspondence was bullying, cajoling, and ultimately threatening in cases where he suspected duties were not carried out in the proper manner.[90] Again a direct analogy with Pepys may be found. Pepys expressed this sort of attitude exactly in noting that 'living as I do among so many lazy people ... the diligent man becomes ... [so] ... necessary that they cannot do anything without him'.[91]

How far was Williamson typical of the administrators who were his peers? Within the select group to which he belongs there are some common characteristics. But something of the spirit of a common method can be found in a document written by Edward Southwell.[92] Edward was the son of Sir Robert Southwell and later succeeded his father as Secretary of State for Ireland. In one of his documents, written in April 1693, he was concerned to lay down a ground plan for cultivating his interest, as he puts it, as Clerk of the Council. His thirteen 'preparatory things to enable mee in my Business'[93] are both a reflection of his character and bear a strong echo of the Williamson priorities outlined above. He noted that he must be in constant attendance at his duties and implied that it should be a learning experience, producing a body of notes and precedent for his own use. He also wished to pass on his awareness of this knowledge to his masters, 'which will resound to my advantage'.[94] Southwell also wished to cultivate a style in his working practices and by so doing he would be using his critical judgement. The differences between the two men, Southwell and Williamson, are primarily those of time, not of administrative skill or priorities. Southwell was writing in 1693 at an early stage of the so-called 'administrative revolution', of post-Revolution Britain, while Williamson was one of a small group of men who prefigured that administrative revolution under the Restoration monarchy. The man at the hub of the office was also at the hub of an expanding intelligence system. Using this methodology he was committed to guarding the regime's security. Here

[89] *ibid.* VII, p. 63. [90] In particular see *CSPD*, 1667–8, p. 545.
[91] Pepys quoted in Ollard, *Pepys*, p. 127.
[92] Bl Add. MSS 38861, fo. 64. [93] *ibid.* [94] *ibid.*

indeed was a man who resembled John Bunyan's Mr Prywell with his 'manner of listening up and down ... Mansoul, to see and hear ... any design against it. For he ... feared some mischief sometime would befall it, either from the Diabolonians within or from power without'.[95] That Williamson was able to blossom in this area was not only the result of his methods, but also a result of the favour shown to him by his immediate political master, Sir Henry Bennet, Earl of Arlington.

V

Sir Henry Bennet, Earl of Arlington, was one of the most talented of Charles II's many ministers and has been undoubtedly underestimated both as a minister and as a statesman.[96] This was as true of contemporary opinion as it has often been of later historians.[97] It is difficult to state exactly why contemporaries disliked Arlington, as his talents and virtues as a minister of state were prodigious. He was prudent in his speech and actions and possessed of the courtier's mentality. He proved subtle in his dealings with the king and highly adaptable in the politics of the court. He could adopt an air of frivolity or sobriety as it suited, yet retain enough mental detachment to gain political advantages. This was matched by a keen and ambitious mind. Charles II found in Arlington an able, personable and much-travelled man, someone who spoke fluent Latin, French and Spanish and was noted for his intelligence, who would work in the king's interests and try to please him in his demands. Qualities such as these no doubt account, at least partly, for Arlington's longevity as a minister of state when so many of his rivals fell by the wayside.

The air of gravity, perhaps even pomposity, which was so obvious in Arlington's nature attracted many enemies at court, from the crusty old Chancellor Clarendon, who despised him, to that dangerous wild card of Restoration politics Buckingham, who loathed Arlington as his greatest rival. The foppish elements in Arlington's character were deceptive.[98] While he might plume himself in his finery and was as satirised as other politicians in the era, he also acquired and retained power. At the same

95 J. Bunyan, *The Holy War* (1682, undated edn), p. 218.

96 There is need for a new biography of Arlington, but until this appears the best introduction remains Barbour, *Arlington*; see also *H of P*, I, pp. 620–22; and *DNB*, Henry Bennet.

97 There are exceptions to this: K. Feiling, *British Foreign Policy, 1660–1674* (1968), pp. 76–8; Hutton, *Restoration*, pp. 192–4; M. Lee, 'The Earl of Arlington and the Treaty of Dover', *Journal of British Studies*, 1, 1961, pp. 58–70.

98 See 'A Lampoon', Anon. in H. Love, ed., *The Penguin Book of Restoration Verse* (1968), pp. 112–13; see also C. Phipps, ed., *Buckingham: Public and Private Man, The Prose, Poems and Commonplace Book of George Villiers 2nd Duke of Buckingham* (New York, 1985), p. 149.

time he was a man imbued with a sense of caution which, while it often kept him silent on official occasions in committees, council or the House of Lords, was useful in private. Even Clarendon grudgingly admitted that Arlington's talents were geared to privacy and secrecy. This air of secrecy was valuable in other ways. It was perhaps acquired in Spain, alongside his Castilian-like stateliness and love of magnificence. Like his master, Arlington was a grandee, and as with the king, Arlington also favoured toleration, proving in the long run to be a closet Roman Catholic. This affection for Catholicism was revealing in itself. It was always sufficiently well covered in public life to be deniable. For Arlington was really a player of roles. He was a politician of easy principles, who was greedy for power and in contrast to some others, willing to work hard to fulfil his ambitions.

In spite of his refusal to be bribed Arlington was a practical politician; he was never unwilling to dirty his hands if it seemed necessary.[99] He was, for example more than willing to persuade Frances Stuart into the king's bed and he had quickly learnt that the court of Charles II was a jungle in which a man, however powerful he seemed to be on the surface, could be swiftly destroyed by his enemies. In this Hobbesian world Arlington was willing to play the pander or flatter alongside the best of them and was also aware that his own interests and survival at court lay in politics on the grand scale, particularly in foreign affairs. He needed to cut a great figure in this arena and this meant that he could not monopolise the business of the office of Secretary of State. While he used the office as a political power base there was simply too much to do and not enough time to do it in. With the trusted Joseph Williamson at his side, however, Arlington was able first to delegate work to Williamson and then forced to do so to enable him to concentrate on high policy. In the matters of intelligence and espionage this need to delegate was even more necessary. While Arlington's role as secretary was to sanction some of the more dubious activities of the regime and have ultimate responsibility as Secretary of State in such matters, he was a shrewd user of the powers of delegation and this enabled Williamson to emerge into a position of unusual prominence in the office.[100] After 1662 Arlington swiftly began to assert his dominance within the secretariat which he used as his ministerial power base. He soon outstripped his partner in the northern office in the confidence of the king.

[99] The same was also true of Williamson, see Feiling, *Foreign Policy*, p. 78; C. L. Grose, 'Louis XIV's Financial Relations With Charles II and the English Parliament', *Journal of Modern History*, 1, 1929, p. 180, for Louis XIVs attempts to bribe both men.

[100] See Bod. Lib. Carte MSS 46, fols. 321v., 357 for examples. For contemporary opinions of Arlington, on which this portrait is based, see Magalotti, *Relazione*, p. 43; René Ternois, 'Saint Evermond et la Politique Anglaise, 1665–1674', *XVIIe Siècle*, 57, 1962, pp. 4–5; Burnet, *History*, I, pp. 180–1; *State Papers Collected by Edward, Earl of Clarendon* (3 vols., Oxford, 1706), III, pp. 81–4.

And as Arlington rose so also did Williamson, who was also out to acquire power and influence for himself. Together this partnership in the period after 1662 conducted what, at times, almost seems to have been a calculated policy of administrative aggrandisement, and it is on the activity of this office during the tenure of these men that the major development of the regime's intelligence system took place. They set the pace and laid down the precedents and it is to their method of work that we must now turn.

Lord Craven, writing to Princess Elizabeth, Electoress of the Palatine in April 1673, noted of Joseph Williamson that he was one of the 'deserving knights of the age for his experience in both forane and domestique concernes and agreeableness in his conversation'. With regard to the Earl of Arlington's view of Williamson Craven noted that 'I must not omit to acquaint your highness that hee is greatly valued by him and in the highest confidences of any person I know'.[101] The relationship between Williamson and Arlington grew over the years 1662–74 and it is crucial to understanding the development of the intelligence system. It was never fully one of master and servant nor one of total equality, it remained somewhere in between. It could not remain the first because the 'servant' occupied too powerful a position within the secretariat. Nor, strictly speaking, could the relationship be said to have been one of equals; at least that is until 1673 when Williamson and Arlington began to go their separate ways.

Williamson ran the office and thus created a role in which Arlington was dependent upon him, for the latter had neither time, nor the inclination to take on the work load necessary for a full understanding of office business.[102] Arlington's interest in high policy, mostly relating to foreign affairs, needed good, solid intelligence in order that he could make the right decisions. Williamson took control of the intelligence-gathering activities of the office, and therefore to a great extent Arlington was also dependent upon him for this. A parallel of this type of situation, which appears to have evolved in the office at a later date and is described by the Earl of Ailesbury, may have some relevance here. Visiting the office when it was under the control of the Earl of Shrewsbury in the 1690s with the intent to ask the earl to accompany him on an excursion into the country Ailesbury found the secretary faced with his newly arrived correspondence. Foreseeing that this would delay their trip Shrewsbury soon put the problem to one side. He noted of the office correspondence,

'What is that to me? I never read or write a letter.' I asking him who did, he told me that Mr William Bridgeman, the first secretary in his office read all the letters and

[101] PRO SP 81/60/61, fo. 87.

[102] See Evelyn, *Diary*, IV, p. 38; also Pepys, who noted on a visit to the office that Williamson 'is endeed the Secretary' when he compared him with Arlington. See Pepys, *Diary*, VIII, p. 318.

reported to him the material contents, on which he drew what answers were requiste, and then set his name to them ... 'that is all I do'.[103]

While it is clear that Shrewsbury may well have been exaggerating a little, it is a useful illustration of what could happen in an office with an efficient under-secretary. However, Arlington did have a little more interest in office business than Shrewsbury. In any event, in return for Williamson's assistance Arlington was liberal with his patronage and care to his under-secretary and in time he cleared the way, for a financial consideration, for the under-secretary to step up into the secretaryship.[104]

The area of intelligence shows in fact how their relationship worked. The exact relationship between the two men on matters of intelligence can be uncovered from the numerous agents' reports which exist in the state papers. Ultimately Arlington, as we have noted, was responsible as Secretary of State for intelligence work. In practice, however, and in the day-to-day running of such affairs he was content to play the passive role he did in the office in general. There were exceptions to this policy,[105] but in the main it was Williamson who was left to run the intelligence-gathering activities of the regime and its agents. It was he who gave out verbal or written instructions to agents, having sometimes discussed them with Arlington, and he received most of their reports. He was also the conduit through which the money to pay these agents passed. He transcribed many of these spies' reports either at the office or in his own lodgings. When we find letters from such people addressed to Arlington, in most instances they had first passed through Williamson's hands. When agents wished to see Arlington personally they were almost invariably referred to Williamson first.[106]

Obviously Arlington had a role to play in the affairs of espionage, but the general trend left Williamson in a powerful controlling position. Moreover the natural air of secrecy about such dealings appears to have worked in Williamson's favour and strengthened his position, making him

[103] Ailesbury quoted in G. A. Jacobsen, *William Blathwayt: A Late Seventeenth Century Administrator* (New Haven, 1932), pp. 16–17. Bridgeman, of course, was a former under-secretary of Williamson.

[104] See PRO SP 105/224, fos. 207–8, 209, 243. But also see Temple, *Works*, II, pp. 296–8 in which Arlington offered Sir William Temple the position of secretary, when the partnership between himself and Williamson was beginning to break up. Temple, as diffident and indecisive as ever, and also thinking 'it no great honour to be preferred before ... Williamson', whom he disliked in any case, refused the offer, but not before Williamson had heard that it had been made.

[105] Exceptions included the close relationship with Temple which also involved overseeing and encouraging him in intelligence work; *Arlington Letters*, I, pp. 62–3, 76–8, 84, 85–6, 90–1, 95–6, 102–3, 106–7, 372–4.

[106] For examples of this see PRO SP 29/193, fo. 165; PRO SP 29/115, fo. 65; PRO SP 29/295, fo. 3; PRO SP 29/447, fo. 20.

positively indispensable. While it is clear that Arlington and Williamson did not tell everything which they discovered by this means to other members of the government,[107] it is also clear that Williamson did not tell the Secretary of State everything he himself uncovered or did in this area.[108] For if in government knowledge was power then secret knowledge was secret power, a fact Williamson also swiftly discovered. A few examples of how this system worked may serve to illustrate the two men's position in relation to the intelligence system. One of the spies of the government, Edward Riggs, makes it clear that he 'waited on Mr Williamson ... for instructions' and received his orders in this way.[109] Williamson would have doubtless discussed with Arlington what these instructions were to be in this case, but it was usually the under-secretary who dealt with such people on a day-to-day basis. William Leving[110] was offered the opportunity to see Arlington in person in special circumstances, and mostly by dogging the secretary's movements, but again for the most part he dealt with 'Mr Lee' as he refers to him in his correspondence, this being Williamson's code name in this instance.[111] Leving and his associates also received money through the under-secretary.[112] Thomas Blood, in whom Arlington took a more than peripheral interest, also came to Williamson to report or get information through to the secretary.[113]

The interrogation of prisoners was an area of intelligence work in which Arlington took a larger role. Interrogation of suspects or prisoners, as we shall see, was one method by which valuable intelligence could be gained about the movements and activities of rebels. It was here in fact that extra-ordinary pressure could be brought to bear. In the period of the plots of the early 1660s Arlington carried out many of these interrogations himself often with other ministers in attendance, usually Albermarle. The ubiquitous Joseph Williamson took the notes at such gatherings.[114] Prisoners could be 'milked' by frequent questioning, then sent to trial and executed. This indeed was what happened to Thomas Scot, the regicide who had been the manager of the Commonwealth's intelligence activities in the

[107] BL Add. MSS 25122, fo. 114.

[108] See below for more on this in the case of Henry Oldenburg.

[109] PRO SP 29/447, fo. 65. For more on Edward Riggs' career see below, Chapter 5.

[110] For more on William Leving's career see below, Chapter 5.

[111] PRO SP 29/129, fo. 236. That the 'Mr Lee' of this letter was Williamson is confirmed by Leving's mention of that individual's illness preventing their meeting; Williamson was in fact ill at this time as PRO SP 29/102, fos. 125, 164 show.

[112] PRO SP 29/115, fo. 65.

[113] PRO SP 29/295, fo. 3; and Marshall 'Blood', pp. 570–1.

[114] See for example PRO SP 29/62, fos. 36–43; PRO SP 29/98, fo. 56; PRO SP 29/115, fos. 71–4. Occasionally interrogations took place on a very high level with the monarch present; see BL Lansdowne MSS 1152, fo. 238.

early 1650s.[115] Some prisoners, however, were 'turned' and then released, or allowed to escape, in order to continue to provide information to the regime. This had two valuable consequences – it ensured a new supply of information about the movements of rebels and also kept the same rebels on edge, as they were never quite sure who was working for the government and who for the 'cause'. Escapes, even from the Tower itself, could be and were arranged and this enabled the new agent to maintain his apparent genuineness with his former friends. The linear progression from capture, to interrogation, 'escape' and the provision of new intelligence to the government was common and well known enough for certain individuals to volunteer their services.[116] A further area in which Arlington took an interest was in the Post Office. He held the position of Postmaster General after 1667 and installed various deputies, including his brother, to supervise its operation.[117] Again, however, it was Williamson who was the more active of the two men, especially when the affairs of the post crossed those of his intelligence-gathering activities, which they frequently did. Arlington's main concern were the profits which could be made out of the office. Having said this it was Arlington as secretary who allowed Samuel Morland the opportunity to install his 'several engins and utinsels' into the Post Office in order that intelligence could be easily gathered from intercepted post.[118]

Something should also be noted about the question of finance in relation to the intelligence work of Arlington's office, for it shows very clearly Arlington's dominance as secretary in the 1660s. The dedicated Elizabethan Secretary of State Sir Francis Walsingham might have been devoted enough to spend his own fortune on matters of state intelligence to save the protestant cause, but the Stuart secretaries were more mercenary. In itself expenditure on intelligence matters is a problematic issue. Quite often such spending was lumped in with the catch-all term 'secret services', which could cover anything from payments to the king's mistresses to those of common informers. It is clear, however, that previous reigns had set a number of precedents by the time that Arlington reached office. Prior to the Civil War an allowance of £1,400 had been made to the two secretaries and usually it was equally divided between them. With the establishment of the English Republic matters altered somewhat. Thomas Scot was initially allowed £800 per annum for intelligence matters in 1649, but this had risen

115 For Scot's interrogation see Firth, 'Thomas Scot's Account', pp. 116–26; Aylmer, *State's Servants*, p. 21.

116 See below, Chapters 4, 5, and 6, for more on this system.

117 Arlington was Postmaster-General from 1667 to 1685. Sir John Bennet was his deputy from 1667 to 1672. See below, Chapter 2, for more on the activities in the Post Office.

118 *HMC*, Finch MSS II, pp. 264–7.

to some £2,000 by the time he had left office. His replacement John Thurloe was, as usual, a law unto himself in such matters. Thurloe initially received two yearly payments of £600, but he spent considerably more than this on matters of intelligence. From April 1656 to April 1657, for example, he spent some £2,234. 3s. 0d. While Thurloe's official payments for intelligence rarely matched the amount he actually spent on such matters, ranging up to and including £2,500, they were nowhere near as high as the figures alleged after the Restoration.[119]

With the return of the king in 1660 such matters returned to the pre-war level, that is a yearly sum of £1,400 with £700 apiece for both secretaries. Arlington's arrival on the scene, however, soon put an end to this. He claimed the whole amount and asked for further payments up to £4,000. With the financial crisis of 1667 the sum for intelligence was fixed at £4,000 and was again meant to be divided between the two secretaries. As might be expected this did not happen. Arlington again seized the majority of the money for his own use leaving the weakened northern office to fend for itself. How much of this £4,000 was actually spent on intelligence matters is next to impossible to say; we must presume that some of it went towards the payment of agents and others. Having said this, given both Arlington and Williamson's penchant for acquiring wealth it is likely some of it must have gone astray. Only when Arlington left office did the question of intelligence payments finally resolve itself. Under the auspices of the Earl of Danby the sum for intelligence was initially fixed at £4,000, with £2,000 for each secretary, and then raised in 1675 by another £1,000 to £5,000. At which point the southern or senior secretaryship, was given £3,000 and the junior or northern secretaryship the remaining £2,000.[120]

One further means by which the relationship between Arlington and Williamson may be explored is by examining the curious case of Henry Oldenburg in 1667. The Oldenburg incident shows many facets in their relationship. Henry Oldenburg was a German *savant*, a man of letters and secretary to the Royal Society who had arrived in England in 1655 as agent for the German state of Bremen to the Lord Protector. In that year, however, he was acting as tutor to Henry O'Brien, later Lord Ibracken and later still husband to Catherine Stuart. Ibracken was to be one of Williamson's most intimate friends, while after O'Brien's death Catherine was to be his wife and their relationship may have begun earlier than this. Oldenburg, after some time in Oxford and a 'grand tour', was one of the first

[119] For a selection of payments see *CSPD*, 1603–10, p. 469; *CSPD*, 1628–29, p. 409; *CSPD*, 1649–50, p. 221; *CSPD*, 1653–4, pp. 454, 458; *CSPD* 1656–7, p. 362; *Thurloe State Papers*, VII, pp. 481–2.

[120] See *CTBks*, II, pp. 397, 439; E. M. G. Evans, 'Emoluments of the Principal Secretary of State in the Seventeenth Century', *EHR*, 35, 1920, pp. 513–28.

members of the Royal Society and was appointed one of its secretaries in 1663, a post he was to continue to hold until his death in 1677. While in this position his foreign correspondence with Europe's foremost scientists and philosophers enabled the Society to become the 'clearing house' for scientific ideas.[121] Oldenburg's burgeoning correspondence also brought him within the range and interest of Joseph Williamson and in 1667 it was to lead Oldenburg to the Tower.

By 1667 Oldenburg had about thirty correspondents ranging from Robert Boyle the scientist and Dr John Wallis, Savillian Professor of Geometry at Oxford as well as cryptographer to the Stuart regime,[122] to Europeans such as the Polish astronomer Lubienietzki and one of Williamson's old correspondents the Frenchman Henri Justel. In that same year England was at the heart of its war with the United Provinces of the Netherlands and thus the exchange of correspondence with Europe, whether scientific or not, was not easy. Conveying the correspondence was a problem in itself, but the possession of too many correspondents could rouse suspicions from a government already fearful of its position and in the midst of a war which was not going well. Thus it may seem surprising that Oldenburg was allowed to continue his activities, especially as the Royal Society's secretary and his correspondents were prone to talk politics as well as natural philosophy. It is clear that not only was this aspect of the business considered but it was controlled and proved useful to the man in control of the government's intelligence activities.

Oldenburg, no doubt through his Royal Society connections, was able to overcome the problems of continuing this correspondence and the expense of postage by striking a deal with Arlington's under-secretary. They were able to reach a mutually satisfying arrangement, which Oldenburg may have regarded as exceptional and flattering, but was not, and was part of Williamson's general policy to gain further sources of information and intelligence. Oldenburg told Robert Boyle that he hoped that he and Williamson 'have so ordered the matter in the point of correspondency, that there will be no exception taken at it'.[123] He then went on to note somewhat naively, and obviously unaware of whom he was dealing with, that 'I could as easily have engaged Mr Godolphin for the same purpose, but that he is gone for Spaine with the Earl of Sandwich'.[124] Oldenburg in

[121] On Henry Oldenburg see *DNB*, Henry Oldenburg; A. R. Hall and M. B. Hall, eds., *The Correspondence of Henry Oldenburg* (13 vols., Madison, Wisconsin/London, 1965–86); M. Hunter, *Science and Society in Restoration England* (Cambridge, 1981), pp. 32–58. Also D. McKie, 'The Arrest and Imprisonment of Henry Oldenburg', *Notes and Records of the Royal Society*, 6, 1948, pp. 28–47.

[122] For Dr John Wallis see *DNB*, John Wallis; also BL Add. MSS 32499, fos. 15, 377. Also see below, Chapter 2.

[123] *Oldenburg Correspondence*, III, pp. 45–6.

[124] *ibid.*

fact was more than happy to go along with the arrangement struck with Williamson, for it saved him money on the Royal Society's correspondence. As with all of Williamson's 'arrangements' there were catches involved. These were explained by Oldenburg thus:

I have employed ... my correspondencing to give advertisments to the Court, such as I thought might be usefull for England; and almost ever since the warr, my letters from France and Holland have, upon my desire, been always deliver'd in the office of My Lord Arlington, where they might be opened at pleasure.[125]

The letters to and from Henri Justel were potentially the most important source of political information. Oldenburg arranged with Williamson that Justel's letters should always go via the secretary's office. To facilitate this, the usual expedient of a cover name was adopted. In this instance Oldenburg formed an anagram of his name. Thus Justel wrote undercover to 'Monsieur Grubendol á Londres' and all of these letters, on reaching the Post Office were taken out and then forwarded to Williamson at his office. Oldenburg then received his letters which, according to some historians, were allegedly unopened, a point to which we will return shortly. He then extracted the relevant political information and sent it back to Williamson. At this point the editors of Oldenburg's correspondence claim that Justel's letters were then destroyed, 'either because they contained little of interest or as a precaution', for few have survived.[126] It is unfortunate that Oldenburg's replies to Justel have apparently not survived[127] for it is quite likely that these also contained the political information which was to get Oldenburg into trouble. However, the system as described begs a variety of questions especially as it led to Oldenburg's incarceration in the Tower.

The exact cause of Oldenburg's two months in the Tower of London remains uncertain. Oldenburg believed he was 'committed for dangerous dessins and practises; and I understand, that that is inferred from some letters and discourses of mine, said to contain expressions of that nature'.[128] John Evelyn, who visited Oldenburg while he was in the Tower, gives the common impression of the reasons behind the secretary's imprisonment. He was there, noted Evelyn, 'for having been suspected to write intelligence ... [but he] ... will prove an innocent person I am confident'.[129] This much is clear, that Oldenburg had been critical of the government's handling of the war, and in the summer of the Medway disaster this was particularly dangerous. It was even more dangerous to commit such criticisms to paper and then send them abroad, which is what

125 PRO SP 29/209, fo. 123. 126 *Oldenburg Correspondence*, IV, p. xxvii.

127 See *Oldenburg Correspondence*, IV, p. xxvii; McKie, 'Oldenburg', p. 46. Oldenburg also used Peter Serraius of Amsterdam to obtain information from the Netherlands.

128 PRO SP 29/209, fo. 123.

129 Evelyn, *Diary*, III, p. 491. See also Pepys, *Diary*, VIII, p. 292.

Oldenburg appears to have done. The problem and controversy really lie not in Oldenburg's 'crime' but how it was detected and who was responsible for pressing the charges against him. Both the editors of Oldenburg's correspondence and Douglas McKie miss the crucial point that the letters which caused Oldenburg so much trouble must have been intercepted and that the man, perhaps the only man, who could have taken on this task was Williamson, who appears to have played a disingenuous role throughout.

Two other candidates have been put forward for the role of prime mover in the case against Oldenburg. The first, advocated by A. R. and M. B. Hall, is Arlington. In this case, they claim, it explains Williamson's apparent inability to assist Oldenburg in his troubles. The under-secretary himself implied this in his correspondence. It might also explain why the petition Oldenburg addressed to the king remained in the office.[130] According to their version of the story, Williamson was helpless to prevent Oldenburg's arrest despite the fact that he was aware of the correspondence in question, and it became partly a case of Arlington asserting his authority over all concerned. The Halls postulate that 'It is tempting to assume that Oldenburg's incautiously phrased indignation [over the war] was intercepted in the post and brought directly to the attention of ... Arlington who may not even ... have known of the arrangement with Williamson'.[131] Arlington thereafter, under pressure from failures of intelligence in the war, used Oldenburg as a scapegoat. While it is true that Oldenburg blamed Arlington for his misfortunes, the Halls miss the point that intercepted post would have most likely have to come through Williamson in the first place. The letters which caused the trouble were outgoing correspondence and therefore the interception of Oldenburg's letters may have been going on for some time. It *is* quite likely, however, that the Secretary of State may not have known of any arrangement with Oldenburg up to that point. The other evidence for Arlington's responsibility may be briefly dismissed here. It is true that Arlington signed the warrants for Oldenburg's arrest and release, directed that Oldenburg be kept 'close prisoner' and accepted the petitions. There is nothing strange in this for these were after all part of Arlington's duties. Arlington signed many hundred warrants in his time as secretary, nor is it clear he read all of them.[132] The Oldenburg documents should thus not be taken out of context. Douglas McKie's tentative solution and the second candidate in the case is the king himself. McKie believes that it was Charles II who came to hear of Oldenburg's criticisms of the conduct of the war and ordered him to be arrested and placed in the Tower. He fails to put forward any real evidence for this

[130] *Oldenburg Correspondence*, IV, p. xxviii. [131] *ibid.*

[132] Certainly Williamson when he reached the secretaryship did not read all he signed; it was this neglect which led to his fall.

view aside from Oldenburg's petition addressed to Arlington. This asks Arlington to 'intercede with his Majesty for me, and to further and facilitate the pardon'.[133] McKie's argument[134] remains a very weak one based on the fact that Oldenburg addressed a petition to the king. This was hardly an uncommon occurrence, nor is it likely that Charles had either time or inclination to read the hundreds of petitions he received, for he employed two Secretaries of State to do this for him.

The third, and the most likely, 'prime mover' in the case of Oldenburg's imprisonment is, of course, Williamson. The arrangement between Williamson and Oldenburg that the 'Grubendol' letters should go through the office before Oldenburg received them and that they should reach him unopened, whereupon Oldenburg would extract the relevant information and send this back to Williamson seems, to say the least, an unlikely one. Indeed Oldenburg noted, as has been seen, that the letters 'might be opened at pleasure'.[135] Undoubtedly, on occasion, the letters were passed to Oldenburg unopened, but it is more likely that Williamson, with his eagerness for knowledge of all sorts, would have had some of the correspondence opened first, read and resealed. The under-secretary had the facilities to do this and the staff in the shape of Isaac Dorislaus.[136] The significant correspondence, of course, would have been Oldenburg's replies. These would also come through the Post Office and could have easily been picked out and read before they were sent on.[137] The question arises therefore as to why Williamson should wish to bring Oldenburg's indiscretions to the attention of his superiors and have a man, with whom he had friendly relations and who was in any case willing to pass on any political information he received to Williamson, arrested. There are a variety of reasons why it may have occurred.

Firstly part of the solution lies in Williamson's character and his inability to brook no rivalry in the field of information gathering and disseminations. For him this was not just a question of money, even if there were profits to be made out of such correspondence and newsletter services;[138] it was a question of the control of information. This is a fact which J. G. Muddiman, apparently blinded by his prejudices, fails to understand.[139]

133 PRO SP 29/210, fo. 59.
134 Given in McKie, 'Oldenburg', pp. 28–47.
135 PRO SP 29/209, fo. 123.
136 See PRO SP 29/209, fo. 118 for an example of Williamson's dealings with Dorislaus and in the same for evidence of Williamson's book of code names kept in the Post Office. Also for other dealings of Dorislaus with intercepted correspondence see for example BL Add. MSS 25125, fos. 31–3.
137 See below, Chapter 2, for more on the interception of the post.
138 Oldenburg was in fact making some profit out of his correspondence and exchange of news. How this worked is not clear. See *Oldenburg Correspondence*, II, p. xxv.
139 See J. G. Muddiman, in *The King's Journalist 1659–1689; Studies in the Reign of Charles II* (1923, 1971 reprint, New York). Despite the errors, and slightly ridiculous hatred of all

Only those favoured by the regime or Williamson himself were allowed to receive Williamson's manuscript newsletter. In this sense they were a select group privileged to receive the information withheld from others. The *Gazette* was stripped of its more interesting news items because they were for the privileged few. This produced a rather bland journal, but that in Williamson's eyes was its purpose.[140] In essence, what we see time and again in the areas which came under Williamson's control was an exercise in power by the curtailment of knowledge and information. Thus Oldenburg's burgeoning freelance correspondence was both a rival and a threat. Of necessity therefore it had to be brought under control and Oldenburg taught a lesson. Those who do not believe that Williamson could be so cynical need only look at his attempts to take over the manuscript newsletter service and the elimination of his rivals Muddiman and L'Estrange.[141] The other darker aspects of Williamson's character are also exposed in this case. Here we have not the amiable *bon vivant* known to his intimate friends, but a ruthlessly ambitious and shrewd under-secretary. Williamson's main idea seems to have been that *all* the threads of intelligence were to be drawn into his hands and any opposition eliminated or brought into line. Muddiman, L'Estrange and Oldenburg form part of the same pattern. It is here that we see confirmation of John Evelyn's barb that Williamson was an able player of 'jeu de Goblets', literally both a juggler and a cheat.[142] The Restoration court was not a place for gentlemen but players and Williamson was very much a player. From an intelligence angle, of course, this was a very sensible way to proceed. It was far better to have all, or as many as possible, of the threads of intelligence in one man's hands than to have them dissipated throughout the government. This was an action in the tradition of the great intelligencers Walsingham and Thurloe, who would not have hesitated to do likewise in similar circumstances. And perhaps we can discern a reading of Thurloe's strategy by Williamson here.[143] Central control equalled efficiency and security. The

who do not agree with the author, or its erstwhile hero Henry Muddiman, Williamson himself comes in for some rigorous criticism from which one can still perceive the more ruthless side of his nature.

[140] As well as to prevent the problems of rumour by providing reliable official news, with more emphasis on the official than reliable. See T. O'Malley, 'Religion and the Newspaper Press 1660–1685: A Study of the London Gazette', in M. Harris and A. Lee, eds., *The Press in English Society from the Seventeenth to the Nineteenth Centuries* (1986), pp. 29–30.

[141] See Muddiman, *The King's Journalist*, pp. 144–207; but for more judicious and less prejudiced views see Sutherland, *Restoration Newspaper*, pp. vi, 4, 10, 123; and Handover, *London Gazette*, pp. 9–20 who also points out that 'Financially the Gazette was insignificant' (p. 19).

[142] Evelyn, *Diary*, IV, p. 39. The correct spelling being 'joueur de gobelets'.

[143] See Introduction.

speeches or letters of Joseph Williamson therefore may well have been full of 'whipped cream' but behind them stood a ruthless and important member of the secretariat determined to get his own way and, within his own terms, feared. The role of Arlington in all of this may thus be clearly discerned. He had, as Evelyn notes,

> remitted all to his man Williamson [and thus] in a short time let him so into the secret of affaires that (as his Lordship himselfe told me) there was a kind of necessity to advance him.[144]

In the intelligence work in the mid-1660s therefore Joseph Williamson set the pace.

It would, of course, be an error to claim that everything ran smoothly in matters of intelligence during Arlington's tenure of office. There were two major failures of intelligence during the Second Dutch War, the division of the fleet in 1666 and the Dutch assault on the Medway in 1667, as well as numerous other minor disasters of English spies lost, plans spoiled and intelligence misread. In terms of domestic policy and fears of conspiracy the government was able to gain a distinct advantage as we shall see, but it may be that in the case of intelligence work abroad the failures were a little more obvious. Certainly the parliamentary committee which investigated the miscarriages of the Second Dutch War laid some blame for the disasters of that war upon the 'want of intelligence' and the secretariat faced the unique spectacle of having its work on this matter turned over by the Commons committee.[145] This was unprecedented and cannot have pleased Williamson who was ordered to attend the committee with his papers.[146] Indeed Samuel Pepys met Williamson on 30 November 1667 when the under-secretary was tight-lipped and 'close, not daring to say anything ... that touches upon news or state of affairs'.[147] Two incidents during the war in particular took the committee's interest. The first was the division of the English fleet in 1666 and the second was the Dutch assault on the Medway in 1667.

In both of these notable failures of the war poor intelligence work was only partly to blame. The division of the fleet in May–June 1666 has been thoroughly investigated by naval historians.[148] They have rightly laid stress upon the problems of a divided command and strategic errors during the

[144] Evelyn, *Diary*, IV, p. 38.

[145] Pepys, *Diary*, VIII, p. 502; *Commons Journal*, 9, pp. 6, 7, 8, 15.

[146] *Commons Journal*, 9, p. 10; *CSPD*, 1667, p. 545; *CSPD*, 1682, p. 601.

[147] Pepys, *Diary*, VIII, p. 556.

[148] Most recently by J. D. Davies, *Gentlemen and Tarpaulins: The Officers and Men of the Restoration Navy* (Oxford, 1991), pp. 144, 150, 151, 153; see also R. J. A. Shelley, 'The Division of the Fleet in 1666', *Mariner's Mirror*, 25, 1939, pp. 178–96.

campaign. The misleading intelligence which began the whole incident can certainly be laid at the door of Arlington's office. Although having said this, in the case of the movements of the French fleet the intelligence came via naval sources in the first instance.[149] Moreover this inaccurate intelligence was compounded by a series of mistakes which were not within the range of the secretary. Clarendon's attempts to foist a large part of the blame for the disaster on his hated enemy Arlington was malicious and his opinions were misleading. In the second affair the blame for the successful assault by the Dutch on the Medway can rather be placed in the lethergy and over-confidence of the regime as a whole and in the way in which de Witt kept his plans close to his chest.[150] The English regime was in fact aware that there would be a landing, but was unable to discover where it would take place. Intelligence that a build-up of Dutch naval forces was underway was also sent to the secretary's office.[151] Whether this was ignored because the regime was more interested in a peace conference or because of mere incompetence is debatable. The former seems more likely. The subsequent debate in the House of Commons on the miscarriages of the war in many senses revealed how little the Commons actually knew about the nature of such work. MPs were well aware of the popular myth of Thurloe's skill in such dealings for they used it as a stick with which to beat the ministry, as well as to attack Arlington, for in the Commons that former servant of John Thurloe, Andrew Marvell, complained of the 'libidinous desire in men, for places [which] makes them think themselves fit for them'.[152] The most sensible comment in fact came from Henry Coventry, the future Secretary of State, who noted that 'Intelligence is like health; we seldom or never have it perfect',[153] while another MP merely damned the whole thing by noting that all intelligence was 'gathered by treachery' in any case and 'we must have what we can get ... not what [we] would have'.[154] Intelligence was therefore unfairly voted a miscarriage of the war. This was far too broad a condemnation of the regime's efforts in that war which were able for the most part and showed little understanding of the difficulties involved. It remained to be seen whether it could do any better in the next few years.

149 See J. R. Powell and E. K. Timings, ed., *The Rupert and Monck Letter Book 1666*, Naval Records Society, 112, (1969), p. 200.
150 Rowan, *De Witt*, pp. 593–4; A. D. Coox, 'The Dutch Invasion of England: 1667', *Military Affairs*, 13, Winter 1949, pp. 224–8.
151 *CSPD*, 1667, pp. 14, 92, 103, 104, 107, 108, 173.
152 Grey, *Debates*, I, p. 71. Marvell was all too obviously attacking Arlington and the secretary knew it; see *Arlington Letters*, I, p. 226.
153 Grey, *Debates*, I, p. 71. 154 *ibid.*, p. 78.

VI

The period 1672–4 was one of war and change in the secretariat. The story of the regime's second war with the Dutch,[155] the break-up of the ministry and the manoeuvres which led Williamson to occupy one of the secretaries' posts cannot be dealt with here.[156] Sir Leoline Jenkins, who shared a diplomatic mission to Cologne with Williamson in 1673–4 noted that the Cumbrian had 'much of [the] philosopher'[157] in him in this period and perhaps he needed it, for once safely installed in office he was faced with a new master, the rising star of the 1670s Sir Thomas Osborne, Earl of Danby. Danby had first risen to prominence as an opponent of Clarendon and as a client of Buckingham.[158] During the early 1670s he had no part in the French alliance or in the indulgence of dissenters, contenting himself with solid administrative work at the Admiralty and then in the Treasury. With the disintegration of the so-called 'Cabal' ministry, however, Danby had taken his chance to become the king's first minister by cutting through his rivals and following his own line of policy. In the main this was to be threefold. Firstly to restore the king's financial independence by reform and thus to make Charles beholden to him. Secondly to bring the crown into line with public opinion on foreign affairs, in effect by dropping the French alliance. Thirdly he wished to work towards such objectives via parliament, in which he intended to build up a political grouping based upon the old ties of church and king. The new Secretary of State Sir Joseph Williamson was inevitably to be caught up in Danby's plans.

Williamson's relationship with Danby, as might be expected, never became as close as had his relationship with Arlington. Danby found the new secretary useful for building up a 'party' in the Commons but there was none of the real trust in secret affairs that Arlington had shown to the Cumbrian secretary.[159] Initially Danby believed that Williamson, as the client of Arlington, had been intriguing against him while in Cologne and he assumed that little trust could be placed in him. Even when they came to work closely together this situation continued[160] for it was rumoured that in 1677 Lady Danby was attempting to persuade her lord that he 'should

155 For intelligence in the Third Dutch War, see below, pp. 226–32.
156 For these manoeuvres see A. Marshall, 'The Secretaryship of Sir Joseph Williamson, 1674–1679' (unpublished paper).
157 BL Add. MSS 28054, fo. 5, part written in cipher.
158 For Danby's career in the 1670s see Browning, *Danby*, I, pp. 105–332.
159 See *CSPD*, 1678, pp. 12–13, 173. See also, Grey, *Debates*, VI, p. 233, where one of the MPs in 1678 argued that 'because of the influence great men [Danby] have upon the Secretaries they must comply, else they lose their places.'
160 *CSPD*, 1678, p. 173.

not rely on any of my Lord Arlington's renegades'.[161] As it was, the Lord Treasurer became prone to keeping the new secretary waiting outside his office some '2 Houres ... before [he] admitted [him]'.[162] This might be seen as a calculated snub to someone as increasingly touchy about such matters as Williamson[163] for there is a lack of real assurance perceptible in Williamson's character after 1674. Consequently, the Venetian ambassador noted that Williamson mostly kept his opinions and counsels to himself, noting that 'although brought up in the midst of these domestic factions and partial to those of Parliament [Williamson] has kept the public in doubt about his politics'.[164] While he remained something of a 'dark horse' to foreign ambassadors there was no real alternative at court and Williamson soon drifted to Danby's party.[165] In so doing he finally, though not totally, disengaged himself from Arlington with whom he had worked so well. At least he could console himself that his own monarch was following a similar line in public affairs.

With Danby's arrival on the scene the balance of power within the Stuart administration also shifted considerably after 1674 from the secretaryship to the post of Lord Treasurer.[166] This was to affect the secretaries' position in the government. The new era was partly the result of a personality bent on the domination of the government. This was necessary in order for Danby to succeed in his plans and to protect his own position. But it was also due to the increasing importance of financial affairs in a regime where such financial problems had become inextricably connected with all areas of government.[167] By using the Treasury as his power base Danby was able to intervene across the wide range of government at Whitehall from foreign diplomacy to domestic affairs. As his power and confidence grew this led to the office of Secretary of State increasingly losing out to the Treasuryship in terms of power and significance.[168]

A further reason for the decline of Williamson's fortunes was related to the fact that the secretaryship itself became divided upon more equitable

161 That is, Williamson and Temple, *HMC*, Ormonde MSS NS, IV, p. 385.

162 *Essex Papers*, I, p. 259.

163 See for example Williamson's complaints about the affronts he had suffered from certain Thames watermen, PRO SP 44/43, p. 152.

164 Williamson's partiality to those of parliament, if true, is rather ironic as will be seen below. *CSPV*, 1673–5, p. 293.

165 Browning, *Danby*, I, p. 135.

166 See S. B. Baxter, *The Development of the Treasury, 1660–1702* (1957), p. 4; also H. Roseveare, *The Treasury 1660–1870: The Foundations of Control* (1973), p. 19.

167 See Browning, *Danby*, I, pp. 128–32. As Southampton had once put it 'The revenue is the centre of all ... business'. Quoted by C. D. Chandaman, *The English Public Revenue 1660–1698* (Oxford, 1975), p. 1.

168 An instance of this is the case for secret service money. Danby deliberately restricted the issue of secret service money to both secretaries. They were not to be paid without his orders. *CTBks*, IV, p. 711. See also, on the peace of Nijmegen, *CSPD*, 1678, pp. 12–13.

terms after 1674. The previously dominant southern secretary's office lost much of its power when Arlington left it. The man in a very real sense had made the office and in so doing Williamson had seized the opportunities which Arlington had put in his way. In the manoeuvres for office in 1674, however, Henry Coventry took over the southern secretaryship while Williamson, much to his and to Arlington's chagrin, was pushed into the northern office which both men had done so much to weaken in the 1660s. Both Coventry and Williamson were to suffer because of the more equitable nature of their position in government. Politically neither was of the significance of Arlington and neither of them could dominate the other, thus in terms of political power both lost out to Danby.

On reaching office Henry Coventry had not in fact been that happy in the position. Arlington's domination of affairs led to his spending most of his time away from the office.[169] This situation continued in the 1670s when Coventry found himself largely excluded from the more significant secret dealings and most of Danby's plans.[170] Williamson, who was more pliable and usually, although not always, ready to bend with the political wind as a 'civil servant' should, also had an unhappy time of it.[171] He was willing to direct his energies to his more formal administrative duties and to colonial affairs, in which he always took a keen interest;[172] but he soon came under the thumb of the overmighty Earl of Danby and thus found himself focusing more upon the activities of parliament as part of Danby's attempt to control the Commons by building up a 'court party'.[173]

The growing significance of the House of Commons as a force on the political scene naturally had an effect on the Secretary of State's office after 1674 and the secretaries' activities there were a pointer for the development in the future years of the secretariat.[174] In fact Danby, in making use of Williamson for such matters, was undoubtedly using a 'weak blade'. Parliament, and the House of Commons in particular, were never Williamson's strongest points and it is true to say that he was never very effective and often increasingly ill at ease in this arena in the 1670s. As a parliamentary speaker he left a lot to be desired and remained largely unconvinc-

[169] See Evans, *Principal Secretary*, p. 139. For Coventry see *H of P* II, pp. 148–53. Also D. T. Witcombe, 'The Parliamentary Careers of Sir William and Mr Henry Coventry 1661–1681', unpublished B Litt. thesis, University of Manchester, 1954.

[170] See Longleat MSS (Marquess of Bath), Coventry MSS 4, Official Home Correspondence, 1, fo. 113, and *Essex Papers*, I, p. 242.

[171] Williamson did not always follow the Danby line; see Browning, *Danby*, I, p. 196; Haley, *Shaftesbury*, pp. 404–5.

[172] For which H. L. Osgood, *The American Colonies in the Seventeenth Century* (3 vols., 1926), III, pp. 146–7.

[173] For which see Browning, *Danby*, I, pp. 146–283; *CSPV*, 1673–5, p. 390.

[174] For this see Thomson, *Secretaries of State*, pp. 23, 25–6.

ing, making him a poor spokesman for the government.[175] He often seems to have bored his listeners with long-winded speeches.[176] Occasionally these speeches were deliberately devised to help the government by 'trifl[ing] away time that the House might be wearied out, and grow thin'. At other times he did not intend to be boring but he was.[177]

That Williamson was out of his depth in parliament as a political and parliamentary leader should not really be very surprising. It took some effort for him to become an MP in the first instance.[178] There is in fact an interesting parallel in this aspect of his career with Williamson's nearest predecessor in character and aptitude for intelligence matters, John Thurloe. Thurloe had also performed poorly in parliament and was out of his depth in the rough and tumble of the Commons. Most commentators on Thurloe's career have noted his limitations in this respect.[179] The area where both men performed their best work, intelligence gathering and assessment, was an area which Williamson in particular, felt was not something which the House of Commons could share or for that matter should be entitled to probe into. As he pointedly told the House, 'It is not happy when such things as this arise in great Assemblies.'[180] This type of remark being redolent of the incipient 'civil service' mentality which had been nurtured on the needs for secrecy.

It was to be Williamson's eventual failure to adapt to the new situation of a parliament flexing its constitutional muscles which was to see him dismissed from office.[181] While he was philosophical enough to regard this as one of the 'casualties of fortune',[182] it was largely self-inflicted. Charles II himself is claimed to have said that 'he did not wish to be served by a man [Williamson] who feared anyone [that is the Commons] but him'.[183] And the situation showed that the Williamson of the 1670s lacked the true politician's ability to adapt to changing political circumstances.

[176] A fault of which William of Orange complained; see S. B. Baxter, *William III and the Defence of European Liberty, 1650–1702* (1966), p. 135.

[177] Grey, *Debates*, V, p. 377. It was also clear that he had no following in the House and according to one source there was 'a long grudge in the House' against him. Possibly this was related to Arlington's activities there in which Williamson had assisted, *HMC*, Ormonde, 4, pp. 475–78.

[178] For details of Williamson's parliamentary problems see *H of P*, III, p. 737; Browning, *Danby*, I, pp. 199–200, 227–8; also G. C. Williamson, *Lady Anne Clifford, Countess of Dorset: Her Life Letters and Works* (2nd edn, Kendal, 1922, reprint, Wakefield, 1967), pp. 285–302.

[179] See Aubrey, *Mr Secretary Thurloe*, pp. 6, 141–2, Aylmer, *State's Servants*, pp. 167, 258.

[180] Grey, *Debates*, VII, p. 309. For Williamson's later and more profitable Commons career see S. N. Handley, 'Sir Joseph Williamson', History of Parliament (unpublished paper). I am grateful to Dr Handley for sight of his draft article.

[181] For this fateful day see Grey, *Debates*, VI, pp. 220–40.

[182] BL Eg. MSS 2678, fo. 62.

[183] Charles II quoted in J. P. Keynon, *The Popish Plot* (Harmondsworth, 1974), p. 155.

As has already been noted the secretaries were deliberately placed in the House of Commons as government spokesmen which made them even more obvious targets as the House became more fractious and less pliable to the government's will. They found themselves in the political front line. They became the mouthpiece of royal policy and managers of the Commons. From the wider perspective of administration and government the position of Secretary of State was thus further transformed from being the king's personal secretary into a front-line politician in parliament. Obviously this meant changes within the office system itself. The elegantly run office system of the pre-1673 Williamson contrasts sharply with that of 1676–8. By 1678 there are hints that all was not well in the office.[184]

It seems clear that the business of the office was being disrupted by Commons affairs. During the debate over Williamson's signing of army commissions for Catholic officers for example, one of the excuses put forward was that the burden of work was becoming too much. Henry Coventry noted that both secretaries had daily to face 'papers brought in all in a bundle and not to be read scarce in a day'.[185] Further revealing comments cropped up in Williamson's own speeches that day. The commissions were 'a trouble', he said, and, rather too revealing of his attitude, 'no [financial] advantage to me'.[186] While the office did obviously retain some interest in security duties, it became much more engrossed in, some might say hindered by, managing the House. It was a factor which at least partly accounts for Arlington's abandonment of the secretaryship for the calmer waters of Lord Chamberlain of the Household after his close brush with impeachment in 1674. For those left in the secretariat, and especially for the uncomfortable Williamson, however, the Commons became a veritable place of perils.[187]

Where did this change of atmosphere and direction leave the English intelligence system? In general terms as the focus of English political life changed in the mid-1670s and as the political environment altered, so the situation in regard to intelligence matters also changed. Perhaps one of the most important factors in this respect was the exclusion of both Secretaries of State from the high-level secret dealings of the regime.[188] Arlington, of

[184] Most obviously shown in Grey, *Debates*, VI, pp. 219, 221–2. [185] *ibid*., p. 221.

[186] *ibid*., p. 222.

[187] It was not so much a problem for Henry Coventry who was more at home in the Commons and, as Roger North put it, 'had the nice step of the House and withal was wonderfully witty'. See Feiling *Tory Party*, p. 144.

[188] Indeed one of the articles brought in for Danby's impeachment in 1678 was that he had 'traiterously encroached to himself ... giving instructions to ... ambassadors abroad, without communicating the same to the Secretaries of State'. There are numerous examples of this occurring. Danby's relations with Sir William Temple, English ambassador to the United Provinces, technically part of Williamson's province as northern secretary, are an example. In Coventry's case, Danby's relations with Ralph Montague,

course, had been heavily involved in such affairs. They were partly responsible for his requiring so much intelligence gathering in order that he could advise the king and make his own decisions. This was a need which Williamson, as has been already seen, was delegated to provide, or chose to fill. Such secret affairs moved from the office of Secretary of State after Arlington had left and naturally fell into the hands of Danby. Danby had his own methods of working which frequently excluded the Secretaries of State, whose position, if not occupants, he saw as possible rivals to his own. An instance of this was his placing of 'secret service' expenditure and affairs into the hands of his client and relation Charles Bertie.[189] As Bertie also acted as Danby's general factotum in other affairs of this sort, this move had an obvious impact on the secretaries' activities.[190] Another area lost to the intelligence system of the 1670s was the result of a clear shift away from government concern over republican conspiracies. In the main this was the result of the action taken prior to the Third Anglo-Dutch War. The Declaration of Indulgence of 1672 had neutralised many of the rebel elements in 1672.[191] Their activities remained of peripheral interest until the late 1670s. The growing significance of parliament and its affairs more than made up for the secretaries' loss of time in investigating plots, but it meant there was less need for the type of intelligence work which had once been so prominent. In the sphere of European affairs the secretaries' intelligence system was also without a major European war to involve itself in after 1674. Thus there was a cutback on its agents abroad with the ending of the Third Anglo-Dutch War. Jerome Nipho indeed had written to Williamson that the correspondent he had recruited for Williamson in Zeeland 'is discharged already, & the other of Amsterdam will bee here this weeke, I will discharge him also'.[192] There was a brief period from 1673 to 1674 when Williamson engaged in some effective counter-intelligence operations[193] but in short, until the period of the 'Popish Plot', the system went, if not into hibernation, then certainly into the doldrums. It became less focused on specific targets, more passive in its intelligence gathering and generally less significant as a result. There was a brief revival in this area with the possibility of a war with France in late 1677 and early 1678. The prospect of

who was ambassador in France, are a further example. In both cases the secretary's knowledge of affairs was limited by the all-powerful first minister. See Browning, *Danby*, II, pp. 247, 577; II, p. 74; Evans, *Principal Secretary*, pp. 139–40. Burnet, *History*, II, p. 173.

189 Browning, *Danby*, I, pp. 195–6; Baxter, *Development of the Treasury*, pp. 182–9.

190 Feiling, *Tory Party*, p. 165; *H of P*, I, p. 641.

191 See Marshall, 'Blood', p. 570; J. Miller, *Popery and Politics in England, 1660–1688* (Cambridge, 1978), p. 117.

192 PRO SP 77/44, fo. 112.

193 An example of which would be the recruitment of Abraham de Wicquefort.

war led Williamson eagerly to begin to activate information networks in northern France with increasing rapidity.[194] He was, or so he claimed, willing to pay any costs to get such networks started. But as there was no real prospect that Charles would really allow a war with France to go forward, much of the effort undertaken by Williamson was wasted and these activities also say something about the secretary's unhappy position in the regime.[195]

To add to Williamson's problems in this area was the reluctance of his partner in office Henry Coventry to take the backseat role which Morrice and Trevor had usually undertaken in such affairs. There was in fact no reason why Coventry should not take an interest in intelligence which was after all part of the secretary's post. But the fact was, as Coventry himself admitted, he was 'neither of a temper or condition to dissemble'.[196] Coventry was hampered both by his own morality and a certain amount of obtuseness. His opinion of Titus Oates is worth quoting as an illustration of this, 'If he be a liar', he said, 'he is the greatest and adroitest I ever saw.' While this was hardly the most perceptive of opinions, Coventry, it is possible to argue, was being employed more for his talents in the Commons than for his intelligence-gathering skills.[197] This did not prevent his actual interference in such matters.[198]

The result of this gradual lapse of the system was only really revealed with the arrival on the scene of Titus Oates and his cronies in 1678. It is clear that at this point the government was overwhelmed by false informations. In any event the actual investigation of the plot was left to Danby and the wider body of the Privy Council, in which the Secretaries of State had a lesser role to play, with tragic consequences. The fault of this may be firmly laid at the door of Charles and Danby. The plot also took its toll on Williamson. He lost his nerve after being sent to the Tower in November 1678 and it eventually led to his removal.

When Christopher Kirkby approached the king with intelligence of a

194 An interesting aspect of this activity was the fact that France was, strictly speaking, within the province of Coventry. Williamson got round this by using intermediaries at Dover and the Channel Islands.

195 See BL Add. MSS 10115, which has Williamson's papers on the 'Projected War with France'; PRO SP 44/43, pp. 179A, 179B, 182, 185, 189, 190; *CSPD*, 1677–78, pp. 584, 604–5, 677, 684; *CSPD* 1678, p. 127; *HMC*, Ormonde MSS 4, pp. 296–7; F. C. Turner, *James II* (1948), pp. 135–6; J. Pollock, *The Popish Plot: A Study in the History of the Reign of Charles II* (1903), pp. 378–79; J. R. Jones, *Charles II: Royal Politician* (1987), pp. 124–6.

196 Bl Add. MSS 25125, fo. 32.

197 *HMC*, Ormonde MSS 4, p. 207.

198 See also Coventry and the Dorislaus affair of September 1677; BL Add. MSS 25125, fos. 31–3. Also on an intelligencer called Monsieur Lubiensque see BL Add. MSS 25122, fo. 3; as well as below, Chapter 2, for his thoughts on intercepting letters at the Post Office.

design against his life on 13 August 1678, it could not have been foreseen by anyone in the government, least of all Charles himself, that the news would lead to months of political trauma for the nation. There had been plots before and this plot, although it bore a resemblance to many of those of the 1660s, had less reality about it than most. In many ways the series of events which come under the heading of the Popish Plot could easily be seen as the revenge of those lesser men and women whom the regime had ruthlessly exploited over the previous eighteen years. They were certainly to pay the regime back in kind. The plot found the ministry of Danby, in which Williamson had a role, an unsteady foundation. The ministry was wandering in the political doldrums. It was both weak and unpopular, if not discredited, by events both at home and abroad.[199] If Danby saw the plot as a chance to revive his fortunes, and there are some doubts about this point of view,[200] it was a severe miscalculation. Once the news had broken the Lord Treasurer was seen to be moving far too slowly in his investigation of the plot. And this was to be held against him. In any case within weeks, urged on by Oates and Tonge, the plot had taken on a life of its own. It overwhelmed the government's capacity for dealing with it and flooded into the unstable political arena of parliament. Fired by the uncovering of Coleman's correspondence, as well as the mysterious death of Sir Edmund Godfrey,[201] parliamentary factions were quick to exploit the latent anti-Catholicism of London and the nation at large. Together they fired the mine which exploded in the face of the government and as a by-product of this managed to bring down many ministerial careers, including that of Joseph Williamson.

It might be thought that with his long experience in such matters and his knowledge of the type of men who invariably brought plots, real or feigned, to the notice of the regime, Williamson would have had a key role to play in the investigation of the Popish Plot. Certainly, given time, he could have provided a 'cool' assessment of the main informants, if not the plot itself.[202] But it is redolent of both how much the political situation had changed and of how quickly the plot spun out of control, as well as the decline in Williamson's own position, that this did not occur. In fact the investigation of the plot, unlike any of those which had emerged in the 1660s, was to spread through various levels of the government.[203] This was an important factor and seems to have been largely ignored by previous historians. Unlike

199 See Browning, *Danby*, I, pp. 283–5.

200 For the doubts see Hutton, *Charles II*, p. 359. For other views Browning, *Danby*, I, pp. 290–1; Kenyon, *Popish Plot*, p. 67.

201 For an interesting, although problematic, approach to Godfrey's death see J. Dickson Carr, *The Murder of Sir Edmund Godfrey* (1936).

202 See for a similar opinion *HMC*, Ormonde MSS 4, p. 308.

203 *ibid.*, pp. 454–7.

the conspiracies of the 1660s there was no single investigation of the plot. The investigations of the conspiracies of the 1660s for the most part had been firmly under the control of the secretariat and examined along these lines. The investigation of the plot of 1678 was never in any one individual's hands. Too many people had a vested interest in it for this to happen. A further difference from the plots uncovered in the 1660s, aside from the fact that a number of these at least had some basis in reality, was the fact that from the first the Popish Plot seems to have been less significant as a plot and more useful as a political tool. Moreover it was a political tool to be used by the various factions both inside and outside the government. Certainly the actual informers themselves cannot have imagined when they concocted their scheme that their invention would get as far as it did. But the fuse which led to the political and religious explosion of 1678–81 was a long one. Its immediate trigger was the distrust engendered from the conversion of James, Duke of York to Catholicism and the possibility of a 'popish' successor to the throne. The uncovering of Edward Coleman's letters and the death of Sir Edmund Bury Godfrey merely added fuel to an already-smouldering bonfire and fears of popery and arbitrary government.

There is little surviving evidence of Williamson's own attitude towards the plot. The various glimpses which do exist of his opinions at least show a healthy scepticism of its genuineness. However, as it soon became impolitic not to believe in the plot's reality, at least in public, Williamson, as did others, kept his own counsel. Of the main informers which the Secretary of State came into contact with there is some idea of his views. Williamson, it should be recalled, had been dealing with such men for years. It therefore comes as no surprise that he thought of the eccentric Israel Tonge as a madman, who was merely intent on gaining an office in the church[204] and so Tonge's initial information was dismissed out of hand.[205] It was a view which Tonge himself seems to have been aware of, for he came to fear the sceptical Secretary of State.[206] William Bedloe was also a type of informant with which Williamson had long been familiar, that is a ne'er-do-well and blackguard.[207] Accordingly Bedloe was encouraged to tell all he knew, which was only a sensible policy. His flattery of Williamson, which

[204] Burnet, *History*, II, p. 156. This was hardly surprising as he was giving out tales of the 1666 Great Fire in which he blamed Colonel Thomas Blood as the agent for a popish/French/Louvestein plot; a very unlikely scenario, *HMC*, Ormonde MSS 4, p. 462.

[205] PRO SP 29/409, fos. 56, 58, 109; *HMC*, Ormonde MSS 4, pp. 455; D. G. Greene, 'Israel Tonge's Journall of the Plot, 1678', in D. G. Greene, ed., *Diaries of the Popish Plot*, (New York, 1977), pp. 34–5; Kenyon, *Popish Plot*, p. 70.

[206] PRO SP 29/409, fo. 65; Kenyon, *Popish Plot*, p. 76.

[207] For more on Bedloe see PRO SP 44/43, fos. 229, 244–5; *HMC*, Ormonde MSS 4, pp. 275, 468.

included telling the secretary that he had informed those MPs who asked that 'they [the Jesuits] looked upon me as an enemy – the same he had told me once before', was regarded with a cool eye.[208] Of the infamous Titus Oates, Williamson never seems to have linked him with the perjurer he had been informed of in 1675, at least in public.[209] The secretary's early opinions of the 'saviour of the nation' are in fact unknown, but in time he did come to fear Oates. This was especially true after Williamson's sojourn in the Tower in November 1678. By this time, however, the secretary's nerve had gone. He was always wary of Oates, however, and invariably took any informations presented to him to the Council.[210]

As the hysteria from the Popish Plot crisis spread outwards it quickly infected the House of Commons. It was to be in the Commons on 18 November 1678 that Williamson faced the verbal battering by MPs which was to wreck his career as Secretary of State. By the end of that day he had been sent to the Tower by the furious MPs, only to be released by an equally furious monarch.[211] Ultimately the effects of this affair upon Williamson's career proved to be disastrous. He could not attend the House for the rest of the session and seems in any case to have fallen ill after his stay in the Tower.[212] The loss of the secretary's political nerve led to increasing doubts about his value in the post to the king.[213] Almost overnight he had become a 'lame duck' minister. Although there was to be a personal compensation for all his travails with his marriage to Catherine O'Brien it probably came as no surprise to him that after a few months he was replaced. At a council meeting on Sunday, 7 February 1679 Charles called Williamson into his private closet and 'Told me, It would be for his service If I would give him ye Seales [of office] (So it was worded ...) I answered as I ought'.[214] The next day Robert Spencer, Earl of Sunderland was installed in the position of Secretary of State, bringing to a close the

208 *CSPD*, 1679–80, p. 3.

209 J. Lane, *Titus Oates* (2nd edn, Westport, 1971), pp. 26–9.

210 See T. S., *The Horrid Sin of Man Catching: The Second Part Of Further Discoveries and Arguments to Prove that there is no Protestant Plot* (1681), p. 20. This relates a curious tale involving Thomas Blood, Titus Oates and Williamson. Blood, according to the author of the pamphlet apparently working for the Catholics or court faction, was to write a treasonable letter to Oates, and then take care to have the informer's papers searched in order to prove his connections with the presbyterians. But Oates took the document to Williamson, who in turn took it to the Council.

211 For Williamson and the House of Commons see Grey, *Debates*, VI, pp. 216–21, 226–40; *HMC*, Ormonde MSS 4, pp. 474–5; BL, Add. MSS 15643, fo. 50; PRO Adm. 77/ Greenwich Newsletters/1, fo. 30.

212 Although this may have been a diplomatic move on his part. *CSPD*, 1678, pp. 531–2, 536–7; *Flemings in Oxford*, I, pp. 266–70.

213 *CSPD*, 1679–80, pp. 25–6.

214 PRO SP 29/366, fo. 417.

nineteen-year career of Sir Joseph Williamson in the government of Charles II.[215]

VII

The later secretaries of the regime were not innovators in the realm of intelligence work, being content to follow the precedents laid down by Arlington and Williamson. In the early 1680s the Stuart regime's intelligence and espionage work was once more revived to be turned against the various factions whom historians, for the sake of convenience, have labelled Whigs. The regime attempted to combat the opposition on a number of levels, especially after the open warfare in the court, parliament and judicial system was forced underground. The result was a clandestine form of political warfare which took place in the taverns, alleys and streets of London and then spilled over into the territory of the Dutch Republic as the Restoration crisis deepened and numerous refugees fled the country. The exile community once more became the focus for the attention of the regime's diplomats and spies. While the pawns on the board on both sides may have changed from the early 1660s, the game remained as cruel as ever. In this game the secretaries had a crucial role to play.

Joseph Williamson's replacement in office was the ambitious and enterprising politician, Robert Spencer, Earl of Sunderland.[216] Gilbert Burnet thought that Sunderland was a man filled with too much 'imagination and passion' to succeed in government, but he did concede that Sunderland had a clear and ready apprehension and 'quick decision in business'. A dangerous political gambler, Sunderland's impulsive manner led him to using his office as a political power base. He was not a man who wanted to be involved in the investigative side of affairs with all of its burdens. Indeed his view in August 1688 that the country was 'never . . . less [in] thought of rebellion', illustrates his limitations in this area.[217] While Sunderland played at politics, therefore, it was left to his partners in office to continue the traditions of their predecessors.

In this respect Sir Leoline Jenkins was a key figure. Jenkins, the son of a Welsh farmer, had been educated at Oxford and remained a stout Anglican royalist throughout his life.[218] This high churchman and stout supporter of monarchy had slowly made his way up from Oxford and then in the legal

215 BL Eg. MSS 3678, fos. 62, 63; PRO Adm. 77/Greenwich Newsletters/1, fo. 31v; *CSPD*, 1679–80, p. 82; *HMC*, Fitzherbert MSS p. 13; Clark *The Life and Times of Anthony Wood*, I, p. 472.

216 For Sunderland the outstanding biography remains that of Kenyon.

217 Kenyon, *Sunderland*, p. 91.

218 See W. Wynne, *The Life of Sir Leoline Jenkins* (2 vols., 1724); also D. F. Taylor, 'Sir Leoline Jenkins, 1625–1685', unpublished M Phil. thesis, University of London.

world of the Court of Arches and the Admiralty Court. In doing so he had acquired a wide knowledge and background in English maritime law. His diplomatic skills, such as they were, were gained through his mission to the Congress of Cologne in 1673–4 as one of the plenipotentiaries there, alongside Sir Joseph Williamson, and as a representative of the king at the Congress of Nijmegen in 1676–8. In character Jenkins was a pedantic and somewhat lugubrious man, 'heavy in his discourse'. Roger North noted that Jenkins on reaching the secretaryship became 'the most faithful drudge of a secretary that ever the court had'.[219] At the same time Jenkins could often lack initiative and self-confidence, finding himself in an agony of indecision when faced with a choice. This, however, did not appear to hinder his progress and in 1680 he was seen as a solid, honest, upright and worthy choice as Secretary of State. While Jenkins managed to gain the respect of most people, his four years in office were to be in administrative terms busy, but devoid of innovation. Jenkins produced no startling insights into the problems of government or intelligence work, merely being content to follow the precedents as they had been laid down under Arlington and Williamson. Not that he was allowed much initiative. His finest hour was in breaking the 'Rye House Plot', although even here he made a number of blunders. His eventual resignation through ill health may if anything have come as a blessed release from the burdens of government. In many respects both Jenkins' and Sunderland's periods of office were typical of the trends which were now to be seen in the office of Secretary of State. The post began to move in two distinctly different directions. A man such as Sunderland followed the Arlington tradition and used it as a potentially powerful political office in domestic and foreign affairs. A man such as Jenkins followed the Williamson line of hard work and unspectacular but positive reform and thus made it something of a rack for administrative drudgery. Jenkins' replacement, Charles, Lord Middleton, took up the reigns of the secretaryship in August 1684. Middleton's background was Anglican, Tory and royalist and he had been a more than capable Scottish secretary. He was also a special favourite of James, Duke of York and struck up a good rapport with Sunderland. Middleton proved another of the diligent and hard-working secretaries. Again he was not an innovator,[220] but remained well placed to uncover the ins and outs of government, while he encouraged the regime's diplomats to deal with the rebels abroad.[221]

Building upon the inheritance left to them by Williamson and Arlington the regime made a variety of moves to counter the threat at home. The Whig

219 *DNB*, Leoline Jenkins.
220 See G. H. Jones, *Charles Middleton: The Life and Times of a Restoration Politician* (Chicago, 1967); Kenyon, *Sunderland*, p. 133.
221 See below, Chapter 7.

leaders in particular were targets, their mail was intercepted and routinely opened, their houses and dwellings as well as their movements were watched. The entourages of the Whig leaders also offered opportunities to recruit double agents. The bravos, retainers and servants who inhabited such suites were often men with slippery loyalties, an eye to a quick profit, or who considered it prudent to keep on the right side of the regime. There were thus spies amongst the Whigs both high and low. The London alderman Sir James Hayes was both a friend of Shaftesbury and a provider of intelligence to the regime. His social position and apparent politics was sufficient to encourage loose talk.[222] Amongst the numerous informers, particularly those the Whigs had imported from Ireland, there were also many unscrupulous men who would easily switch sides, for a price, and could be bought and sold. Where money was not used pressure could be applied in other ways. Edward Fitzharris and Stephen College were pressured into implicating prominent Whigs in treason. James Hayes also recommended the seizure of Samuel Wilson, Shaftesbury's secretary, but Wilson was to stand firm in the face of attempts to persuade him to inform upon his master.[223] Of course, intelligence gathering went both ways and there is little doubt that the Whigs had means of gathering information from inside the Stuart regime. Rather than by paid informers, these links were created from social acquaintances, former friends or 'trimmers' anxious to placate both sides. A system of secret meetings in safe houses, use of ciphers and canting letters to protect plans was also set up to assist the Whig cause.[224]

As the crisis deepened the Whigs were eventually forced into more extreme measures and into plans for a rising as well as an assassination plot against the royal brothers. In this murky arena the regime had considerable advantages. A rising would mean the involvement of many people and the more who became involved in such conspiracies the greater the chances that it would come to light. Having skirted on the edges of treason for some time, there were bound to be some involved whose loyalty was dubious or who lacked the courage of their convictions. The government was able to wait and eventually penetrated the schemes. The decisive break emerged on 12 June 1683 with the appearance of Josiah Keeling before Sir Leoline Jenkins. Keeling's information added to the already-growing rumours and enabled the gloomy Secretary of State to break the plot. Whether there really was an assassination plot was debated at the time and subsequently.[225]

222 BL Stowe MSS 186, fos. 39–46; Ashcraft, *Revolutionary Politics*, p. 343.
223 Haley, *Shaftesbury*, pp. 669–70.
224 See Ashcraft, *Revolutionary Politics*, pp. 338–405.
225 For the Rye House Plot see Ford, Lord Grey, *The Secret History of the Rye House Plot and of Monmouth's Rebellion* (1754); T. Sprat, *A True Account and Declaration of the*

As it has come down to us the 'plot' derived its name from the plan to murder Charles and his brother as they passed the Rye House near Hoddesdon in Hertfordshire on their return from Newmarket to London in March 1683. This assassination was to be followed by a rising in London and elsewhere.[226] It seems likely that plans for a rising at least were under discussion amongst the Whig leadership on the so-called Council of Six in 1681–3. At the same time a group of lesser figures, the heirs of the plotters of the 1660s, who were among the more extreme elements of the Whig movement, were debating assassination as a way out of the problems they faced. The connection between the two schemes was blurred then and remains so now, and questions over the legitimacy of their actions disturbed even the participants. In retrospect the Rye House Plot resembles a great many of the alleged schemes in the 1660s and probably had as much chance of success.[227] The government's tactics at the plot's discovery were certainly remarkably similar to those of the 1660s and it also had the experiences of the Popish Plot to draw on in its dealings with it. However, the chance to break the Whigs was too much to resist and it was exploited for all it was worth, although the king himself was remarkably restrained in his actions.[228]

One thing was clear, with everything in England in ruins many Whigs were forced to flee to the comparative safety of the Low Countries and the focus of the government's attention shifted to the cities of the Dutch Republic in particular. Here the diplomats of the Stuart regime were urged to curb the exile problem. In so doing they recruited spies to watch them and turncoat Whigs to inform the regime of the exiles' plans, and attempted to persuade the Dutch authorities to allow the seizure of troublemakers.[229] And so the reign ended as it had begun, with the secretaries involved in security matters.

During the period 1660–85 the office of Secretary of State was the centre of the government's intelligence system. At its height the physical environment of the office, a place Williamson humorously labelled his 'shop', would have been one of crowd, bustle and a businesslike atmosphere. Amongst the numerous visitors to these offices who were seeking advice, patronage, money, or news would be the occasional spies or informers operating in the London area or further afield. They would, no doubt arrive in the office to report or receive instructions, or, alongside the rebels they

Horrid Conspiracy against the late King, his Present Majesty and the Government (1685); Ashcraft, *Revolutionary Politics*, pp. 338–405; Greaves, *Secrets of the Kingdom*, pp. 133–206; Haley, *Shaftesbury*, pp. 707–24; D. Milne, 'The Results of the Rye House Plot', *TRHS*, 5th series, 1, 1951, pp. 91–108.

226 *ibid.* 227 For more on the assassination aspect of the plot see below, Chapter 8.

228 See Miller, *Charles II*, pp. 367–68; Jones, *Charles II*, pp. 181–2.

229 See below, Chapter 7.

spied on, to be interrogated. Thomas Blood, after his rehabilitation into an agent of the government in 1671, was noted for haunting the office attempting to establish his royalist credentials.[230] It was the secretary's duty as Williamson put it, 'watch all the Parts of the Businesse of my Trade',[231] and it is the details of this trade which we now explore.

[230] See Marshall, 'Blood', p. 570. [231] *Flemings in Oxford*, I, p. 199.

2

Intelligence and the Post Office

I

In the late seventeenth century the postal system was at the forefront of the Stuart intelligence system. It was one of the means by which intelligence could be both gathered and controlled. The origins of the English postal system lie in the later middle ages, but it is significant that a genuine postal system really emerges under the Tudors and early Stuarts. The new nation-state's wish to control the flow of information on both the domestic and foreign fronts and the need for points of contact between officials through correspondence meant that the Post Office rose in importance. As the nation-state arrived so did its bureaucracy and agencies of control. As John Brewer has noted, the 'power of governments has been and always will be in large part dependent upon their capacity to order and manipulate ... information'.[1] The development of a Post Office was one of these elements. It was established in effect as a preventative monopoly. Once again the control of information was a key factor. As literacy developed so, allegedly did 'dangerous' and 'seditious' ideas. Indeed too much knowledge, according to one contemporary, 'overheat[ed] the people's brains and [made] them ... overbusy ... with state affairs'.[2] One of the ways in which such ideas could be transmitted was through correspondence. The best means to control such correspondence therefore was a government-sponsored agency. The suppression or absorption of rival postal services by the state in the period goes some way to proving this.[3]

Although it was never stated explicitly, the Act of 1660, which established the Restoration Post Office, clearly had this in mind when it noted 'the well ordering ... [of a correspondence] ... is a matter of a general

[1] J. Brewer, *The Sinews of Power: War, Money and the English State, 1688–1783* (1989), p. 221.

[2] The Duke of Newcastle in Margaret, Duchess of Newcastle, *The Life of the First Duke of Newcastle and Other Writings* (1911), p. 159. Also T. P. Slaughter, ed., *Ideology and Politics on the Eve of the Restoration: Newcastle's Advice to Charles II* (Philadelphia, 1984).

[3] See for example *CSPD*, 1667, p. 570.

concernment'.[4] Moreover with the letter the only means of communication other than the spoken word in the period, the Post Office was uniquely placed to assess what the literate public had on its mind. It could be used to assess the political state of the country. Of course, this meant intercepting and reading the correspondence it handled, but as the pivotal point in the English Post Office was the General Letter Office in London it was easily accessible for such purposes.

The letter services of the early Stuart period were first systematised by Thomas Witherings, who was created by proclamation Postmaster of England. The post was then farmed out to Witherings and his successors, relieving the government of the cost of maintaining it and providing a flow of money into the Exchequer and later still during our period into the pockets of the Duke of York. The state monopoly on the post, however, was firmly established, along with much else, under the English Republic. The Act of 1657 fixed the rate of postage and the make-up of the system. It also gave the Secretary of State a means of access into this important area for intelligence purposes by making it a monopoly and therefore easier to control. The Restoration Act of 1660 concerning the Post Office was essentially a legal re-enactment of that of 1657.[5] With these Acts a general Post Office was established in London for the transmission of foreign and domestic correspondence, while the sole right of receiving and despatching letters was vested in the office of Postmaster-General. The occupant of this office was naturally to be a royal appointee.[6]

The importance of the Post Office to the Restoration regime was recognised by the purging of the office in 1661 of disaffected and republican elements under the control of John Wildman and his intermediary Henry Bishop. It was alleged that Bishop had been employing former republicans and was in any case believed to be of a doubtful political background.[7]

[4] 12 Car. ii c.35 'An Act For Erecting and Establishing a Post Office'.

[5] The 'Ordinance Touching the Office of Postage of Letters' is printed in C. H. Firth and R. S. Rait, eds., *Acts and Ordinances of the Interregnum, 1642–1660* (3 vols., Florida, 1972), II, pp. 1007–13.

[6] For the early history of the Post Office see *The Post Office An Historical Summary* (HMSO, 1911), pp. 5–7; J. Wilson-Hyde, *The Early History of the Post in Grant and Farm* (1894); J. C. Hemmon, *The History of the British Post Office* (Cambridge, Mass., 1912); H. Robinson, *The British Post Office: A History* (Princeton, 1948); K. Ellis, *The Post Office in the Eighteenth Century : A Study in Administrative History* (Oxford, 1958). For the Post Office's activities in the field of intelligence see *Report from the Secret Committee on the Post Office 5 August 1844*. Parliamentary Papers Report Committees, 14 (1844); E. R. Turner, 'The Secrecy of the Post', *EHR*, 33, 1918, pp. 320–7. For communication in general see K. Sharpe, 'Crown, Parliament and Locality: Government and Communication in Early Stuart England', *EHR*, 101, 1986, pp. 321–50, especially p. 345.

[7] For the purge of the Post Office see M. Ashley, *John Wildman: Plotter and Postmaster* (1947), pp. 155–67; 196–7. See also M. Ashley, 'John Wildman and the Post Office', in R. Ollard and P. Tudor-Craig, eds., *For Veronica Wedgewood These* (1986), pp. 204–16.

Despite this purge of its officers for the time being nothing much was done about Bishop, but in 1663 he lost his franchise to the more acceptable royalist Daniel O'Neill.[8] However, it was not until late in 1667 that the Post Office finally came under the direct and official control of Arlington's office. Unlike John Thurloe who had almost immediately been able to encroach upon this important area of government, Arlington faced difficulties in taking the Post Office under his control. He tried to secure the office of Postmaster-General in 1662 mainly for its financial benefits rather than the intelligence angle, but hostility from Clarendon scotched his plan.[9] This had not, however, prevented the secretariat from carrying on its work of interception, copying and 'dead letter' drops for its agents' correspondence. Behind most of this work was the ubiquitous Joseph Williamson.

Williamson's connections with the illicit side of the Post Office's activities were mainly through various intermediaries most of whom were drawn from the staff the regime had inherited from John Thurloe. They included men such as Isaac Dorislaus, son of the murdered Commonwealth envoy, who had been employed by Thurloe to intercept and copy letters in the Post Office and who was to continue these tasks under the new regime,[10] Sir Samuel Morland, a diplomat, inventor and mathematician,[11] and Dr John Wallis, Oxford mathematician and cipher expert. Another name which might be added to this intelligence team was Henry Oldenburg who translated from obscure tongues intercepted or stolen documents for the secretariat.[12] Of the actual forty-nine or so officers employed at the General Letter Office (located in Clock Lane, Dowgate until 1666), Williamson's main points of contact were James Hickes, the senior clerk of the establishment, who had assisted him in the attempted destruction of Muddiman's newsletter service, as well as a man to whom Dorislaus was close in the 'Foreign Office' section of the Post Office, Jeremiah Copping.[13]

The procedure for letters in the General Letter Office was fairly simple and governed the covert activities which the secretariat involved itself in.

[8] For more on Daniel O'Neill see D. F. Cregan, 'An Irish Cavalier: Daniel O'Neill in Exile and Restoration, 1651–64', *Studia Hibernica*, 5, 1965, pp. 42–76. It was O'Neill who had handled the delicate situation of Lucy Walter in 1656 along with other secret services for the king and his father. See also Hutton, *Charles II*, pp. 97, 184.

[9] For Thurloe and the Post Office see Aylmer, *State's Servants*, pp. 258–9, a very shrewd portrait of the man and his work. See also Evans, *Principal Secretary*, pp. 113–16; and for Arlington in 1662 below, Chapter 5; Barbour, *Arlington*, pp. 54–5.

[10] For Dorislaus see *DNB*, Isaac Dorislaus. His knowledge of French, Spanish and Dutch made him especially useful. See also *Thurloe State Papers*, I, pp. 303, 480; II, p. 231.

[11] For Morland see H. W. Dickinson, *Sir Samuel Morland Diplomat and Inventor, 1625–1695*, The Newcomen Society Extra Publication, 6 (Cambridge, 1970); and *DNB*, Samuel Morland, as well as the sources cited below.

[12] For Wallis see below and for Henry Oldenburg see above, Chapter 1.

[13] For the staff at the office see Wilson-Hyde, *Early History of the Post*, pp. 258–9; Robinson, *British Post Office*, pp. 53–6. For Copping and Dorislaus see PRO SP 29/209, fo. 118.

Letters for domestic or foreign destinations might be handed in at the General Letter Office, or at one of the London receiving stations, which would then pass them on to the General Letter Office. Within the Inland section of the central office were the eight clerks of the roads who had charge of the mails on the six great roads to Holyhead, Bristol, Plymouth, Edinburgh, Yarmouth and Dover. The domestic mails, including those for Ireland and Scotland, left for their destinations on Tuesdays, Thursdays and Saturdays. Domestic mail arrived in London on Mondays, Wednesdays and Fridays. Foreign correspondence went through the three clerks in the Foreign Office, hence the significance of Copping. The mail for France, Spain and Italy left each Monday and Thursday; that for the Netherlands, Germany and Northern Europe each Monday and Friday, while there was a daily post to Kent and the Downs. Arrivals of post from the continent were of the same number, although they were naturally subject to the vagaries of the weather.[14] In fact the duties of the officers of the main Post Office required much of their work be done at night. This was fortunate for it meant there was a convenient period of time to enable the government officials to work quietly intercepting the mail.

If Samuel Morland is to be believed, and he had had long experience in its affairs, the Caroline regime's basic philosophy towards the Post Office was that 'a skilful Prince ought to make a Watch Tower of his Gen[era]l Post Office ... & there ... place such carefull Centinels as that by their care and diligence he may have a constant view of all that passes'.[15] It was in the interest of the 'skilful Prince' to use his Post Office in such a way so as to spy upon his own people, or to manage 'successfully the lopping men of so many different Parties, & the Heroes of the populace, who like untamed horses have thrown their unskillfull riders many times within these fifty years'.[16] Anyone who undervalued such arts, claimed Morland, pointedly, need only review the troublesome reigns of 'Chas I & James the 2d'.[17]

The regime used the Post Office to intercept, open and read the mail and the interception, opening and reading of the mail was a well-known phenomenon in the later seventeenth century, and not just in England. Comminges noted, however, that the English 'have tricks to open letters more skillfully than anywhere in the world'. Moreover he claimed that in

[14] Hemmon, *British Post Office*, pp. 27–8; and H. Robinson, *Britain's Post Office* (Oxford, 1953), pp. 35–6. See also BL Harleian MSS 7365, H. Gardiner, 'A General Survey of the Post Office'.

[15] BL Add. MSS 47133, fos. 8–13. 'A Brief Discourse concerning the Nature & Reason of Intelligence by Sr Samuel Morland'. There are two copies of the document, both of which appear to date from some point in the period 1689–95. Morland died in 1695. There are minor changes in the text of the second version from that of the first.

[16] *ibid*. See also for a comparison the advice of Machiavelli, *Discourses*, pp. 398–424.

[17] BL Add. MSS 47133, fos. 8–13.

England it was commonly thought that 'it is not possible to be a great statesman without tampering with packets'.[18] Unofficially, for at this point such activities had no basis in law, the interception and reading of the correspondence was the prerogative of the Secretary of State, although other ministers and lesser fry made attempts to play a part where they could.[19]

The actual policy of the Stuart regime towards the interception of letters was outlined by secretary Henry Coventry in 1677. Coventry was writing to Arlington who was still Postmaster-General, in answer to Arlington's complaints about the treatment of Isaac Dorislaus and 'invading your [Arlington's] office of Post Master'. Coventry noted that 'a Secretary of State may demand an Account of any letters that come to the Posthouse from anybody'. Furthermore Secretaries of State 'have not ... to ask anybodys leave but the King's but to all inferiors their order is sufficient'. As to the opening of letters, Coventry made it clear that although he thought that morally 'the opening of letters is what no man can justify', the regime was justified in using 'reasons of state, or the king's particular demand'.[20] This position was not formalised until the reign of Queen Anne,[21] but up until that point, as Arlington well knew, having ordered them himself often enough, interceptions were justified mainly on the basis of precedents and the king's 'particular command'.[22]

In general there were two main routes in which the regime proceeded when intercepting the mail: firstly by making specific interceptions and secondly by a more general rifling of the post. Henry Coventry, for example, was asked by the king in December 1676 to intercept the letters of Edward Coleman in order to discover what 'correspondency' Coleman was holding both at home and abroad.[23] Coventry, as has been seen already, was something of a stickler for the legalities and wary of such methods. He therefore asked Charles for a signed order for the interception. Charles prevaricated at this and 'told mee there was no neede of an order because the matter was to be kept secrett'.[24] Coventry, unlike Arlington or Williamson, was a blunt individual and told the king that he did not want a signed order to make the affair public but 'to justify myselfe to himselfe ... in case of his [Charles] forgetting' and the story getting out. Charles,

[18] Comminges quoted in Dickinson, *Sir Samuel Morland*, p. 96. Not that Louis XIV's France was entirely innocent of intercepting letters, as Denzil Holles pointed out to Arlington. See PRO SP 78/119, fo. 35.

[19] See for example, *HMC*, Various Collections, 3, p. 116; and *Essex Papers*, I, 209. Also the activities of the Bishop of Durham below, pp. 105–6.

[20] BL Add. MSS 25125, fos. 31–3. Compare this with Morland's philosophy outlined above.

[21] 9 Anne c.ii clause 41.

[22] See *Report From the Secret Committee for the Post Office* (1844).

[23] Longleat MSS Marquess of Bath/Coventry Papers, 9, fo. 168.

[24] *ibid.*

whose memory for such matters could at times be conveniently forgetful, replied that 'hee would remember it well enough'.[25] So the secretary had to be satisfied with that. His next move therefore was to inform Colonel Roger Whitley, who was Deputy Postmaster at that point, to intercept and copy Coleman's correspondence with 'severall Roman Catholiques both at home and abroad'.[26] The results were then to be passed to Henry Coventry. This then, was a normal enough course to follow in such cases, although it is intriguing to note in this particular case the exclusion from the process of interception of any letter directed to or coming from James, Duke of York. This particular correspondence was 'not in the least disturbed or revealed'. In light of what is known about Coleman's correspondence at this time and in particular the compromising references to James, Duke of York in it, it can easily be seen why Charles wanted his brother's correspondence left untouched.[27]

An example of Williamson's involvement in the specific interception of mail can be found in a memorandum of August 1666 which advocated the interception of all letters coming from Ireland which were addressed to John Knipe, Aldergate Street, or all of 'Potter's' letters going to Ireland addressed to Daniel Edgerton, Cook Street, Dublin. This partly related to the regime's attempts to uncover the author of the radical tract *Mene Tekel*. Obviously the addresses and names would be supplied to officials in the Post Office in order that any such letters could be picked out and passed to Williamson.[28] Williamson also involved himself in the use of interceptions within the regime itself. Williamson had used his influence at the Post Office to intercept Muddiman's newsletter service in order to undermine his rival. He did this through Hickes. The latter stopped Muddiman's letters so that their news could be read, extracted and then included in the newsletters of Williamson.[29]

There is little doubt that the general interception of the mail during the Restoration period followed similar lines to the work undertaken by John Thurloe in the late 1650s. This is to be expected for Williamson had inherited Thurloe's staff. Under Thurloe, Isaac Dorislaus had been given a private room next to the Foreign Office. It was here on post nights that Dorislaus was able to search through the mail, remove, open and copy the more interesting letters. Occasionally Dorislaus had the assistance of

[25] *ibid.* [26] *ibid.*, fo. 170.

[27] See Kenyon, *Popish Plot*, pp. 42–3; and also J. Miller, 'The Correspondence of Edward Coleman, 1674–78', *Recusant History*, 14, 1977–8, pp. 261–75. For Coleman see J. Gillow, ed., *A Literary and Biographical Dictionary of the English Catholics* (6 vols., 1885–1902), VI, pp. 532–6.

[28] *CSPD*, 1666–7, p. 64.

[29] See *CSPD*, 1665–6, pp. 77, 246; *CSPD*, 1667–8, p. 102; Evans, *Principal Secretary*, p. 293. It is quite likely that Henry Oldenburg's correspondence was also intercepted in this way.

Morland. The results of their activities were then brought to Thurloe.[30] The letters which were generally opened were those of ambassadors, an obvious target, and 'publick ministers'.

Thurloe had also been especially interested in the letter office when there was danger of a royalist rising. Nothing much changed in this respect after the Restoration, only that radical and republican elements replaced the royalists as targets. Although the interception of letters may have been less systematic in some ways after 1660 it is clear that it was more elegantly carried out. Moreover it was sufficiently thorough enough to give ordinary folk grounds to worry about what they were writing and to be afraid of the regime reading their correspondence. When even an innocent man such as Edward Arden, secretary to Bishop Cosin of Durham, feared to write much 'for letters are open'd and nothing is certaine', it is clear that the government's activities were having an effect.[31] For it was not only in prospect of catching treasonable letters that interception was useful, it was also effective in preventing the use of the established letter service for carrying such correspondence and in teaching the ordinary subject to behave with respect, or at least with circumspection. As Morland put it 'By [such] arts, and by the frequent inspection of letters ... a king soon knows the temper of all his principal and active subjects.'[32] Interception also forced conspirators to use alternative and naturally more insecure routes of communication. One way of countering this was to use false cover addresses. Another was to resort to the alternative of using the common carriers. According to John Wildman, such people in Cromwell's time were subject to arrest in order to see what they were carrying, but he said this was to 'shoot at rovers'.[33]

Problems also existed for correspondence at the higher diplomatic level. Dutch diplomatic correspondence and despatches from England, for example, were sent by a circuitous route to avoid interception.[34] Samuel Morland pointed out that ambassadors tended in any case to send out their despatches as late in the day as possible to the General Letter Office so that the people there had no time to open them.[35] In fact such interceptions were all part of the diplomatic game of cut and thrust and English actions were repaid in kind by both the Dutch and more particularly by the French.[36]

[30] Firth, 'Thurloe and the Post Office', pp. 530–1.

[31] Durham University Archives, Cosin Letter books, 5, a/b, 1666–70, fo. 54.

[32] *HMC*, Buccleuch MSS 2, pt 1, p. 50. [33] Firth, 'Thurloe and the Post Office', p. 531.

[34] See for a report on this PRO SP 84/174, fo. 131. In 1678 Williamson was also to tell the House of Commons that the Florentine ambassador had been under suspicion for giving covert to [illicit] Letters [during] the Dutch war of 1672–4. Grey, *Debates*, VI, p. 165.

[35] *HMC*, Buccleuch MSS 2, pt 1, p. 50.

[36] For French activities in this area see as an example PRO SP 78/119, fo. 35. See also J. B. Wolf, *Louis XIV* (New York, 1968), p. 167; and P. Burger, 'Spymaster to Louis XIV: A

Dorislaus' actual methods of opening letters had been rather crude when he worked for Thurloe, a fact which 'caused great mutterings and many complaints to be made'.[37] These methods mainly consisted of the use of a hot knife placed under the seal with a drop of wax to re-seal it afterwards.[38] During the Restoration period the actual opening of letters took on a more scientific bent with the assistance of Sir Samuel Morland. Morland had been born in 1625 and educated at Winchester School and then Magdalene College, Cambridge. He was a zealous supporter of the parliamentary cause and undertook some diplomatic service in the early 1650s. John Thurloe evidently found him useful enough to employ in the secretary's office, but Morland was an unpleasant sort of man, a shifting personality and always lacking in funds he proved to be more than willing to work his passage as the Restoration drew nearer by betraying the old regime in order to find new success under the Stuarts. The Italian Lorenzo Magalotti described Morland's temperament as more than a little 'melancholy and ... queer', and nearing death in 1695 Morland allegedly became extraordinarily pious.[39] Morland's involvement in secret affairs was not solely confined to postal duties. He also became involved in the betrayal of the French protestant adventurer Claude Roux de Marcilly in 1668. Roux trusted Morland because of his previous connections with the Waldensians in the 1650s. Morland used his friendship to entrap Roux, by having the French ambassador, Henri de Ruvigny, concealed behind a curtain making notes during their conversations. These soon found their way back to Lionne, Louis XIV's Foreign Minister.[40]

Morland's work for the new regime in the area of the Post Office is, however, the most interesting part of his long career. In 1664 he went to see

Study of the Papers of the Abbé Eusèbe Renaudot', in E. Cruickshanks, ed., *Ideology and Conspiracy: Aspects of Jacobitism 1619–1759* (1982), pp. 111–37. For the French Post Office see A. Corvisier, *Louvois* (Paris, 1983), pp. 233–40; and for an aspect of the Dutch Post Office see E. Schrijver, 'Jacob Quack and Maritime Intelligence', *History Today*, 1977, pp. 134–6.

[37] Firth, 'Thurloe and the Post Office', p. 531.

[38] *HMC*, Buccleuch MSS 2, pt 1, p. 50.

[39] Magalotti, *Relazione*, p. 62. See Dickinson, *Sir Samuel Morland*, pp. 112–19 for Morland's autobiography. This prints the manuscript in Lambeth Palace Library MSS Lambeth, 931. Orign. See also BL Add. MSS 47133, fos. 8–13. Also Pepys, *Diary*, I, pp. 141, 221; IV, pp. 274–5. One of his most extraordinary inventions, which might well account for the melancholy Magalotti found in him, was a mechanical glyster for delivering enemas to himself without leaving his bed. Morland was also to marry an adventuress in 1687 in an attempt to get himself out of debt, but in the end this succeeded in making his financial position even worse. See Pepys, *Diary*, X, p. 251. Also on his career in general see Anon. *A Brief Account of the Life, Writings and Inventions of Sir Samuel Morland* (Cambridge, 1888).

[40] For more on Roux de Marcilly, J. Noone, *The Man Behind the Iron Mask* (1988), pp. 176–7; and Aimé-Daniel Rabinel, *La Tragique Adventure de Roux de Marcilly* (Paris, 1969); A. Lang, *The Valet's Tragedy and Other Studies* (1903).

Arlington and they 'fell upon the subject of intelligence'.[41] Ever one to push things Spanish, Arlington told Morland of a method in Spain of sealing up letters which were impossible to open without it being discovered. Morland saw this as a challenge and undertook to examine and copy a letter written by Arlington and sealed in the Spanish fashion so that it would not be observable. This he did and returned to Arlington not only the original, apparently unopened, but three or four copies. Arlington was startled to discover that he was unable to tell which was the original. As a consequence, an interview with the king was arranged in the secretary's office late one night where Morland showed the latter 'modells in little of several engins and utinsels' with some experiments showing how the trick was done. Morland thus found himself working in two rooms in the General Letter Office where his inventions were put to some practical use.

After about three months the king, Arlington and 'one more' – almost certainly Williamson[42] – visited Morland in his rooms to see the machines at work. For over three hours they witnessed the counterfeiting of wax seals, wafers and 'any handwriting whatever, so as not to be discovered by him who writes the original'. They also saw a safe and easy way of opening letters far removed from the crudities of Isaac Dorislaus, as well as 'A most dextrous and expeditious way of copying out any sheet of paper close written on both side in little more then a minutes time'.[43] Charles gave orders for all of these activities to be put into practice. They continued in operation until the Great Fire of 1666 put an end to them. Morland revived the question in the 1690s but William III was not as enthusiastic as Charles had been about his ideas.[44]

The exact methods used by Morland are unknown. Dickinson has suggested that some type of plastic material was used to make copies in the

41 For what follows see *HMC*, Finch MSS 2, pp. 264–7, *HMC*, Buccleuch MSS 2, pt 1, pp. 48–51 for a different version of the same paper; and *HMC*, Downshire MSS 1, pt 2, pp. 594–95; Dickinson, *Sir Samuel Morland*, pp. 98–100.

42 Morland does not say who this third man was but he was writing in the 1690s when Williamson was still alive, which may account for his reticence. Moreover intelligence was Williamson's area and the fact was known in government circles. See for example Sir George Downing who in 1668, when faced with a petitioner who claimed that her late husband had discovered a plot in 1662 and wanted some money as a reward, turned to Williamson to discover the truth of the matter. *CTBks*, 1667–8, p. 432; and *CSPD*, 1667–8, pp. 125–6.

43 *HMC*, Finch MSS 2, p. 456. For an Italian version of Morland, named Celio Malapina, who offered to forge letters for the Council of Ten of Venice, see H. F. Brown, *Studies in the History of Venice* (2 vols., 1907), I, pp. 248–9.

44 William III, who was not adverse to intelligence work, showed a remarkable reluctance to sponsor the scheme and thought it better that the idea should die with Morland. See *HMC*, Buccleuch MSS 2, pt 1, p. 51. See also Dickinson, *Sir Samuel Morland*, p. 96; and for William's involvement in interceptions as king see S. P. Oakley, 'The Interception of Posts in Celle, 1694–1700', in R. Hatton and J. S. Hatton, eds., *William III and Louis XIV. Essays 1680–1720. By and For Mark A. Thomson* (Liverpool, 1968), pp. 95–116.

case of counterfeiting seals. In the case of copying the documents he suggests an offset process of pressing damp tissue paper against the ink: a method later used by the inventor James Watt for business copying purposes. It is clear that Watt's machine needed the correct type of ink to work successfully, so it may well be that Morland exaggerated his own machine's capabilities. Having said this, in October 1655 John Evelyn visited the 'ingenious' Samuel Hartlib who informed him that he possessed an 'inke that would give a dozen copies moist sheetes of paper being pressed on it and remaine perfect' without injuring the original. Hartlib's invention may well have come to the knowledge of Morland.[45] It is clear that Morland's methods and his machines were very useful to the regime while they continued in operation.

Most of the spies writing their reports back to Williamson would have wished to keep their identity secret from prying eyes and part of this activity also came under the province of the Post Office. The methods which had worked so well under John Thurloe were continued when this area fell under the control of Williamson. Wildman had previously informed the regime that it had been Samuel Morland, under Thurloe's direction in the 1650s, who gave out to the Republic's agents 'some false address whereby to direct all their letters, as for example: [For John Adams at the Sugar Loafe in Milford Lane] or the like'. At the same time this address was given to Isaac Dorislaus at the Post Office who would put it on his own list 'so that when he opened the maile, and found such an addresse, he might know whether [*sic*] to send them'.[46]

An identical procedure found its way into Williamson's system and there is little doubt that Williamson had borrowed Thurloe's methods. The agent was given a cover name, or one of the 'borrowed names' as Williamson himself put it. This would be written on the cover of the letter going to England. Two illustrations of this policy may be useful to show what exactly went on at this point. In 1679, for example, the letters written between Henry de Vic and Sunderland, who had just replaced Williamson as secretary, were to come to the earl under three different addresses and in three different languages:

English For Mr Henry Wilmot at the Three Pigeons in
Wapping, London.
For Mr Wm. Parker at his house in the Strand,
London.

[45] See H. W. Dickinson, *James Watt, Craftsman and Engineer* (Cambridge, 1936), pp. 115–17, also Plate VII(b) for a photograph of Watt's device; and Evelyn, *Diary*, III, pp. 162–3.

[46] Firth, 'Thurloe and the Post Office', p. 533.

Dutch Aeen mÿn Heer Francois de Mol Koopman
tot London.

Aeen mÿn Heer Hendrich Adamson noonende
in Covent Garden tot London.

French a Mademoiselle
Mademoiselle du Pré
proche la Bourse
a Londres.

a Monsieur
Monsieur de Launcy
dans le Pell Mell
a Londres.[47]

The other example is an entry in Williamson's own address book, which reads: 'Mr T. B. fró Holl Zealand writing under ye address of Jo. Taylor at ye Post House London & of Thomas Harris'.[48] Any foreign or domestic attempt to intercept such letters would be thrown off the scent by such seemingly innocuous addresses. Once these addresses were agreed upon, the names would be added to a list which was kept in the Post Office and when the mail was sorted the relevant letters could be removed with safety. It might be thought that sorting through all of the mail might be rather time-consuming, as indeed it was, and led the ordinary members of the public to become suspicious of the inevitable delays in receiving their letters. They did, of course, have just cause to suspect the post. However, as it was the Post Office's proclaimed policy not to release or deliver any letter until those of the king had arrived at the court, delays could be partly explained away. This policy obviously gave the intelligence team some time to perform their tasks.[49]

Occasionally things did go wrong with the system of cover addresses. One of the letter carriers in July 1667, a Mr Herbert, had a letter addressed to 'Samuel Cottrington' a merchant.[50] This individual he could not find despite 'much enquiries amongst many persons'. It was only when Herbert asked Isaac Dorislaus if he knew 'Samuel Cottrington' that he was told that the gentleman was in fact Williamson using a pseudonym. Being an honest man and aware of the trouble it could cause him if he fell foul of the powerful under-secretary, Herbert took the letter to James Hickes, and told him the tale. Hickes writing to Williamson wanted to know how Dori-

[47] BL Add. MSS 40677, fo. 296. The information is written on the cipher key.

[48] PRO SP 9/32, fo. 213. Also Marshall, 'Blood', pp. 563, 576–77. See also PRO SP 106/6, fo. 18. 'Projet de la Méthode pour tenir une Secrete Correspondence'.

[49] See *CSPD*, 1672–3, pp. 8–9.

[50] PRO SP 29/209, fo. 118; and *CSPD*, 1667, pp. 291, 296.

slaus knew where to send the Cottrington letters and if he had seen Williamson's address list kept in the Post Office. Hickes, Ellis and O'Neill were apparently aware of the book but not of the reasons behind Williamson's methods and were unaware of the exact status of Dorislaus. This might be expected with something so secret and a policy of divide and rule is typical of Williamson's methods elsewhere. It seems clear that it must have been Dorislaus who held the list or book. Hickes expected trouble to arise from the incident but only one Smartfoot, another letter carrier who had put the letter with that of some real merchant's correspondence, lost his post because of the blunder.[51] It is also clear that it was well known that on no account were Williamson's letters to be opened in the Post Office, but his very secrecy about such methods and devices as well as the plethora of cover names occasionally seems to have had its drawbacks, as has been seen. It seems to have allowed the occasional letter to go briefly astray while the Post Office clerks attempted to puzzle out to whom such letters were supposed to go.

A glimpse of the covert route by which secret English correspondence flowed out of the United Provinces to Williamson is provided in the Third Dutch War. One Henry Dale, an acquaintance of Silas Taylor, keeper of naval stores at Harwich and himself used as a spy by the under-secretary, was located in the port of Briel. Dale kept lodgings in the town and supplied the passengers of the packet-boat with meals on board ship. He was thus able to pass through the guards around the dock with the letters on his person. Once on board the correspondence was given to the master of the packet-boat who in turn, on reaching England, passed them on to the under-secretary's minions for forwarding to Williamson. For this dangerous activity, and his own information, Henry Dale received 200 guilders.[52]

II

Another means by which information and intelligence, as well as names, might be kept secret from prying eyes was through the use of codes and ciphers. The art of cryptography was a long and ancient one stretching back to at least the time of the Roman Empire.[53] No major innovations

[51] PRO SP 29/209, fo. 118; *CSPD*, 1667, pp. 291, 296. The Dutch also used merchant cover addresses see *CSPD*, 1672, p. 403.

[52] See *CSPD*, 1671–2, pp. 462–3; *CSPD*, 1672, pp. 464, 484.

[53] For Julius Caesar's cipher, which makes an interesting comparison with the early modern ones, see Suetonius, *The Twelve Caesars* (Harmondsworth, 1977), pp. 34–5. For a general history of codes and ciphers D. Khan, *The Codebreakers: The Story of Secret Writing* (1968); and C. G. Cruickshanks, *Elizabeth's Army* (1966), pp. 73–4. For a near-contemporary view, P. Thicknesse, *Treatise on Deciphering and Of Writing in Cipher* (1772); J. Wilkins, *Mercury or the Secret and Swift Messenger: Shewing How a Man May With*

took place in this area during the period 1660–85 but codes and ciphers remained important for a variety of reasons. Used correctly they did protect the authors of certain secret correspondence from discovery, as long as the key to them remained unbroken. This fact allowed information to pass freely and without hindrance even if the mail was intercepted by interested parties. To the late-seventeenth-century mind 'Cypher ... [was] ... a kind of Magick'.[54] Thus codes and ciphers were in common use in the period, whether in the correspondence of kings, such as Charles II, or of diplomats, such as Sir William Temple, or in that of a man who believed that he had something to hide, such as Colonel Joseph Bamfield. Indeed it often seems as though the English in particular were obsessed with covering their tracks.[55]

Ciphers used by the English regime and its agents in the period were mainly of three types. By far the most common of these were simple numerical substitution ciphers with a set of numbers replacing individual characters, dipthongs or words. Correspondence could be drafted out by a trustworthy clerk, or by the person concerned, and then the letters replaced for figures drawn from the cipher key and the occasional 'null', or meaningless number, in an attempt to conceal the actual word. Paragraphs or even the whole letter could be wholly or partially replaced by a series of figures which had the effect of concealing the important information. The more complicated ciphers would attempt to conceal the actual words in a form of anagram called transposition. Thus 'SECRET' would become 'ETCRSE' which could then be replaced by numbers drawn from the cipher key.[56] However, the typical English cipher used in this period would invariably have the numbers written in the correct order, replacing the relevant letters so that the recipient could simply fill in the letter above the number and read the message. In the main this was because the English, despite their obsession for secrecy, seem to have also been subject to the inclination to make ciphers easier to use or, to put it in rather more blunt terms, were merely too lazy to use the more complex and time-consuming

Privacy and Speed Communicate His Thoughts to a Friend at any Distance (1641); L. Potter, *Secret Rites and Secret Writing: Royalist Literature 1641–1660* (Cambridge, 1989).

[54] A. de Wiquefort quoted in D. P. Heatley, *Diplomacy and the Study of International Relations* (Oxford, 1919), p. 245.

[55] Relevant in this context are the private shorthand and ciphers used by men such as Samuel Pepys and Robert Hooke.

[56] See Khan, *Codebreakers*, p. xiii; C. H. Carter, *The Western European Powers, 1500–1700* (1971), pp. 233–60; W. J. Roosen, *The Age of Louis XIV; The Rise of Modern Diplomacy* (Cambridge, Mass., 1976), pp. 137–44, 199–200.

systems which were available.[57] This actually made such ciphers easier to break, for certain words and letters, such as 'the' and 'e', occur with great regularity in the English language and enable the illicit decipherer to break down the correspondence and create his own key; hence the attempts to break down the regularity by using 'nulls' or meaningless numerical indicators.[58] The actual recipient of such a letter, as opposed to someone who had intercepted the correspondence, would use his copy of the key to reveal the information by deciphering the relevant sections of the letter. Some of the keys used by the regime and its agents were fairly large and complicated and printed forms were available to make the construction of these much easier. These forms printed the numbers, and less rarely, code words, next to blank spaces allowing both parties to fill in the actual letters and words in ink themselves. The second type of cipher used in the period was indeed created by using substitute names or symbols for the actual names. Such a code by itself seems to have been fairly rare in English government procedure at the time; the English seem to have favoured a mixture of the two. The names of persons, places or things were replaced in the correspondence by substitutes drawn from mythology, or mere pseudonyms mixed with merchant jargon.[59] Unfortunately the users of such a system would rarely have fooled anyone who came across their efforts.

A further type of cipher to be found in English correspondence was that recommended by Dr John Wallis in 1692. This he claimed was 'an easy Cipher, which yet might be tolerably safe'.[60] The cipher merely consisted of moving letters forwards or backwards in the alphabet. Thus a–z, would become b–z with the letter 'a' of the second series becoming 'z' of the first. Thus the world SECRET for example, would become TFDSFU. The problem here is again obvious. The letter E occurs twice and thus become F and with a little common sense the illicit decipherer could work out the system being used. Alternatively one could use the next letter but one, or two, either before or after the original letter. To make the cipher a little more difficult numerical figures or Greek characters could be intermixed. Wallis claimed that such ciphers were safe for four reasons:

> 1) 'Tis a chance, whether, or no the letter be intercepted. 2) If so, 'tis yet a further chance whether those who have it will attempt its being deciphered (& not rather

[57] Examples can be found in PRO SP 106/6, 'Charles II Ciphers'; and BL Add. MSS 40677, 'A Collection of Late Seventeenth Century English Diplomatic Cypher Keys'. See also P. S. Lachs, *The Diplomatic Corps under Charles II and James II* (1965), pp. 172–3.

[58] For a useful and clear introduction to these problems see Edgar Allen Poe's story 'The Gold Bug', in *Selected Writings* (Harmondsworth, 1976). The story hinges on the breaking of a cipher.

[59] For the opposition use of this tactic Ashcraft, *Revolutionary Politics*, p. 343.

[60] Wallis quoted in D. E. Smith, 'John Wallis as a Cryptographer', *Bulletin of the American Mathematical Society*, 24, 1917, p. 95. Compare this with PRO SP 77/40, fo. 274.

neglect it as thinking it to no purpose). 3) 'Tis a further chance whether they light upon one who can do it 4) If deciphered 'tis yet a chance whether it do you any considerable mischief (for I presume you will not intrust anything of very great moment therein).[61]

The purpose here, and usually elsewhere amongst English statesmen, was for a rapid and easy to use cipher. Wallis suggested more complex ciphers if some real security were needed, the disadvantage with them being that they took time to construct. In fact it was the opinion of many that though any number of new ciphers could be invented, 'The industry of men whose wits are sharpened by necessity and by self-interest, will not fail to discover the key to them'.[62] De Callières, however, believed that it was corruption and betrayal which were the worst enemies of the well-made cipher rather than experts such as Wallis.[63]

Another method favoured by some was to conceal the piece of correspondence, whether ciphered or not, in invisible ink. An apparently innocent piece of correspondence might thus have hidden depths. The usual substance for such attempts was lemon juice or milk. The invisible writing might be on the back of a piece of correspondence or in between the lines. When placed before a candle or other source of heat, however, the hidden writing miraculously appeared. Such schoolboy techniques were used with all seriousness by some men.[64]

Whatever the method of cipher or code chosen, its use was always a long and often time-consuming process over which considerable care had to be taken. Sir Robert Southwell was to recommend that for the Secretary of State's office a specific clerk should be delegated with this rather onerous task. He noted in 1689 that a new secretary coming into office should get 'Cyphers ... and [let them be] ... studied by one of the Clerkes, who is to be relyed on, for Cyphering and Uncyphering what occurs'.[65] It was only in the early eighteenth century, however, that more settled arrangements in the office took place and that a regular salary was paid out for a 'decipherer'.[66] This still left the actual ciphering to be carried out by a clerk, and problems could occur.

The best example of such problems emerges in the correspondence of Sir William Temple in 1668. Temple wrote to Arlington that he was in 'despair' over the new cipher which he had been given. According to him 'we cannot make out one syllable of ... the two long paragraphs in one

[61] *ibid.* For more on Wallis see below, pp. 93–5.
[62] F. de Callières, *The Practice of Diplomacy*, translated by A. F. Whyte (1919), p. 142.
[63] *ibid.*
[64] Colonel Joseph Bamfield is a case in point. For other examples of secret writing see J. Pollock, *The Popish Plot: A Study in the History of the Reign of Charles II* (Cambridge, 1903), p. 378.
[65] BL Add. MSS 38861, fo. 46.
[66] See Sainty, *Secretaries of State*, pp. 51–2.

letter'. Temple blamed the cipher itself noting that 'I am apt to imagine the exactness required to this cypher is more than can agree with the haste often necessary in your lordship's office'.[67] A hastily ciphered letter, or a cipher that was merely too complex, could lead to errors and unintelligibility. The natural haste which occurred within the secretaries' office seems to have made this inevitable. John Richards, writing to Williamson while the latter was in Cologne in 1673, seemed surprised that the cipher he was using 'gave noe occasion of complaint more than what all cyphering produces, being sometimes little mistakes'.[68] The actual numbers of ciphers floating about cannot have helped the situation. When Lord Preston was sent to Paris on a diplomatic mission he was given five different ciphers to use. If this allowed him a certain flexibility of choice, it could have just as easily made things confusing for the recipient.[69] The attempts to ease the situation by new inventions rarely succeeded.[70] The process of ciphering the deciphering thus remained a tedious, as well as a difficult, but important part of the intelligence system.

For the Stuart regime part of the answer in deciphering intercepted letters lay in the employment of Dr John Wallis.[71] Wallis had acted in a semi-official capacity for most of the governments of the mid to later seventeenth century. His career as a decipherer of intercepted letters had begun in the 1640s when he had been brought a letter in cipher which he had managed to decipher in two hours.[72] Wallis worked for the parliamentarians during the Civil War and was well rewarded for his services.[73] His work in this period was also to bring him trouble at a later date when accusations were made that it was Wallis who had deciphered some of the captured correspondence of Charles I after Naseby. The implication was that he was one of those who by his actions had helped the king onto the scaffold. It was an accusation which Wallis strenuously denied.[74] Be that as it may, there is no doubt that Wallis was willing to assist the Cromwellian regime and the Republic of 1659–60 in its deciphering tasks.[75] It is, of course, quite possible that he saw this as merely an intellectual challenge and ignored the political implications. If so he was being politically naive. In any event the Restoration did the mathematician no real harm and he

[67] Temple, *Works*, I, pp. 410–11. [68] *Williamson Correspondence*, I, p. 110.
[69] *HMC*, 7th Report, p. 261.
[70] See for example Samuel Morland's ideas about a 'circular cypher', *CSPD*, 1667–8, p. 143; and Dickinson, *Sir Samuel Morland*, pp. 34–5.
[71] For Wallis see C. J. Scriba, 'The Autobiography of John Wallis, FRS', *Notes and Records of the Royal Society*, 15, 1970, pp. 34–40.
[72] *ibid*; *DNB*, John Wallis.
[73] See C. Webster, *The Great Instauration: Science, Medicine, and Reform 1626–1660* (1975), pp. 40–1, 79–80.
[74] See BL Add. MSS 32499, fo. 377.
[75] See Underdown, *Royalist Conspiracy*, pp. 295–6.

was made a chaplain to the new king. Wallis himself claimed his policy was always to play the 'trimmer' and that 'It hath been my endeavour all along to act by moderate principles, between the extremities on either hand in a moderate compliance with the power in being'.[76] This is a statement that a modern intelligence operative would no doubt be proud to proclaim for himself – although the validity of it would be just as suspect.

His work for the new regime was as a decipherer of the most difficult of the captured documents and he was well rewarded for his services. Wallis received 200 guineas for one piece of work.[77] Wallis later reminded his Williamite masters that Arlington had sent for him in 1672 and given him 50 guineas as a downpayment and promised another 50 guineas per quarter for deciphering letters. Wallis had received 200 guineas by the time Arlington left the secretary's office.[78] The large fees were probably quite justified for it could be hard work and Wallis was famous throughout Europe for his skill.[79] The German philosopher Leibniz apparently wrote to him to learn his methods, but Wallis refused to disclose them to him, although in the later years of his life he did agree to train a successor. Wallis occasionally deciphered documents for other powers if he was asked.[80] Wallis appears to have been an effective decipher expert more than probably because he was an expert mathematician, although François de Callières, who probably had experience of such men in his diplomatic work, was rather dismissive of professional decipherers as a group. In general they gradually increased in numbers as the seventeenth century progressed. De Callières believed that their reputation rested rather on 'the ineptitude of poor ciphers rather than upon their discovery of a good cipher'.[81] Clarendon, had also at one time underrated John Wallis's skill, but he was to later praise his 'industrie and sagacity'. Clarendon noted that the most 'accurate cifers ly[e] as open as a common Alphabet' to him.[82] Wallis himself claimed that he had 'seldom failed of any ... Though the labyrint[h]s of Cipher have from day to day grown more difficult.'[83] Wallis therefore remained a most important member of the regime's intelligence system. It

[76] Scriba, 'Autobiography of John Wallis', pp. 42–3.

[77] See J. A. Kemp, ed., *John Wallis: Grammar of the English Language with an Introductory Grammitico-physical Treatise on Speech or on the Formation of Speech Sounds* (1972), p. 11. Wallis received £100 for his services in 1691, BL Add. MSS 32499, fo. 303. As an example of his relations with Williamson see *CSPD*, 1677–8, p. 405. His salary and that of his self-chosen successor, William Blencowe were regularised in 1701. See Sainty, *Secretaries of State*, pp. 51–2. Blencowe committed suicide in 1712. His successor, Dr John Keill, was thought to be 'a booby' and was swiftly replaced in 1716 by the Rev. Edward Willes. D. B. Horn, *The British Diplomatic Service, 1689–1789* (Oxford, 1961), p. 227.

[78] Smith, 'John Wallis as a Cryptographer', p. 91.

[79] *ibid.*, p. 84; and Kemp, *Grammar*, p. 10.

[80] Kempk, *Grammar*, p. 10.

[81] de Callières, *The Practice of Diplomacy*, p. 245.

[82] BL Add. MSS 32499, fo. 15.

[83] Scriba, 'Autobiography of John Wallis', p. 38.

is therefore very ironic that Wallis was a good friend to John Locke and it was in Wallis' house that Shaftesbury stayed during the Oxford Parliament.[84]

The postal service and the covert activities which took place within it had a crucial role to play in the Restoration regime's intelligence system on a variety of different levels. Most importantly it was through the Post Office that the flow of illicit information could be controlled, or even manipulated. Indeed the Post Office in the period provides one element of continuity which the early modern English espionage world might otherwise lack. It was a central core to the system in which John Thurloe and Thomas Scot had operated and in which Williamson followed them with much the same staff. This cannot have but been of value to the Restoration regime in its espionage system as the Republic's system provided the groundwork and in its covert postal work the Restoration regime learnt from the Republic's mistakes and experience.

[84] See Haley, *Shaftesbury*, p. 625. Wallis also worked for secretary Jenkins in the aftermath of the Rye House Plot. See *CSPD*, July–September 1683, pp. 25, 102–3.

3

Local intelligence networks in the north of England

Restoration government could only govern the provinces with the assistance of the local community, in the shape of its county officers, and even then the process was often a 'combination of sticks and carrots'.[1] The extensive and important work undertaken on the county community has increased both our knowledge of how this relationship came about as well as how it worked in practice, but one area which has been generally neglected has been the question of intelligence work in the local arena.[2] It is the purpose of this chapter to explore some aspects of this area of local government in the Restoration period, particularly in the north of England. We can say at the outset that many local officers were involved in intelligence work. Directives from the centre may often have given contradictory signals about the persecution as well as the prosecution of radicals and dissenters, but an underlying theme in the period was the encouragement of local officials to uncover as wide a variety of information and intelligence as possible in order to comprehend, as well as direct, public opinion at the county level. From such sources vital insights into the mood of the people could be obtained, local responses to government policy could be assessed and with luck moulded to the central government's needs. The maintenance of security and order was a further consideration. Indeed Andrew Coleby has noted that the Restoration regime's primary concern in the early 1660s was to prevent politically inspired unrest at the local level.[3] Both of these factors, information and security, therefore led the Stuart regime to take more than a passing interest in the affairs of local government. The maintenance of royal influence in the localities was a necessary part of government. This meant developing a relationship between the Secretary of State and the offices of Lords Lieutenant and more especially the local justices of the peace. For their part the county officials were simi-

[1] J. S. Morrill, *Seventeenth Century Britain, 1603–1714* (1980), p. 125.

[2] See, however, T. G. Barnes, *Somerset 1625–1640: A County's Government During The 'Personal Rule'* (Oxford, 1961), pp. 86–91.

[3] A. M. Coleby, *Central Government and the Localities: Hampshire 1649–1689* (Cambridge, 1987), pp. 125–6.

larly interested in the activities of those they saw as enemies of the state. These enemies could range from old Cromwellian soldiers and politicians to the local dissenting communities, but whatever the opposition the local officers usually needed little encouragement to develop the means of ensuring that these troublemakers did not get out of hand.

In matters of intelligence and security the justices of the peace were certainly regarded as the most significant officials on the local level. The justice of the peace was the workhorse of local government in the period and someone upon whom much depended. His duties were wide-ranging, from enforcing the criminal law, to matters of national security on the local level.[4] It was the latter area which carried them into the world of espionage. While it was not laid down that a justice should create his own local intelligence network, the penal laws against recusants and dissenters allowed for the use and the reward of informers and it *was* one of the justices' functions to be on the watch for suspicious characters and seditious words. The secretariat, spurred on in the 1660s by the information-hungry Joseph Williamson, also pushed many justices into the gathering of local news for the government. The reward for such activities in the 1660s, aside from the strong sense of public duty already present in most justices appears to have been official news of the affairs at court and abroad in the shape of a manuscript newsletter from the secretary's office. This was something any intelligent gentleman would be eager to obtain. Indeed this is part of the reason why Joseph Williamson at least played upon their needs and attempted to restrict the official news and information reaching them. There is no doubt that he at least wished to bond the local officers into a reciprocal weekly correspondence. From the gathering of local news for the under-secretary that such a relationship necessitated, it was but a short step to the actual use of informers and spies for other areas of intelligence work.

It can also be argued that the nature of society on the local level often seems to have been conducive to the general gathering of such information. While one would not go as far as Lawrence Stone and claim that life in the provinces was characterised by an 'exceptionally oppressive atmosphere of neighbour[hood] hostility and espionage',[5] it was a society where most local people knew everyone's business and where the presence of any curious stranger, or even political grumbling, would be commented on. It

[4] For a useful and clear introduction to the work of the justice of the peace and other local officials see S. A. Peyton, ed., *Minutes of Proceedings in Quarter Sessions held for the Parts of Kesteven in the County of Lincoln 1674–1695*, The Lincoln Record Society, 25 (1931), pp. xxv–xxxvii. See also Pollock, *Popish Plot*, pp. 269–76 for more on the justices' inquisitorial activities against recusants.

[5] Lawrence Stone quoted in A. Fletcher, *Reform in the Provinces: The Government of Stuart England* (New Haven, 1986), p. 281.

would also at some point, invariably come to the attention of the guardians of the law.[6] This was especially true in times of political stress for the state. Such stress at the centre invariably caused reverberations which easily swept through to the county level. As Norrey points out there was also a 'constant stream of directives [flowing] from London ... [with] insistent calls for care and vigilance' for the local officers to contend with.[7] Frequent examples of this occur in the early 1660s.[8] It was then partly this environment that Williamson and the regime managed to plug into with an extensive list of domestic correspondents from Cumberland to Kent.[9] How reliable and useful the officers of the county were in this field is another matter. They invariably communicated by post or on visits to London and the reports of particular local officers might well be less than candid on occasion. Thus there was some effort to spread the network of information gathering as widely as possible by using a patronage network of friends, clients and relatives. The question of evaluation of information at the central-government level thus remained a critical one. In matters of local conspiracy and plot the ministers were often sceptical, wishing to assess both the sources and motives of the intelligence they received from such quarters, cross-checking the intelligence to ensure that the problem was not merely some over-zealous official.

II

Perhaps the best means by which local-intelligence activities may be examined is to analyse them in one specific area of the country. In this sense the north of England in the early 1660s may serve as a typical example of what went on at this level of government. One of the most significant figures on the scene of local government in the counties of Cumberland and Westmorland in the early 1660s was the staunchly royalist Sir Philip Musgrave. The family of Musgrave was of long-standing in the north-west of England and Sir Philip himself was of proven loyalty as a lifelong royalist and Anglican. Certainly Musgrave, who had suffered for his beliefs, was often as fanatical as those he persecuted. At the Restoration he was reinstated as a justice of the peace in both Cumberland and Westmorland, made Custos Rotulorum in Westmorland, as well as a deputy lieutenant in both counties. He was also given the governorship of Carlisle.[10] It may thus be seen

6 See for example Cumbria RO (Kendal), WD/Ry, 34 (Fleming Papers) fo. 1120.

7 P. J. Norrey, 'The Restoration Regime in Action: The Relationship Between Central and Local Government in Dorset, Somerset and Wiltshire, 1660– 1678', *HJ*, 31, 1988, p. 792.

8 See Coleby, *Hampshire*, p. 106.

9 *Williamson Correspondence*, II, pp. 161–5.

10 See G. Burton, *The Life of Sir Philip Musgrave, Bart.* (Carlisle, 1840), pp. 33–9; *Flemings in Oxford*, I, p. 140, and *CSPD*, 1661–2, p. 498. J. Nicolson and R. Burn, *The History*

that owing to the local offices he held Musgrave emerged as a very substantial figure on the county scene in the north-west. He and his son were also close to Joseph Williamson, himself a native of the area and quite willing to exploit these connections.

Musgrave was a rather high-handed local officer and was especially hated by dissenters, although even his county neighbours nicknamed him the 'Grand Vizar and Bashawes Begge ... of Westmorland' having frequently suffered under his rule.[11] He was, however, an exemplary local official having great experience in local government, war and, more significantly, in matters of conspiracy. The latter skills had been gathered under the difficult circumstances of the Civil Wars and the Republic when he had been deeply involved in royalist plotting.[12] If nothing else this valuable experience must have given him a unique insight into the minds of conspirators. Conversely such experiences could also have had a negative side. Musgrave does seem to have become slightly hysterical, if not obsessive, in some of the cases which came before him in the early 1660s. His persecution by the republican authorities, both local and national in the 1650s may possibly have warped his judgement enough to foster ideas of revenge when he came back into power in 1660. Musgrave was certainly very zealous, if not overzealous, in his prosecution of recusants, nonconformists and anyone he considered dangerous to the Stuart regime. He considered himself a 'state physician', well able to purge his region of all forms of dissent. In religious terms he also thought that the 'dregs of schism are so deeply settled in men that indulgence will never purge them out'.[13] It may be he was correct in this assumption for in terms of religious dissent the north of England did prove troublesome. The Anglican church structure in the northern counties was weak in many respects. Michael Watts has estimated that on average the parish was usually four times as large in the dioceses of Durham and Carlisle, and in Yorkshire twice as large, as in the southern counties. There were for example only fifty-four rectories in the whole of Northumberland and in Musgrave's own area the parish of Kendal covered most of the Lake District.[14] The Anglican church was therefore under some pressure in the north of England and often chose to maintain itself by fierce persecution. Of the various dissenting groups the strength of Presbyterianism was particularly notable. The Quaker movement was of course born in the north-west of England and proved par-

and Antiquaries of the Counties of Westmorland and Cumberland (2 vols., 1776), I, p. 597; also *DNB*, Philip Musgrave; *H of P*, II, pp. 120–2.

[11] Cumbria RO (Kendal) WD/Ry, 34 (Fleming Papers), fo. 594.

[12] For Musgrave at this time Underdown, *Royalist Conspiracy*, pp. 114–15, 167.

[13] Musgrave quoted in *H of P*, II, p. 121.

[14] M. Watts, *The Dissenters from the Reformation to the French Revolution* (Oxford, 1985), pp. 277–82, 285.

ticularly resilient despite harsh treatment in the region from 1660. The Quakers saw Musgrave as one of their chief persecutors.[15] It is also clear that he was not alone in holding strong views about the problem of dissent in the north-west. In the county of Westmorland Sir Daniel Fleming, another close friend of Williamson, acted equally harshly towards the local 'fanaticks', citing their 'boldness [and] their great disaffection to the present government', which he hoped 'so long as I am in authority ... to helpe punish them when they shall offend'. As did other local officials, he looked to central government for some guidance as well as encouragement in his tasks.[16] Conversely another local family, the Braithwaites of Ambleside Hall, who had both Catholic and dissenting relations, were somewhat more liberal in their views and attempted to check the aggressiveness of their colleagues.[17] Thus there was ample room for friction on the county level between the local officials on the problem of religious dissent, to say nothing of the political differences. It was something which could be exploited by men such as the rebel and spy Robert Atkinson to the detriment of the regime.[18]

As a good county officer, Musgrave was also zealous on the questions of intelligence. Dr Isaac Basire of Durham put it to Musgrave that Sir Philip was regarded as one who nourished intelligence; good intelligence, as Basire saw it, being 'the mother of prevention'.[19] Musgrave did indeed put considerable effort into his work in this area being willing to travel in person as well as to employ spies in order to obtain information. In one instance he travelled up to Jedburgh on the Scottish border in order that he might gain news of Scottish affairs,[20] a journey which at his age showed his keenness in such matters. Furthermore he employed agents to provide him with intelligence. It is unfortunate that many of Musgrave's own papers are scattered or missing and consequently only a fragmentary picture of his apparently extensive intelligence network, which covered the three northern counties, can be pieced together. An additional problem for historians in this area, and one which is common to most of these local networks, is that they often lack the fine details that are to be found at the national level. The references to their employees by their local masters are

15 See J. A. Nickalls, ed., *The Journal of George Fox* (1986), p. 454 and W. C. Braithwaite, *The Second Period of Quakerism* (1919), pp. 29–34.

16 *HMC*, Le Fleming MSS, p. 68.

17 See B. Nightingale, *The Ejected of 1662 in Cumberland and Westmorland: Their Predecessors and Successors* (2 vols., Manchester, 1911), I, p. 75; Nicolson and Burn, *Westmorland and Cumberland*, I, pp. 126–7, 190, 604.

18 For Atkinson's story see below, pp. 108–15.

19 Durham University Library MSS, Cosin Letter Books, 1 (b), 132, Basire to Musgrave, 17 May 1665.

20 *CSPD*, 1667–8, p. 454.

invariably to 'my spies' or 'an intelligencer' rather than any specifically named individuals, except where the local officer thought the secretaries might be interested. It also appears likely that many of the reports delivered to Musgrave were of a verbal nature and thus not many written reports from his spies would be expected to survive. What is known about Musgrave's method and system can be compared with other systems in the northern counties at that time and tends to support this view. A good example of what we mean emerges in the work of Musgrave's Yorkshire contemporary Sir Thomas Gower. He noted that he was frequently forced to visit one of his intelligencers 'who might not be seen with me in publique much less in York[,] being yet unsuspected'.[21] Obviously therefore the communication between the two men was invariably spoken rather than committed to paper. Some of the local spies were in any case unwilling to commit themselves to paper for fear of discovery. One of Gower's most notable agents, Major Greathead, proved very reluctant to send his information to Gower directly for fear of news of his dealings leaking out.[22]

There is no doubt from the information which does survive that Musgrave at least was at the centre of a regional network of spies and informers and supplemented their information with that provided by his fellow justices of the peace, militia officers[23] and deputy lieutenants. In turn he forwarded his gathered intelligence, depositions and interrogations, where they warranted it, to the Secretary of State. The alternative was to incarcerate the individuals concerned and await orders from Whitehall. These orders would either be to forward the most important suspects to London, or to hold them for trial at the local assizes. Occasionally those conspirators who reached London and suffered interrogation there were, when the central government had no further use for them, sent back for trial at the county assizes. An alternative to this was the prospect of new employment under the control of the Secretary of State's office.[24] The most frequent employees on the ground level for such local systems appear to have been ex-soldiers. This was sensible enough as their targets were usually ex-New Model Army men. Such employees were certainly as typical of Musgrave's system as they were of Sir Thomas Gower. Musgrave also had his spies not only in Cumberland and Westmorland but also across the county boundaries in the Palatinate of Durham. One Durham agent of Sir Philip's was engaged jointly with Christopher Sanderson, a justice of the peace from

21 PRO SP 29/81, fo. 187. 22 PRO SP 29/83, fo. 70.

23 For the militia officers as detectives see P. J. Norrey, 'The Restoration Regime in Action: The Relationship Between Central and Local Government in Dorset, Somerset and Wiltshire, 1660–1678', *HJ*, 31, 1988, p. 792.

24 As an example of this see the case of William Leving below, Chapter 6.

Barnard Castle, for the princely sum of £60 per annum.[25] Indeed the local officers were often willing to pay quite large sums of money in some cases to employ local spies. Sir Thomas Osborne, the future Earl of Danby, when High Sheriff of Yorkshire paid out £15 each to six men (£72 per annum), whom he set to spy on ex-New Model Army men in the early 1660s. Osborne was keen to let it be known that large rewards were available in order to encourage informers to come forward.[26] Such monies were, it was hoped, to be reclaimed from central government. Indeed Musgrave was given £10 for intelligence purposes by Sir Edward Nicholas during the latter's tenure of office.[27]

The names of a few of Sir Philip Musgrave's employees in this area have survived and provide some example of the type of men he hired. One of them was Captain John French 'formerly a Captain in Cromwell's army'.[28] In November 1663 a Captain French was sent under guard on Musgrave's orders by Daniel Fleming to Sir William Carleton in Penrith in the aftermath of the Northern Plot.[29] This seems to have been the beginning of French's career as Musgrave's spy and he turned from alleged conspirator to agent at this time. According to the knowledgeable Joseph Williamson, French was either then, or later, an innkeeper in Kendal and a native of Westmorland.[30] As such he would have been in a useful position to listen to the local gossip as it came through his tavern and then pass his information onto Musgrave. By such methods an intelligence relay could be built up, with French on the ground level, Musgrave at the intermediate and the secretariat at the centre. Another informant who wished to keep his name quiet after the events of October 1663 was Andrew Huddleston. Musgrave kept Huddleston's name secret in order that he could be used again to obtain further information,[31] and Huddleston is known to have caused his son-in-law some problems in November 1663 when he implicated him in the plot of that autumn.[32] In general most of the men used on this level have been 'small fry' on the national scene, but they were typical of the type of men a justice of the peace such as Musgrave would have had at his command. As such, and in comparison with the type of spy used by the central government, their information has a distinctive local flavour, if not a 'gossipy' feel to it, except when it impinges on the concerns of

[25] *CSPD*, 1665–6, p. 300; for Sanderson see also 'Selections from the Diary of Christopher Sanderson of Barnard Castle', in *Six North Country Diaries*, Surtees Society, 118, (1910), pp. 34–63.

[26] *CSPD* 1661–2, pp. 537–8; and Browning, *Danby*, I, p. 27; II, pp. 26–8. Osborne's penchant for paying for what he wanted was perhaps a foreshadowing of his later activities with parliament in the 1670s.

[27] BL Egerton MSS 2543, fo. 115. [28] PRO SP 9/32, fo. 219.

[29] PRO SP 29/83, fo. 170.

[30] PRO SP 9/32, fo. 219. [31] PRO SP 29/83, fo. 24. [32] *CSPD*, 1663–4, p. 342.

national security.[33] There are frequent accusations against neighbours which show all the signs of personal vendettas or old scores being paid off.

Occasionally things could become confusing if each Lord Lieutenant or justice refused to co-ordinate their activities in intelligence. The result of this was often an increased tension between local officials. The idea of the county boundary was in any case deep-seated amongst local officials, particularly in the north of England. Running alongside this was the view that only in their own county were the officers really efficient, while across the border anything might be expected. This, as one historian has noted, was both a source of strength and weakness.[34] Belief in one's own abilities was a strength, but might also prove to be an illusion; no confidence in the local officers across the county border might mean lack of co-ordination in security matters. It could also cause local government to present a far from united front on occasion. We can see this most obviously in the relations between the local authorities of Durham and those of Yorkshire in the aftermath of the Northern Plot of 1663. Relations between the two turned so sour that one of the major conspirators, John Joplin, was found not guilty at his trial.[35] Richard Neile of Durham was one of those who openly criticised the 'malice and backbiting of Yorkshiremen against this country', that is Durham, which he considered partly responsible for the Joplin affair.[36] Indeed Durham was at the centre of some long-standing controversy in local government in the north. The local officers of the burgeoning city of Newcastle-upon-Tyne were very reluctant to accept the authority of the bishopric.[37] The Palatinate authorities were also criticised for the failure of the 1660 experiment to place the bishopric with the North Riding of Yorkshire under one lieutenancy. Once the Bishop of Durham, John Cosin, returned to the Palatinate the experiment was deftly replaced by the old system of the bishop himself as Lord Lieutenant.[38]

Having said this, secrecy could have beneficial effects when it occurred

[33] See for example Cumbria RO (Kendal) WD/Ry, 34 (Fleming Papers), fo. 1120.

[34] G. Scott Thomson, 'The Bishop of Durham and the Office of Lord Lieutenant in the Seventeenth Century', *EHR*, 40, 1925, p. 351.

[35] See *Memoirs of the Life of Ambrose Barnes*, Surtees Society, 1 (1867), p. 397; G. Ormsby, ed., *The Correspondence of John Cosin, DD, Lord Bishop of Durham*, Surtees Society, 52 (2 vols., Durham, 1869–72), II, pp. 99–100, 104–5, 107–8, 314–17. Also J. Walker, 'The Yorkshire Plot', *The Yorkshire Archaeological Journal*, 31, 1935, p. 358; and R. Surtees, *The History and Antiquities of the County Palatine of Durham* (4 vols., 1920), II, p. 391; H. Gee, 'A Durham and Newcastle Plot in 1663', *Archeologia Aeliana*, 3rd series, 14, 1917, p. 156.

[36] Surtees, *Durham*, II, p. 391.

[37] See J. C. Hodgson, ed., 'Papers Relative to the Plot in the North in 1663 Extracted from the 31st Volume of the Mickleton and Spearman MSS', *Archeologia Aeliana*, 1st series, 1, 1822, pp. 143–8; R. Howell, *Newcastle-upon-Tyne and the Puritan Revolution: A Study of the Civil War in North England* (Oxford, 1967), p. 63.

[38] Scott Thomson, *The Bishop of Durham*, p. 360.

between the employer and his various employees. Sir Thomas Gower, the judicious local official, who by his use of Major Greathead was largely responsible for breaking the Yorkshire section of the Northern Plot of 1663, employed numerous spies 'who know not of one another'.[39] Such a policy not only enabled him to cover the county but to check one set of informations against another. This was invariably a good sign for it proved Gower to be a man unwilling to believe everything he heard, unlike many of his contemporaries. It was partly responsible for his confident prediction to Buckingham, on the latter's arrival in Yorkshire in late 1663, that the affair had blown over.[40] This cross-checking of information was not something all local officials undertook to do and it is occasionally responsible for the sometimes panicky nature of their correspondence with the Secretary of State's office. Equally, Norrey has pointed out that in the south-west the officials were often confused by the directions from Whitehall and the resulting sometimes overzealous actions had to be curbed by the regime.[41]

The actual tasks set such spies by local officers could vary. One of Sir Thomas Gower's men was 'sent ... purposely [to be] inquisitive in inns and private houses, informing himself also of the opportunity to watch bridges and to beat the highway at night'.[42] Another man was sent out by Gower to track down John Atkinson the Stockinger, a conspirator of October 1663, who was lurking about Durham in 1664 dressed 'in laborers habit and colored ... face'. Gower was confident that his agent, whom Atkinson 'does not at all distrust', would never 'dare ... play double with me'.[43] Inns and local taverns provided the classic environment for the local informer and spy. Musgrave's agent Captain French, as has been seen above, operated in his own tavern. Robert Philipson[44] trailed three men and a boy from Troutbeck Bridge in the county of Westmorland one evening in February 1669 and attempted to engage them in conversation at a tavern. As they were not very forthcoming he left, but only after he had 'charged mine host, to take notice not only of their words but actions'.[45] Philipson was later told that after he had left, in the tediously time-honoured tradition of conspirators, one of the men 'pulled a letter out of his pocket [and] said "Now I thinke wee may safely read [this]."' They

[39] PRO SP 29/80, fo. 231.
[40] *ibid.*, fo. 127. See Albermarle's comments below, Chapter 4.
[41] P. J. Norrey, 'The Restoration Regime in Actions: The Relationship Between Central and Local Government in Dorset, Somerset and Wiltshire, 1660–1678', *HJ*, 31, 1988, p. 805.
[42] PRO SP 29/81, fo. 186.
[43] PRO SP 29/83, fo. 77. John Atkinson is not to be confused with Robert Atkinson.
[44] Robert Philipson was a justice of the peace who had fallen on hard times in the aftermath of the Civil Wars. See *Flemings in Oxford*, I, p. 208.
[45] Cumbria RO (Kendal), WD/Ry 34 (Fleming Papers), fo. 1120.

subsequently retired to a private room while 'mine host' listened at the door, but heard nothing.[46]

The techniques used in tavern life on the local scene were even sufficiently well known to have appeared in the drama of the period. In the 1607 play by Beaumont and Fletcher, *The Woman Hater*, for example there is a speech which illustrates the classic techniques used by such men in such locations. According to one character in the play the spy and informer lived

> in alehouses and taverns and ... [thought] ... to discover ... much out of the talk of drunkards in Taphouses ... informations pick'd out of broken words in men's common talke which he with his malitious misapplication hopes will seem dangerous.[47]

There was therefore a role for the *agent provocateur* in the local intelligence system. This is something which Sir Thomas Gower was certainly accused of encouraging. He was alleged to allow his 'privileged' spies to persuade local people into conspiracies.[48] In many ways, viewed from a worried local official's perspective, the criticism of local officers using *agents provocateurs* is unfair. There is no doubt this practice took place. One Dobson confessed that he spoke treason to others on Gower's orders to see if he could make any discoveries[49] and it is more reasonable to see this tactic as part of the 'game' of espionage in which the stakes were thought to be high.[50] There was always a fine line, however, between involving innocents and egging on active conspirators in order to uncover a whole plot.[51] There is little doubt the local justice of the peace faced with this dilemma would have argued that if the victim were really innocent he wouldn't have become involved with such people in the first place. In the case of some of the more prominent ex-Cromwellians in the early Restoration, they had little choice in such matters as they were subject to informers and spies putting words into their mouths.[52] But there were few moral qualms in the period to curb such tactics. No lead was given from the established church; indeed clergymen themselves were not above using spies if they felt it necessary. The Bishop of Durham can perhaps be excused of this as he was fulfilling a dual role as both bishop and Lord Lieutenant, but the Bishop of Lichfield was willing to use spies against his

[46] *ibid.*

[47] *The Woman Hater*, in F. Bowers, ed., *The Dramatic Works of the Beaumont and Fletcher Canon* (Cambridge, 1966), I, pp. 168–9.

[48] PRO SP 29/85, fo. 25. [49] *CSPD*, 1663–4, p. 463.

[50] Compare this with Machiavelli, *Discourses*, pp. 398–424.

[51] See below in the Tonge Plot, pp. 142–50.

[52] See *Original Memoirs Written During the Great Civil War: Being the Life of Sir Henry Slingsby and the Memoirs of Captain Hodgson* (Edinburgh, 1806), pp. 167–8.

own local clergy whom he suspected of laxity. He wrote that he could 'hit on no better remadie then to send out ... spies to the most suspected parishes; and upon proof of ... neglect, to suspend the incumbent'.[53] John Cosin, Bishop of Durham, also had the local post rifled to obtain evidence[54] and required Dr Isaac Basire, rector of Egglescliffe, to make secret lists of those 'that have served as souldiers of officers aginst the King' as well as to find out which of them were still possessed of 'ill principles'.[55] Bishop Ironside of Bristol used gangs of informers against dissenters.[56] One individual from Yorkshire, who evidently possessed some classical learning, complained that it was just like the reign of a new 'Tiberius' in the England of the early 1660s.[57]

Certainly the type of men employed by local officials often left much to be desired. Gower's spy, Major Joshua Greathead, alias the Ironmonger, was described as a 'cunning knaveish man ... hated by all good men'.[58] A man such as Greathead seems always to have been bent on trouble of some sort and was possibly better off under Gower's control. Having said this Captain John Hodgson, who suffered considerably at the hands of local officers in Yorkshire, was alleged to have said he would join the 1663 plot if Greathead were involved in it.[59] Certainly a description of Greathead's character inspires little confidence in his morals. His neighbours are said to have stood in some awe of him and it was well known that 'it was a very dangerous thing to be in his company'.[60] Gower was evidently satisfied enough with Greathead's work, as well as in his faithful service, for the sheriff to recommend the major to the Secretary of State. He wrote that Greathead was 'not obstinate but ... sensible of his duty'.[61] But it is notable that Gower was not foolish enough to rely on Greathead's information alone. However much he nurtured and cajoled his spy he pointed out that 'I have more strings to the bow nor shall he be the single witnesse'.[62] Greathead was later briefly employed to collect the Hearth Tax before misbehaving himself and spending some time in the King's Bench

53 Bishop of Lichfield quoted in F. Bate, *The Declaration of Indulgence: A Study in the Rise of Organised Dissent*, (1908), p. 69.

54 *Cosin Correspondence*, II, p. 108.

55 *ibid.*, p. 108. Basire was prebendary of the seventh stall of Durham Cathedral and had been persecuted in the Civil Wars. He had thus left for foreign parts visiting Constantinople and Syria. See *Cosin Correspondence*, II, pp. 6–7.

56 J. Latimer, *The Annals of Bristol in the Seventeenth Century* (Bristol, 1900), p. 355.

57 PRO SP 29/85, fo. 25.

58 'An Exact Relation of Severall Occurrences', printed in S. J. Chadwick, *The Farnley Wood Plot*, Thoresby Society, 15 (1909), p. 126.

59 *Original Memoirs*, pp. 187–8.

60 'An Exact Relation', p. 126.

61 PRO SP 29/83, fos. 70, 84.

62 PRO SP 29/80, fos. 231, 214; and also PRO SP 29/109, fo. 47.

prison. He did write to Williamson, in March 1678 seeking a return to his old employment, but little came of this.[63]

The local justices could, of course, on occasion be over-zealous in their persecution of those they suspected of sedition in their areas. Captain John Hodgson was an ex-army officer living in Yorkshire who suffered in this way. Hodgson found a particular enemy in Sir John Armitage, a justice, who according to one source was to come to no good end when he 'was slaine with a fall from his horse & broke his neck'.[64] According to Hodgson, Armitage was drunk at the time.[65] Prior to this he had conducted a campaign of harassment against Hodgson, which is typical of the way in which old Cromwellians in the north were treated in the early 1660s. Armitage always hoped of catching Hodgson in some conspiracy, of which there were more than enough to go round, but he never succeeded in this despite employing all of the weapons at his disposal. These ranged from the use of informers, to armed raids on Hodgson's home in the middle of the night. At times Armitage appears to have conducted something of a personal vendetta against the ex-officer which certainly smacks of an obsession. Armitage may have had good reason for this, for it is clear that Hodgson was never as innocent of active conspiracy as his official memoirs make out.[66]

That the plots of 1663 in the north were stifled before they got off the ground was partly the result of good local intelligence and the activities of the local officers. A vigilant officer such as Sir Thomas Gower, or Sir Philip Musgrave who kept his ear to the ground and employed local spies to supply him with information which he in turn could pass onto the central government, was doing a good job for the Stuart regime. Indeed Gower had word of conspiracies in his area as early as March 1663. The local officers in Durham also picked up on the information given to them by the informer John Ellerington.[67] Ellerington's information by itself was fairly crude but it set the local officers seeking the names of other conspirators. In time Gower was able to penetrate deeply into the Yorkshire section of the conspiracy and he was able to gain intelligence from up to three sources within the planning group of the conspiracy. Gower's intelligence meant a confident approach to plotters was possible. It might thus be said that the plot was doomed from the start. But as events were to prove the leaders of such schemes were to be more resilient in their activities than anyone could guess. A man such as Robert Atkinson, and there were more dangerous

[63] See *CSPD*, 1678, p. 49. [64] 'An Exact Relation', p. 125.
[65] See *Original Memoirs*, p. 189.
[66] See *ibid*., pp. 189–93; and Walker, 'The Yorkshire Plot', p. 357; Greaves, *Deliver Us From Evil*, pp. 31, 199.
[67] *Cosin Correspondence*, II, pp. 314–17.

men than he involved in plotting, as the years 1664–7 were to show, could exploit the differences between local officials for his own ends.[68]

It was the local officials who received the information and took the depositions of those brought before them. Most of them certainly knew the local conditions in the north of England and it has been seen above how they operated. Occasionally they provoked those whom they suspected into errors. The good local officers checked the evidence that they received with some care before alerting London. They were, however, nervous men. Any failure would fall inevitably upon their own heads. Thus psychologically they might have often been more willing than most to believe in a nation-wide conspiracy, if only because this would throw the burden from themselves onto central government or others across the county border.

In its dealings with information supplied from the local level Whitehall was often cautious. Those concerned at the centre, were not fools and they rejected many of the tales of plots emanating from the provinces which came before their gaze. Secretary Nicholas indeed told Sir Henry Coker to calm down and show more restraint.[69] Occasionally it was clearly seen as necessary to treat a plot as genuine, or to exaggerate its importance in order that the regime might benefit. This cannot be said of 1663, but even then the regime cannot really be faulted for this. In the world of *realpolitik* which Charles II's government played it was much better to have republican or dissident elements under lock and key, or at least for the regime to know where they were, than have them roaming the country. Such a stance discouraged many a large scheme from emerging and many a plotter from plotting. In many senses therefore the early 1660s in the world of espionage and conspiracy saw a war of attrition between government and those who would not be governed or refused to accept the new situation. In the early 1660s especially the counties were still suffering from the post-Civil War and republican traumas. In this sense then 1663 proved to be a good year for the Stuart government, although this was not at first apparent. Numerous troublesome individuals were laid to rest, or forced into the open. By the end of 1663 and the beginning of 1664 the regime had extensive lists of both known and potential troublemakers and urgently took on the task of hunting them down.

III

Late on the evening of 12 October 1663 John Waterson of the village of Great Musgrave in Westmorland was slowly making his way home from

[68] See below, pp. 113–115.

[69] P. J. Norrey, 'The Restoration Regime in Action: The Relationship Between Central and Local Government in Dorset, Somerset and Wiltshire, 1660–1678', *HJ*, 31, 1988, p. 805.

Kirkby Stephen when he came across a body of mounted men on the road. They commanded him to stop and state his name. Their leader, armed and mounted on a white horse, was Captain Robert Atkinson, formerly governor of Appleby Castle in the time of the Commonwealth, an ex-soldier under Cromwell and also, though his companions were unaware of it, an ex-spy for Sir Philip Musgrave who was then royal governor of Carlisle. As the group had a spare horse Waterson was included in the band. He was swiftly informed that this night the north would rise against King Charles II. Indeed he was told that men were already up in arms in Scotland and throughout all England; further that Fairfax himself had joined the fray and had decided to lead them.[70] The party was poorly armed but rode on towards an inn called Spittle on Stainmore Common close to the Durham border. There it hoped to link up with larger forces coming from the Palatinate and if necessary engage against any royal forces in the area. Atkinson's own plans were to seize the excise money in the hands of the clerk of the peace at Appleby as well as to take Sir Philip Musgrave prisoner. The word was to be 'God be with us.' Both Atkinson and his followers soon discovered that they were virtually alone on the moors and that no help or assistance was going to come from Durham or anywhere else. As they neared Kaber-Rigg their numbers also began to dwindle. Atkinson decided to stop his company at this point and cut their losses telling his followers to quietly disperse to their homes. Having come this far some of them proved reluctant to do so and wished to go on. When the group did eventually move on to Birka they drew up together in a military fashion before disappearing into the night. They were assured by Atkinson that they had done nothing wrong and had little to fear from the authorities. Unfortunately for all concerned the authorities, led by the strong-minded 'grand vizar' Sir Philip Musgrave himself, were already aware of the 'rebellion' and took immediate action to arrest the would-be rulers of England. They began to round up suspects and incarcerated thirty-five of them, including Atkinson, in Appleby gaol prior to interrogation, thus putting an end to what became known as the Kaber-Rigg Plot – part of a northern conspiracy which was meant to take place that night.[71]

In hindsight those involved on the night of 12 October 1663 seem to have had little, if any, chance of success. The rebel numbers were unimpressive and they had barely reached the Durham border before they broke up. Moreover it is difficult to imagine where they could have gone onto

[70] For the events on this night see the interrogations and depositions of the Kaber-Rigg (Northern Plot) rebels located in PRO ASSI/45/6/3, fos. 178–222. Some of these are printed in J. Raine, ed., *Depositions From the Castle of York, Relating of Offences Committed in the Northern Counties in the Seventeenth Century*, Surtees Society, 40 (1861).

[71] *ibid.*

from that point. Westmorland was a bleak place in the late seventeenth century, far from the centres of power and Stainmore was moreover one of the bleakest places in the county. A rebellion here would have soon faltered for lack of numbers and the basic necessities needed to supply it. A night on the wind-swept moors seems to have been the only result of the rebels' efforts in the north-west and retribution, in the shape of the due legal process of the law, was to be the price paid for their folly. The botched rebellion does, however, highlight some interesting aspects of intelligence at the local level and was the peak of the career of one man in particular: Captain Robert Atkinson of Mallerstang.

In an era when the origins of most spies and rebels remain obscure Robert Atkinson stands out as a man about whom a little more than usual is known. He was native to Westmorland and was born in the village of Winton between 1614 and 1624. According to Sir Philip Musgrave, Atkinson was originally a yeoman farmer worth about £30 per annum. It is also known that he was a tenant of Anne Clifford, Countess of Pembroke on her estate at Mallerstang. His religion he described on the scaffold as 'moderate Presbyterian'.[72] Atkinson was active for parliament in the Civil War and served as a captain of horse and afterwards as 'Colonel of the County troop'.[73] He also became governor of Appleby Castle in the 1650s and was again active in securing royalists in the county. It may be at this point that Atkinson and Musgrave clashed for they certainly came to dislike each other. While they were poles apart politically, in many ways they also held certain traits of character in common. Atkinson in the 1650s had been as much given to an authoritarian style in his dealings as governor of Appleby as Musgrave was to be in the 1660s. When the local mayor and his officers threw up their offices in the early 1650s, after having had the new Protectoral charter forced upon them, Atkinson brought his soldiers into the town to choose the new mayor and is alleged to have clapped his hand upon his sword saying 'I'll do it by this.'[74] He also set himself up as a man of the people in this period by urging on the legal suit of some of his old landlady's tenants against her estate at Mallerstang. After this Lady Anne Clifford regarded Atkinson as her great enemy.[75] With the Restoration of course, such activities came to an abrupt end and Atkinson's fortunes took a turn for the worse.

[72] PRO SP 29/95, fo. 111; also Cumbria RO (Carlisle), D/Mus Letters, Bundle 6, fo. 3; Williamson, *Lady Anne Clifford*, p. 269; J. Nicolson and R. Burn, *History of Westmorland and Cumberland*, I, pp. 315, 547. For Mallerstang see *An Inventory of the Historical Monuments in Westmorland* (Royal Commission on Historical Monuments, 1936), p. 163; R. R. Sowerby, *Kirby Stephen and District*, (Kendal, 1948).

[73] PRO SP 29/95, fo. 111.

[74] See Nicolson and Burn, *History of Westmorland and Cumberland*, I, pp. 315–16.

[75] PRO SP 29/95; fo. 111; Williamson, *Lady Anne Clifford*, p. 398.

By a not so unusual twist of fate in the 1660s the roles of Musgrave and Atkinson became reversed. While the royalist came back into his own, the 'Roundhead' captain of horse lost his power and eventually found himself playing the spy for the new authorities. This new role seems to have begun in early 1662.[76] In return for information Atkinson wanted a pardon and some money for his own security. The deal could be said to have been fairly shrewd on both sides, for Musgrave was well aware of Atkinson's background and the former soldier's potential for causing trouble. Engaging him as a spy would have been at least a way of curtailing the troublesome captain's activities. Moreover as an erstwhile staunch Commonwealthsman, with a well-known local reputation to prove it, Atkinson would be able to gain the trust of his ex-army colleagues and neighbours, who would readily reveal to him their plans and schemes for returning to power. For a price Atkinson agreed to pass his intelligence to Musgrave. Musgrave possessed a low opinion of men such as Atkinson and probably thought he had bought the captain's loyalty cheaply enough. For his part Atkinson, without this change of roles and with his political background could have easily expected years of persecution in the early 1660s, much as a fellow Cromwellian, Captain John Hodgson was to experience in Yorkshire.[77] Some security, along with a little political leeway and some ready cash, would have come from working for Musgrave. How genuine the information was that Atkinson passed to his new master is much more debatable. Musgrave later argued that Atkinson had provided him with some 'considerable truths', but it is equally possible that Atkinson was feeding the royalist false information to calm his fears and take the pressure from himself and his friends' activities. It was clear to all concerned that someone of Atkinson's background and temperament was hardly likely to settle down under the royal regime and in due course Atkinson became involved in the Northern Plot of 1663.[78] Long before this, however, Musgrave had thought better of the association and decided to dispense with Atkinson's services as a spy. He had found him to be 'unfaithfull to mee & [so] laid him aside'. Musgrave came to the conclusion that Atkinson's motives were dubious to say the least and his information even more so. Having decided this, he then settled on a view of Atkinson that bordered on mania, seeing in him all the former ills of the state as well as a very 'subtle & false person'.[79] Perhaps he was, to Musgrave at least, for by the spring of 1663 Atkinson was deeply involved in

[76] See *CSPD*, 1661–2, pp. 368, 542. [77] See *Original Memoirs*.

[78] See PRO SP 29/81, fos. 148–148v, 'Sir Thomas Gower's Papers Concerning the Intended riseing in Yorkshire'. See also Cumbria RO (Kendal), D/Mus/Letters, Bundle 5, unfoliated: headed 'Proceedings at York', and J. D. Whitaker, *Loidis and Elmete* (1816).

[79] PRO SP 29/91, fo. 11.

consultations across the county border with other conspirators. Nor is there any need to doubt Atkinson's genuine affinity to the new scheme. He had revived his old views and was not attempting to trepan the conspirators. Musgrave's distrust of Atkinson grew with the passing days and the increasing rumours which he picked up led to Atkinson's arrest in August 1663. Musgrave had Atkinson placed on an open bond for his good behaviour[80] but, as we have seen, this did not prevent him from leading the abortive Kaber-Rigg rebellion.

The collapse of the Kaber-Rigg rebellion on the night of 12 October 1663 left Atkinson and his companions in desperate straits. Atkinson having reassured his companions that they had done nothing wrong returned to his home, hoping that their activities had gone unnoticed. In due course Atkinson's home was raided and he was arrested and then sent to Appleby gaol to join his companions.[81] The night before his examination, however, he escaped from the weakly held gaol. He also fled from the custody of one Hugh Atkinson, possibly a near relative. The captain swiftly retreated into the hills of Westmorland while Musgrave sent out a hue and cry to search for him and then put a price on the now outlawed captain's head.[82] Atkinson was not daunted by his experiences and his strength of character made him even more dangerous in adversity. At his trial, and later on the scaffold, where humility was usually expected and penitence required,[83] Atkinson's manner was thought 'very insolent' and haughty by the authorities and it disturbed them greatly. Atkinson was alleged to have arrogantly informed his guards that no one could draw any more information from him 'then he had a mynde to declare'.[84] It must have come as no surprise that rumours soon reached the local authorities that Atkinson was bragging that if he could get twenty men together he would make a daring raid on the gaol at Appleby and rescue his comrades from Kaber-Rigg, while at the same time revenging himself on 'some perticular gentlemen'.[85]

The interrogation of some of the Kaber-Rigg rebels had already revealed to Musgrave that his particular fate during the rebellion was to have been to have his throat cut[86] and this made him even more determined to recap-

[80] PRO SP 29/82, fo. 186. [81] *ibid.*, fo. 104; *CSPD*, 1663–4, p. 315.

[82] PRO SP 29/99, fo. 120; PRO SP 29/95, fo. 111.

[83] See J. A. Sharpe, '"Last Dying Speeches": Religion, Ideology and Public Execution in Seventeenth-Century England', *PP*, 107, 1985, pp. 144–67.

[84] Cumbria RO (Carlisle), D/Mus Letters, Bundle 6, fo. 3. But compare this statement with his interrogation.

[85] Cumbria RO (Kendal), WD/Ry, 34 (Fleming Papers), fo. 567.

[86] PRO SP 29/83, fo. 138. The interrogations and depositions of the Kaber-Rigg rebels are located in ASSI/45/6/3, fos. 178–222. Some of these are printed in Raine, ed., *Depositions From the Castle of York*.

ture Atkinson. Fortunately Robert Atkinson may have had more than enough of the life of an outlaw. It may be that he was thinking of his family at this time, or after three weeks 'sculking' in the hills with the onset of winter in the offing the costs may have seemed just too high to pay. News of the collapse of the rebellion in Yorkshire must have also reached him and made the impossibility of his situation clear. However, rather than flee to the Low Countries, the usual course in such situations, Atkinson was still confident enough in his own abilities to feel that he could talk his way out of his problems. Whatever his reasons Atkinson decided to surrender, not to Musgrave, whom he had every reason to fear, but to some men who may have been relations on his wife's side, the Braithwaites.

Atkinson surrendered himself to Thomas Braithwaite a Catholic and the son of Richard Braithwaite of Burnside near Kendal. As a Catholic Thomas would have been compromised by this so Thomas decided to involve Richard Braithwaite of Warcop, their wives being cousins. Richard Braithwaite was the local justice of the area who had already been vigorous in his examination of the rebels. However, according to Musgrave's later investigations, the Braithwaite and Atkinson association had been a suspiciously early one. It was claimed that Richard Braithwaite's servant had 'held intelligence with Atkinson immediately after his escape from Appleby'.[87] When Atkinson came in the Braithwaites made no move to tell Musgrave or Sir Daniel Fleming that they had Atkinson in their custody. Instead they decided to take Atkinson to York to see the Duke of Buckingham who had been sent north to deal with the rising. These highly unusual actions smack of local politics in the raw. Atkinson himself was again playing a new game, hoping for a pardon in return for turning informer, but intending to play the Braithwaites and everyone else false if he could. He was later to swear that he 'would rather be hanged then come to the barr' and give evidence against anyone.[88] Buckingham was in York to supervise the round-up of the Yorkshire rebels and was an important figure in the north, so the duke's patronage could have been very useful to both Atkinson and the Braithwaites.[89] As we shall see, Buckingham's association with rebels was to become well known. The angry Musgrave claimed that it was Thomas Braithwaite who persuaded his cousin to take this course and that his only motive was that of greed. It was claimed that Thomas was after a reward of sorts. Musgrave was, however, a slightly biased source as he seems to have personally disliked Thomas Braithwaite and claimed the Braithwaites' actions went against the good of the county.

[87] PRO SP 29/93, fo. 77. For the Braithwaites see *Flemings in Oxford*, I, p. 26; and B. Nightingale, *Ejected of 1662*, p. 75.

[88] Cumbria RO (Carlisle), D/Mus, Letters, Bundle 6, fo. 3.

[89] See *Miscellenea Aulica*, pp. 317–18.

Moreover Musgrave later became convinced that Thomas Braithwaite was guilty by association and was not slow to give out 'sleites and contempts' to Thomas.[90] As Musgrave saw it, taking Atkinson out of the county was a crime in itself.

Unfortunately for the two Braithwaites Buckingham had left York by the time they arrived. Seeing that all was well and there was little glory to be had the duke had swiftly retired to the pleasure and politics of the court. Instead the Braithwaites decided to talk to Judge Turner who was presiding over the trials of the Yorkshire rebels. Recognising Atkinson as a possibly important figure in the rebellion Turner advised them to take the rebel to London. The party therefore returned to Westmorland and then turned south. Again the Braithwaites did not seek to inform the other local officials of their actions; indeed they seem to have deliberately concealed them.[91] By the time Musgrave had received word of what was taking place he could only write to Williamson to deny he had any part of the scheme.[92]

Atkinson's 'weekend' in London took place in February. According to Atkinson himself, he and the Braithwaites arrived in the city on the Saturday and he was then interviewed by the king and Buckingham. He had left London by the Monday following. One of Thomas Braithwaite's letters mentions that Atkinson actually escaped while in London and on Thomas' horse, to add insult to injury.[93] When Musgrave heard of this he clearly thought it might be a trick and that Atkinson was 'still at command'.[94] The latter phrase being a euphemism for spying for the government while appearing to be a rebel. If so, then a deal had been struck without Braithwaite's knowledge and Atkinson was allowed to escape. In fact the Braithwaites were left at a loss as to how to proceed and obviously their plans had come adrift. Thomas noted that the 'escape had rendered me obnoxious to the sensure of severall in this towne' and that Atkinson had thrown 'dirt . . . in my face'.[95]

It is, of course, highly possible that Atkinson's 'escape' may well have been officially sanctioned, as many such 'escapes' were.[96] Certainly Atkinson seems to have believed that he had secured his pardon while in London and he hurried back to Westmorland. As yet none of this had filtered through to the county level. In Westmorland Atkinson was still a rebel 'on the run' from the local authorities, but it is possible that he was operating as an agent for the government and was, so to speak, on approval. In other words he would receive a pardon as and when he came up with some significant information. Atkinson was to make yet another offer to spy in May 1664, when he wished to be placed amongst those that 'are already

[90] Cumbria RO (Kendal), WD/Ry, 34 (Fleming Papers), fo. 594; PRO SP 29/92, fo. 12.
[91] PRO SP 29/91, fos. 11, 21. [92] PRO SP 29/92, fo. 12. [93] PRO SP 29/93, fo. 17.
[94] *ibid.* [95] *ibid.*, fo. 81. [96] See Chapter 4.

suspected to know the Plott and are now in prison; by which artifice he might find out what they know'. Alternatively he sought to be 'employed in Holland'.[97] It is therefore probable that he was allowed to escape at this earlier date by the regime, but was found to be so untrustworthy that they renounced the deal. More plausibly, the local authorities, in the shape of Musgrave, made too much of a fuss about the situation for it to work. Certainly Braithwaite later noted the fact that in April 1664 he had again 'delivered Capt. Robert Atkinson to the Tower of London where he is secure but [the Musgrave's] knowe not anything of itt'.[98] By this stage Musgrave himself was intent on proving that Thomas Braithwaite had 'concealed several perticulars considerable to the king's service'.[99] Whatever the truth behind the tale Atkinson had caused enough trouble between the county officials to make none of them altogether happy with the situation.

Atkinson's ultimate fate was by this stage inevitable. He was recaptured, underwent a brutal interrogation and sent for trial, which led to his execution at Appleby in September 1664. The regime regarded Atkinson as a key figure in the plots of 1663 and was concerned to milk him for as much information as possible before disposing of him.[100] In spite of this he was convinced he would receive last minute pardon. Asked his opinion of Atkinson and his fate Musgrave revealed his attitude as a local officer to such people in general. Atkinson he noted

> did not performe his engagement to the king for he did not reveale the uttermost of his knowledge in the plott, nor did [he] intend any service to his Majesty by testifying the truth against those he knew to be traitors ... His death I suppose hath breaked those of his humor as much as the loss of any friend they had in these parts and given more satisfaction to his Majesty's Loyall subjects who were acquainted with his wicked wayes.[101]

One man at least was entirely satisfied that Captain Robert Atkinson came to the end he did.

97 PRO SP 29/98, fo. 80.
98 Cumbria RO (Kendal), WD/Ry, 34 (Fleming Papers), fo. 594.
99 PRO SP 29/99, fo. 119.
100 Atkinson's interrogations took place in February, April, May (twice) and June 1664.
101 Cumbria RO (Carlisle), D/Mus Letters, Bundle 6, fo. 3.

4

'Taking the ruffian's wage': spies, an overview

I

In the espionage world of Restoration politics the infantry were those men, and even the occasional woman, who were members of what Clarendon had once called the 'ignominious tribe' – the spies. Any intelligence system in the period, whatever its other sources of information, was ultimately dependent upon men and women actually going out to gather information on the ground. It was such people who would perform the dangerous tasks which otherwise could not be carried out. It was the spy who would take the 'ruffian's wage', to mix with the 'hired slaves, bravos and common stabbers, Nose-slitters [and] alley-lurking villains'.[1] They became a necessary, but often double-edged asset to the political and diplomatic life of any regime. They were essential because the late-seventeenth-century world was both physically and mentally a large place for its occupants, and factors of time and distance played a significant part in seventeenth-century government as well as in international politics. Instantaneous communication, other than face to face, was impossible. It took days, sometimes weeks, to communicate by letter, even if one allowed for human or natural intervention. Furthermore in places otherwise out of reach, or in places where no government officer could go openly, it was necessary to have 'eyes' to do so. This, as well as the need to counter subversive activity, and to prevent the interference of foreign government in domestic affairs, made the trade of the spy essential if not respectable and in such a world, especially one prone to violence, war and conflict, the trade of the spy could also thrive.

There has always been a mixture of hostility and curiosity about such people. The word spy itself has always had pejorative overtones and those who undertook such activities were more often despised than praised for their actions. Those who used them and those upon whom they practised their trade invariably held them in contempt. Espionage was also a trade

[1] T. Otway, *Venice Preserved* (1682), Act III, sc. ii.

fraught with moral ambiguity. It might mean the betrayal of one's friends, acquaintances, kin, country, religion and even, in the end, oneself. Spying and espionage also raised other questions. Spies operated in a secret world; often the results they obtained were shadowy insubstantial things, rumours or guesses at movements and motivations. This naturally raises questions about their usefulness and the practical value of the intelligence they obtained. The spy, of course, had an interest in proclaiming the value of what he did; others were not so sure. Marchmont Nedham claimed that the use of such 'pestiferous creatures' merely 'heap[ed] a world of hatred upon Governors' and that it was 'very rare that they bring them any benefit at all by their service'.[2] Others were inclined to rate the spy's value more highly. Very few, however, doubted their necessity in political life and this leads us to some of the questions which this chapter examines. How useful were the spies used by the Restoration regime? How were they recruited and how many were there? What did they do and how reliable were the men and women who took the ruffian's wage and sometimes 'cut the throats of wretches' as they slept?

II

As a whole the Restoration regime employed a very mixed bag of men and woman in its espionage activities. They ranged across most of society from ex-ministers of the church, to the professional spy, to complete rogues and rank amateurs. There were men who betrayed their long-held beliefs as well as their former comrades-in-arms; there was even a man, Nathaniel Desborough, who betrayed his father.[3] In this period there was no fixed social grouping from which the spy could be drawn. He could be a foreign aristocrat, an outcast from the London slums, or a once-respectable gentleman of the middling sort. Many of them were rootless ex-soldiers who had moved from home during the English Civil Wars or the conflicts of Europe and never really found another footing. Yet more were poverty-stricken government officers or foreign officials forced to make their way in the world, keen for patronage and reward, preferably in cash. In the latter years of the reign of Charles II many of the spies used by the regime were drawn from the London slums and were criminal opportunists or rogues desperate for the next meal or drink. They often clung to the label 'gentleman' or invented military titles for themselves because it gave them some prestige and credibility. We may say therefore that the intelligence system of the Restoration regime was a catholic organisation in its recruits,

[2] M. Nedham, *Certain Considerations Tendered in all Humility to an Honourable Member of the Council of State, August 1649* (1649), p. 13.

[3] I. Jones, 'Captain Nathaniel Desborough: A Post-Restoration Sidelight', *History*, 42, 1951, pp. 44–56.

it drew them from wherever was most suitable. Even the world of the theatre and literature had a part to play. It is perhaps not surprising to find dramatists, actors and the men of a literary bent in this area. Such individuals have always been drawn to espionage for authors and actors traditionally hide behind a mask and it may have been merely another role to play. What is clear is that very few of the agents of the regime died quietly in their beds. The wastage rate of such people was naturally high and it was a squalid, high-risk, short-term occupation for the most part, with only the very lucky, or the very devious, lasting the course.

In numerical terms the average number of agents in the regime's employ could vary considerably at any one time. In general in any one year there would be usually no less than twelve to twenty men employed as spies by the regime. Of course, in times of war these numbers could expand. In 1666 we find some twenty-two or three agents being used. Such a figure would then decline in peacetime as agents, particularly those employed abroad, were paid off. At the end of the Second Anglo-Dutch War many individual intelligencers in the Low Countries were simply dropped by the regime. This policy was also carried forward into 1674 at the end of the Third Dutch War. With the conclusion of English interest in that conflict Jerome Nipho in Flanders wrote to Joseph Williamson that the correspondent which he had recruited for Williamson in Zeeland 'is discharged already &c the other of Amsterdam will bee here this weeke, I will discharge him also'.[4] This occurred in 1674, as it had in 1667, while in 1677–8, when faced with the possibility of a war with France, Williamson had to go through the whole process of placing 'correspondents' in St Malo, Nieuport, Dunkirk, Calais, Dieppe, St Valery and Boulogne. Such people then would be used for the duration of a conflict and then dismissed. Another reason why they were not permanently available was one of cost. The limited financial resources available to the Secretary of State's office for intelligence could not be wasted.[5] We may also note that, the diplomatic scene being a notoriously changeable one, the needs of foreign policy naturally dictated the employment of such people. To retain the numbers of spies the regime had in wartime would have been wasteful. In terms of foreign relations therefore the general policy appears to have developed to recruit and place individuals to gather specific military and naval intelligence as and when the situation demanded. At the end of the war such people could then be paid off. The circumstances, as well as commonsense, dictated that this side of the intelligence system lacked permanence and fluctuated in numbers according to the needs of the country's foreign policy and wars. There was nothing novel in this, nor did it detract from

[4] PRO SP 77/44, fo. 112. [5] See above, pp. 54–5.

the regime's permanent interest in illicit activities, at home and abroad, where these affected its vital interests. While it may not have been a very forward-looking policy on the whole, it has a generally discernible pattern.

In reality, of course, as we have already noted the actual pool of information available to the state at any one time would be greater than that gained from spies. There would also be a range of informers, invariably ensconced in the legal system with its penal laws, and a wealth of unsolicited information which could be supplemented by the activities of the Post Office, in the 1660s by a newsletter system, and local officers. Joseph Williamson's address book, dated to between 1663 and 1667 has around fifteen or so entries who may be labelled as spies.[6] A further set of figures also exists in Williamson's disbursements on behalf of Sir Edward Nicholas for intelligence between midsummer 1660 and October 1662 and shows that the secretary had something in the region of twelve to fourteen men on the payroll as spies in this period.[7] In both cases Williamson would have access to this wider pool of intelligence. Indeed it was essential for cross-checking of information that this was so. We may note by way of contrast that the numbers of agents employed by John Thurloe during his period as Secretary of State was around eighteen, with around 104 informers to supplement them. A further list of agents from 1659 to 1660 gives a figure of twenty-nine individuals who were acting as 'Correspondents & Spyes' for Cromwell.[8] Only three of these men have the actual label of spy in the information provided about them, the others were merely correspondents who provided general intelligence.[9]

It must therefore be inferred that the actual number of spies employed by the Stuart regime at any one time would vary with the circumstances, but would on average be about eighteen to twenty-two. In retrospect this might seem a startlingly low figure, especially in light of the modern multi-million-dollar intelligence corporations; but for the employer it was not just a question of numbers but of effectiveness and how they were used. The myth that John Thurloe's intelligence gathering was based upon a huge number of individuals working as spies, a myth frequently used to berate the Stuart regime in the 1660s, can also be exposed here. The pattern in numerical terms from the 1650s through to the 1680s is clear. At any one time there would have been a small group of paid agents working for the government, with a larger group of informers operating on various levels throughout the country. Supplementing this would have been such techniques as the newsletter system, and in wartime, correspondents in the

6 PRO SP 9/32, fos. 211–30. See also PRO SP 104/77, fo. 10.
7 BL Eg. MSS 2543, fo. 115.
8 PRO SP 18/220, fo. 114; BL Stowe MSS 185, fos. 183–4.
9 BL Stowe MSS 185, fo. 183v; Baker, 'John Thurloe', p. 550.

ports and towns on the south and eastern coasts of England who could observe ships, English or foreign, passing at sea and inform the secretary's office of their movements. Add to this mixture the work of the diplomats and their minions and we have, by modern standards, a small, but usually effective, intelligence system.

III

It is as well to ask just how reliable the information supplied by such people to the government was. Again, contrary to popular myth, it was in the spy's own interest to tell the truth in his reports, or as much of it as he could uncover. The reason behind this is clear. It was in his interest to tell the truth about what he saw if he wished to obtain any reward. It was also in his interest because he would never be the only spy available to the regime and his information could often be checked. It would thus be highly dangerous for him to attempt to deceive his master. That some of the government's spies did exaggerate the information they uncovered there is no doubt. All spies exaggerated to some extent and thus the information they acquired had to be handled carefully. But there was always a fine line between outright lies, usually detectable, exaggeration and the truth of the matter, and only by working well could the spy justify his continued employment. The question of loyalty in such matters, however, was often blurred. The spy was frequently in the awkward position of being squeezed on all sides. In addition to the day-to-day pressure, the double game might well also warp his judgements with its own addictive kick; secrecy and mystery being rather addictive things and according to Doctor Johnson at least, naturally leading to 'vice and roguery'.[10] The addictiveness lay in the power of being aware of things hidden to others. As knowledge was power, so secret knowledge was seen as a source of secret power.

Once entered into such a life moreover it was also often difficult to break away. Many of the weak-willed men who became spies were soon locked into a dependent relationship, neither able to break the link with the authorities, nor appeal to those upon whom they spied. For the master and spy there would always be some element of loyalty, but usually the spy-master saw his spies as twice traitors and although essential for security prone to fail or to turn upon him. While some of the spies themselves had their own peculiar codes of honour,[11] all their statements and activities had to be handled with care. With this in mind the Stuart regime's attitude to the spies in its employ was a naturally cautious and practical one. George

[10] P.J. Smallwood, ed., *The Johnson Quotation Book* (Bristol, 1989), p. 105.
[11] See Edward Riggs or Thomas Blood below, pp. 151–2; 201–6.

Monck, Duke of Albermarle, who was as sound and sober in the matter of spies as he was in so much else, noted that 'Concerning spies you must always be suspicious of them; because [as] it is a dangerous task for him that undertaketh [it is equally] so ... for him that employeth them'.[12] Albermarle's other observation was that 'the most effectual means to be well served by these ... men is to be very liberal to them; for they are faithful to those who give them most'.[13] This was not just a guarantee for the present, he also believed that without it intelligence could fail in the future.[14] Obviously this could rebound as the more money available the more the spy might be tempted to exaggerate and this no doubt accounts for the tight control of the purse strings in this area, for the regime, contrary to Monck's views, was never lavish with its money to its spies and chose rather to keep many of them in penury to ensure their loyalty.[15] A firm hand was needed with such men. There were, however, few qualms about the business their spies engaged in from the officers of the king who sat in the office of the Secretary of State. Morality, or faith in the inherent goodness of human nature, played no role in this area of the regime's work. There is little doubt that Joseph Williamson and the others who came into day-to-day contact with such men would have agreed with that spy from a later age, Captain Dudley Bradstreet. Bradstreet noted that nothing was of

> plainer proof than that this business [espionage] is the universal and natural propensity of humankind [than] if we consider how neighbours and friends watch each other, the pleasure they take upon the least hint given them in mangling the reputation or interest of those they professed a friendship for before, and all these without the least expectation of fee or reward.[16]

In short, as he went on to put it, as 'nine out of ten are minding other peoples affairs more than their own',[17] why not exploit this fact. This type of attitude pervaded the whole business of espionage and filtered through to the running of the intelligence system: human nature was intrinsically bad and must be treated as such. A mixture of pragmatism, cynicism and shrewdness therefore marked the relationship between master and spy in Stuart England.

IV

The men and women used by the government in espionage work entered government employ by a variety of means. It may be said, however, that

12 Monck, *Observations*, p. 59. 13 *ibid.*, p. 60. 14 *CSPD*, 1665–6, p. 526.
15 PRO SP 104/177, fo. 106.
16 G. S. Taylor, ed., *The Life and Uncommon Adventures of Captain Dudley Bradstreet* (no date), p. 111; *DNB*, Dudley Bradstreet.
17 *ibid.*, p. 112.

three or four main avenues of recruitment stand out from the evidence available. Firstly there were those individuals who volunteered for the task. Secondly, and by far the largest and most interesting category from a psychological viewpoint, were those acting under duress. Thirdly were those who for all intents and purposes may be seen as professional spies and intelligencers. The European continent had many such individuals who knew no other occupation, unless it were that of soldiering and were willing, at a suitable price, to volunteer their sometimes unreliable services. We might also add to this list a fourth category of men, those who were recruited on what might be termed a 'sub-contract' basis. Spies were recruited by other spies and as 'Great fleas have little fleas upon their backs to bite 'em' so some spies had their own agents to assist them in their work.[18] Indeed, it was part of the duty of any espionage agent of the regime to set up his own network of informants who would, he hoped, continue to supply intelligence after he had left the area.

Volunteers

There were, and always have been, men who find the idea of spying upon their fellows very appealing. Thus there have always been those who will volunteer for the task. Their actual motivation may be very mixed, from an incipient patriotism to plain greed, or some form of deep-seated psychological gratification. It is clear from the literature that in this area at least it was part of human nature to be thrilled by the possession of secret knowledge, and to be involved in secret activities, for it brought with it a form of secret power, and pandered to a form of vanity and a sense of self-importance not available to most men. Nor should the simpler motive of hope of adventure be discounted. Espionage brought with it excitement to mundane lives and was one way in which an otherwise insignificant individual might make an impact upon the world. If it were not so we could not otherwise explain the story of the Scot John Fraser. He was executed during the Third Dutch War by the Dutch authorities on the accusation of a seaman that he had come out of England armed with his home-made 'fire-instruments' with the intention of firing Amsterdam and the ships in the harbour there. He was betrayed by his companions, freely confessed and was 'broke on a crosse from his legs upwards'.[19] There is no evidence he was working for any government. It is clear that during the Restoration period the position of the volunteer spy was in a transitional phase. The role of religion as a motive for volunteering for such work had shown a

[18] Augustus de Morgan, 'A Budget of Paradoxes', quoted in *Collins Dictionary of Quotations* (1980), p. 315.
[19] Swart, *Netherland-Historian*, p. 134.

considerable decline since the volunteers who had once served Elizabeth I's secretary Sir Francis Walsingham.[20] While a religious motivation for taking up the trade of espionage cannot be totally ruled out in the Restoration period, a general decline in fanaticism and a greater degree of cynicism amongst such men is observable. Conversely many of the informers of the period would have still used religion as a motive for their work, although it almost invariably disguised base motives of greed and jealousy.

What were the motives of the average volunteer spy in the Restoration period? The best means by which they may be uncovered is by looking at a specific example: the case of Thomas Carr. In March 1678 Carr wrote to Sir Joseph Williamson volunteering for espionage work.[21] He had had previous experience of espionage; as he put it he had spent 'some tyme formerly in negotiations of ... [that] ... kind'.[22] Carr also clearly had his ear to the ground and believed that England and France were drifting to war under the policies of Danby. On the surface at least he was apparently correct in his assumptions.[23] In the event of war between France and England agents would be needed on the continent to gather military and naval intelligence as well as political information. In fact, on the strength of the information received from the king, Williamson had already begun to set up information networks in northern France based on intermediaries in Jersey, Guernsey and Dover.[24] Carr obviously believed that it was a good moment to volunteer his services as an agent as the time was fast approaching for 'imployments of secret trust'.[25]

In any event Carr's qualifications for such a task, according to his own opinions, were considerable. Aside from previous experience, the main point in his favour was that he was not much known at any court, or indeed to Williamson himself, 'but in a secondary and remote way to some letters' and was a little way off the 'roade of such imployments'.[26] He was in fact living near the village of Belford, which is close to Bamburgh in Northumberland, about as far from the royal courts as one could get.[27] This, of course, could provide an obvious advantage in using him. Being unknown at any court, he could, if employed at one, provide information

20 See Conyers Read, *Mr Secretary Walsingham and the Policy of Queen Elizabeth* (3 vols., 1967), II, p. 336 for an example.

21 PRO SP 29/402, fo. 64. 22 *ibid.*

23 See BL Add. MSS 10115, which is Williamson's notebook on the 'Projected War With France'; also Jones, *Charles II*, pp. 124–6.

24 See PRO SP 44/43, pp. 179A, 179B, 182, 185, 189, 190. 25 PRO SP 29/402, fo. 64.

26 *ibid.* Carr's previous correspondence with Williamson had been in the early 1670s. See PRO SP 29/367, fo. 115; *CSPD*, 1672, p. 638; *CSPD*, 1675–6, pp. 25–6; *CSPD*, 1676–7, p. 431.

27 See E. Bateson, *A History of Northumberland* (15 vols., 1893), I, pp. 362–4. Carr was postmaster there in 1672; see *CSPD*, 1672, p. 638.

to Williamson about its inhabitants. As for his other qualifications for the job, Carr claimed 'fidelity, secrecy and quicknesse of dispatche, and fortitude to undertake anything for my Kinge, lett the imploy be never soe dangerous'.[28]

Carr's main motivation, however, aside from any reward which might come his way, appears to have been an incipient patriotism to king and country as a faithful subject. Such motives may be often be disregarded by the cynic because they must also be weighed with the fact that, in an age when patronage and power lay in London, there was precious little chance of Carr receiving any of these things in the wilds of Northumbria. It is also clear that Carr was attempting to attract a patron in Williamson. In fact as financial rewards for such services were fairly poor Carr was also probably of an optimistic nature, which in itself was not a bad attribute to have in a potential spy of this or any period. Dudley Bradstreet was to note that the volunteer spy also needed to have a degree of fatalism about his life and to be reconciled to death should it come to him. He needed an ingratiating manner in order to be able to fall into the 'vices, follies and appearences ... [of] those who are enemies'.[29] In other words he needed to be able to uncover the 'foibles' of the human heart which would enable him to attack his enemies at their weakest point. But he also needed courage to perform his tasks.

By June 1678, Carr's previous letter having apparently fallen upon deaf ears in London, he made another attempt. This time he was willing to be taken 'on approval' as it were. He first offered the bait of some local news; this was invariably a good move if he was aware of Williamson's voracious appetite for intelligence. Carr then offered to go to Edinburgh to attend the 'convention of the Estates of Scotland' there 'to give you frequent intelligence of the passages of it'.[30] Carr's offer was not apparently taken up by the Secretary of State. It may be because Williamson was beginning to be distracted by problems closer to home in the summer of 1678.[31]

Entering the system: the rebel

The second area of recruitment was that of men and women who were dragooned in to espionage by the regime and it is useful at this point to examine the archetypal spy used against conspirators against the regime, particularly in the 1660s, for many of these were indeed acting under duress. In a sense, of course, all the men so used were rather untypical, but a number of general characteristics do stand out. The first point to note is

28 PRO SP 29/402, fo. 64. 29 Taylor, *Bradstreet*, p. 111.
30 PRO SP 29/404, fo. 170.
31 His parliamentary problems in particular.

that the spy used against the rebel elements in the reign would invariably be male. This general trend was true in all espionage of the day. As with all seventeenth-century occupations successful women appear to have been very few and far between. The espionage community was therefore male-dominated for the most part. The *femme fatale* figure, so beloved of spy fiction, had not yet arrived in seventeenth-century espionage.[32] The potential spy used against the surviving republican elements in the state would also invariably be an ex-soldier of the parliamentary forces who had seen a little active service.[33] A man who was fairly radical in his politics and of a Commonwealth rather than the Cromwellian persuasion. He would also be a man who was discontented with the Restoration political climate. He would not, however, be so tied to his beliefs that he could not be persuaded to betray his companions if his life depended upon it. These men were usually weak characters at bottom. The potential spy might also well be a man who having been pensioned off from the army in 1660 had not resumed his former occupation, but who had either gravitated towards London, despite the government proclamations designed to keep him out of the city, or who had gone home to brood upon the country's misfortunes.[34] Most of these men, it seems, felt some sense of betrayal and perhaps this made it easier for them to betray others. In any event the potential spy would invariably become involved with those of like mind and either conspire, or talk about conspiracy, until the group were betrayed by one of their own number, who might have become worried at the consequences of his actions. At this juncture the government would have our potential spy arrested along with his comrades and thrown into the Tower for interrogation; it was at this point that his real career as a spy would begin.

Spies acting under some form of coercion are by far the largest category of recruits in the period. Indeed if we are to believe historians studying modern espionage they are still the most common recruits to be found in the lower levels of the espionage world.[35] Examples of the careers of such individuals abound. The major question with such people is why they should serve the regime by fear alone? Clearly the threat of government action hung over their heads, as well as those of their families, which in itself might be thought motivation enough. Of course, other elements existed. The situation of a captured conspirator was a desperate one in

32 But see below for Mrs Aphra Behn. See also, for Margaret Swann, *CSPD*, 1671–2, p. 57.
33 For other types of spy see below.
34 T. B. Macaulay, *History of England From the Accession of James the Second* (2 vols., 1889), I, p. 76.
35 See R. Cecil, 'The Cambridge Comintern', in C. Andrew and D. Dilks, eds., *The Missing Dimension: Governments and Intelligence Communities in the Twentieth Century* (1984), pp. 173–4.

psychological terms. Plotters and conspirators for the most part lived in a mental world where most things seemed to be possible. One has only to read the rumours believed by such people to realise that their world was sometimes filled with optimistic fantasy. Armies of thousands, for example, were often alleged to be gathering all over England or abroad at various times in the 1660s. Yet the sheer physical problems of maintaining and supplying such forces in secrecy, either at home or in the Low Countries, the most suitable point for invasion, rarely seems to have crossed their minds, or the minds of some historians.[36] Delusions of grandeur may be seen as one of the major faults in the conspirators of the period. More practically the larger any conspiracy grew, the more impossible secrecy became.[37] Plotters in the 1660s were also tempted into plots by the involvement of famous names such as John Lambert or, perhaps more surprisingly, Fairfax, who never had any intention of rebelling, or more usually Edmund Ludlow, who, as far as can be known, remained in Switzerland throughout the period and in his own particular mental prison. Only in the 1680s were genuinely formidable names really involved in conspiracy. The involvement of men such as Shaftesbury, Russell and even Monmouth made these schemes appear that much more plausible. The captured plotter on the ground, however, was usually in for a bitter disappointment when he discovered the reality of the situation, or when he was told that his plot was all the fantasy of a 'trepanner' – the contemporary term for an *agent provocateur*. It undoubtedly led to depression, given the strain. Incarcerated, in gaol or the Tower, an unpleasant experience in itself, with the threat of death above him and blind despair around him, he might well give in to defeatism. With the realisation that there was little real chance of overthrowing the Stuarts, again he would be left to succumb to the blandishments of the government, whether verbal, or in some cases physical.[38] It is known that the 'experience of defeat' caused grave problems for many of the former high-ranking officers and officials of the republican government.[39] Among the lesser ranks it can have been no different.

The option of becoming a spy at the very least offered a chance of life and freedom from imprisonment. By itself the latter could last a long time

[36] See Greaves, *Deliver Us From Evil*, pp. 112–13.

[37] As an example of this see *CSPD*, 1663–4, p. 49 and above.

[38] Such as the cell 'Little Ease' in Newgate into which Miles Prance was placed until he 'changed his mind'. See Kenyon, *Popish Plot*, p. 150; G. R. Scott, *The History of Torture Through the Ages* (1959), pp. 246–7. The classic exposition of this theme in the period, although in a different context, remains Christian's despair in the dungeons of Doubting-Castle: see John Bunyan, *The Pilgrim's Progress* (Oxford, 1984), pp. 93–7. Also important in this context is Underdown, *Royalist Conspiracy*, p. 199. Underdown deals with the case of Sir Richard Willys. It is also a book equally as important for the psychology of the royalists after 1660.

[39] See C. Hill, *The Experience of Defeat: Milton and Some Contemporaries* (1984).

and lead to sickness if not death.[40] Perhaps of more relevance here is the opinion of a modern spy in a similar position. Wulf Schmidt, caught by the British in 1940, became a double agent. He had experienced similar pressures and noted that the reason he turned 'was really very straightforward. It was simply a matter of survival. Self-preservation must be the strongest instinct in man'.[41] Having once been turned, or course, there was no real way back for many of the late-seventeenth-century men who had already betrayed their cause and were not willing to betray their former comrades. Broken mentally after frequent interrogations the new spy would perhaps have felt penitent enough to welcome the attentions of his new masters and attempt to serve them faithfully at least for a time, after which the regime could safely discard him.

The usual course was that after some time in gaol the captured rebel would undergo some form of interrogation. The regime would 'milk' him for all the information he possessed. Interrogations in the period were often brutal exercises, for the inquisitor's art was always a mixture of subtlety and brutality.[42] The interrogation would have been conducted in stages, mainly through repetitive questioning and intimidation. At some stage, to prevent either apparently endless interrogation, or execution, the prisoner would crack and then either offer himself or be asked to go back among his associates and make further discoveries. In this respect it is worth noting, by way of example, the interrogations in 1664 of a man we have already met above, Captain Robert Atkinson. Great pressure was brought to bear upon Atkinson, with the usual blend of subtlety and brutality. By the end of these examinations the exhausted Atkinson claimed that he could 'speake nothing now then what he hath already said'. He therefore offered to go to the Netherlands as a spy, or to go amongst his fellow rebels in gaol and provide information about what they were saying to each other merely in order to escape the pressure.[43]

As has been said, the interrogations of rebels could be very severe. It would usually stop short of physical torture and there is in fact little evidence of torture being used by the English government in this period, although much depends on how the word is defined. Captured rebels in Scotland, particularly in the 1680s, were another matter. There physical torture was legally permissible. Ideally the pressure applied in cases where the eventual intention was to 'turn' the prisoner would in any case be

[40] *CSPD*, 1665–6, p. 397. [41] Wulf Schmidt quoted in Andrew, *Secret Service*, p. 671.

[42] See for example Samuel Atkins questioning before the Whig leaders. See *State Trials*, VI, pp. 1473–92. Also J. H. Wilson, *The Ordeal of Mr Pepy's Clerk* (Ohio, 1972), pp. 33–40.

[43] PRO SP 29/98, fo. 80.

psychological rather than physical.[44] The interrogations of such men could be carried out on various levels of government. Charles II himself was occasionally involved in the interrogation of his wayward subjects and if his cross-examination of Titus Oates is typical of his techniques the king was rather good at it. The king had the blend of wit and nastiness in his character which would have been valuable in such an area, although on other occasions he was less effective. His remarks to Mrs Cellier in her examination were a case in point.[45] More often the task would be delegated to the king's ministers.

Naturally in the 1660s this meant the Secretary of State, invariably Arlington and more often than not George Monck, Duke of Albermarle. These were the two ministers whom John Atkinson, the Stockinger, faced for example.[46] Robert Atkinson, who has already been mentioned above, was brought before Arlington, Buckingham and the Lord Chief Justice Hyde.[47] Two spies whose interrogation was made into an official investigation were the Dutch agents Gerbrand Zas and William Arton. Zas was certainly threatened with physical torture. The record shows that 'if he did not answer clearly & make true discovery ... it was like to be forced from him by torture'. The committee actually sought out precedents for torture at this point, noting that torture could not be 'extended to the lameing, disjoynting or dismembering of ... their bodies'.[48] The committee seems to have had a rack in mind for the unfortunate Dutchman. Certainly the Earl of Lauderdale, clearly inured to torture in Scotland, heartily recommended its benefits.[49]

The techniques of Joseph Williamson were a little more subtle than this, as one might expect from that gentleman. Lorenzo Magalotti noted that

[44] See P. Watson, *War on the Mind: The Military Uses and Abuses of Psychology* (Harmondsworth, 1980), p. 198. For a history of torture in England see J. Langbein, *Torture and the Law of Proof: Europe and England in the Ancien Regime* (Chicago, 1977), pp. 83–5; P. Deely, *Beyond Breaking Point* (1971); J. Heath, *Torture and the English Law: An Administrative and Legal History From the Plantagenets to the Stuarts* (Westport, 1982). For an example of threats used by local officers see Cumbria RO (Kendal) WD/Ry 34 (Fleming Papers), fo. 594.

[45] A bored Charles was more interested in Cellier's sexual exploits, see E. Collier, *The Matchless Rogue: Or a Brief Account of the Life and Many Exploits of Don Thomazo, The Unfortunate Son* (1680), p. 28. For Oates see Lane, *Titus Oates*, p. 105.

[46] PRO SP 29/115, fos. 71–4.

[47] PRO SP 29/98, fo. 80. For other interrogations see PRO SP 29/98, fo. 56; PRO SP 29/62, fos. 20–4; BL Lansdowne MSS 1152, fo. 238.

[48] Codrington Library, All Souls College, 220, Various MSS, fos. 103b–107b. See also Swart, *Netherland-Historian*, p. 187.

[49] Zas was almost certainly shown the instruments of torture in the Tower; see Haley, *William of Orange*, pp. 84–5. Thomas Tonge, the alleged conspirator of 1662, also said at his trial that he had been 'in the Tower ... threatened with the rack'. See *The Impartial Narrative of the Indictment, Arraignment: Tryal and Sentence of Thomas Tonge ... December 11 1662* (1662); also *State Trials*, VI, p. 259.

Williamson 'is very inquisitive in getting information'[50] and subtle questioning was more in his line than physical torture.[51] On his way back from Cologne in 1674 Williamson interviewed some informants in his attempt to uncover the ramifications of the Du Moulin affair.[52] The questioning of the men, Crouch and William Carr, was both subtle and lengthy. He cross-checked what the first man said with the second and their answers were assiduously noted down.[53] This was in fact a technique recommended by Albermarle. He noted that to prevent the spies giving 'false advice', as Albermarle put it, 'they should be examined severally ... and by the verification of those which speak true or false, you shall know those who betrayeth you or doth you true service'.[54] In such a way, by threats, coercion and lengthy questioning, many a rebel would begin, and continue, his life as an agent of the government.

Once turned the new spy might well be provided with a pass to see him through difficult situations with the local authorities. Most of these people would not be aware of his actual status and some form of verification was often an essential item.[55] He might also then, or later, receive a cipher or a code name for his correspondence with the Secretary of State's office. An arranged escape was one of the more usual methods of providing an agent such as this with suitable cover and he would soon disappear into the alleyways of London, or move to Holland to spy on the exiles there. Once in situ, he would be instructed that he should supply regular information on the activities of his comrades to the Secretary of State's office. Alternatively he might use a go-between. More usually, at least in the 1660s, he would have been in touch with Joseph Williamson and would have written to him as well as received money or further instructions from the under-secretary.[56] Such men often had very brief careers as spies, a few years perhaps, or even less if their cover were blown; by necessity if the government required witnesses, by accident or possibly by design if the government thought the situation merited it. Most of the regime's agents were unwilling to be compromised by appearing as witnesses in court against their victims as this could lead to physical danger after the trial was over, but sometimes there was little choice.

[50] Magalotti, *Relazione*, pp. 44–5.

[51] See Williamson's comments on the Dutch plenipotentiary at Cologne, PRO SP 105/229, fos. 20v, 153.

[52] See PRO SP 105/222, fos. 105, 122–8; also Haley, *William of Orange*, pp. 194–7. Pierre du Moulin ran a Dutch intelligence network in England during the Third Anglo-Dutch war.

[53] PRO SP 105/222, fos. 126–7 and the case of Ludlow and Venner's daughter.

[54] Monck, *Observations*, p. 59. See also Sir Thomas Gower's techniques, above pp. 103–4.

[55] PRO SP 29/103, fo. 21; PRO SP 29/109, fo. 12; PRO SP 29/116, fo. 19; and *HMC*, Earl of Westmorland MSS, pp. 112–13.

[56] See PRO SP 77/38, fo. 88.

Often the cover used by the spy could be an adopted profession. One of the commonest occupations chosen by spies and conspirators alike seems to have been that of a doctor or medical man, such as an apothecary for example. The reasoning behind this may be something to do with the ease with which such people could come and go at various hours of the day and night without attracting that much suspicion. Perhaps a further reason is to do with human psychology. Individuals are never more vulnerable than when they are ill, or more loquacious when talking with a medical man and were, no doubt, even more so when he was a fraud with winning ways. They are thus easy prey for subtle interrogation. London in particular seems to have been awash with quack medical men, faith healers as well as legitimate doctors, so one or two more would not have attracted that much attention. In any case quack medical men tended to make capital out of their mysterious origins and their secret potions. This was matched by a gullible audience to whom 'the very notion of secrecy had a guaranteed mystique'.[57] Who better therefore to give off this air of secrecy than the undercover spy. Most of the examples cited below would have had little, if any, medical training and the problems of the qualifications necessary to practise 'physick' never seem to have arisen; needless to say, it does leave the historian some little concern as to the exact fate of the patients who were left in the hands of such quacks as Edward Riggs and Thomas Blood.[58]

[57] R. Porter, *Health For Sale: Quackery in England 1660–1850* (Manchester, 1989), p. 195.

[58] As will be seen below, both sides, rebel and spy, used medical covers, see for example *CSPD*, 1661–2, p. 79, *HMC*, 7th Report, p. 393. For 'Quackery' in general see Porter, *Health For Sale*. For the background to the legitimate medical profession at this time see Holmes, *Augustan England*, Chapters 6–7. The connections of the republican radicals with legitimate medical men, as well as healers such as Valentine Greatrakes, the Irish Stroker, are also well known. Quite a few medical men had served the Republic. See Aylmer, *State's Servants*, pp. 276–7. One of the most notable conspirators was, of course, Dr Edward Richardson who took his MD degree at Leiden in the Netherlands, a notable centre in Europe for medical training, as well as a gathering point for republican exiles. For the University see Holmes, *Augustan England*, pp. 176–7; and for Richardson see Sprunger, *Dutch Puritanism*, pp. 415–16. Lack of space precludes an examination here of Valentine Greatrakes' activities and the use the republicans apparently tried to make of him. See for the background: Bod. Lib. Carte MSS 46, fos. 257–257v; also David Lloyd, *Wonders no Miracles: Or Mr Valentine Greatrates Gift of Healing Examined upon Occasion of a Sad Effect of His Stroaking, March the 7 1665 at one Mr Cressets House in Charter-House Yard* (1666); H. Stubbe, *The Miraculous Conformist: Or An Account of Severall Marvailous Cures Performed by the Stroaking of Physicall Discourse Thereupon* (Oxford, 1666); V. Greatrakes, *A Brief Account of Mr Valentine Gratrak's and Dives of the Strange Cures by him lately Performed* (1666); see also *DNB*, Valentine Greatrakes; Edmund Godfrey; K. Thomas, *Religion and the Decline of Magic* (Harmondsworth, 1980), pp. 240–42; N. Steneck, 'Greatrakes the Stroker: The Interpretations of Historians', *Isis*, 73, 1982, pp. 160–77; B. Beigun Kaplan, 'Greatrakes the Stroker: The Interpretation of His Contemporaries', *Isis*, 73, 1982, pp. 178–85; J. R. Jacob, *Robert Boyle and the English Revolution* (New York, 1977), pp. 164–76; and J. R. Jacob, *Henry*

Invariably, whatever his adopted role, the agent would have a hard time of it while at his task. He would constantly claim lack of funds and express fear of the dangers involved; he was caught in the situation of demanding more money from a regime whose policy was often to play him along with promises in the hopes of squeezing more information out of him. Psychologically, of course, he would *indeed* be having a difficult time of it. The life was not an easy or a glamorous one. The spy's life was secret and was often held cheap by both his masters and opponents alike. Further it is also alleged by some modern interpreters that the prolonged concealment of the spy's actual motives and identity could eventually debilitate judgement, belief and character. In the late seventeenth century among people with already-limited capacities in this respect, who formed the bulk of the men employed by the government, this could be nothing short of fatal. Alternatively the spy could become too confident and self-assured, too clever for his own good and thus become carried away on the headiness of former successes and the sheer thrill of being in such a situation of secrecy and this also could lead to failure.

The stakes in this game were, of course, usually very high – his own life – so it must be asked why anyone would wish to undertake such an occupation with all of its hazards? Most, of course, had no choice, but again this begs the further question of why, having been released, they did not just disappear back into the world and abandon the whole enterprise. Such an alternative was not possible. Often there was a genuine change of heart and a feeling of repentance which should not be underestimated, for confession, it was thought, was good for the soul as it led to redemption.[59] Of more significance perhaps was the fact that retribution could be also meted out in this world in a variety of ways, either to the individual himself when he was caught, as he almost always was, or to his immediate family. Moreover, the men who entered the government's service in this way were already under threat of death; a traitor's death at that, with all the pain and horror that implied. The lucky spy would retire to some small post in the excise or the navy or government, the unlucky spy would, if he had not done so already, perhaps turn to crime or come to a bad end in some other way.[60]

Stubbe: Radical Protestantism and the Early Enlightenment (Cambridge, 1983), pp. 50–6, 59–63 *et passim*; J. R. Jacob, 'Robert Boyle and Subversive Religion in the Early Restoration', *Albion*, 6, 1974, pp. 175–93.

59 See J. A. Sharpe, 'Last Dying Speeches', *PP* 107, pp. 144–67.

60 See the threats made to Edward Riggs, below. For spies after retirement see *CSPD*, 1667–8, p. 281; *CSPD*, 1668–9, pp. 157, 196; for spies with pensions see *CSPD*, 1670, p. 174; PRO SP 29/366, fo. 11; *CSPD*, 1671, p. 265.

Professionals

The English intelligence system also recruited its spies from the professionals of the espionage world. By the term professional it is not meant that they were more intelligent, or indeed any better equipped for the tasks set them than any others. It is rather that aside from soldiering, usually as mercenaries, or minor diplomatic work, they knew no other occupation. Amongst the professionals we can also find the bravos, murderers and assassins who could be hired if the government wanted more violent tasks carried out. The professional spy, ever slippery in his loyalties, was more mercenary in his outlook than most. He served a variety of masters, sometimes all at once. Many were of foreign extraction and drawn from a coterie of professional rogues, adventurers, or dubious diplomats who haunted the staterooms and corridors of the palaces of Europe. Their actual value was often questionable and their loyalty to themselves usually cut across any national boundaries. In the main the professional spy operated in the world of diplomacy and warfare. Johann Böekell was one such. He was recommended to the secretariat by King Charles, Prince Rupert and the diplomat Jerome Nipho. Böekell worked for cash rather than any sense of loyalty to England. Having said this he did perform creditably in the Second Anglo-Dutch War.[61] Wilhelm van Schrotter was another of this type. He was originally a native of Saxe-Gotha who went to Vienna under the pretext of matters of trade and was regarded there as a spy in the service of the English crown.[62] There were others, and it was well known that such men were commonly bought and sold in Europe. A man with the alias of Samson, for example, was a private agent who specialised in military intelligence. Samson did not work for the English, but he was employed by the French to spy on Austrian troops in Germany in the 1670s. Unfortunately for him the French government discovered that he was also working for the Holy Roman Emperor, as well as the King of Spain. Louvois ordered him kidnapped and brought over the border into France. He was then incarcerated in the fortress of Pigenol as an example of what it meant to betray the Sun King. Louvois described Samson as 'one of the biggest scoundrels in the world'.[63] Of most of the professional spies something similar could have been said.

In the service of the Stuart regime the professional might find himself spying in the Low Countries, a familiar hunting ground for such people. To provide a broader picture of the type of man who found himself

[61] PRO SP 29/232, fos. 211–12, 217–18. [62] PRO SP 29/368, fo. 272.
[63] J. Noone, *The Man Behind the Iron Mask* (1988), pp. 162–4.

involved in the service of the English regime a scribbled note from 1666 by Joseph Williamson may give us some clues. The document reads:

In Holld.
Bu[at] who dyed for it
V[a]n R[uyven] who was banished [with] wife & children
Dr M[a]c D[owell] who was imprisoned & banished
Mr Corn[y] who was imprisoned & banished
one [man] at Rotterdam
[one man] at Zealand
. . . Beaulieu in Fr[ance] . . . lost his life
Petit carried away to Pignorol.[64]

Once broken down the document uncovers the following men in English employment. Henry de Buat was an Orangist Franco-Dutch officer who was executed by de Witt's government for his conspiracies with the English. While not a spy himself Buat was eager to forward the position of the young William of Orange during the Second Anglo-Dutch War. In doing so he engaged in treasonable correspondence and thus crossed John de Witt's government. The English side to the Buat conspiracy was directed from Arlington's office, hence the involvement of some of Williamson's spies.[65] One of them was Dr William Macdowell who had been placed in the city of Delft in 1665 in order that he could spy upon the Dutch. He was a basic intelligence agent. A professional man, he was sent out to gather naval intelligence for the Secretary of State's office.[66] In the wake of the collapse of the Buat affair, Macdowell was one of a number of English agents who were arrested.[67] The others included a clerk who worked for Kievit, a Rotterdam magistrate and Tromp's brother-in-law, who managed to escape and Dirk van Ruyven, also mentioned in this document, who fled from the United Provinces. John Nisbett, another Englishman, also fled as part of this general round-up of English agents.[68] Macdowell was kept a 'close prisoner' and apparently suffered one of the hazards of espionage when he was rumoured to have been tortured.[69] Thomas Corney was another English agent who went the same way.

Of more substance was the Chevalier de Ghet, Abbé de Beaufort, alias 'Beaulieu' in Williamson's note. He was a highly placed English recruit in

[64] PRO SP 101/Newsletters/96, fo. 109.
[65] For Buat see Feiling, *Foreign Policy*, pp. 197–201.
[66] *CSPD*, 1664–5, p. 300.
[67] *CSPD*, 1666–7, pp. 192, 198; *CSPD*, 1667–8, p. 201; Rowen, *De Witt*, p. 621.
[68] For Nisbett's accounts while in Amsterdam see H. T. Colebrander, *Zeeoorlogen: Bescheiden uit vreemde archieven omtrent de Groote Nederlandsche Zeeoorlogen, 1652–1676*, (2 vols., Rijks Geschiedkundigne Publication, The Hague, 1919), II, pp. 295–6.
[69] *CSPD*, 1666–7, p. 192.

France. The abbé was the brother of Francois de Vendôme, Duc de Beaufort, Admiral of the French fleet. The abbé was also 'accustomed to amuse ... [Louis XIV] every day, speaking to him even in the chamber of Madamoissle la Valiere'. He was eventually arrested by Louvois in person on 24 August 1666 and his papers seized. After this he was placed in the Bastille. The Venetian ambassador reported that the abbé was generally believed to be a double agent, taking and giving intelligence to and from London, but reporting 'differently from what was written to him'. The fact that his brother was a French admiral would have no doubt attracted the Stuart regime's interest.[70] Williamson's note confirms the English end of the story. The recruitment of abbés at the French court seems in any case to have been a popular pastime for the Stuart regime. Sir Bernard Gascoigne wrote from Turin in 1664 offering to procure the services of one 'Abbot Siry' for Williamson. 'A man', Gascoigne pointed out, who would be 'very glad of your friendship and of the King our Master'. For the provision of 'secret intelligence' the, no doubt, godly abbé wanted to have £300 per annum.[71]

Rene Petit was also based in France at the court. He had served as secretary to Ralph Montague in 1662 and then as secretary to Denzil Holles, the irascible English ambassador. Petit continued at the French court after Holles had left and also continued to provide the Stuart regime with intelligence. In June 1666 Louis XIV's government took exception to Petit's activities and particularly his writings and sent him to the fortress of Pigenol which was frequently used for political prisoners.[72] The fact that Petit's letters to Williamson had been intercepted and then opened in order to discover his libels against the King of France seems to have been deftly, and conveniently, ignored by the French. In any case the French regime was less concerned with the libels and more with the fact that Williamson had 'good intelligence' from the French court. 'What greater proof', complained William Perwich to Williamson, 'can we have of them opening our letters'. Petit was later released, but new information against him led Louis XIV to demand that he be removed from the vicinity of the court. Petit was sent to Rouen to manage English commerce there. His activities had been partly those of a newsletter writer but he had all too obviously become involved in the seedier activities of espionage.[73]

Another prime area in which potential spies might be found was in the entourage of an ambassador. In 1675 Joseph Williamson engaged an agent in the entourage of Don Pedro Ronquillo, the Spanish ambassador in

[70] *CSPV*, 1664–6, pp. 184, 188. [71] *ibid*.
[72] PRO SP 29/95, fo. 79; PRO SP 29/99, fo. 76.
[73] At least according to Williamson, although there is no trace of Petit in H. F. T. Jung, *La Vérité sur le Masque le fer (Les Empoisonneurs) d'après des Documents Inèdits ... (1664–1703)* (Paris, 1873).

London. Don Pardini was a clerk or secretary to the ambassador who was given £100 per annum for his information.[74] Williamson was interested in Ronquillo's relations with members of the House of Commons and how much money he had to bribe the MPs. The spy reported that the Spanish ambassador had not brought any money for bribes and that he wished to settle in before he saw any parliament men.[75] This did not prevent numbers of them visiting him, however. This news and other intelligence Pardini passed to Williamson by letter and occasionally even in person.[76]

In contrast to the Cromwellian regime the Restoration regime used spies drawn from the European Jewish community rather sparingly. The exception appears to have been the colonial possession of Tangier. The Earl of Peterborough had employed several 'Arabian spies' to gather intelligence in order to protect the English colony.[77] Colonel John Fitzgerald, the deputy governor of the city, also made full use of the services of a Jewish merchant of Tetuan 'whose concerns make him an enemy to both Guyland [the Moorish chief] and the Spaniards'.[78] This unnamed Jewish spy had access to the negotiations between the Spanish and Ghaïlán and he set out to get a copy of the treaty itself.[79] On the whole, however, the Jewish diaspora with its European-wide connections were never fully exploited.[80]

V

The type of information the regime wished its agents to gather may be placed under five broad headings. Firstly there was intelligence concerning the whereabouts and activities of rebels, whether at home or abroad. Secondly there was obviously a need for intelligence on any possible conspiracies which might be emerging from that quarter. Thirdly the spies sent into the Low Countries were, of course, required to obtain military and naval intelligence. A fourth area of concern was political intelligence. This for the most part would relate to the host country's monarchy and its court politics, or the activities and political make-up of its legislature, or even the state of public opinion in certain important areas, such as the province of Zeeland in the United Netherlands for example. Lastly there was also

[74] Compare with Petit see PRO SP 9/32, fo. 225; *CTBks*, IV, pp. 739, 761, 785; *CSPD*, 1673–5, pp. 562–3; also M. B. Curren, ed., *The Despatches of William Perwich, English Agent in Paris 1669–1677*, Camden Society (1903), p. 47.

[75] PRO SP 29/366, fo. 11.

[76] *CSPV*, 1673–5, p. 467 also Haley, *Shaftesbury*, pp. 372–402; Browning, *Danby*, I, pp. 146–84. *CSPD*, 1675–6, pp. 143, 268, 476.

[77] See below Chapter 5.

[78] *A Description of Tangier the Country and People Adjoyning with an account of the Person and Government of Gayland* (1664), pp. 27–8.

[79] PRO CO 279/2, fo. 152. [80] *ibid.*

sometimes a need for some basic economic intelligence, such as the movements of the host nation's merchantmen for instance. The instructions given to the individuals who worked for the regime in the espionage field would obviously vary with the task in hand. Moreover as they were often of a verbal rather than a written nature no evidence of them can be found in the historical record. Having noted this, however, there are certain documents extant which do give some idea as to what exactly was required by the Stuart regime of its agents in the field. The instructions given to Mrs Aphra Behn in 1666 are a case in point.[81]

Mrs Behn has long since become the doyen of feminist historians and English literature scholars. While this in itself is all to the good, there is an unfortunate tendency in such work to exaggerate both her importance, and distort her adventures, as a spy. This is understandable in one sense as there has been little knowledge of the background of her activities heretofore. One point that should be made at the outset is that she was not the daring and important agent her biographers attempt to make her out to be. In fact her talents in this area were generally poor. Thomas Corney, who it is true, disliked her and thus may be prejudiced, could not conceal his disappointment in the choice of Behn for the tasks given to her. He claimed she was 'indiscreet' and despite her 'greate deele [of] witt . . . shee understands not' such affairs, which he thought was of great dishonour to the king's government.[82]

Behn's task was to contact William Scot, adventurer, soldier and son of the deceased Commonwealth intelligence chief Thomas Scot, who was then living in the United Provinces as an exile. Aphra Behn's task was first and foremost to win Scot over to the new regime. One attempt to do this had already gone disastrously wrong when Scot, to save his own skin, had betrayed both of the men sent to deal with him to the Dutch authorities.[83] Mrs Behn's task was to approach him to see if he had any 'resolution to become a convert'[84], if so he was to be promised both a pardon and a reward. The written instructions for Mrs Behn can be divided into subjects. She was to attempt to gain naval, military and merchant intelligence from

[81] These are printed in W. J. Cameron, *New Light on Aphra Behn* (1961), pp. 34–5; along with all of the Behn correspondence in PRO SP 29 from which the following notices are taken. For Mrs Behn see *DNB*, Aphra Behn; A. Goreau, *Re-constructing Aphra: A Social Biography of Aphra Behn* (1980); also the popular biography by M. Duffy, *The Passionate Shepherdess: Aphra Behn 1649–89* (1989). By far the most sound of the burgeoning literature on Aphra Behn is Sara Helen Mendellson, *The Mental World of Three Stuart Women* (1988).

[82] PRO SP 77/35 fos. 91–2.

[83] One of whom had been Thomas Corney; he was imprisoned and then banished for his pains. See above and *CSPD*, 1667–8, p. 281; and PRO SP 77/35, fo. 77 for Corney's opinions of Scot.

[84] Cameron, *New Light on Aphra Behn*, p. 34.

Scot; that is, to uncover the state of the Dutch fleet, its readiness, movements, numbers of men and the passage of any merchant vessels. This was normal fare for any agent of the regime, especially in wartime as access to such information, while not entirely restricted, was difficult to obtain. Invariably such intelligence was also nearly always out of date by the time it arrived, due to the vagaries of wind and weather, so a continual supply of it was necessary in order that military–political decisions could be made with an easy mind. Mrs Behn was also to gain from Scot some idea of what plans the Dutch had in the offing, including any possible landing in England. Further written instructions take the reader into what would in present-day parlance be termed 'counter-intelligence'. She was to attempt to learn through Scot who, and where, the Dutch agents were in England, Scotland and Ireland. The regime was also interested to discover who amongst the exile community was most active. Mrs Behn was to broach with Scot the possibility of setting up directions for frequent correspondence in the country with all 'secrecy imaginable', using cover names and addresses. Thus when she and Scot left the area the supply of intelligence would, theoretically at least, continue. This last instruction was a common requirement amongst the agents of the regime. It may have stemmed from Joseph Williamson's obsessive need for information even when there was little enough to tell. It was also a logical outcome of a spy's moving on elsewhere in what was often a short-term occupation. Leaving a route behind for further intelligence was a potentially sound investment for the future.

Very similar in tone and style to the instructions given to Mrs Behn are those in a captured document giving the Dutch point of view.[85] These instructions were for Dutch spies operating in England, but it is clear that English agents were working on similar lines. There were quite a number of Dutch agents, operating in England throughout the reign. Some were Dutchmen, others native-born Englishmen. The republican rebels in the country were also used by the Dutch. Christopher Pooley, for example, was arrested on 'suspition of holding intelligence with the Hollanders' in June 1667. He was eventually released on a £200 security.[86] Zacharias Taäckin was arrested in Ipswich in April 1667 and eventually brought before the Privy Council.[87] All this is evidence not only of Dutch activity but of the wariness of local-government officers towards all strangers.

85 PRO SP 29/187, fo. 148.

86 PRO PC 2/60, fo. 69; de Witt had spies near the Medway in 1667; see Rowan, *De Witt*, pp. 592–3.

87 PRO PC 2/59, fos. 190v, 203v, 219v. Taäckin was discharged from the Gatehouse prison on 10 May 1667; PRO PC 2/59, fo. 213v. For the arrest and examination of some other alleged Dutch agents *CSPD*, 1672–3, pp. 90, 100, 135.

The spies in the case of the Dutch instructions were to give weekly intelligence, something which Williamson in the 1660s and 1670s was very insistent upon with all of his correspondents. He appears to have considered this the solid foundation of a good intelligence system. The intelligence was to consist of what forces were raising in the country, their movements and destinations, what ships of war were building, their numbers, guns and men needed to man them. Further items of intelligence to be gathered included victualling, the actual commanders and their conduct and so on. In the modern high-tech. espionage world such information would be considered very low-grade material, easily available from published sources or newspapers. But it must be remembered that access to such material in the late seventeenth century was difficult – it *had* to be observed and seen by the human eye *in situ* and moreover was in a constant state of flux as the political, naval or military situation demanded.

Once again these agents were to leave behind or engage such 'as shall correspond weekly ... [and] ... what a[g]reed for shall be payd'.[88] This in effect gave carte blanche to the Dutch agents to sub-contract agents. Similar policies are to be found in the case of English spies. Although money was often promised, payment by results was also required. The Dutch authorities also wished for the usual wide scope of news about merchant shipping and individual contacts were to be made with noted rebels in England such as Colonel Henry Danvers and William Scot's brother-in-law. The agents were to lay down a network of correspondents 'at what place is fitting ... to watch the motion of all that comes, & give advice of all'.[89] Such places were invariably in London or the sea ports. These men were also to gauge the mood of the country and to drop hints on the return of the republican exiles alongside actual written propaganda in the shape of a declaration. All the latter areas were used, from a different perspective, by the Stuart regime – we need merely to insert Orangist elements in place of republican exiles to complete the picture.

Heinrich Hildebrand's contract with the regime illustrates a further aspect of the duties of an agent of the Stuart regime. Hildebrand engaged himself to write intelligence every post-day giving 'punctual' advice of all that was passing in the States General. It was also made clear in the contract that this was not to be the common news of the *Gazette* 'but what is secretly consulted'.[90] Aside from this, presumably, top-grade political intelligence, Hildebrand also contracted to give 'Mr Bankes', which was Williamson's pseudonym in this instance, notice of naval intelligence: the movement of men of war or merchantmen, their numbers and strength. He also promised to go in person (or to send his son) to Zeeland, the rivers

[88] PRO SP 29/187, fo. 148. [89] *ibid.* [90] PRO SP 101/55, foliated at 222.

Maas, Texel and the Vlie once a week to observe activities in these areas. The intelligence gathered was to be the names of ships and numbers of crews and captains. In return Hildebrand was to be financially rewarded, but the contract also contained the undisguised and more sinister threat of public exposure as an English agent by Williamson should he fail in his tasks.

Hildebrand was sub-contracted from the original spy in the area who had been passing through the Netherlands and had engaged him for Williamson. In turn Hildebrand guaranteed a supply of information to Williamson from himself, or from his son. For this he wanted 100 Rixdollars per annum and travelling expenses; he had, however, to submit a detailed breakdown of expenditure every quarter in order to receive his wages. If he died during the course of the contract, provision was made for his son to take over the position.[91] This sub-contracting, as has been seen in the instructions above, was a common means of proceeding. Other examples may be cited. Johann Böekell noted in his expenditure that he had paid £1,100 per annum 'For entertaining some Spyes to [send] from one place to another, where I could not come myself'.[92] Colonel Joseph Bamfield wanted to use 'his man' to infiltrate the English sectaries at Rotterdam or Amsterdam.[93] Such sub-contracts also took place on a domestic level. They were a means of security for the agent, for the authorities would tend to pick up the lesser fry first, as well as a way of keeping information flowing through to Williamson.

The other side of this picture is the domestic scene. Here the spy might be asked to attend conventicles, to lurk in London's taverns and inns, to go into prison in order to listen to the conversations of prisoners and report them, or rejoin his former comrades in order to betray them. There are some instructions for the messenger and *agent provocateur* John Bradley in existence. Bradley was ordered in June 1676 to pick up one Macquire, alias Jackson. He was ordered to enquire 'very slyly at the next alehouses' to the addresses he was given. Macquire was said to be lurking in these areas. He was to ask the customers if they had seen any persons going in or out of the buildings and to pretend that he was interested in someone who owed him money. Moreover he was told to say that he would pay a reward for any information.[94] The domestic spy's life, as that of those who went abroad, was often dangerous, dirty and humiliating. In general, however, the gathering of such information was not a thing of physical brutality. It was far better to cultivate the art of listening, a fawning manner and to put the

[91] *ibid.* [92] PRO SP 29/232, fo. 218. [93] *CSPD*, 1663–4, p. 386.

[94] *CSPD*, 1676–7, pp. 180–1. Bradley was also involved in breaking the Tonge Plot of 1662. He resigned from the post of King's Messenger on 23 October 1682. See V. Wheeler-Holohan, *The History of the King's Messengers* (1935), p. 272.

victim at his ease. The unwritten rules seem to have been to gain the victim's confidence, never to drop your guard and to achieve the purpose of your masters.

There were a variety of means by which the agent would be able to pass on his information once he had obtained it, to obtain further instructions and occasionally gather his salary. Often these tasks were carried out by letter, hence the surviving correspondence. On occasion they would be the result of furtive visits to the office of the Secretary of State, late in the evening, usually between seven and nine o'clock, after dark. Such visits would be kept to the minimum, indeed only 'when necessity require[s] it',[95] for such surreptitious visits could be dangerous. It is for this reason that it is not often clear where these illicit meetings would have taken place. The most obvious meeting place would have been the lodgings of a man such as Williamson, or Whitehall Palace. Unfortunately these places might have been obvious to others. When John Thurloe had to meet his agents they seldom came to Whitehall for the secretary's rooms were always watched. John Wildman noted that Thurloe always had 'a convenient roome or two in some private places in the Citty, which ... [were] hired by the year in another's name, on purpose to meet such persons in a disguise and receave their intelligence'.[96] There is no reason to doubt that with this example before them the Stuart regime also used such safe houses for similar purposes.

The financial and personal rewards for a spy in the service of the Stuart regime were not that high. Much depended upon the quality of the information, the use of the agent, his position and the regularity of his intelligence. For the most part service as an English spy was relatively poorly paid. The sums of money were often small, at the lower end averaging from £10 to £100. The actual payments were irregular and getting hold of the money was a long-drawn-out process.[97] The Irishman Philip Alden, for example who had served as a spy both for the Duke of Ormonde and the Secretary of State in the early 1660s, eventually retired with a pension of £100 per annum for his past services. Predictably he had difficulty in collecting the money he was due and his pension was invariably in arrears.[98] The lower down the social scale the spy was located the lower would be his or her wages. Presumably it was thought that poverty and the occasional sum of money would be the best policy. The spy who was better placed to exploit his position in society or office would be more highly paid. Certainly a well-placed man such as Don Pardini in the Spanish ambassador's entourage might receive £100 per annum for his work, while

[95] PRO SP 29/102, fo. 176. [96] Firth, 'Thurloe and the Post Office', pp. 532–3.
[97] *CSPD*, July–September 1683, p. 427.
[98] *CSPD*, 1671, p. 267; *CSPD*, 1670, p. 174.

Edward Riggs, working in a different area and under threat of death if he was caught, was sent off to the Netherlands with only £35 to serve his purposes.[99] Joseph Bamfield received various amounts, invariably small cash or bill-of-exchange payments; how such payments were received can be judged by the fact that in one instance a payment of £50 sent him in to a prolix response of servility. Aphra Behn was given £50 and soon fell into debt partly because, if we can read between the lines of her correspondence, she was ruthlessly pillaged by the importuning adventurer William Scot.[100] Thomas Blood on the other hand received the spectacular sum of £500 worth of Irish lands, and some cash when he eventually came in, but Blood was always in a peculiar relation to the king's government. The professional spy Johann Böekell, who had a number of overheads and employed spies himself, spent the sum of £506. 16s. 0d. in two and a half years in his work for the regime.[101] One of Sir George Downing's 'friends' located in the States General was offered £400 per annum,[102] while Dirk van Ruyven was given £100 per annum for his news and intelligence and John Bradley, the messenger and *agent provocateur*, had to be content with the occasional £10.[103] After his career as a spy William Carr obtained a consulship in the Low Countries and took up travel writing. On the other hand Ignatius White, part of the White clan which looked upon espionage almost as a family trade, fared rather better than most. He was given the titles of Baron de Vicque and then Marquis of Albeville for his services to the Spanish and the Holy Roman Emperor, while James II rewarded him with an ambassadorship to the United Provinces, which turned out to be a disastrous move for James.[104] The life of a spy therefore tended to be financially varied and could be a mixture of feast or famine. The Stuart regime then was not very liberal in its payments.

[99] *CSPD*, Addenda, 1660–70, p. 666; for Pardini see above, pp. 134–5.
[100] For Behn see above.
[101] For Böekell see below, Chapter 7.
[102] *CClSP*, V, pp. 121–2.
[103] BL Eg. MSS 2543, fo. 115.
[104] See below, Chapter 7.

5

The spies of the early Restoration regime, 1660–1669

I

The 1660s were a time of trial for the Stuart regime. Rumours of republican conspiracies were rife, trouble was expected and four actual risings took place, in London in 1661, in Dublin and in the north of England in 1663 and in Scotland in 1666. The regime also had a problem with the exile community in the Netherlands which increased as it drifted into a war with the Dutch. To survive in the clandestine side of government and to counter its many problems the Stuart regime was forced to develop the use of spies and informers to penetrate and betray any potential plot and gain secret knowledge of foreign affairs. In the following pages it has been possible to trace the careers of some of the men who were used by the regime for this work.

II

The history of the alleged Tonge Plot of 1662 has long been a contentious one. Two sides to the argument which emerged over the break-up of this supposed design exist. The first viewpoint has it that the scheme was at least partly genuine and that minor figures who were arrested, convicted and executed were part of a more general and nation-wide scheme. The second view, however, was that the plot had little validity outside the fevered and greedy imaginations of a group of *agents provocateurs*, who were mainly concerned to exploit the situation as much as they could; moreover that what emerged was then taken up by a rattled government, who ruthlessly exploited it in parliament and sent a group of, comparatively, innocent, and certainly misguided, men to a bloody death for its own purposes. The reality, as might be expected, lies between these two extremes. Those arrested *had* been involved in something, even if it were only seditious talk, but they had also been provoked into this by government agents. The latter were out to incriminate as many men as possible and thereby gain in wealth as well as position.

Contemporaries were half inclined to believe in the design as it emerged from the government's managed interrogations and the trials which followed its discovery. But even secretary Morrice noted that it was 'an inconsiderate design'. He also toed the government line, though, noting that 'the very thought and ... debate will forfeit the lives of seven or eight of them'.[1] Arlington similarly noted that those involved were 'meane people', yet even he was not confident enough to 'affirme that they have not been encouraged by higher springs and such as perhaps they are very ignorant of'.[2] In fact it was clear that it was not the design itself that was the real crime in 1662, but rather the actual thought of rebellion. It was this which had to be punished in order to prevent future problems. The result was described by another contemporary, whose sympathies evidently lay with the victims, as a 'bloody tragedy'. He also lamented the unhappy state of a government 'which [found] it necessary [to] support so thievish, such accursed instruments',[3] for according to him the men who set up the scheme, the government's agents, were the real plotters. In order to discover what had really happened in London in 1662 we must re-examine the careers of some of the men who became involved in what became known as the Tonge Plot.

The main *agent provocateur* in the Tonge Plot was not William Hill as Professor Greaves has suggested, although as will be seen, Hill did loom large in the design, but John Bradley. In the 1650s John Bradley had been employed as a messenger for the Cromwellian Council of State and Edmund Ludlow later remembered him as a man more than capable of telling 'many untruths'.[4] After the Restoration Bradley's fortunes are obscure, but he almost certainly took payment to become a 'trepanner'. It was to be stated openly in court that Bradley was a man who 'when there was notice of [a] design ... was employed to find it out, and give [the regime] an account of it'.[5] His work took him amongst the ex-soldiers, sailors, ejected ministers and former Cromwellians who haunted the London streets and alleyways – those whom Greaves has rather dubiously named the 'radical underground'. Certainly there were disgruntled elements in the community whom the regime thought fit to worry about and for men such as Bradley they remained prime targets. His eventual reward for his somewhat insalubrious occupation was his reinstatement as a messenger, this time for the king. It was a post which he was to hold for some twenty years. During this career Bradley was to continue his work for

1 *HMC*, Heathcote MSS, p. 48.
2 Bod. Lib. Carte MSS 46, fos. 12–12v.
3 PRO SP 29/85, fo. 15: an anonymous, but valuable letter, evidently intercepted by the government in 1663–4.
4 Ludlow, *Voyce*, p. 942.
5 *State Trials*, VI, p. 246. Bradley did receive a regular wage from the secretariat, see above.

the regime in London, making enquiries and then arresting the disaffected to be found in the city. In June 1676 for example he was set upon the trail of one Macquire, alias Jackson, already mentioned and lurked near alehouses which his quarry was known to haunt. He made enquiries amongst the customers, asking who went into and out of certain nearby buildings, he also pretended to seek Macquire for the repayment of some debts. The spy was willing to pay for information. In 1662 his enquiries amongst the radical community would not have been that different or that difficult. He possessed a politically correct background from the 1650s, financial backing, and there were many victims ready to fall into his hands.

Amongst the people with whom Bradley became involved there were many who had been disheartened by the Stuart regime's policies during its first two years. Discontent was growing amongst political radicals and sectaries alike. The introduction of the Act of Uniformity in May 1662 and the repercussions of 'Black Bartholemew', an ill-fated day which the sectaries immediately linked with the massacre in Paris ninety years before,[6] had stirred this discontent still further. In fact the men who were to become implicated in the plot shared this discontent, whether religious or political. One element also common to those involved was the evident loss of social standing they had experienced after the Restoration due to the government's harsh laws and persecution. Bradley himself was a victim of this. Others who were to be involved in the plot, such as John Baker, the ex-lifeguard turned knife-grinder, Edward Riggs, the ex-minister and chaplain to Robert Blake, turned brewer's clerk, Thomas Tonge, the military man and defender of the 'good old cause', who was forced to turn to tobacco selling and distilling for a living, had all suffered in this way. Even William Hill, the other 'trepan' who became involved in the scheme had lost out at the Restoration, but at least his and Bradley's self-seeking air was to bring them profit. To the others, men in a formerly prominent or respected place in their community, the social decline must often have seemed an insufferable burden, leading to bitterness and frustration. Amongst ex-ministers such as Riggs, who had a calling, but were not allowed to practise it, it must have produced something close to despair.[7]

The other *agent provocateur*, William Hill, emerges from the plot as a decidedly unsavoury and self-serving character. He was an ejected minister whose father had been a keen supporter of the 'good old cause'. Ludlow came to believe that Hill had been hired by no less than the Bishop of London, Gilbert Sheldon, to act in the scheme. There were undoubtedly some elements of free-enterprise in Hill, but the fact that he was to receive

[6] Burnet, *History*, I, p. 327.

[7] See G. C. Cragg, *Puritanism in the Period of the Great Persecution, 1660–1688* (Cambridge, 1957), p. 9.

a living in Gloucestershire for his pains is perhaps confirmation of Ludlow's claim. Some historians have based their interpretation of the plot upon Hill's *Brief Narrative*, which he published as a part-justification and part-profit making enterprise. While undoubtedly a valuable source, much that Hill later wrote and claimed at the trial should not be taken at face value for very few men had much good to say of him; a 'spirit uncleane ... grosse [and] open in proclaiming [his] villainy', as one contemporary put it.[8] For a proclaimed man of God his methods were also particularly reprehensible. While adopting the language of the sectary to inveigle himself amongst the victims of the plot Hill's *Brief Narrative* was to openly mock their godliness, naivety and trust in him. As he sarcastically put it 'there was all of God's glory [and] in Ze[a]l we were up to the eyes [as] I began exactly to speak their language'.[9] At least Bradley was no better than he claimed or deserved to be, Hill was nothing more than a hypocrite.

Edward Riggs, the third main element in the plot, was the 'godly' man of the scheme. He was 'the darling of the Churches' according to William Hill.[10] However, such attitudes were not to prevent Riggs from betraying his former comrades. Riggs, with Admiral Blake's death, took up a living in Deal, before moving to one on the Isle of Thanet in the late 1650s.[11] At the Restoration he was ejected and, needing to support his wife and children, who seem to have loomed large in his affections, Riggs gravitated towards London seeking employment and eventually became a brewer's clerk in a brewery located in Cat's Hole, near the Irongate in St Catherine's.[12] This was obviously something of a humiliation, given his former calling, and may have been enough to foster his resentment against the new regime. As with so many others in the city it seems almost inevitable that he should have become involved in conspiracy. His declining fortunes would, no doubt, have thrown him into the company of others in a similar plight, especially ex-navy men. In such circumstances it would have been natural that their discussions would turn to the past and present political situations. In the event Riggs took a forward part in the Tonge Plot. Indeed he was seen by William Hill as 'the most intelligent person among' the plotters and Hill also claimed that Riggs had at one point intended to be

[8] PRO SP 29/85, fo. 15. See also J. Ralph, *History of England* (2 vols., 1744), I, pp. 83–4.

[9] W. Hill, *A Brief Narrative of that Stupendeous Tragedie Late Intended to be acted by the Satanical Saints* (1662), (p. 4).

[10] *ibid.*

[11] E. Calamy, *The Nonconformists Memorial* (3 vols., 2nd edn, 1802), II, p. 340; also A. G. Matthews, *Calamy Revised* (Oxford, 1934), p. 412. See also B. Capp, *Cromwell's Navy: The Fleet and the English Revolution, 1640–1660* (Oxford, 1989), p. 382 and, for naval chaplains of the period, see pp. 307–21.

[12] See *The Impartial Narrative of the Indictment, Arraignment, Tryal and Sentence of Thomas Tonge ... December 11 1662* (1662); also *State Trials*, VI, p. 253.

one of the six leaders of the scheme, but unfortunately 'he had engaged himself in business in a Brewhouse ... that he could not defer'.[13] In retrospect this seems a rather feeble excuse in light of what the plot was intended to do. Riggs, from the evidence of Hill's *Brief Narrative*, certainly emerges as someone deeply involved in furthering the conspiracy. However, at the trial he was to shift most of the blame to Tonge[14] and it may be that Riggs was all along being duped by Bradley and Hill to bring others into the plot.[15] In any event the involvement of Riggs was not only to lead to his arrest and interrogation but also to a career as a government agent.

Edmund Ludlow later alleged that Bradley and Hill were working for others, one of them being no less than Gilbert Sheldon, Bishop of London, whom Bradley claimed had given him £200 to further the design. The other man said to be involved was Major-General Richard Browne, a former lord mayor and a zealous persecutor of religious and political dissenters. The involvement of Sheldon in this rather murky sphere of life might seem surprising at first, but in August 1662 he was noted to be particularly hostile towards dissent. As a skilled politician his view was that only 'a resolute execution of the law [could] ... cure this disease, all other remedies serve and will increase it'.[16] To a man such as Sheldon nonconformity and rebellion were one and the same. Moreover, as we have seen, the Anglican church itself was not generally adverse to employing the 'children of Judas' in a variety of ways. John Cosin, Bishop of Durham used such men, while John Hackett, Bishop of Lichfield and Coventry was capable of using informers against his own clergy whom he suspected of laxity.[17] In 1670 Bishop Gilbert Ironside of Bristol had a gang of spies at his call to penetrate conventicles in order to identify those who attended such meetings.[18] The other man who it was claimed backed Bradley in his work was Sir Richard Browne.[19] A distinguished commander of the London trained bands during the Civil War, he had been excluded at Pride's Purge and later still forced into hiding after Booth's rising. In post-Restoration London he was responsible for dealing with Venner's rising in 1661.

13 Hill, *Brief Narrative*, (pp. 4–5). 14 *Impartial Narrative*, pp. 21 *et seq*.

15 *State Trials*, VI, p. 247; *CSPD*, 1661–2, p. 541; Abbott, 'English Conspiracy', pp. 513–14. For a radical viewpoint of the plot see Ludlow *Voyce*, p. 1117. For Riggs' naval connections in the plot and the general concern of the regime over the reliability of the navy see Capp, *Cromwell's Navy*, pp. 371–94; see *CSPD*, 1663–4, p. 68.

16 Gilbert Sheldon quoted in J. Spurr, *The Restoration Church of England, 1646–1689* (New Haven, 1991), p. 47.

17 F. Bate, *The Declaration of Indulgence, 1672* (1908), p. 69.

18 J. Latimer, *The Annals of Bristol in the Seventeenth Century* (Bristol, 1900), p. 355; also R. Hayden, ed., *The Records of a Church of Christ in Bristol, 1640–1687*, Bristol Records Society (Bristol, 1974), pp. 149–57.

19 *H of P*, I, pp. 732–3.

Browne was keen to show his loyalty to the regime and vigorously persecuted dissenters, who hated and feared him. Browne clearly egged on his two or three trepanners to incriminate as many people as possible. The royalist press, of course, saw his methods in a rather different light as they praised his 'extraordinary care and vigilance'.[20]

In 1662 Captain John Baker, formerly of Cromwell's Lifeguards and latterly of New England, had been reduced to grinding knives for a living and it was whilst thus occupied that John Bradley came across him and asked why he was in such a lowly condition. Baker's reply was that he needed to make a living somehow. Seizing his opportunity Bradley's next move was to claim that there was a design afoot to suppress the government and he gave the impecunious ex-soldier 2s. 6d. for his pain. It was later alleged that he then took Baker to see a secret arms cache which Ludlow believed Sir Richard Browne had collected as a deliberate ploy to draw men in.[21] Baker, a man of violent temperament by all accounts, was all for the scheme. He was drawn in by those four standbys for a Restoration plot: discontent, intrigue, secret knowledge, and money. At this point William Hill also met Baker in the street in Cheapside. He found the former officer all too obviously fired up and railing against the government. Hill, with his eye for the main chance from which he could profit, soon put himself upon the sifting of Baker. He persuaded the ex-soldier to tell him all he knew. As Baker had already been primed with information about the bogus plot he had a lot to tell Hill. Whether Hill knew Bradley was behind the scheme is difficult to say. Spies who worked in teams were not unknown in the period. But it is quite likely that at first Hill and Bradley were unaware that they were working to the same end. As Baker and Edward Riggs were also to give evidence against the 'plotters', initially there was the ridiculous situation of four members of a bogus plot with no-one to plot against except themselves. Edward Riggs seems at least to have genuinely believed in the plot. But obviously such a situation could not continue and he, with the others, was to draw in the plot's real victims, Thomas Tonge, Sergeant George Phillips, Francis Stubbs, a cheesemonger, John Sellers, a compass maker, Nathaniel Gibbs and James Hind, a gunner.

The alleged design, which emerged through the 'confessions' and at the trial, was to seize the persons of the king, his brother, Albermarle and Sir Richard Browne. The latter may have been added for effect and to flatter Browne's ego, although he *was* hated by the nonconformists. The plotters were alleged to have debated how best they could attack the palace at

[20] *The Kingdom's Intelligencer*, no. 44, 3–10 November 1662.

[21] Ludlow, *Voyce*, p. 942. This is an interesting possibility, especially in light of the frequent rumours of existence of such arms caches.

Whitehall. They rejected the routes through St James's Park and Charing Cross in favour of coming through King Street and emerging into the Privy Garden. The plotters had also allegedly planned to seize and ultimately kill Charles as he went to Greenwich to visit the Queen Mother. High on the list of places to be taken and held was the Tower of London. They had already corrupted a sergeant and gunner at Windsor Castle and were apparently ready to surprise a further two strongholds in Kent. Meanwhile, the Guildhall's treasure was also to be seized. Already 600 arms had been handed out and it was to be said that only the plotters' capture had prevented a further distribution.[22] It was also argued that the whole design was at first guided by a council of forty, then by an inner council of six. This council was created to unite the congregational interest from the Fifth Monarchists, who were to be in the van of the rising, to the so-called fighting Quakers. All-Hallows eve was chosen as the day of the rising. As a spur to the country copies of a forged letter claiming that the papists were about to rise and massacre the protestants were also sent out. After the rising a declaration for a Commonwealth government was to be issued. Those members of the former Rump Parliament who had not deserted their principles were to be called up to serve in it.

The reality was, of course, somewhat different to this. Much, if not all, of the alleged scheme was invention, designed to trepan some 'mean inconsiderable people'. How the government could square the lowly position of the men involved with the massive planning that such a plot would have entailed was a question not really dealt with. As Ralph was later to put it 'all [these] mighty things were to be perform'd by six of the meanest of the people, unaided and uncounternanced, either by the Grandees at home, or any sovereign state abroad'.[23] It is also clear that many of the details given in the published narratives of the plot were to set something of a precedent and details were to find their way in to other alleged plots: the Tower of London as a target, the murder of king and ministers, the secret councils, arms caches and all were to emerge time and time again. Parts of this well-publicised plot were to surface in 1678, as Titus Oates had undoubtedly heard of it and his compatriot Israel Tonge may have been a relative of Thomas Tonge. The forged letter alleging a papist design and linked to the Presbyterian churches was similar to the rumours of schemes in 1679.[24] It is also interesting to view this plot of 1662 in light of the so-called 'Meal-Tub' conspiracies of Thomas Dangerfield and his friends,

[22] Or so it was claimed at the trial.

[23] J. Ralph, *History of England* (2 vols., 1744), I, p. 83.

[24] It is also possible the letter might have had a real precursor in the notorious Mounteagle letter of the Gunpowder Plot of 1605. For a text see H. Ross Williamson, *The Gunpowder Plot* (1951), p. 66.

for there also we find the same dangerous exaggerations.[25] There were also undoubtedly links with the fears of a popish plot prior to the Civil War. It may be that the trepanners thought it necessary to spice up their device with the addition of the traditional popish bogeyman, without whom no plot in seventeenth-century England was complete.

The old soldier Thomas Tonge seems in retrospect to have been guilty of little more than holding true to the 'Good Old Cause' in difficult times. Under interrogation and on the scaffold Tonge did admit to being involved in a plot, but scaffold speeches were part of the theatre of punishment,[26] whilst interrogations could produce many wild claims and those undergoing them could easily tell the interrogator exactly what he wished to hear, especially when faced with torture on the rack as Tonge had been. Tonge's mistake was to be drawn into the company of the men who had really contrived the business for which he was to die. He was caught up in a web of lies which had been spun by Bradley, Hill and their dupe, Riggs. The others involved were also drawn in this way, words were put into their mouths and their actions distorted. Tonge serves as the best example of the men involved. As an ex-soldier he knew many of the men who, it was claimed, had a part in the wider scheme. In fact he knew a lot less about the business than some claimed. Tonge plaintively pointed out at his trial that it was Riggs who was 'continually at my shop and would not let me alone, prompting and inducing me to these things'. His confessions therefore need not be taken as proof of his guilt. Another of the alleged conspirators pointed out the plot was in actual fact very much 'a report [of what] I received from one man and told to another, [as] the original was a lie ... there was no such matter'.[27] So it is clear that the plot was stitched together out of a variety of meetings in public houses and in the homes of men such as Tonge, where drink, bravado in desperate times, complaints, thoughts of the good old days and other rumours were mixed together. The Tonge Plot was in reality little more than a deadly game of Chinese whispers. The truth, a complex concept in such an arena at the best of times, was slurred over and often buried beneath an avalanche of lies and deceit. To reconstruct the chronology of the plot therefore would be both time-consuming and ultimately fruitless. Some of its details were blatant lies, though carried off with great skill by Bradley and Hill, and by Riggs who was under pressure to perform. There was even the occasional grain of truth in some aspects of the story and there were no doubt some connections between the plotters and the more dangerous men who lived in London at the time.

[25] For the Meal-Tub Plot see below, Chapter 6; also W. C. Abbott, 'The Origin of Titus Oates' Story', *EHR*, 25, 1910, pp. 126–9.

[26] See J. A. Sharpe, 'Last Dying Speeches', *PP*, 107, pp. 144–67.

[27] *State Trials*, VI, p. 258.

There was however little resembling the potential widespread insurrection depicted by the government and others.[28] When captured the men involved were soon forced to accept their role in the drama which unfolded around them. Their path could only lead to the scaffold, but for Edward Riggs fate had something else in mind.

III

After his capture Riggs was taken before the Secretary of State but he proved to be rather stubborn and at first he would confess little. On 25 October 1662 he found himself before the king.[29] For this interrogation Charles was accompanied by Lauderdale, a minister not noted for his gentle ways, and James, Duke of York. Riggs was threatened quite severely by James, who quickly probed and found the former clergyman's weakness: his wife and 'five small children'. The Duke of York played on this point, amiably pointing out that they would no doubt starve to death when Riggs was hanged, as he undoubtedly would be, whereas the alternative was that he might save his life and provide for them.[30] At which point Riggs broke down, 'ask'd his Majesty's pardon, [and] confessed the whole design'. He confessed all he knew of the alleged scheme and probably more than he knew.[31] Brought back again before the Secretary of State he confessed it all again and agreed to serve as witness in the trial of his confederates. This took place in December 1662 and he was then returned to the Tower until the regime found a use for him.

In April 1663 Riggs was released on bond of £500 with two others and at the same time given three months to leave the country.[32] The three months' grace is perhaps significant as it gave him time to settle his family and more importantly to re-establish himself with any potential rebels. He was in London in this period and in August, at the end of his three months, he wrote to James Halsall, cupbearer to the king and a man who was often used as a go-between. Riggs made it clear that all was now ready and contact was to be made with Williamson. He also asked for more money for his wife as he was preparing to leave the country.[33] Two days later a warrant was issued for his arrest.[34] On the surface at least it must have seemed as if Riggs was about to have been re-arrested by the authorities. However, Williamson's note in his Index book makes it quite clear that he at least had no intention of allowing the arrest of the former minister.

[28] For another view see Greaves, *Deliver Us from Evil*, pp. 109–34.
[29] *CSPD*, 1661–2, p. 530.
[30] J. S. Clarke, ed., *The Life of James II, King of England, etc. Collected out of Memoirs Writ of His Own Hand* (2 vols., 1816), I, pp. 396–7.
[31] *ibid.* [32] *CSPD*, 1663–4, p. 108. [33] *ibid.*, p. 248. [34] *ibid.*, p. 250.

Williamson was well aware of where Riggs was living in the city and noted that 'his wife dwells on the backside of the Falcon on the backward side but in all searches for him wee must not search there but elsewhere – Holland now'.[35] Under cover of the arrest warrant, pursuit by the king's messengers and apparent persecution by the Stuart regime, with a variety of cover names and a direct line to Williamson, Riggs' main mission began. It was to take him into the Low Countries and the centre of the exile community in Holland – Rotterdam.

Having left London on 23 August 1663 Riggs arrived in Rotterdam the next day.[36] He had been given £35 for his expenses by Arlington's office and bemoaned the fact that this had been insufficient for his needs. 'Holland', as Riggs pointed out, was 'a dear place'.[37] His complaints did him little good, even when he was asked to return to the Netherlands in the following year the regime was only willing to give him an extra £5 to take his salary up to £40.[38] As a comparison it is notable that Mrs Aphra Behn was given £50 when she left England, £15 more than Riggs, but like the amateur agent she was, she had spent most of it by the time she reached Flanders and she had to resort to pawning her rings.[39] It is fortunate that in two letters to Williamson Riggs gave some idea as to what his expenditure as an agent of the government was. Taking account of his actual expenditure when he was in Holland, the £35 had not gone very far and only just covered his lodging and diet when he was there. He was also able to supplement this by money given to him by the Dutch ministers and by practising 'physick'.[40] His other letter on expenses is more detailed. He claimed that the new sum of £40 per annum was still impossible to live on 'conside[r]inge its the dearest place beyond [the] sea'.[41] According to him a house with three or four rooms cost 150 guilders per annum to rent, the equivalent of £15. His expenditure on business, such as 'goeing from place to place to meetinges as I did & must doe', he estimated would cost him at least 20 guilders. This he claimed was the equivalent of £10, which seems either a little improbable or a miscalculation. This would have left £15 but he claimed that 'I must have victualls[,] which is dearest of all & cloathes . . . which £15 p[er] an̄n cannot do it'.[42] Riggs thought it was impossible to live in the United Provinces on a small allowance and even considered £100 per annum would need to be supplemented by an extra 300 to 400 guilders

[35] PRO SP 9/26, fo. 131. [36] PRO SP 29/93, fo. 163.
[37] For the £35 see *CSPD*, Addenda, 1660–70, p. 666; and for the possible second trip see PRO SP 29/93, fo. 162.
[38] *CSPD*, Addenda, 1660–70, p. 666. Aphra Behn also noted that the Low Countries was an expensive place to live.
[39] Cameron, *New Light on Aphra Behn*, p. 39.
[40] *ibid.*, and also PRO SP 29/98, fo. 56.
[41] PRO SP 29/93, fo. 162. [42] *ibid.*

which he hoped 'my ingeneuity leads me to gett in my practise ... [of] ... phisick'.[43]

Another problem mentioned by Mrs Behn for English spies in the Low Countries was the low monetary exchange rate of pounds for guilders. While Mrs Behn was in the Low Countries in wartime she was still losing 8 per cent on the exchange rate. Beginning with £50 this was only worth £40 in Antwerp, but she had bills to pay and lacked the initiative to avoid her creditors, a simple enough task one assumes for a spy. Apparently Aphra made rather a poor showing and was dogged by her creditors who, as she rather plaintively put it, 'do come out of theire way ... [and] ... will be payd'. Behn was soon in real financial trouble and also asked, as Riggs had, for at least £100 to live on.[44] Further financial problems arose for Riggs because he was sending money back to his wife in order to keep his family. In fact, as has been noted already, he could and no doubt had, made a little out of the Dutch ministers and the money which came from 'the churches in England'. In the case of the latter he noted, with no trace of irony, that 'I doubt not but to share a little [in it], my interest is soe considerable'.[45] We can compare the expenditure, actual or claimed, of Edward Riggs with that of Johann Böeckell.[46] Böeckell estimated he had spent some 50 stuivers a day on his 'ordinary' over a year. He also spent another 365 florins per annum on his daily 'extraordinaries'. Some 200 florins had gone on his travelling expenses to various places in the United Provinces and a further 100 florins per annum 'For entertaining some spyes to [be] sent from one place to another, where I could not come myselfe'.[47] Böeckell's lodgings in Amsterdam were more than the ex-minister Edward Riggs had paid in Rotterdam, at 270 florins per annum for both his lodgings and fuel. It is possible he had more in the way of appearances to keep up. Böeckell had paid out some £506. 16s. 0d, or 5,086.15 florins over two and a half years in the United Provinces. Finally a comparison of the cost of living for these agents with the ordinary Dutch people in the period may be pertinent. In the mid seventeenth century Schama has estimated that that the weekly wage of a skilled worker was 2.8 florins or some 104.8 florins per annum, and the annual stipend of a schoolmaster or predikant was 200 florins. He also estimates the average price of a house 'in town' was some 300 florins.[48] There are other English agents who quote various

[43] *ibid.* [44] Cameron, *New Light on Aphra Behn*, pp. 53, 54.
[45] PRO SP 29/93, fo. 162. See above also, pp. 140–1.
[46] See PRO SP 29/232, fos. 217v–218. [47] *ibid.*, fo. 218.
[48] Schama gives prices in *guilders* and *stuivers* where one florin was equal to 20 *stuivers*. See S. Schama, *The Embarrassment of Riches: An Interpretation of Dutch Culture in the Golden Age* (1987), p. 6176. Aphra Behn also found problems in Antwerp in 1666, as there was little in the way of cheap accommodation there either. See Cameron, *New Light on Aphra Behn*, p. 53.

figures for their pay and again these make an interesting comparison with Riggs, Behn and Böeckell. Frederick de Blewston, using the alias of Wasserburg, noted that he had been promised £100 a quarter during the Third Dutch War. However, three years later he was still attempting to get hold of most of the money due to him from the government.[49] Captain Anthony Deane offered Williamson a man who was willing to go as a spy into France in 1670. This man's demands were rather high. He wanted £60 for his family, £40 to defray his expenses and bills of credit for all his wants on the journey to Toulon. If Williamson wanted to engage him for six months he wanted £100 reward plus expenses, £200 for twelve months and so on in proportion to the time he spent in Williamson's employ. Alternatively if he went by sea to Toulon he required £100 every six months for his trouble and victuals and another £50 for his family.[50] These large amounts were apparently justified because he feared that Turkish pirates might seize him, but in light of Williamson's noted reluctance to pay anything without good reason to such men there is little chance the offer was ever taken up.

Riggs' actual mission was to penetrate the exile community as an apparent friend to all and sundry while providing detailed information on their activities. He deliberately went to Rotterdam because there were more exiles in Rotterdam than anywhere else.[51] At first he was lodging in the house of a member of his church, but on his third night there he was visited by Mr Lawrence and Mr Thorne, two exiled church ministers. Both these men appeared in due course in Williamson's 'Index list' of nonconformist ministers and other dangerous people which was compiled at around this time. It is clear that Williamson's intelligence about them was coming directly from Riggs.[52] It was, claimed Riggs at a later date, these ministers' task to 'visitt afflicted banished friends; and to acquaint them that the churches was [*sic*] upon a designe'. They came to see if Riggs was willing to be included in the design which, they assured him, was already preparing in the north and west of England. Riggs hastily sent in his first reports of this news to Williamson with the promise of more to come. He also gave intelligence of one Mr Knowles, a Baptist minister. The information Riggs gathered about Knowles also passed into Williamson's Index book. Knowles, noted Williamson, was 'a good schollar ... now in Amsterdam maintained by the Churches ... one Theobalds (his Elder) in

49 For De Blewston, see *CSPD*, 1676–77, pp. 6, 500. See also Colenbrander, *Zeeoorlogen*, II, pp. 295–6.

50 *CSPD*, 1670, p. 592.

51 *CSPD*, 1663–4, p. 426. But Amsterdam had its fair share of 'the Basest Villanes'; PRO SP 29/50, fo. 100. See also for Sir George Downing's opinion on the exiles BL Eg. MSS 2537, fo. 349; For more on Rotterdam see Sprunger, *Dutch Puritanism*, pp. 427–76.

52 PRO SP 9/26, fos. 83, 147.

Tower Street corresponding with him'.[53] Theobalds' congregation was obviously one that Williamson was very interested in, more especially as money from these gathered churches was apparently passing into Holland to sustain the exile community. For the most part Riggs forwarded intelligence about the northern conspiracy of 1663 from its Dutch end. It was now in its crucial phases and there is no doubt that this information was especially valuable to the regime.[54]

One of the most fascinating aspects of the work of Riggs is that he gives one of the rare glimpses of the exile community in Holland from the inside. Because the exiles moved around so often and their lives were precarious very few of their papers survived. Riggs was placed right in the heart of this community and because the regime had given him such a good cover he was able to provide intelligence which must have reassured Williamson and the regime about the lack of unity amongst the exiles. The damage wrought by Oliver Cromwell's *coup d'état* of April 1653 was still to be seen in the exile community and effectively crippled its activities. Cromwell's action had certainly not been forgiven by many of the more radical elements who had seen their hopes of a Godly Commonwealth dashed by the soldiers. One of the most interesting images of the exiles presented by Riggs therefore is of a meeting he attended in Rotterdam at which the unfortunate Colonel Thomas Kelsey was upbraided by one of his fellow exiles, Mr Cole, over 'Oliver the new king'. Cole said that he hoped that the soldiers 'now ... see there error ... [that] in setting up Oliver the[y had] brought in the Kinge'. Kelsey, noted Riggs, was 'much troubled, but he and the rest hoped ere longe to be ingaged for the Ould Cause a Commonwealth'. This they hoped 'would be much pleasinge to the Generality of England, then Monarchy'.[55] What the 'Ould Cause' was to such men is clear enough. It referred to that period of the Republic from 1649 to 1653 when the English cause, and by implication God's cause, was at its highest. It is the period praised by Milton, Algernon Sidney and Thomas Scot who noted of that time 'We never bid fairer for being masters of the whole world'.[56] The exiles' despair at the situation in which they found themselves comes through in Riggs' reports of their activities as they attempted, in vain as it turned out, to repair the political unity which the same divisions and their own folly in the 1650s had broken.

[53] *ibid.*, fos. 76, 147. Not much is known of Theobalds who is merely listed as 'an elder in Tower Street'. Presumably the congregation was a Baptist one as Knowles is called an 'Anabaptist Minister'.

[54] For all this see PRO SP 29/93, fos. 163–5.

[55] PRO SP 29/93, fo. 163.

[56] Thomas Scot quoted in J. Scott, *Algernon Sidney and the English Republic 1623–1677* (Cambridge, 1988), p. 103. For more on the impact of this regime on such Englishmen see this work pp. 102–5; and B. Worden, *The Rump Parliament, 1648–1653* (Cambridge, 1974), p. 185.

It may be assumed therefore that the Stuart regime had little to fear from such a divided group of men. However, this assumption would be an error. It is true that the Tonge Plot was something of a 'non-event', and many of the conspiracies of these people were penetrated, often before they had begun, but a hard-core of genuine conspirators still remained a danger to the regime with their ultimate aim being to overthrow Charles II. Riggs was told that they 'did hope before longe to have some thing to doe in England and that the kingley party should know the ould souldiers and phanatiques had not lost their courige and all that I talked with of that had the same hopes'.[57] With their long memories of an exile in which the republican and Cromwellian regimes had also once seemed to be impossible to bring down and their own counsels just as divided, the royalists feared such a hope. The same men who had experienced the nadir of their fortunes in the 1650s now ran Charles IIs government and they knew exactly what the combination of time and good fortune could bring. This experience must always be borne in mind when examining some of the plots of the 1660s.

Fortunately Riggs was able to continue to send Williamson intelligence of the exiles' plans and activities. Their collection of arms was noted by him in his correspondence to Williamson in order that they could be seized by the government when they entered English ports. He also told Williamson of the comings and goings of the various men involved in the designs of 1663. Mr Lawrence for example was to go back to his former haunts at Great Yarmouth and Riggs told Williamson when he was due to arrive. Other information concerned the exiles' correspondence and the cover names by which it was addressed, which Riggs advised Williamson to search for at the English end.[58] He wanted above all to maintain his cover and safety in such matters. In February 1664 Riggs moved to Delft and then caught a ship back to England, driven home by a lack of money, which the government had promised and then failed to deliver, as well as a concern for his wife. Once there he wrote up a final account of all his activities since leaving England the previous August, as well as supplying lists of the exiles in the various places in Holland. As has been noted already, Williamson tried to persuade Riggs to go back to the Netherlands later in the year, but it is clear that this journey never took place. However, as he had served the regime faithfully, in time Riggs was rewarded by being made a muster-master at sea in the Royal Navy. Edward Riggs, as far as can be discovered, never served as a spy again, but his span of life was violently cut short when he was killed in the Four-Days Battle in 1666.[59]

[57] PRO SP 29/93, fo. 163. [58] *ibid.* [59] Clarke, *Life of James II*, II, p. 397.

IV

William Leving or Leeving, was a native of the Palatinate of Durham who had served as a junior officer in Sir Arthur Heselrige's regiment during the Civil War. In 1659–60, he took the part of John Lambert in the divisions which arose in the army and as a consequence lost both his post and any arrears of pay which might have been due to him. Leving was another man whose involvement in conspiracy seems to have been almost inevitable given his background, and in due course he appeared, in the company of his father, as one of the major plotters in Durham in the planned rising of 1663.[60] When the plot was broken he was captured by the authorities and placed in a cell in York Castle. The evidence against Leving was particularly strong, for Sir Thomas Gower claimed to have had 'two witnesses against him which will hang him upon a triall'.[61] However, while he had been engaged in plotting, Leving had become nervous and decided to betray his friends. He claimed it was not fear that made him do this, but pangs of conscience, along with the hopes of the king's pardon.[62] Even so his subsequent arrest left him languishing in gaol. Fortunately for Leving the authorities decided he could be more useful to them than merely dangling from a gibbet in the north. The suggestion of using Leving as a spy came from Sir Roger Langley the High Sheriff of Yorkshire and was almost certainly prompted by Leving himself. When Langley wrote to Arlington in April 1664 he noted that, 'if a way could be founde to gett ... [Leving] ... out of the gaole soe as he might not be suspected by his owne party he might be of greate use, for he assures me if hee were out he would not question to let you knowe some of the [names of the rebel] Councell now in London'.[63] In the meantime, in order to establish his usefulness, Leving had been busy reporting the conversations of his fellow prisoners to the local authorities, a technique he was to use on other occasions. Indeed when placed in the Tower he was to complain to the secretary that he could not give news of the prisoner's conversations there because he was kept a close prisoner.[64] The idea of using him as a spy was soon taken up and Leving was sent to London in May 1664. To encourage him Langley gave Leving £10. This left the sheriff out of pocket but as he informed Williamson 'since Mr Secretary is pleased to command it I dare not doubt that I will be ... reimbursed'.[65]

[60] PRO SP 29/81, fos. 48–48v.; PRO SP 29/99, fos. 216–19; Cumbria RO (Carlisle), D/Mus/Letters, Bundle 5, unfoliated, 'Proceedings at York'.

[61] PRO SP 29/97, fo. 41v. For Gower see *H of P*, I, pp. 425–7; and above, Chapter 3. Leving was to claim that Gower was a little heavy handed in his dealings with the captured conspirators; see *CSPD*, 1663–4, p. 608.

[62] *CSPD*, 1663–4, p. 615. [63] PRO SP 29/97, fo. 41v.

[64] PRO SP 29/97, fo. 75; *CSPD*, 1663–4, pp. 615–16.

[65] PRO SP 29/98, fo. 132. Langley was reimbursed, see *CSPD*, 1664–5, p. 314.

On his arrival in London Leving spent some time in the Tower. Here he wrote letters to Arlington claiming that if released he would 'give an account of every plot that may be hatched between London and the Tweed'.[66] Leving suggested that he escape and 'shift as a banished man'.[67] This was a common-enough procedure. The use of the escapee enabled the government to release its new agents back into the world in comparative safety.[68] In the meantime Leving was able to keep up his reputation with his former friends by assuring them by letter that they need not doubt his loyalty to the 'cause' and that he would submit to suffering rather than abandon them.[69] When his engineered escape did eventually take place it was fortuitously mixed up with other escapes which occurred at the same time. It is not clear whether all of these escapes were deliberately engineered in order to give Leving some cover. It is unlikely, however, that the regime would have wished to lose Captain John Mason, who made his escape out of York Castle at the same time as Leving 'escaped' from the Tower, for Mason was a dangerous individual whom the regime would have preferred to have under lock and key. It is, of course, possible that Leving, with his connections with the rebels both inside and outside of prison, became aware that these gaol-breaks were being planned and took the opportunity, after due consultation with Arlington and Williamson, to 'escape' at the same time.[70] The fact that Leving escaped from the Tower should not come as any real surprise. Security at the Tower, even for notable prisoners such as John Lambert, could be lax and it says something for the security there that Thomas Blood in 1671 was able to walk off with the Crown Jewels under his arm and nearly get away with them.[71] Moreover security at local gaols was often worse than this.

In any event Leving was now sent out amongst his friends and wrote his intelligence to the secretariat under the alias of 'Leonard Williams'.[72] He was soon providing valuable information to the regime about the activities of the hard-core of the rebel community in London. One of the first men

[66] *CSPD*, 1663–4, p. 616. [67] *ibid.*

[68] Another example can be found in the clipper and highwayman Henry Hutchins whom Williamson allowed to escape in February 1672. See *CSPD*, 1672, p. 162.

[69] *CSPD*, 1663–4, p. 629.

[70] Mason escaped with George Rumford, Robert Davies and Colonel Thomas Wogan, all men implicated in the conspiracy of 1663. At the same time Edward Carey escaped from a messenger. See PRO SP 29/100, fo. 54; *CSPD*, 1663–4, p. 652; also PRO SP 29/99, fos. 216–19.

[71] For Blood and the security at the Tower see below. For Lambert's escape in 1660 see G. Davies, *The Restoration of Charles II, 1658–1660* (Oxford, 1955), pp. 334–5.

[72] Greaves makes no connection at all between Leving and 'Leonard Williams' apparently believing that they were two separate individuals, despite the fact that the manuscript sources make it clear that Leonard Williams was Leving's alias. See Greaves, *Enemies Under His Feet*, pp. 11, 17.

the regime was interested in was John Atkinson, the Stockinger. Atkinson had fled from Yorkshire after the collapse of the plot there and moved to London where he lived in the city under the false identity of 'Doctor Johnson'. His alias may have been useful because it was easier for a doctor to come and go at all hours of the day and night without attracting suspicion.[73] In any event Leving supplied the regime with intelligence on Atkinson's activities as well as his address. Atkinson was living in Worcester Court upon Garlick Hill 'and may be found any morning betwixt the houres of 5 & 8, going to the Greyhound Ordinary opposite Worcester-Gate'.[74] He described Atkinson' as 'a little man [with] sad browne haire something thin ... seemes to be about 40 yeares old'.[75] In fact a series of meetings were taking place in London at this time, the chief meeting place for the rebels being in the widow Hogden's house in Petty France. There they were planning a design to seize the Tower and to fall upon Whitehall Palace. The rebels intended to take some houses near the Tower, as well as one near Whitehall, one in Southwark and two or three in the city itself. They had a small sum of money set by which they used warily. They also had hopes of assistance from abroad; the more especially so as England and the United Provinces were drifting into war.[76] Unlike the alleged Tonge Plot the seriousness of these men was not in doubt for they were the hard-core of conspirators in the 1660s: men such as Captain John Mason, John Atkinson, Captain Lockyer, the one-handed Major Lee, Nathaniel Strange, Captain Roger Jones, who was the author of the notorious underground pamphlet *Mene Tekel: Or the Downfall of Tyranny*[77] and a man 'not heard of formerly' named Mr Allen, whom someone, seeing the name in the document written by Leving, wrote above it 'his true name is Bludd'.[78] They took to moving from place to place as soon as the regime picked up their trail and if their safe lodgings were found or suspected they sent messages to their comrades to 'forewarne them lest they should be snapt'. If any of the rebels were arrested the rest dislodge and so [it is] hard to find any of them'.[79]

It must obviously be asked just how serious a threat these men were to

[73] PRO SP 29/102, fos. 48–9; and see above, p. 130.
[74] PRO SP 29/102, fos. 48–9. For this area of London see W. G. Bell, *The Great Fire of London in 1666* (1951), pp. 71–2; and B. Weinreb and C. Hibbert, eds., *The London Encyclopedia* (1983), p. 303.
[75] PRO SP 29/102, fos. 48–9.
[76] *ibid.*; and *CSPD*, 1664–5, p. 6. For the area of Petty France see J. Stowe, *A Survey of London* (2 vols., Oxford, 1908), I, p. 264.
[77] R. Jones, *Mene Tekel: Or the Downfall of Tyranny* (1663).
[78] PRO SP 29/102, fos. 48–9.
[79] PRO SP 102, fo. 175 and PRO SP 29/115, fo. 72v. R. H., the author of the earliest biography of Thomas Blood, also describes the rebel's security system and it confirms Leving and Atkinson's revelations to some extent. See *Remarks*, p. 222.

the regime. Their seriousness should at least not be doubted for most were ex-soldiers with a genuine grudge and one assassin's bullet aimed at a king who was notoriously lax in security for himself could have caused chaos. Of their organisation I have already argued that it was rather loose and they were certainly a little bit more fissiparous than Greaves has argued. Moreover they lacked the genuine leadership a Lambert or a Ludlow could have provided to make their schemes successful. There was not one man amongst them above the rank of colonel and they were held together by negative attributes rather than any positive sense of political will. It might be said that while they knew what they did not want, they were never quite clear what they did want. Despite this they had motivation and fertile planning minds, and the intelligence system of the government was efficient enough to forestall them. It was not, however, *that* easy to capture them because of the nature of the environment in which they operated and it must be recalled that they were taken very seriously by the regime itself, for had not many in the Stuart regime itself been conspirators in the 1650s? The ministers were well aware of what went on in such men's minds. Thus the rebels should be taken seriously by the historian who must eschew hindsight in his dealings with them.

Leving soon set up for the government an opportunity to seize Atkinson in September 1664 by providing the information of his whereabouts. The men employed to take Atkinson at Worcester Place unfortunately botched the job by going into the house too soon, in spite of Leving's information. When they raided the house very early in the morning they discovered another man in bed there. This was one Richardson, who was using the alias Fawcett. Questioning him about the whereabouts of 'Doctor Johnson' Richardson managed to talk his way out of the situation. He got clear and immediately rushed off to inform Atkinson, who had been due to turn up at the house that afternoon. In turn Atkinson sent out messages to warn all the others who used the house including, ironically enough, Leving himself. Leving claimed that the release of Richardson was the worst thing that the messengers could have done, for his interrogation could have proved invaluable in tracking down the other rebels and no doubt it would have thrown some of the blame for what would have followed from the agent himself. It was fortunate that Leving was not suspected himself by his compatriots and that the blame for the affair fell upon 'the jealousy ... of a woman' who lived with Atkinson in the house,[80] a fact which provides a brief glimpse into the private lives of such men. However, Leving was forced to 'bee in a shifting condition' to prevent his exposure and keep up the pretence that he was a rebel. The vagaries of

[80] For this raid see PRO SP 29/102, fo. 175.

such a life meant he soon fell into financial difficulties. These grew worse the longer the secretary's office wanted him to remain in London. To all intents and purposes, however, he was on the run and thus unable to work openly at any trade. Leving was also anxious to receive an indemnity for his activities, for he was still a proclaimed traitor and escapee, a fact which could, and was to, lead him into trouble if he was discovered by those authorities not in the know.[81] It also meant that without a protection the regime could cut him off when they felt like it. His agitation eventually drew a certificate out of the Secretary of State. The survival of such documents is rare for the all too obvious reason that the recipients led such dangerous lives. It is therefore worth quoting in full.

This is to certify all whome it shall concerne that the bearer hereof William Leving is emploid by mee and consequently not to bee molested or restrained upon any search or enquiry whatsoever.
Henry Bennet.[82]

Leving's means of gathering his salary and further instructions was by furtive visits to 'Mr Lee'. Mr Lee was none other than Joseph Williamson.[83] It is clear that such visits to Williamson took place quite late in the evening. Seven and nine o'clock are two of the times mentioned, which would have been after dark, of course, but the visits to see the under-secretary only took place 'when necessity require[d] itt'[84] and it is possible that Williamson created a safe house, as John Thurloe had to interview such people. Leving did occasionally ask to visit Arlingon's own residence, but this request was granted only in exceptional circumstances.[85]

Leving's curious twilight life also began to affect his character and there is little doubt that the degeneration of his character over the period of his employment as a spy must have come from the oddity of his existence. There was always a fine line between protecting himself, calming the fears of his associates and providing intelligence. The question of to whom exactly he was loyal would have caused him problems as he began to be squeezed on all side. Initially Leving's main problems came from his lack of funds to sustain him in his tasks. His salary as a government agent remained sporadic to say the least. Despite his later claims that he had

[81] *ibid.*, fo. 176. [82] PRO SP 29/103, fo. 21. It is a copy of the original.

[83] This is proved conclusively by the fact that Mr Lee's illness prevented Leving seeing him when he wanted to in late September 1664 and Williamson was in fact ill at the time. See PRO SP 29/102, fo. 236; also PRO SP 29/102, fos. 125, 164; letters from Williamson's doctor, Quartremaine.

[84] PRO SP 29/102, fo. 176; Williamson had a house in Scotland Yard and later in his career in the Mews. Only in 1679 did he move to the more prestigious James Street. See *CSPD*, 1667–8, pp. 533, 544; *CSPD*, 1668–9, p. 488; *CSPD*, Addenda, 1660–85, p. 501. See also Firth, 'Thurloe and the Post Office', pp. 532–3.

[85] PRO SP 29/102, fo. 176.

originally been engaged at £20 per annum to act as a spy,[86] this money was paid infrequently if at all and he was soon arguing in his letters that he should be dismissed if the regime did not wish to give him a regular salary. In his early career he displayed a curious morality about his profession, not sharing Edward Riggs' view that those he was spying upon should also provide money to maintain him. Leving did not wish to be beholden to those he inevitably had to betray. It may be that he felt a sense of guilt about what he was doing. A more practical reason for this was that Leving had apparently told his associates that he was in a better financial condition than he was. Perhaps this was in the vain hope that the appearance of large sums of money from the government was a possibility and would need explanation if it were not to become suspicious. Leving's attempt to gain the moral high ground, however, soon passed away and he became as greedy and grasping as the others in the employ of the regime.[87] In late 1664 and early 1665 he was still associating with John Atkinson who was planning to leave London for the Low Countries in the spring of 1665. Leving himself had thought of going there but his lack of funds as well as lack of orders prevented him from going on the trip. Instead the rebels' business being, as Leving put it, 'at a stand' at the beginning of 1665 they began to search for a possible informer in their midst. They suspected Fawcett, but the activities of another man, Henry North, enabled a different picture to emerge. Henry North became acquainted with Leving's business and was, alongside William Freer, or Fryer, to form part of a team of agents over whom Leving was, in theory, to have some control.[88] North was also associated with the Duke of Buckingham as an 'intelligencer' and allegedly acted as a direct line for Buckingham into the rebels. Despite Leving's warnings North began to ingratiate himself with Fawcett and thus came under suspicion himself. Finding himself in trouble with the rebels North immediately informed them that Leving was a spy and that Buckingham sent his assurances that he, the duke, would appear for them, given a suitable opportunity. This, at least was Leving's version of the tale which he gave out in February 1667. As will be seen, however, the use of Buckingham's name at this time is suspect as in his original relation it does not appear.[89] However, the difficulties faced by Leving from this act of betrayal soon emerged.

The still unsuspecting spy had a visit late one Sunday night in February

[86] See PRO SP 29/115, fo. 65 Leving received £40 from Williamson which he shared with John Betson. Although Betson was to later claim that £60 had been paid for the seizure of Atkinson. See *CSPD*, 1667, p. 285.

[87] PRO SP 29/110, fos. 16–17.

[88] See *CSPD*, 1665–6, p. 173 for Leving, North and Freer. Also PRO SP 29/113, fo. 108.

[89] Compare *ibid.* and *CSPD*, 1666–7, p. 511.

1665 by two of his friends. They asked him to come to a meeting about some business and took him 'through many turnings into an obscure place'.[90] In a house at the end of this journey Leving was faced with several men who put their swords and pistols to his chest and accused him of being the spy who had betrayed them. Forced to bluster, he claimed that they had little reason to suspect him and wished to know his accuser's name. He also claimed that if he'd wanted to he could have betrayed them many times as he knew all their secrets. Faced with his plausible denial the group sent out to get hold of North, intending to interrogate him further in order to obtain some more specific accusations. In the meantime Leving, although still being held as a prisoner, had held off a further interrogation until the Tuesday morning. It was then that North was secretly brought into the house. At this point his captors came to him again and told him that they now had their 'evidence' against him. Some of the rebels who still remained friendly to Leving let slip the fact that it was North who was his accuser, and Leving's protestations against North were persuasive enough for him to be regarded in a new light. Despite his obvious guilt the rebels decided with a curious liberality to set North at liberty with the understanding that he go nowhere near the Secretary of State or his minions.[91] Leving having just escaped the exposure of his real identity decided to take his revenge by arranging the capture of John Atkinson, the Stockinger.

By March 1665 Leving had linked up with another partner, John Betson, with whom he hoped 'to performe considerable service'.[92] At around the same time, with Leving's assistance, John Atkinson was finally arrested. He was then interrogated by Arlington and Albermarle on 18 March 1665 and claimed that the leaders of the group were Lockyer, who was using the alias of Rogers, Jones, Carew, Lewis Frost of South Shields who had been prominent in the Durham Plot of 1663 and had planned to use the port to bring in arms for the rebels,[93] Nathaniel Strange, Colonel Henry Danvers

[90] PRO SP 29/113, fo. 108.

[91] For other references which may relate to this story see *Remarks*, pp. 222–3; and more importantly Bod. Lib. Rawlinson A 185, fos. 473–5. The story in the pamphlet may be a distorted version of Leving's tale with Blood being given a more prominent role. Certainly the two men accused in that story were released in a like manner, from which it may be possibly inferred that someone did not want to have the deaths of two government agents on his hands for reasons of his own. The notes from Blood's pocket book imply that the events took place in Coleman Street and are in any case full of references to the area of London in which the rebels were operating, the movement of their arms and meetings in various taverns in the area.

[92] PRO SP 29/115, fo. 65.

[93] The town had something of a tradition of covert activities. During the 1580s South Shields had been part of a covert route from Middleburg used to smuggle Roman Catholic priests into northern England. See A. Dures, *English Catholicism, 1558–1642*, (1983), p. 24.

and Blood. Ironically Atkinson also attempted to protect Leving by admitting that he knew him but not his present whereabouts. Arlington and Albermarle's questioning was both probing and subtle, giving the impression that their spy Leving was still a wanted man, as well as confirming that Leving's true nature was not suspected by the rebels.[94] The seizure of Atkinson, who despite his protests to the contrary, was a significant catch, threw the rebel group into some confusion. As Leving put it they were more 'afraid of each other . . . [and] . . . are fitter at present to trappan one another then carry on any designs'.[95] In spite of this Leving and another member of the group remained suspect and his work over the next few weeks must have increased this suspicion as the government raided various places in the area of Thames Street. Thus it comes as no surprise that in April 1665 he requested permission to leave the city and along with William Freer was granted a pass to travel overseas if he should wish to do so.[96]

Having left the metropolis Leving and Freer were soon in trouble again when they found themselves under arrest in Leicestershire in May 1665. They were forced to write to Whitehall to get the Secretary of State to release them.[97] Leving's plans at this time were to visit the authorities in Yorkshire and Durham pretending to have 'come in' in the hope that his associates would follow him. In fact it seems to have been a quiet period of his life and he soon returned to London in the company of John Betson. By this time the plague was sweeping through the city, but the entrapment of the rebels still continued.[98] The general abandonment of the city by the political world meant that London was ripe for further plotting. However, the strong hand of Albermarle came down hard on any who attempted anything unusual.[99] Leving tried to ingratiate himself with Albermarle and draw some money out of the duke; a difficult task in itself considering Albermarle's character.[100] Leving was also afraid of the plague, from which he lost most of his family, but could not leave the city. He lacked the necessary funds to carry out his tasks, he could neither contact Arlington or his under-secretary as both men had left London with the court. The spy also fell out with his colleagues. Henry North and William Freer had returned and both were proved troublesome charges for Leving. They refused to take his orders. Freer in particular was, according to Leving, behaving irresponsibly and did not care who knew what he was doing as long as he got some money. He kept pestering Leving to visit Williamson

94 PRO SP 29/115, fos. 71–4; see also PRO SP 29/97, fo. 98; and PRO SP 29/117, fos. 136–7.
95 PRO SP 29/116, fo. 15; *CSPD*, 1664–5, pp. 271, 293. 96 *CSPD*, 1664–5, p. 314.
97 *ibid.*, pp. 357, 361, 419–20. 98 *ibid.*. pp. 442, 472.
99 See Abbott, 'English Conspiracy', pt 2, pp. 699–700.
100 *CSPD*, 1664–5, p. 650. See also above, Chapter 4.

and demand money from the under-secretary; he refused as he was no doubt well aware of what Williamson's reaction would be to such a request. As a consequence of these squabbles Leving sought to have Freer dismissed.[101] The new year brought no better fortunes for him and Leving begged the Secretary of State to provide him with some funds as his salary was in arrears, even requesting that a post in the customs service be provided to give him an excuse to remain in London. Apparently the rebels were growing increasingly suspicious of him because he had no real reason to remain there.[102] However, Leving was told to stay where he was and wait on developments which would take him to Ireland.

The intelligence system which Dublin Castle ran in the 1660s has its own separate and, as yet, unwritten history.[103] The most interesting aspect of its relationship with the secretaries' intelligence work is the latter's unwillingness to interfere with Irish affairs without the permission of the Lord Lieutenant. Arlington was circumspect in his dealings with Ormonde. In August 1666 he wrote to the duke that 'some of my informers have offered to goe ... [to Ireland] ... towards which I have not yet positively pitcht upon & am unwilling to doe it till your Grace, desparing of doeing it better there shall call upon mee for it'.[104] This general reluctance to intervene in Ormonde's territory, at least openly, is perhaps significant as the Secretary of State's office was never usually loath to intrude elsewhere. In this instance Arlington's offer was accepted and Leving and William Freer spent nearly two and a half months in Ireland in late 1666. They were back in December 1666 and would have stayed there longer at Ormonde's own request according to Leving, but they found someone for the duke who was willing to do the service required.[105] It may be that Leving found the tasks set him not very profitable, but his return to England was to lead directly to his death.

John Heydon, as astrologer and member of the Rosicrucian movement, had, according to his own account, been in the royalist forces and later travelled extensively in Europe.[106] In 1655 he had entered Lincoln's Inn but

101 *CSPD*, 1665–6, p. 173. 102 *ibid.*, p. 326.

103 The introduction has already touched on the reasons why this book does not deal with the Irish intelligence system.

104 Bod. Lib. Carte MSS 46, fo. 357.

105 See Bod. Lib. Carte MSS 46, fos. 383, 392v; *CSPD*, 1666–7, pp. 132–3, 349.

106 For Heydon and what follows the basic sources are Clarendon, *Life*, pp. 1230–3; BL Add. MSS 27872, fos. 6, 13; *CSPD*, 1666–7, pp. 428–9, 511–12, 533; *CSPD*, 1667–8, pp. 286–7, 298, 342–3; *HMC*, Fleming MSS, p. 45; Browning, *Danby*, I, pp. 45–6; Barbour, *Arlington*, pp. 104–5; F. A. Yates, *The Rosicrucian Enlightenment* (1975), p. 230; Thomas, *Religion and the Decline of Magic*; M. C. Nahm, ed., *The Cheats*, by John Wilson (Oxford, 1935), pp. 195–6; Ashley, *John Wildman*, p. 205; Lady Burghclere, *George Villiers, Second Duke of Buckingham, 1628–1687: A Study in the History of the Restoration* (1903), pp. 163–82; see also Jacob, 'Robert Boyle and Subversive

had swiftly acquired a reputation for casting horoscopes. As a result of these activities he had spent some time in gaol during the Protectorate. After the Restoration he had again run foul of the law and, it was said, his wife, for he was something of a philanderer. He had again been thrown into prison, this time because of debt, only to be released in 1663 as a result of the influence of George Villiers, Duke of Buckingham. Buckingham had apparently begun to take an interest in Heydon's astrological work. Whether Buckingham was an actual member of Heydon's Rosicrucian circle is not clear, but the interest shown by the duke in Heydon was to cost him dear.[107] By the 1660s Buckingham had also begun to set himself up as a leader of the people, especially those of more dangerous persuasions. Unfortunately for the duke he was also rather good at making enemies at court. Arlington and Buckingham in particular were mortal enemies. The two men despised each other heartily and it is clear that Arlington had received several informations concerning Buckingham's activities and words which could be seen as treason. The time being not yet ripe to use them Arlington had put these to one side for the future. Buckingham had also alienated Clarendon and perhaps the secretary saw a potential ally against his enemy. In court politics, however, Buckingham was more than capable of taking care of himself. Unfortunately his antics had also drawn on himself the wrath of the king. Charles had uncovered a line of intelligence into Buckingham's servants through a man called Braithwaite, an ex-Cromwellian and as such typical of the type of man Buckingham gathered around himself.[108] As the duke had already damaged the parliamentary session through his antics, Charles was more than willing to believe that Buckingham was involved in more dangerous activities.[109] Braithwaite told the king that his master had 'fallen into the conversation of some men of very mean condition, but of desperate intentions', claiming that Buckingham used to meet them at 'unseasonable hours and in obscure places'.[110] All of this had led Braithwaite to presume, partly because there was more profit that way, that Buckingham had some design afoot. Fearing the worst and as a 'loyal' subject he had left the duke's service and gone straight to inform the king. Charles certainly believed something was going on for he was later to inform Sir Thomas Osborne that Buckingham had

Religion', pp. 277–80 for contemporary beliefs that the Rosicrucians and the radical sects were connected and that Heydon himself was directly involved in sedition. Certainly it was reported that some radical conspirators involved in one of the plots of 1666 had chosen their timing of their rising, 3 September, by using astrological prediction. See the *London Gazette*, 48, 26–30 April 1666; also Thomas, *Religion and the Decline of Magic*, pp. 353–4.

107 Jacob, 'Robert Boyle and Subversive Religion', p. 277.

108 Burghclere, *Buckingham*, pp. 162–7.

109 *ibid.* 110 Clarendon, *Life*, p. 1230.

'very ill intentions ... [having] tampered with his [the king's] spies [and] writt divers letters to Headon and alwaies called him brother in them'.[111]

With the king primed it was at this point that Arlington conveniently stepped in with his informations about the astrologer John Heydon. According to this side of the story Buckingham had asked Heydon to cast the king's horoscope, an action, which as Keith Thomas has pointed out, in popular estimation was not far removed from 'malevolent conjuration to take away the ruler's life'.[112] Naturally Charles was furious and ordered Arlington to have Heydon arrested and thrown into the Tower. These activities had also involved Leving and Freer through their association with Henry North, who clearly had some connections with both Buckingham and the rebels and against whom Leving, at least, had a grudge. Leving and Freer were to be used as witnesses and, according to Andrew Browning, Sir Roger Langley was also involved in this scheme. The evidence is obscure, but it may be that Arlington had used Langley as an intermediary to enlist the men in the plot so as to distance himself from it, although Langley had reasons of his own to dislike Buckingham as he had been prevented from obtaining a parliamentary seat in York in 1664 in order that it could be given to Buckingham's client, Sir Thomas Osborne.[113]

With Heydon already in the Tower, and as he put it 'an unjustly abused ... [and] close prisoner, tortured in the Dungeon to speake their poisons against' Buckingham,[114] Henry North was arrested and his papers seized.[115] This was after Leving had made a statement which implicated both North and Buckingham and also claimed that the latter had plans to assist the rebels.[116] The evidence was then brought before the king to add fuel to his anger. Charles brought it to the notice of Clarendon who, though he was later to claim no prejudice against Buckingham, had no great love for the duke either and he was more than willing to advise Charles to have Buckingham arrested.[117] Buckingham's eventual escape from punishment need not concern us here. He went to ground after the warrant for his arrest had been issued and when he finally entered the Tower was able to talk himself back into Charles' good grace again, for the king's anger never lasted for very long.[118] While Arlington and Clarendon were immune from Buckingham's anger at their actions, the tools they

[111] Charles quoted in Browning, *Danby*, II, p. 31.
[112] Thomas, *Religion and the Decline of Magic*, p. 407.
[113] Browning, *Danby*, I, pp. 29, 45–6. [114] BL Add. MSS 27872, fo. 6.
[115] *CSPD*, 1666–7, p. 512.
[116] *CSPD*, 1666–7, p. 511. [117] Clarendon, *Life*, p. 1231.
[118] *ibid.*, pp. 1231–3; and Burghclere, *Buckingham*, pp. 179–82. See also BL Add. MSS 27872, fo. 13, which is the transcript of Buckingham's somewhat farcical examination before Arlington, Morrice, Coventry and Clifford in July 1667.

had used were not and the Duke of Buckingham's anger, as others were to find, was not something to be taken lightly.[119]

While the affairs of court went on, however, William Leving's career had taken a decided turn for the worse. In company with William Freer he had moved north and taken to highway robbery in the area of Leeds. He was as unsuccessful at this as at most of his other attempts to make a living. The authorities arrested the highwayman and brought him to York Castle.[120] From there he wrote a plaintive note to Joseph Williamson asking for his release. In due course Leving's cry for help had a response when he was transferred to Newgate.[121] Then at the end of July 1667 Leving was suddenly returned to York to act as a reluctant witness against Roger Jones, John Atkinson and Robert Joplin, who were implicated in the plot of 1663. His companions on the road were to be Corporal Darcy and seven cavalry troopers. The main reason for such a strong guard, however, was not the presence of William Leving, but the transfer of the prisoner Captain John Mason who had been recaptured in June 1667. Mason was on his way north to York for his trial, and probable execution, for he was a notable rebel who had been heavily implicated in the Northern Plot of 1663 and conspiracies in London subsequent to this.[122] The presence of Leving in this company is itself suspicious and probably not entirely fortuitous, for we may recall that Leving had begun his career as a spy reporting on the conversations of prisoners and was probably there to perform a similar role with Mason. It would have provided useful material for his appearance as the crown's star witness in York. In the event the little party was ambushed in the town of Darrington on 25 July 1667 by Thomas Blood, taking time off from his medical practice, and his associates. It is unlikely that Blood, or the others, had any intention of rescuing Leving; their interest was in Mason. In any case during the ensuing struggle, in which one man was killed and Corporal Darcy with three of his men were wounded, Leving made himself scarce by hiding in a nearby house.[123] In spite of this he was able to recognise the men involved in the rescue of Mason and informed the authorities.[124] He was then sent onto York Castle. Leving himself had apparently been recognised by Blood[125] and was never to testify in court. By the first week of August 1667 he was dead, poisoned by his enemies, according to his erstwhile friend William Freer.[126]

It must be asked who ordered the killing of William Leving. There were

[119] As Thomas Blood found out. See below, pp. 222–3.
[120] *CSPD*, 1667, pp. 107, 114.
[121] *ibid.*, p. 285. [122] PRO SP 29/231, fo. 42.
[123] PRO SP 29/231, fo. 42; PRO SP 29/210, fo. 151; *CSPD*, 1667, p. 337.
[124] PRO SP 29/210, fo. 151. [125] See Bod. Lib. Rawlinson A 185, fo. 473v, entry 51.
[126] PRO SP 29/212, fo. 70, and *CSPD*, 1667, p. 427. There seems no reason to doubt Freer's claim that Leving was poisoned. He was certainly frightened enough to know the facts.

really three main suspects. The first of these was Thomas Blood. Blood certainly had the ability and the motive for murder. Moreover he may well have had the means, for he had recently spent some time as a 'doctor of Physick' in Rumford. His motive would have been to save his friends who were to stand trial in York and to get revenge on Leving for revealing the names of the rescue party at Darrington. Also by now the rebels must have been well aware of Leving's actual status. Unfortunately Blood is precluded for two reasons. The first of these is that the use of poison was not in his style, which was certainly more flamboyant than that of a mere poisoner. The second reason is more important, in that Blood was badly wounded in the fight at Darrington and forced to 'lay close' for a while in a friend's house in Yorkshire.[127] Another suspect is John Atkinson, who has at least the merit of being in the same prison when Leving died and may, by this date, have been aware of who betrayed him in London. But a far more obvious candidate offers itself in the shape of George Villiers, Duke of Buckingham.

Buckingham, it should be recalled had the right Yorkshire connections. Moreover, the trumped-up charges against him had not long been withdrawn. He had only just emerged from the Tower in the previous month and his enemies, still as numerous as ever, would be happy to revive the charges and cause him further trouble. If one of the 'witnesses' against him were eliminated then it would make it more difficult for them. Moreover a man such as Buckingham, who had a violent, as well as cruel, streak to his character, would have no compunction in ordering the murder of someone as insignificant as Leving. An important element to this argument is that in his defence of his private life Buckingham felt the need to defend himself against the specific accusation of poisoning. As he saw it 'let any man show that [he was] really poisoned and he will do me the greatess kindness imaginable, let the matter of fact be but once proved and I'll undertake to tell for what reason it was done'.[128] This ambiguous answer may have concealed many crimes. In any event, whoever ordered Leving to be murdered it was carried out with skill and his life came to a squalid end.

V

The Marquis of Louvois' statement that most of the professional spies of his acquaintance were 'scoundrels' was entirely correct of one professional

[127] Bod. Lib. Rawlinson A 185, fo. 473v, entries 47–53; and *Remarks*, pp. 223–6.

[128] A. Pritchard, 'A Defence of his Private Life by the Second Duke of Buckingham', *HLQ*, 44, 1980–1, pp. 157–77.

spy at least: Colonel Joseph Bamfield.[129] Bamfield's name is a familiar one to most seventeenth-century historians and his career in espionage was a lengthy one of some forty-one years. His reputation was largely deserved and his covert activities had begun early in his career in 1644. They only ended with his death in 1685. Bamfield was a man who had lived most of his life engaged in spying on someone or something and so his career illustrates many of the facets of the professional spy. He began as a soldier at the age of seventeen in the First Bishops War of 1639. According to Clarendon, Bamfield was an Irishman whose real name was Bamford, although there is no real evidence for this statement.[130] With the outbreak of the Civil War he became a colonel of a royalist regiment. His apparently natural gifts for intrigue and espionage, however, appear to have attracted the king's attention and Charles sent him to London in 1644 to spy on the activities of parliament. He was reliable enough in secret dealings to be trusted in arranging the escape of James, Duke of York in April 1648 from St James's Palace. He disguised James as a woman and took the duke to the Netherlands. Bamfield then returned to London where he continued a liaison with Anne Murray, afterwards Lady Halkett,[131] who had assisted him in the duke's escape. Their relationship reveals Bamfield's penchant for roguery in that he was not only capable of outrageous lies but also bigamy. Having decided to offer his hand to Anne he blithely informed her that his wife had just died. If nothing else Bamfield seems to have had a way with the ladies, which in itself is not unusual with a man so heavily involved in espionage. Many of the men involved in such practices throughout history have been notorious philanderers and have fancied themselves as 'ladies' men'.[132] After the execution of Charles I, however, Bamfield prepared to leave London for Scotland, mainly it seems to pursue Anne Murray, but he was captured by the authorities and only just managed to escape. He then fled to Holland. By this time his bigamous activities were well known and as a consequence he fought a duel with Sir

[129] There are various spellings of his name. I have taken the version given by *DNB*, Joseph Bamfield, as well as his own biographical pamphlet, which remains essential reading for his career. See J. Bamfield, *Colonel Joseph Bamfield's Apologie Written by Himself and Printed at His Desire* (1685). Unfortunately, or perhaps predictably, he suppressed most of the references to his espionage activities. For Louvois see Noone, *The Man Behind the Iron Mask*, pp. 162–3. See also *Dictionnaire de Biographie Française* (15 vols. so far, 1933–) XI, cols. 1075–76; see also Wolf, *Louis XIV*, p. 175; and G. A. Ellis, *The True History of the State Prisoner Commonly Called The Iron Mask* (1826); Jung, *La Vérité dur le Masque de Fer*, pp. 234–40.

[130] Clarendon, *Life*, p. 479.

[131] For this see Clarke, *Life of James II*, I, pp. 33–9; and J. G. Nichols, ed., *The Autobiography of Anne, Lady Halkett*, Camden Society (1875), pp. 19–24; also J. Lofts, ed., *The Memoirs of Lady Anne Halkett and Anne, Lady Fanshawe* (Oxford, 1979), pp. x–xiv.

[132] See Colonel John Scott, below, p. 236.

Henry Newton, Anne's brother-in-law, who happened to be crossing the Channel on the same ship. As Bamfield managed to shoot Newton in the head he failed to win the confidence of the exiled king and his court despite his former services. He returned to England, but in 1652 was brought before the Council of State and he was told to leave the country. According to his own version of events he then visited Vienna, eventually ending up in Utrecht. He continued there for about five years, 'frequently agitated betwixt hope and despair' as he put it.[133]

Anne Murray's description of Bamfield's character at this time gives us an informal portrait of the spy in his formative years and displays the characteristic traits he was to carry through the rest of his life. There is little doubt that she thought too much of her lover and that he was able to make a fool of her. She was only the first. Anne claimed he was 'unquestionably loyall, handsome, a good skollar, which gave him the advantage of writing and speaking well, and the cheefest ornament hee had was a devout life and conversation'.[134] In reality, of course, she was totally wrong as Bamfield's loyalty rarely stretched beyond himself and he was something of a lugubrious personality with a singular inability to even think in a straight line, let alone tell the truth. A more perceptive contemporary called him the 'most closl[e]y cunning fellow in the world'.[135] Doubtless Anne Murray's emotional involvement prejudiced her in favour of the adventurer, but then Bamfield was the type of man who would betray nearly everyone he ever came into contact with in one way or another.

Clarendon's opinion of him therefore is perhaps more sound for, while he marked Bamfield as a 'man of wit and parts' as well as a 'restless unquiet spirit', he also saw him as possessed of an 'active and insinuating nature ... dexterous enough in bringing anything to pass that he had the managing of himself'.[136] In spite of a wide variety of faults, in his time Bamfield was to be variously employed by Charles I, John Thurloe (who was certainly no fool), Clarendon, Arlington and Williamson, as well as John de Witt, another man of singular intelligence. During the 1660s Bamfield also associated with various English exiles and apparently fooled them into believing his loyalty to the 'Good Old Cause'. At the latter end of his career in the 1680s he was also in touch with Secretary of State Jenkins. There is no doubt that many trusted him who should with hindsight have perhaps known better, all of them at one time or another were warned that he was dangerous and Bamfield happily betrayed them all. His

133 Bamfield, *Apologie*, p. 54.
134 Nichols, *The Autobiography of Anne, Lady Halkett*, p. 26.
135 See Cameron, *New Light on Aphra Behn*, p. 37.
136 Clarendon, *Life*, pp. 479, 645, 670.

aims, if indeed he had any beyond his immediate gratification, seem to have been simple enough: to return to England and preferment at the court, but they were always marred by personality faults and actions which took that target ever further away from him.

Bamfield began the 1650s engaged in espionage work for the Lord Protector's regime under John Thurloe and using the alias of 'John Nowmane'. He was hired to provide intelligence on the exiled royalists and was later to claim that 'insupportable necessity' or lack of funds had driven him to this course. Again such a statement must not be taken at face value. Bamfield was a blatant and prolific liar and his prolonged cries of poverty were a constant theme, or wail, throughout his life. He worked for Thurloe until Cromwell's death in 1658, although at various points he had played a double game.[137] After this he decided to return to England. At the Restoration Bamfield was a marked man. The new king, who disliked him personally, and his ministers were well aware of Bamfield's actions during the Protectorate and indeed the spy's name appeared in both of the lists of Thurloe's agents which were handed over to the new regime.[138] Naturally enough the government rounded up the individuals on those lists, both because of their previous activities and because it intended to interrogate them further to learn Thurloe's methods. Consequently Bamfield was arrested and thrown into the Tower and there he was to remain for nearly a year.[139] The general opinion of the king and his ministers was openly hostile. One of Bamfield's petitions for release was simply endorsed by Nicholas 'not to be released'.[140] The spy had offended far too many important people during the 1650s and had backed the losing side, a sign that this professional agent at least was singularly lacking in judgement. Some judicious trimming would perhaps have saved him from the Tower. More important to his future was the hostility shown by the king, for Charles simply regarded Bamfield as a traitor and the king was to prove particularly unforgiving on some matters.[141] Indeed one of the main themes running through Bamfield's relations with the regime after 1660 was his attempt to cultivate the forgiveness of Charles, but neither the king nor his

137 Bamfield, *Apologie*, p. 57. For Bamfield's work for Thurloe see Underdown, *Royalist Conspiracy*, pp. 62–6; and Gardiner, *Commonwealth and Protectorate*, III, p. 142; Aubrey, *Mr Secretary Thurloe*, pp. 94–5, 98, 116–17, 120.

138 PRO SP 18/220, 114; and BL Stowe MSS 185, fo. 183. Bamfield's name is the one constant in the lists.

139 See Bamfield, *Apologie*, p. 61. Another example of one of Thurloe's former spies who ended up in the Tower in 1660 was John Risdon. *CSPD*, 1660–1, pp. 251, 263, 272, 372. He is also listed in PRO SP 18/220, fo. 114. Very few of these men, however, succeeded in the manner of Bamfield in crossing the divide to find new employment under the Stuarts.

140 *CSPD*, 1660–1, pp. 171, 600.

141 See A. Bryant, ed., *The Letters, Speeches and Declarations of King Charles II*, (1935), p. 29.

regime was of a forgiving nature and both were to insist that Bamfield work his passage back into favour. Due to the spy's personality, this was something he was never able to fully achieve. Of course, it might be argued that if the regime never treated Bamfield very well why should he respond, however, it was all too well aware of his past.

In the event Bamfield was released in 1661 with the assistance of Clarendon. The Chancellor had known the spy in the 1650s when, in the process of a double game, Bamfield had continued to supply dubious intelligence to the royalists. It seems to have been obvious to all concerned that Bamfield could not remain in England, especially as he was soon in trouble again. Clarendon, who was at this point at the peak of his powers, sent the reluctant spy to the United Provinces. This in itself might be thought surprising, for Clarendon has traditionally been seen as someone who viewed espionage with distaste. On the whole, however, this is a false impression and with the Chancellor in control of the foreign affairs of the country he was not averse to using the necessary tools to undertake certain less salubrious aspects of that job. Unwilling to soil his hands with Bamfield personally, however, Clarendon used a mutual acquaintance as an intermediary to communicate with the spy. This acquaintance was Sir Allen Apsley who held the office of Master of Hawks, and had also held military posts in the Civil War in the West Country, where Bamfield himself had spent some time.[142] Other than this Apsley was an odd choice. He was not that friendly to a twice traitor and moreover he himself was a dangerous man to know, as his brother-in-law Colonel Hutchinson found out. Apsley promised to protect Hutchinson from persecution, but at the same time he also sent information about Hutchinson's activities to the Secretary of State's office.[143]

Arriving in the United Provinces Bamfield quickly found something to occupy his time: aside from spying on all and sundry and sending, usually unwanted, advice to Clarendon, he took service in the Dutch army as had so many English exiles. In his first years in the Netherlands Bamfield based himself in the town of Middleburg in the troubled province of Zeeland. Bamfield's espionage career then became a complex web of secret intrigues and double dealings. The enterprising colonel often found himself in opposing camps sometimes at the same time, in a juggling of roles which must have eventually taken its toll. Two main associations stand out in this period. Firstly there were his links with the various English parties involved in, interested in, or living in the Netherlands. Secondly there were his dealings in the domestic politics of the Dutch Republic. In the first category we

142 *CClSP*, V, p. 390.

143 *CSPD*, 1663–4, p. 441; *H of P*, I, pp. 541–3; C. H. Firth, ed., *Memoirs of the Life of Colonel Hutchinson by his Widow Lucy* (1906).

can find Bamfield's dealings with Clarendon, usually via Apsley, Sir George Downing, and Arlington's office. He also became involved in the intrigues of the various exiles, endlessly plotting a return to power. On the Dutch side Bamfield found himself embroiled in the struggles between De Witt and the Orangist faction in Zeeland.

Bamfield had opened his correspondence with Apsley by providing information about the situation in England as well as the Netherlands. He also struck up an acquaintance with Sir George Downing. Downing, who could recognise a rogue when he saw one, did not trust the spy, but strung him along in any case with hopes of favour and money in return for what he could turn up. By 1663, obviously aware of the way the wind was blowing in the court of Charles II, Bamfield decided to contact the Secretary of State's office, now under Arlington. In general the correspondence which followed was not very enlightening for either side for it oozed so much servility on Bamfield's part that it may have rebounded on the hapless spy. It certainly seems to have made the recipients suspicious of Bamfield's motives and he received little by way of financial encouragement. Two themes emerge from the correspondence. Firstly Bamfield was determined to get back into England by any means. Secondly he was clearly out to make some money. Sir Leoline Jenkins, who was to have dealings with Bamfield in the 1680s, claimed the spy's letters were inevitably of little use.[144] The secretary's office was in fact rightly suspicious of Bamfield's motives. In a tortuous career he was too often tempted by his contacts with the exiles and the Dutch government. He began to play all sides off against the others in a confused triple game. Situated as he was in Zeeland Bamfield also gained the confidence of John de Witt. De Witt had also been warned that the Englishman was a 'notorious rogue', probably in the pay of the Stuarts,[145] but he wanted to use him as an expert on English affairs, as well as to spy on the English exiles, the Orangist party in Zeeland and to keep an eye on the activities of Downing. He was also useful as a military adviser. Bamfield was to continue in the Dutch forces until in 1672 loss of favour and a breakdown in health led to a sojourn in Leuwarden. With this his career apparently came to an end, but Bamfield did correspond with Jenkins towards the end of his life.

Whether he was claiming to be 'in' with the 'Presbyterian party' in exile abroad, or why he could not make a 'considerable inspection into what-

[144] *CSPD*, 1683–4, p. 318. For Bamfield's relations in the early 1660s with the English government: PRO SP 84/167, fos. 109, 128, 137, 138, 150, 151, 182, 211; PRO SP 84/170; fo. 51; *CClSP*, V, pp. 390, 403, 418, 421–2, 487; *HMC*, Ormonde MSS VI, pp. 460–1; *CSPD*, 1683, pp. 97–8.

[145] For Bamfield and de Witt see R. Fruin and N. Japikse, eds., *Brieven aan Johan de Witt, 1660–1672* (Historich genootschap, 1922); Rowen, *De Witt*, pp. 664–5, H. H. Rowen, *John de Witt: Statesman of the True Freedom* (1986), p. 182.

ever the French could have designed', Bamfield produced a tedious prose, which, as with its author, promised much and delivered little. This was another theme which continued throughout his career. Jenkins wearily noted in 1684 that Bamfield's letters 'were too general and very obscure, there being in them no designation of persons, actions or other circumstances [he] speaks of so oft'.[146] There is little doubt that this was partly a result of Bamfield's own personality and partly deliberate. Hidden behind the ciphers and invisible lemon-juice writing was a large percentage of rumour and hearsay. This mixture Bamfield hoped would produce some results, but his penchant for intrigue would eventually prove too much for all of his masters.

While Bamfield did provide some interesting news concerning the Dutch political scene and spied on the activities of certain of the English exiles, most of his correspondence, often of seven or ten pages per letter, was taken up with the one subject which interested him above all others – himself. Bamfield's utter self-obsession continued throughout his career. His correspondence of the 1680s repeated the same arguments, complaints and mistakes. Endless wails about his 'insupportable ... and violent despair' which he had tried twenty years previously on Thurloe, Arlington, Williamson and Clarendon were replayed for the benefit of Jenkins. This only confirmed to Jenkins that the man was a waste of his valuable time. Taken out of context the attitude of Bamfield might show a man in the throes of some psychological crisis, but if we place them in context they clearly show Bamfield merely attempting to squeeze yet more money and favours out of his employers. His employers ultimately all came to the conclusion that while Bamfield was at least useful enough for them to be kept sweet by the occasional sum of money in general he was a timeserver. The money was designed to get him to continue to supply any information he did pick up, but they clearly never provided him with too much by way of funds in case he should dry up as a source. In any case gifts of money could often merely lead to lengthy letters leading nowhere. To take an example from 1663, the passing of a bill of exchange worth £50 by the secretary's office led to a prolix response, in exceedingly 'humble' language, in which Bamfield promised from, the 'bottome of my soule [to] beseech almighty God to inflict an exemplary vengence upon mee in this life and to withdraw his mercy eternally from me at my last and greatest extreamity, if ever I shall prove unfaithful to any of his most sacred Ma[jesty] ye king of great Brittaynes commands'.[147] It is likely that such crude self-abasement, which was part of Bamfield's style, fell on stony ground. The world of espionage was a brutal and practical one and few

[146] *CSPD*, 1683–4, p. 318. [147] PRO SP 84/167, fo. 182.

were more practical than the men in the office of the Secretary of State during the reign of Charles II.

VI

In the port of Cadiz in October 1663 the English consul Mr Martin Westcombe listened uneasily to a Swedish engineer, Martin Beckman, as he flourished extracts of the correspondence of King Philip IV of Spain and his minister the Duke of Medinaceli. These, claimed Beckman, had been taken from the desk of Medinaceli himself and proved that the Spanish crown had plans to ally with the Moors, and take the recently acquired English colonial city of Tangier by *coup de main*. The consul was clearly troubled by this news. Could Beckman's intelligence be trusted? Was he not after all a spy? If Beckman's intelligence could be trusted then he must immediately inform his masters in London, especially the Secretary of State, Lord Arlington. Westcombe soon decided on this option and also decided at the same time to write to the deputy governor of Tangier in Lord Teviot's absence, Colonel John Fitzgerald. Martin Beckman must have thought his fortune was made, but in the murky world of espionage in relation to international politics in the 1660s nothing was ever certain.

The nexus of Martin Westcombe's problem and Martin Beckman's opportunity was the city and port of Tangier which lay upon the north-west coast of Morocco, or 'Barbary' as the English of the seventeenth century called it. The city had a legendary air about it, and according to one English writer of the period, 'Tangier ... was by Seddai the Son of Had, compassed about with walls of Brass and the roofs of them covered with Gold'.[148] Although the anonymous author then went on to rather deflate the image of the golden city by the sceptical addition, 'believe it [those] who can'. The 'jewel of Tangier' came into the possession of the English crown in 1662 as part of the marriage dowry of Catherine of Braganza. The offer of Tangier proved to be a tempting one to English eyes. It was reasoned that the port would give England a strong naval and commercial advantage in the Mediterranean, although the harbour was in need of some protection from the elements and this major engineering project was to prove expensive. The English acceptance of Tangier would also cause problems elsewhere. Most obviously it would increase the displeasure of the Spanish monarch, Philip IV. Spain was not only at war with Portugal, but also considered the town a Spanish possession.[149] The local

[148] *A Description of Tangier, The Country and the People Adjoyning with an Account of the Person and Government of Gayland* (1664), p. 4.

[149] See Sir Richard Fanshawe, *Original Letters* (1701), p. 41. Also E. M. G. Routh, *Tangier: England's Lost Atlantic Outpost, 1661–1684* (1912), pp. 49–53; R. A. Stradling, 'Anglo-

Moorish chieftains also looked askance at any Europeans in occupation of what they considered to be their territory. In reality the political situation in the interior of the country was not conducive to the survival of English ambitions. A state of virtual civil war existed. The local monarch, Er Rasheed II, or 'Tafiletta' as the English called him, lost in the Arabic pronunciation, was under pressure from another faction who sought to install his brother, Mohammed, on the throne. Also prominent amongst the opposition was Abd Allah Ghaïlán, whom the English called 'Guyland' or 'Gayland'. Ghaïlán was an ambitious warlord intent on carving himself a kingdom out of the area and who claimed Tangier as his own. He was to prove a troublesome and dangerous enemy for the English beleaguered in Tangier.[150] Contemporary English opinion of Ghaïlán, whom the Spanish were to attempt to use as an ally, was not favourable: he 'hath two Qualities ... Perfidiousness ... and ... Cruelty' noted one observer.[151]

Surrounded by a myriad of enemies, Tangier and its garrison proved to be both difficult and expensive to maintain and the cause of a steady drain upon the never very healthy finances of the English crown.[152] As the garrison remained in a more or less perpetual state of siege from hostile forces both within and outside its walls some at home began to question its value. The local residents of the city, who had been abandoned by the Portuguese, were equally unfriendly. The town itself oozed little of the so-called mystic charm of the east. It was quick to degrade or kill off the unwary European. Samuel Pepys described it as a place of 'vice ... swearing, cursing, drinking and whoring'. 'Everything', he wrote, 'runs to corruption here.'[153] Indeed the occupants of the English garrison were quickly overcome with lethargy and drunkenness, when they were not carried off by disease and sickness. In addition the local conflict with the 'Moors' became a particularly nasty little war in which neither side gave any quarter and atrocities were common.[154] Nevertheless the town was accepted by Charles

Spanish Relations From the Restoration to the Peace of Aix-la-Chapelle, 1660–68', unpublished Ph.D Thesis, University College, Cardiff, 1968; Childs, *Army of Charles II*, pp. 115–16.

150 Essential reading for understanding the background to the local problems of Tangier is to be found in BL Sloane MSS 505, 'The Present State of Morocco & Fez with somewhat of Gayland's Original Rise', fos. 83v–110; and Routh, *Tangier*, pp. 12–35. For Ghaïlán's later history see pp. 89–112. See also N. Meakin, *The Moorish Empire: A Historical Epitome* (1899), pp. 136–54; J. Davis, *The History of the Second Queen's Royal Regiment* (3 vols., 1887), I, pp. 271–81; and J. B. Wolf, *The Barbary Coast: Algiers Under the Turks, 1500 to 1830* (1979), p. 228. I have adopted Routh's spellings of the Arabic nomenclature.

151 *A Description of Tangier*, pp. 12–13.

152 John Childs has estimated that Tangier cost the crown some £75,388. 21s. 6d. in 1662 aside from the human cost in disease and deaths in action. See Childs, *Army of Charles II*, p. 118.

153 See R. Ollard, *Pepys: A Biography* (1985), p. 273.

154 Routh, *Tangier*, p. 65.

anuary 1662 it was occupied by the E
ough with 3,000 foot and 200 horse.[155]
r was to have a troubled history, but fo
s an interesting glimpse into certain aspec
of espionage in the Restoration period.
e fore in Tangier because of the increasingly
England and Spain. At the Restoration of
the two states gradually deteriorated as the
Stuart regime began to reorganise its foreign policy. From the very beginning the English occupation of Tangier had met with Spanish hostility, which was to hinder any prospect of prosperity for the port. Ships from Tangier, for example, were prevented from entering Spanish ports because the Spanish government had spread the rumour that they carried the plague. As a result Tangier could only draw its supplies from England which was a long and dangerous sea voyage away. Spanish grievances were in fact reasonable and genuine ones. Part of the army holding off the Spanish in their attempt to recapture Portugal was made up of English troops. These men were mostly taken from the old army of the English Republic; and the war provided a convenient dumping ground for men who otherwise could have proved to be troublesome if they had remained in England. Tangier itself was also used in this way. In the early days of the occupation of the city, republican sentiments were commonplace.[156] To the Spanish the city of Tangier also provided the English with an ideal base for raids on the Spanish coast.[157] The occupation of Tangier by the English was made to appear even more reprehensible by Charles II's sale of the former Spanish possession of Dunkirk to Louis XIV in 1662. In response to these provocations Spanish policy grew more hostile and aggressive. The Stuart regime's many enemies were given assistance by the Spanish crown. King Philip and his ministers even went so far as to attempt to undermine the newly restored regime by backing conspiracies against it.[158] In the case of Tangier a different strategy was followed by Philip. Under the auspices of his minister and governor of Andalucia, the Duke of Medinaceli, he contacted the Moorish chieftain Ghaïlán in order to make various offers to him.[159]

[155] BL Sloane MSS 505, fo. 89.

[156] For the troops in Portugal see P. H. Hardacre, 'The English Contingent in Portugal, 1662–1668', *Journal of the Society for Army Historical Research*, 1960, 38, pp. 112–25. Naturally enough the exiles sent to Tangier created a disturbance in the port. See PRO CO 279/3, fo. 24, for information on John Davis of 'seditious principles'.

[157] The republican Admiral Robert Blake had noted the strategic importance of the place.

[158] For these plots see R. A. Stradling, *Philip IV and the Government of Spain, 1621–1665* (Cambridge, 1988), p. 299; and also R. A. Stradling, 'Spanish Conspiracy in England, 1661–1663', *History*, 87, 1972, pp. 269–86.

[159] See *CSPV*, 1664–6, p. 4; and Feiling, *Foreign Policy*, p. 40.

we have seen, news of a possible Spanish–Moorish
ugh to the English government when in October 1663 Ma
ought to Westcombe, the English consul at Cadiz, evidence
y the Spanish and the Moors to take Tangier by *coup de ma*
Moors were to lay siege to the city by land, whilst the Spanish invad
sea.[160] Martin Beckman had originally been employed by the Eng
crown as an engineer and hydrographer and had seen some service in th
Civil War.[161] He had accompanied the Earl of Sandwich to Tangier in 1662,[162] and was known to the Earl of Teviot, who became the governor of Tangier, as well as to 'other persons of honour about the Court', including Prince Rupert and the Duke of York.[163] However, Beckman lost his place to the clients of the new governor and decided to leave the city, later claiming 'ill usage' by the Earl of Peterborough. His decision may also have had something to do with Colonel John Fitzgerald, the deputy governor, in Teviot's absence. Fitzgerald was a quarrelsome man who actively disliked Beckman.[164] He later claimed that Beckman merely became discontented and, as mercenaries will, had decided to offer his services elsewhere.

Beckman's deficiencies of character were therefore apparently well known to all and sundry. An image emerges of 'a man of valor . . . [and] . . . great knowledg[e] in his profession, but [also] of an ambitious inconstan[t] vengefull natur[e]'. He was moreover possessed of a 'cozenus appetite' for money.[165] As a military engineer Beckman also knew all about the fortifications and garrison of Tangier – information which could be useful to the city's enemies.[166] He had assisted in the construction and repair of the

160 PRO SP 94/45, fo. 115; and PRO CO 279/2, fos. 130–3.

161 Bod. Lib. Rawlinson MSS D, 395, fo. 190.

162 Little is known of Beckman, who is also called Börkman in some documents, but see *DNB*, Supplemental Volume, Martin Beckman; and especially Bod. Lib. Rawlinson MSS D, 916, fos. 99–101; BL Sloane MSS 2448, fos. 15, 46–7; Pepys, *Diary*, III, 37; X, 24; E. G. R. Taylor, *The Mathematical Practitioners of Tudor and Stuart England* (Cambridge, 1924), p. 252; H. C. Tomlinson, *Guns and Government: The Ordnance Office Under the Later Stuarts* Royal Historical Society (1979), p. 49; E. Chappel, ed., *The Tangier Papers of Samuel Pepys*, Naval Record Society, (1935), 73, p. xliv; R. F. Edwards, ed., *Roll of the Officers of the Corps of Royal Engineers From 1660–1898* (Chatham, 1898), p. 1. His nationality is variously described as German, Dutch or Swedish and he later became a naturalised Englishman; see *HMC*, House of Lords MSS, p. 285.

163 PRO CO 279/2, fo. 134; and BL Sloane MSS 2448, fos. 46–7.

164 *CSPD*, 1663–4, p. 414. For a brief biography of Fitzgerald see S. Saunders Webb, *The Governors-General: The English Army and the Definition of Empire, 1569–1681* (Williamsburg, 1979), p. 506.

165 Bod. Lib. Rawlinson MSS D, 916, fo. 99. For all his faults Beckman was brave. See *HMC*, Dartmouth MSS, p. 52.

166 PRO CO 279/2, fos. 122–122v. In the 1680s the Moors were to have the assistance of English deserters who were experienced in siege warfare and came close to taking the city. See Childs, *Army of Charles II*, p. 147.

city's defences; and intelligence such as this would have been invaluable to the Spanish if passed on to Ghaïlán. It is not surprising therefore that Beckman went to Spain after leaving Tangier.

Initially the Swedish engineer decided to offer his services to Philip IV of Spain through the auspices of the Duke of Medinaceli. The king told his minister to take Beckman into his service, but to remain uncommitted until the negotiations with Ghaïlán had come to fruition.[167] As encouragement Beckman was also promised, and apparently received, a substantial down-payment of money, although Beckman evidently decided it was not substantial enough for his tastes nor was it paid in a timely fashion. Thus 'he reflected within himselfe to betray his owne plott ... under the notion of haveing by great providence made discovery and pryed [into] it with full curiosity in order to the service (as he stiled it) of his Master the king of great Britaine'.[168] In the hope of increasing his profits then, Beckman approached the English consul at Cadiz. To Westcombe he flourished extracts from the correspondence of Philip and the Duke of Medinaceli whilst proclaiming his 'signall service' in getting hold of such information.[169] From the purloined correspondence it was clear that the Spanish were attempting to buy the alliance of Ghaïlán and in due course they were to send both money and envoys to the Moorish chieftain. Unfortunately they were to meet with little success. English diplomatic opinion later came to the conclusion that Ghaïlán was an unstable character who was more interested in the Spanish monarch's present of 40,000 pieces of eight than any real alliance.[170]

The historian J. S. Corbett has offered an alternative view of Beckman's manoeuvres, claiming that Beckman 'was apparently given to understand that he might make himself useful as a spy in Spain'.[171] However, it is clear that Beckman was not working for the Caroline regime on his Spanish sojourn, but for himself, although he had, as we shall see, acted earlier in such a role for the regime. In any case his espionage activities, as well as his greed, were to get him into trouble with the English government this time.[172] Beckman was to be thrown into the Tower for his pains in late 1663. This makes it highly unlikely that he was being directly employed by the government's intelligence system, for the latter rarely rewarded its agents in this way unless it believed that the Stuart regime was being betrayed.[173]

In fact Beckman's activities are clearly characteristic of a freelance agent in the period. There were many such men in Europe at the time. They were

167 *HMC*, Heathcote MSS, p. 130. 168 Bod. Lib. Rawlinson MSS D, 916, fo. 100.
169 *ibid*.; and PRO CO 279/2, fo. 130v. 170 See PRO CO 279/2, fos. 152, 154–5.
171 J. S. Corbett, *England in the Mediterranean, 1603–1713* (2 vols., 1904), II, pp. 39–40.
172 Bod. Lib. Rawlinson MSS D, 916, fos. 100–100v. 173 See *CSPD*, 1663–4, p. 414.

the mercenaries of the espionage world who offered their services for hire and often played a double game. Louvois, as we have seen, described them as 'scoundrels' and they were rarely to be trusted too far.[174] Beckman was already a mercenary soldier and it would have taken little for him to turn to espionage. Intelligence of enemy fortifications always had a market value. Indeed Samuel Pepys, who met Beckman in the 1680s, was told by the engineer himself that during the period of his so called 'ill usage' by Peterborough he had undertaken some secret work disguised as a servant, making plans of Tetuan, Ceuta and perhaps most significantly of the Spanish port of Cadiz. Such activities could prove to be dangerous. Colonel John Scott, who worked as a spy for a number of governments in the early 1670s before he attracted notoriety during the Popish Plot, had been caught drawing the fortifications of Bruges and told by the authorities there to get out of town, but he was unusually lucky.[175] Beckman's work may have been for the Governor of Tangier or may have been simply free-lancing, with the hopes that he could sell the plans at a later date to any interested parties. He was a man motivated by the financial possibilities of espionage. Further suspicions of Beckman's motives must certainly be aroused by the fact that he did not go back to Tangier after telling his story to the English consul at Cadiz. Instead he offered to go directly to England with the documents he had obtained from the Spanish.[176] This was clearly because rewards and preferment lay at court and not back in Tangier with its disease and dangers.

The dubious nature of Beckman's morality and his general untrust-worthiness also raised the suspicions of Colonel Fitzgerald. He wrote to Arlington that 'Beckmann the Intelligencer is to be feared', although he conceded that 'I conceave what hee gives us [is] not soe far to be neg-lected'.[177] As a result of this suspicion and his other activities, Beckman was to spend at least six months in the Tower. He claimed that this was through the 'malice of one person'[178] and this person may well have been Fitzgerald, who also later informed Arlington, in what looks suspiciously like jealousy of a rival, that Beckman who is now 'soe much spoke of' had received 'a good quantitye of money' from the Spanish in his initial deal-ings with them[179], news which would damn the Swedish engineer in Arling-ton's eyes.

While Beckman returned to England Colonel Fitzgerald had other prob-lems to contend with. He was hampered by the absence of his superior

[174] Louvois quoted in Noone, *The Man Behind the Iron Mask*, pp. 162–3.
[175] See Bod. Lib. Rawlinson MSS A, 175, fos. 68, 164; Swart, *Netherland-Historian*, p. 233.
[176] PRO SP 94/45, fo. 115. [177] PRO CO 279/2, fos. 122–3.
[178] *CSPD*, 1663–4, p. 414.
[179] PRO CO 279/2, fo. 162.

officer, the Earl of Teviot, as well as by a lack of supplies, ships and men. Nevertheless he did try to make Tangier secure.[180] Beckman's advice had been that the fortifications should be strengthened. This was commonsense, but Beckman could also have been motivated by self-interest. Fitzgerald rejected the idea of strengthening the fortifications as being impossible at the time, but he was willing to make an attempt to strengthen the castle which would have been a last refuge in the event of a disaster.[181] An important part of Fitzgerald's attempts at securing Tangier included his own schemes to gather intelligence from Ghaïlán's camp. A boat was sent up the coast on the pretence of trade, but in reality to gather information about the enemy's movements. Another strategy was to employ some individual to spy in the Moorish camp. Earlier in the year the Earl of Peterborough had himself employed several 'Arabian spies' to gather intelligence, so that this avenue of approach may still have been open to Fitzgerald.[182] Fitzgerald made use of a 'Jew of Tetuan' who had an 'interest there and whose concerns make him an enemy to [both] Guyland and the Spaniards'.[183] This unknown Jewish spy had access to the negotiations between the Spanish and Ghaïlán and he also attempted to obtain a copy of the treaty itself.[184] The spy claimed that the Moors had plans to build a string of forts round Tangier to 'curb our libertie'. Doubtless it was for this reason that they wanted a military engineer, which the Spanish had hoped to supply in the shape of Beckman.

The use of a Jew as a spy for the garrison is rather surprising, given that the Jewish community in the city was not usually trusted by those in command at Tangier. The Jews had already gained some notoriety as carriers of information for both sides. They acted as merchants as well as interpreters, but were suspected of taking out as much information as they brought to the garrison. Little distinction was made between the Ashkenazi and Sephardic communities. Lord Dartmouth's instructions in 1683 on the eve of the English abandonment of Tangier clearly stated that especial care should be taken that the Jews in the city did not hear of the impending withdrawal by the English, lest they betray the information to the Moors.[185] In fact outside Tangier, as has already been noted, the use of Jewish spies was rare in the Caroline espionage world. Oliver Cromwell and John Thurloe had used the Jewish community for this purpose, but both Joseph Williamson and Arlington, the men in command of the

180 *ibid.*, fo. 122; Saunders Webb, *Governors-General*, p. 506.
181 PRO CO 279/2, fo. 122.
182 *A Description of Tangier*, pp. 27–8.
183 PRO CO 279/2, fo. 152. Tetuan was 13 miles from Tangier; see *A Description of Tangier*, p. 5.
184 PRO CO 279/2, fo. 152.
185 *HMC*, Dartmouth MSS, p. 83.

Restoration regime's intelligence activities from 1662 to 1674 never really tapped this resource. The diaspora, with all of its Europe-wide connections, was never exploited. Why this was so is not clear. It cannot be explained by any overt or latent anti-Semitism on the part of the regime, because in their exile the royalists had used Jewish agents for various purposes. It was left to William III and Marlborough to pick the Jewish connection up where Cromwell and Thurloe had left it.[186]

As well as sending out his own agents Fitzgerald also had to content with Spanish spies in Tangier itself.[187] A Spanish officer visited Tangier two or three days after Fitzgerald's boat had embarked on a 'like pretence'; he claimed to be investigating the possibilities of trade with the colony, but the Spanish gentleman was obviously spying out the land. In a diplomatic game of cat and mouse the deputy governor used the Spaniard with civility, for the two countries were not yet at war, but neither he nor the officer got very much out of each other.[188] In general Fitzgerald's assessment of the emerging intelligence was that Tangier's security ultimately depended upon the negotiations between the Spanish and the Moors. If, as seemed likely, these floundered on mutual distrust then the city was secure. On the other hand, if a deal was struck the town was indefensible to a joint attack.

Meanwhile Martin Westcombe, consul at Cadiz,[189] was approached by 'a Rambling English man' whom he had known for some '20 yeares'. This Englishman was a Dominican friar by the name of Father Peter Martin who had once been employed in the West Indies to discover what had happened to Prince Maurice, Prince Rupert's brother.[190] Westcombe, however, had last seen Martin in 1660, in secular dress, in the Spanish ambassador's house in London. The consul clearly didn't trust this man, despite the fact that he had given Westcombe a variety of intelligence including the news of growing poor relations between England and the Dutch. As a good diplomat Westcombe did not trust anyone in Cadiz and his suspicions were quickly aroused by the dubious friar. Martin, a short corpulent man with a ruddy complexion, who also claimed to be a 'true Englishman', was too 'subtle' a character for the consul's tastes.[191] Friar

[186] See L. Wolf, 'Cromwell's Jewish Intelligencers', in C. Roth, ed., *Essays in Jewish History* (1934), pp. 91–114; L. Wolf, 'The Jewry of the Restoration, 1660–1664', *The Jewish Historical Society of England Transactions*, V, 1908, pp. 5–34; J. Israel, *European Jewry in the Age of Mercantilism 1550–1750* (2nd edn, 1989), pp. 127–32, 158–60.

[187] For Spanish activities in the field of intelligence at an earlier date, but still relative to the 1660s, see C. H. Carter, *The Secret Diplomacy of the Habsburgs, 1598–1625* (1964).

[188] PRO CO 279/2, fo. 152.

[189] For more on Westcombe see Barbour, 'Consular Service in the Reign of Charles II', *American Historical Review*, 33, 1928, pp. 561–2, 565–6, 571–2, 577.

[190] Prince Maurice had gone missing in a storm at sea in 1651. Gardiner, *Commonwealth and Protectorate*, II, pp. 144–5.

[191] PRO CO 279/2, fos. 32v, 152.

Martin wanted Westcombe's assistance to go to Tangier, alleging that only from there could he catch a ship for England. The friar claimed that as he was a Roman Catholic the masters of the ships who were going to England refused to have him on board. Westcombe clearly believed that something was not quite convincing about Martin's tale, especially as the erstwhile friar often went under the name of Captain Crofts and tended to travel in secular dress. He therefore wrote to Fitzgerald giving him advanced warning of the man's arrival in Tangier.[192]

Fitzgerald naturally took precautions and in due course the friar arrived using his alias of Captain Crofts, 'I gave the frier ... fitting libertie', Fitzgerald later wrote to Teviot, 'and yett have a watchfull eye on him endevouring to intercept some of his letter[s]'.[193] In a further attempt to unmask this man and his aims, Fitzgerald set one of his junior officers, Major Knightly, to talk to Friar Martin. Knightly's amateurish blunderings did not gain much in the way of intelligence except that there was a Spanish fleet. This was made up of galleons from the India fleet and the galley squadron at Cadiz.[194] He did gather that the Spanish would do their utmost to 'compass' Tangier. Fitzgerald was also able to confirm by this source that the Spanish were still negotiating with Ghaïlán. Knightly, appealing to Martin's Christian sensibilities, bluntly told him that it was wrong for Christians to join in an alliance with the Moors. In reply the friar said that the Spanish 'would joyne with the devile' if they could have Tangier.[195]

The English ministers decided to act on the intelligence in order to curb continued Spanish aggression. They decided on a diplomatic warning shot across Spanish bows.[196] Sir Richard Fanshawe was chosen as the new ambassador to Madrid, his instructions making it clear how he was to use the information that had come into English hands. He was not to flaunt his knowledge, but was to 'lett [the] Duke de Medina les Torros know wee are not ignorant of it & wee could not easily be persuaded such a design would be sett on foot at the same time that wee receive such Professions of Friendship'.[197] The regime attempted to convey in diplomatic language the warning of possible retribution if Philip IV and his chief minister the Duke of Medina de las Torres, continued their schemes. It also revealed to the Spanish that the design had been uncovered and that the Tangier garrison as well as the English intelligence system were on their guard. In fact Philip IV was finding that his plotting with the Moors had achieved very little so

[192] *ibid.*, fos. 130–3. Friar Martin was not the only member of his order involved in espionage, see *Essex Papers*, I, pp. 138–9, 231.

[193] PRO CO 279/2, fo. 150.

[194] Corbett, *England in the Mediterranean*, II, p. 40.

[195] PRO CO 279/2, fo. 150.

[196] Feiling, *Foreign Policy*, p. 82.

[197] PRO SP 94/45, fos. 187v–188.

far and that without the aid of Ghaïlán the Spanish could never attack the city alone and be sure of success. The wily Ghaïlán clearly had no more intention of turning the city over to the Spanish than had the English. He was more than content to take Spanish money and to play at diplomacy with Philip's envoys. The negotiations continued in a rather desultory fashion, but there was very little chance of their proceeding much further. Philip then made soundings to try to gain control of the city by treaty with the English; this also came to nothing. The poor relations between England and Spain over Tangier reached a peak in June 1664 when the Earl of Teviot and a large part of his command were massacred outside the walls of the city by the Moors. Arlington reacted strongly to what he saw as Spanish complicity in this deed. He told Fanshawe to 'observe very well the Spaniards Counternance in this accident, and whether they are transacting anything with Guyland'.[198] In fact, although Medinaceli, who was a violent Anglophobe, had been supplying guns as well as technical advice to the Moors, the disaster which overtook Teviot was something which needed no Spanish help.

By that time Martin Beckman had long since arrived in England. His appearance at court did not go well, despite meeting Arlington personally. He had hoped that Prince Rupert would help him gain a reward for revealing the plot, but the English government, as so often happened, proved as dilatory in its rewards as had the Spanish. Disappointed yet again, Beckman's head was filled with a 'new chimera'. He went to see the Dutch ambassador 'admitting him to a free discourse of Tangier' and its affairs.[199] He was obviously hoping for some form of pecuniary advantage with this information. This act proved to be his undoing. The government was quickly 'inform'd of this peece of villany', for in Restoration England ambassadors' comings and goings, as well as those of their visitors, were watched and their mail was routinely opened by Arlington's office. King Charles himself ordered enquiries to be made.[200] This led to Beckman's arrest and a spell in the Tower for his pains. There he languished for at least six months. After his eventual release he left England and moved to Germany. His later rehabilitation, however, was to lead him back to England after 1667 and to the position of third engineer of the state in 1670. In 1677–8 Sir Joseph Williamson sent him to survey the Channel Islands' fortifications as the possibility of a war with France was imminent. In 1683–4 he was also back in Tangier and was responsible for the demolition of Tangier's fortifications when the English finally abandoned the city. For his part in the evacuation of Tangier he was to be knighted in

198 *Arlington's Letters*, II, p. 26; and for the Teviot massacre see *DNB*, Teviot.
199 Bod. Lib. Rawlinson MSS D, 916, fos. 100v–101.
200 Bod. Lib. Rawlinson MSS D, 916, fo. 101.

1685, when he also became Chief Engineer and Master-Gunner of England.[201] For a man who had chosen a role in the squalid profession of spy he had not done too badly.

The affairs of Colonel Bamfield and those of Beckman at Tangier show how the work of intelligence and diplomacy went hand in hand in this era. The information uncovered by the English government through its agents abroad could sometimes be skilfully exploited to keep any foreign opposition in check. The alertness of English diplomats and soldiers as well as its paid spies could therefore pay dividends. Both cases also illustrate some of the murky world of Restoration espionage. Fired by the greed of certain freelance spies it was one of the elements which lubricated the English intelligence system. The gathering of intelligence then worked its way through the diplomatic undergrowth to affect the foreign-policy decisions of the nations involved. On the other hand the activities of Edward Riggs and William Leving show how the regime contained and managed its covert domestic problems in the 1660s. Both men were ex-rebels who were used to penetrate the designs of plotters. While some of these designs were undoubtedly sham plots there were equally some genuine schemes which were stifled by such men as Riggs and Leving.

[201] See *DNB*, Supplemental Volume, Martin Beckman; and Pepys, *Diary*, X, p. 24.

6

The spies of the later Restoration regime, 1667–1685

I

In the second half of the reign of Charles II the world of espionage and conspiracy continued to be as perplexing for the government as in the first half. The 'problem' of Catholicism also began to loom, to explode in the Popish Plot of 1678. There were a number of men employed as spies by the regime in this period and while it is not possible to trace all of their careers here, lengthy case studies are given of two of the most notable and complex individuals who enlisted as covert soldiers in the regime's espionage wars: Thomas Blood and John Scott.

II

Sir Joseph Williamson, who came to know Thomas Blood quite well, noted on the day after Blood's attempt on the Crown Jewels that it was 'one of the strangest any story can tell'.[1] There is no doubt that Thomas Blood was the *nonpareil* of the seventeenth-century spy, rebel and adventurer. There is no-one quite like Blood in the Restoration regime's service, or for that matter out of it. He was distinctive in many ways, but most of all his is the only fully rounded figure of a spy in the period we can uncover. The others involved in the Restoration regime's intelligence system remain at heart shadowy figures. With Blood, however, we have a man whose thoughts we can actually penetrate through his own personal writings. Yet in spite of this there are great mysteries both concerning the man and his career. Notorious in his day, he was also adept in covering his tracks. Having said this, there is little doubt that Williamson the spymaster thought Blood a good catch on the morning of 10 May 1671. As he put it, 'God has made us Masters of Blood [and] it is of ten times ye value . . . of the Crowne itself'.[2]

Thomas Blood was born in Sarney, county Meath, in Ireland around the

[1] Bod. Lib. MSS Eng. Letters d.37, fo. 84. [2] *ibid.*

year 1618. The circumstances surrounding his early life are obscure but his father was said to have been a blacksmith and ironworker of 'no inferior credit'.[3] Blood's first real appearance in the historical record occurs during the survey taken in Ireland in the period 1654–6. In this he is listed as a protestant who had owned some 220 acres of land at Sarney since at least 1640.[4] In between these dates, however, Blood had undertaken some military service. The evidence concerning this is often slight and contradictory and there is at least the possibility that his later claims about an army career were partly bogus, or certainly inflated to suit his particular company.[5]

In a newsletter, written soon after his capture in 1671, Blood is described as being 'formerly ... a captain in the old king's army under Sir Lewis Dyve'.[6] There is a later claim that Blood had served under Monck in Ireland. While he does not appear in any of the major royalist army or regimental lists[7] there *is* a reference to a 'captain Bludd'[8] in the 'Indigent Officers List' of 1663. It is clear, however, that this man did not make a claim for any of the money on offer; he was merely noticed as the captain of John Harris of Dorset. Harris himself was the quartermaster of the regiment of Sir Lewis Dyve. During his interview with the king in 1671 Blood also claimed to have fought in England, on the royalist side, under Prince Rupert; and it was alleged the latter remembered him as a 'very stout bold fellow'. Again there is no firm evidence of such service and it is possible that Rupert, as with so many others, may have been seduced by Blood's natural eloquence.[9] In any event, with his marriage in 1650, if not before, Blood appears to have deserted the royalists for the cause of parliament and again he later claimed the rank of lieutenant in the parliamentary armies. In fact other than this lieutenancy, which seems genuine enough, there is no trace of any further rank being awarded to Blood. This fact did not prevent his regular self-promotion in the 1660s, from captain, to major

[3] *Remarks*, p. 219.

[4] R. C. Simmington, ed., *The Civil Survey AD 1654–1656, County of Meath*, Irish MSS Commission (Dublin, 1940), V, p. 126.

[5] It may also be noted here that in 1650 he married a young Lancashire gentlewoman, Mary Holcroft. She was the daughter of Lieutenant-Colonel John Holcroft of Holcroft Hall. For this marriage see W. Johnson-Kaye and E. W. Wittenburg-Kaye, eds., *The Register of Newchurch in the Parish of Culcheth: Christenings, Weddings and Burials*, Lancashire Parish Register Society (Cambridge, 1905), pp. 15, 217; J. Gillow, *Lord Burghley's Map of Lancashire in 1590* (1907), pp. 44–5.

[6] BL Add. MSS 36916, fo. 233.

[7] See E. Peacock, *The Army Lists of the Roundheads and Cavaliers* (2nd edn, 1874); H. G. Tibbutt, *The Life and Letters of Sir Lewis Dyve, 1599–1669*, Bedfordshire Record Society, 27 (1948); P. R. Newman, *Royalist Officers in England and Wales* (New York, 1981).

[8] *A List of Officers Claiming to the Sixty Thousand Pounds Granted by his Sacred Majesty, for the Relief of the Truly Loyal and Indigent Party* (1663), p. 39.

[9] *HMC*, 6th Report, p. 370; also *CSPD*, 1671–2, p. 373.

and eventually to colonel as he became more notorious. Also at some point subsequent to 1651 Blood and his family moved back to Ireland and his later career proves that, to some extent at least, he became committed to the 'Good Old Cause'.

Although we know very little about Blood's activities prior to the Restoration in 1660, it was this event which was to launch him into a new career of conspiracy and espionage. The period from the Restoration to May 1663 may be regarded as an apprenticeship for him. As an Irish protestant the fears and discontents of his fellow protestants were something he shared. Their discontent grew quickly into a serious conspiracy which could have led to a nation-wide Irish rebellion in the early 1660s. Blood found himself at the heart of this conspiracy, though the exact reasons for his involvement remain obscure. During the period 1660–1 it is possible that he was deprived of some of his lands, such 'hard usage' turning him against the new regime. What is certainly clear is that he was very active in engaging men to join the plot in Dublin in 1662.[10]

When the plot collapsed in May 1663 Blood found himself on the run from the authorities and in danger of certain execution if caught. That this did not happen was partly the result of his unusual talents for clandestine activities, disguises and, it must be said, an ability for disappearing at the appropriate moment. Despite the dangerous circumstances Blood remained undaunted and made repeated efforts to re-unite the remaining conspirators. Such activity meant that Ireland eventually became too dangerous and so he took ship to England. The next few months he spent wandering around the north of England.[11] The Northern Plot, which had run parallel to that in Ireland, was broken in the autumn of 1663. With this Blood appears to have made the decision to travel south to London and then on to that asylum for political refugees in the seventeenth century, the Dutch Republic.[12] Blood's first visit to the Netherlands was a short one and he was almost certainly back in London by 1664. Unrest in the country was growing as war with the Dutch approached and plotting amongst the radicals resumed with renewed fervour. During the next few months Blood was allegedly involved in a variety of plots.[13] In May 1665 he was reported by one government agent to be organising meetings in Coleman Street, an area notorious in the city as a stronghold of the disaffected. It is also clear that

[10] For the problems of Ireland and the plot see *Calendar of State Papers Ireland*, 1663–5, pp. 111, 265, 269. Also T. Carte, *A History of the Life of James Duke of Ormonde* (3 vols., 1736), II, pp. 261 *et passim.* Also Bod. Lib. Carte MSS 35, fo. 52. T. W. Moody, F. X. Martin and F. J. Byrne, eds., *A New History of Ireland*, III *Early Modern Ireland, 1534–1691* (Oxford, 1991), pp. 424–5. For Blood's land see *HMC*, 9th Report, pp. 126, 176.

[11] Bod. Lib. Rawlinson MSS A, 185, fos. 473–5.

[12] PRO SP 84/168, fo. 48.

[13] In association with John Lockyer. For Lockyer see *BDBR*, II, pp. 198–9.

he remained in London during the plague which afflicted the city. He survived, a fact which he considered a sign of God's blessings on his activities.[14]

It is reasonable at this point to ask how Blood managed to remain at large for so long, for he always appeared to be one jump ahead of the authorities – that is if we presume he was in fact regarded as hostile to the regime. As will be seen, there is some evidence to suggest otherwise, or at least it suggests that Blood was not all he appeared to be on the surface. Part of this evidence lies in the address book of Joseph Williamson. The Williamson document contains an entry concerning correspondence which was coming from a 'Mr T. B.' in Zeeland in the United Provinces and we have Blood's own evidence that this is where he landed in the spring of 1666 while on a mission of importance for the rebel cause.[15] If we assume that Blood was an agent of the government at this time, and the evidence is further examined below, then the cautious Williamson would have studiously avoided having him arrested, having done exactly this in other cases.[16]

Blood's mission to Europe began around March 1666 when he undertook to travel with John Lockyer to the United Provinces. The eventual destination was to be Switzerland and, as Edmund Ludlow later recollected, the mission was to 'perswade me on behalf of friends in Holland to repaire with Col[onel] Sidney to Paris & there to treate with that King & the States Agent for the carrying on of a designe against our common enemy, and for ye accompanying of me thither'.[17] The mission to Ludlow is significant. Blood and another exile, John Phelps, met Ludlow at Lausanne and Blood was not impressed with either Ludlow's attitude or with the man himself. He considered Ludlow 'very unable for such an employment'. Ludlow, he claimed was more content in 'writing a history as he called it'[18] and rejected the overtures made to him. The mission thus ended in failure and by September 1666 Blood was back in London, for on his own evidence he was nearly arrested in the city during the period of the Great Fire.[19] It is also clear that he became peripherally involved in the Pentland Rising in Scotland later in that year. When this was crushed Blood, by now entirely predictably, escaped. He returned briefly to Ireland, but was pursued by the authorities there and soon left. This interest in his

[14] PRO SP 29/121, fo. 131; Bod. Lib. Rawlinson MSS A, 185, fo. 474.
[15] PRO SP 9/32, fo. 213; Bod. Lib. Rawlinson MSS A, 185, fo. 473v, entries 38–44; Ludlow, *Voyce*, pp. 1111, 1114, 1265.
[16] See PRO SP 9/26, fo. 131.
[17] Ludlow, *Voyce*, p. 1265.
[18] Blood quoted in *A Modest Vindication of Oliver Cromwell from the Unjust Accusation of Lieut-Gen. Ludlow* (1698), p. 2.
[19] Bod. Lib. Rawlinson MSS A, 185, fo. 473v.

whereabouts continued both in Lancashire and then in Westmorland.[20] At this juncture in his career, evidently tiring of the 'mutinous courses of life',[21] Blood took his family back to London. The investigations made by the government after the attack on Ormonde in 1670 uncovered the fact that Mary Blood and her family set up in an apothecary's shop in Shoreditch. Using the alias of Hunt, Blood's eldest son, also called Thomas, was soon apprenticed to an apothecary in Southwark.[22] Thomas Blood himself took on the identity of one Doctor Ayliffe or Allen and proceeded to 'practise physick' in a form of semi-retirement. The question of the qualifications necessary to practise medicine does not seem to have arisen; or if it did Blood had the necessary guile, or help, to overcome it.[23] In the event he was not in practice for very long.

July 1667 saw the country in an uproar over what was considered a 'most insolent act against the king and the government'.[24] The cause of this furore was the organised escape of the notable rebel, Captain John Mason. An ex-army general Baptist and Northern Plot conspirator, Mason had been on his way to trial and probable execution at York until Blood and his men had appeared at a small village not far from Doncaster called Darrington, shot and wounded five of Mason's guards and absconded with their friend. This incident was described by Edmund Ludlow as 'agreeable work for ye Lord'.[25] Having briefly and dramatically surfaced, Blood just as quickly disappeared to resume his bogus medical practices.

On the evening of 6 December 1670 five men stopped at the Bull's Head, a tavern in Charing Cross. They remained there for some time until a coach passed by the tavern on its way to the Haymarket and Pall Mall. It carried the sixty-year-old James Butler, Duke of Ormonde, and was taking him back to his residence at Clarendon House. The visitors left quickly after the coach had passed and according to one eyewitness they were led by a very 'fine man' in a brown periwig.[26] Thomas Blood, now by some obscure means advanced to the rank of colonel, was intent upon the

[20] For the rising see I. B. Cowan, *The Scottish Covenanters, 1660–1688* (Edinburgh, 1976); J. Buckroyd, *Church and State in Scotland 1660–1681* (Edinburgh, 1980), pp. 65–7; C. S. Terry, *The Pentland Rising and Rullion Green* (Glasgow, 1905), R. Louis Stevenson, 'The Pentland Rising: A Page of History 1666', in *The Scottish Stories and Essays* (Edinburgh, 1989), pp. 204–18. For Blood in Lancashire see PRO SP 29/189, fo. 20; *CSPD*, 1667, pp. 1–2. Also Bod. Lib. Carte MSS 35, fo. 54.

[21] *Remarks*, p. 223.

[22] *HMC*, 8th Report, p. 155; *Remarks*, p. 223.

[23] One of his associates and the man to whom he apprenticed his son was formerly 'a surgeon in Goffe's regiment & then in ... Briens'. See House of Lords RO Main Papers HL, 352 (e6), fo. 76v.

[24] A. Browning, ed., *The Memoirs of Sir John Reresby* (Glasgow, 1936), pp. 69–70.

[25] Ludlow, *Voyce*, p. 1265. One of the men with Mason was the spy William Leving. See above, Chapter 5.

[26] *HMC*, 8th Report, p. 155; Carte, *Ormonde*, II, p. 421.

abduction and assassination of his old enemy Ormonde. In the three years since the rescue of Mason, Blood, despite rumours of his death, had been relatively quiet.[27] There is little doubt that his various activities had continued but without much success. At various times warrants had been issued for his arrest and searches made for his person. The authorities were perhaps justified in being apprehensive for the scheme to abduct Ormonde was undoubtedly being hatched at this time. Moreover it was, as with most of the schemes in which Blood was involved, a plan somewhat outlandish in its style. This was not only to abduct the duke but also, according to one source, hang him at Tyburn. An alternative given to Arlington by an informer was that the attempt was made 'not to rob or kill . . . [Ormonde] . . . but to carry him to some obscure place and oblige him to ransom himself at ten or twenty thousand pounds'.[28] Although Blood later claimed that revenge had been the principal motive in this mission it seems clear that another person of note had engaged him to do the deed. The suspicion falls heavily upon the decidedly wayward George Villiers, 2nd Duke of Buckingham.

Buckingham's associations with a variety of prominent dissidents, radicals and republicans are well known. There is little doubt that he regarded them as useful for his political ambitions. Buckingham, according to Roger North, 'sought to set up for one of the heads of that faction'.[29] He was a friend to nonconformists and in favour of toleration, stressing its economic advantages to the state.[30] These connections had eventually led him into trouble in 1667, as we have already seen.[31] We may add to this his frequent and occasionally violent feuds with his rivals at court; he took part in the political destruction of Clarendon in 1667, created an intense rivalry with Arlington, quarrelled with the Duke of York and 'hated the duke of Ormonde mortally'.[32] Buckingham was thus a dangerous mixture of the frivolous courtier and interfering politician. He may well be seen as a dilettante of politics in the period: lightweight perhaps, but with a ruthless streak. In other words he was a dangerous man to cross lightly.

K. H. D. Haley has pointed out the possibility of some personal animosity between Buckingham and Ormonde due to a breakdown of a proposed marriage alliance between the two families in 1664.[33] In any case, mutual antipathy between the two was a natural result of both temperament and

[27] *CSPD*, 1667, p. 488. He had been seriously wounded during the Darrington incident.

[28] *HMC*, 8th Report, p. 155. Also Echard, *History of England*, III, p. 363; D. Hume, *The History of Great Britain* (2 vols., 1754–7), II, pp. 207–8.

[29] R. North, *The Lives of the Norths* (2 vols., 1896), I, p. 68. Also Clarendon, *Life*, pp. 1197–201, 1231.

[30] See M. Lee, *The Cabal* (Urbana, 1965), pp. 173–4.

[31] See above, Chapter 5.

[32] Carte, *Ormonde*, II, p. 424.

[33] Haley, *Shaftesbury*, p. 188.

political outlook. Buckingham was generally thought to have instigated the recall of Ormonde from Ireland in February 1669. There are still some doubts about Buckingham's actual influence on this question and it may well be that the removal of Ormonde was a calculated step by Charles himself.[34] Even if he was being used as a cover for the king's political manoeuvres, Buckingham was certainly out to consolidate his power. He kept up the attack on Ormonde even after the latter's return to England. If, in Buckingham's mind, Ormonde was far better out of the way, then there is little doubt that it would have been best for the duke's interests if this situation could be made permanent by the old man's death. Buckingham's associations with the political underground would have soon uncovered the right man for the task. The obvious choice would have been a man who was not only intelligent enough to do the job well but who also had a grudge against Ormonde. That man was Blood.

The connections between Blood and Buckingham at this stage of the former's career are somewhat tenuous, but they undoubtedly existed and contemporaries were quick to perceive them.[35] A letter from Blood to his wife in November 1670 suggests an agreement was being reached with someone in that very month. There is every possibility that it was Buckingham.[36] The association between the two men was also to continue after Blood's capture in 1671. In the event Blood's attempt on Ormonde on the evening of 6 December 1670 went badly wrong. The would-be assassins, or kidnappers, having caught their man were forced to flee, leaving a prostrate Ormonde in the highway.[37] The audacity of such a scheme being perpetrated on such a notable as Ormonde outraged the authorities sufficiently to allow the sitting of a special committee. The discovery of the three principals, Thomas Blood, Thomas Blood junior (alias Hunt the highwayman), and Richard Halliwell did not take very long. Indeed the speed with which Arlington discovered the names of those involved is suspicious in itself. The homes of the three were raided but they had long gone. A price of £1,000 was set on their heads for the outrage but they continued to elude the authorities.[38]

In the late seventeenth century the Tower of London was the main citadel of the kingdom. The Tower was, and remains, a formidable structure. For the casual visitor to Restoration London it retained a variety of entertainments. Of these the menagerie and the jewel house were the most

[34] See J. I. McGuire, 'Why was Ormonde Dismissed in 1669?', *Irish Historical Studies*, 18, 1973, pp. 295–312; and J. C. Beckett, 'The Irish Vice-Royalty in the Restoration Period', *THRS*, 5th series, 10, 1970, pp. 53–72.

[35] Carte, *Ormonde*, II, p. 425; also House of Lords RO Main Papers, HL 352 (g6), 17 November 1670.

[36] *ibid.*

[37] *Remarks*, p. 226; Carte, *Ormonde*, II, 420–2; *HMC*, 8th Report, pp. 154–6.

[38] *ibid.*; *CSPD*, 1670, p. 567.

popular. The latter held, in the words of Samuel Pepys, the 'crown and scepters and rich plate'[39] of the king. The actual regalia were not in fact as valuable as they seemed and the security immediately surrounding the Crown Jewels was also poor. They fell under the authority of Talbot Edwards, an aged ex-soldier, who was the assistant keeper of the jewels. He lived with his family above the room in which they were kept in Martin Tower. Edwards was permitted to make some profit out of his charge by taking a fee from curious tourists, such as Pepys for example. It would therefore come as no surprise to him that in April 1671 he had the dubious honour of a visit from one Doctor Ayliffe and his 'wife'. The doctor, dressed in the 'habit of a parson'[40] had been most interested in the jewels. His 'wife', however, had unfortunately been taken ill. The obliging Edwards allowed the lady to recover in his own apartments and she was there tended to by his wife and daughter. Doctor Ayliffe, pleased that such Christian charity should be shown to strangers, became a frequent visitor to the Edwards household as a result and a friend of the easily flattered Edwards. As a sign of this burgeoning friendship Ayliffe suggested that a match might be made between Edwards' daughter and his nephew. It was, of course, eagerly accepted. Thus did Thomas Blood, alias Doctor Ayliffe, gain frequent access to the Tower.

Terms for the match were soon agreed and on 9 May 1671 at around 7 o'clock in the morning five men rode up to the Tower. One of them remained outside to look after the horses.[41] Blood, disguised as Ayliffe, Thomas Blood junior, alias Hunt the highwayman, Captain Robert Perrot[42] and Captain Richard Halliwell made their way to Martin Tower.[43] There they were met by Edwards. To pass the time until his 'wife' arrived Blood suggested that the regalia be shown to his friends. Halliwell remained on guard while the others proceeded to the room on the lowest floor of the Tower. Once in the proximity of the jewels Edwards was quickly overpowered by several 'unkind knocks on the head'.[44] The jewels were then distributed between the three men. At this point, in true seventeenth-century fashion, 'providence' took a hand. Edwards' son, who had been abroad as a soldier, took this rather inopportune moment to return home from the wars after many years. He naturally went to see his father. Forewarned by Halliwell, Blood and his men had left the jewel house and were on their way to their horses. The younger Edwards on discovering the

[39] Pepys, *Diary*, IX, p. 172.

[40] BL Harl. MSS 6859, fos. 1–17, fo. 1. Calling himself Ayliffe or Ailoffe.

[41] This was William Smith, a Fifth Monarchist and a known accomplice of Blood. He was captured in 1678 and Blood interrogated him for the regime. *CSPD*, 1678, pp. 300–1.

[42] Perrot later fought at Sedgemoor and was interrogated by James II before his execution. See BL Lansdowne MSS 1152, fo. 238.

[43] BL Harl. MSS 6859, fo. 5.

[44] *Remarks*, p. 228.

crime naturally raised the alarm. He and Captain Martin Beckman led the chase after the men.[45] Although Halliwell and Hunt reached their horses and rode off, the latter ran straight into the pole of a cart which had turned in front of him and was subsequently arrested. After a brief struggle, in which a shot was fired, Blood and Perrot were also taken. Typically Blood seems to have been undaunted by the experience and is alleged to have merrily told Beckman, 'It was a gallant attempt ... [but] ... it was for a Crown'.[46] A statement which sums up both a part of his character and the attitude he was to take.[47]

The capture of such a formidable set of outlaws did not provoke the set of consequences which were generally expected. When examined by the magistrates in the Tower, Blood demanded to see the king to answer the charges and to everyone's surprise Charles agreed to the request. While this may have been idle curiosity on Charles' part, it is unlikely. Charles had interrogated and was to continue to interrogate, rebels or informers on occasion and thus this should not be seen as particularly unusual. However, it is clear that Blood had other great persons working on his behalf. One of these is thought to have been Buckingham and the other was almost certainly Arlington, perhaps prompted by his right-hand man Joseph Williamson. It may be that Charles and Buckingham both had motives for keeping Blood quiet and granting him an interview where the audience would be more select than in an open court. One theory which has been postulated is that the attack on Ormonde had not been Blood and Buckingham's alone and that Barbara Villiers, Countess of Castlemaine, Duchess of Cleveland, and erstwhile mistress to the king may have had a share in the plot.[48] Thus both mistress and minister may have had cause to shield their former employee. Charles himself is unlikely to have escaped criticism if Blood had denounced the king's mistress as one of the authors of his attempt. However, there were other equally important reasons for keeping the valuable Blood alive.

The interview with Charles took place on 12 May 1671. The known details of what passed between the two men are sparse, but some hints do exist. Blood admitted his involvement in the rescue of Mason and the attack on Ormonde; he refused to name his fellow conspirators, lied about

[45] This was the same Martin Beckman who had also been a spy in 1662–3, a case of a poacher turned gamekeeper.

[46] BL Harl. MSS 6859, fos. 1–17, fo. 5.

[47] For all the events see BL Harl. MSS 6859, fos. 1–17; *Remarks*, pp. 227, 229; Carte, *Ormonde*, II, p. 422; *CSPD*, 1671, pp. 225, 237, 244, 300, 414; *HMC*, 6th Report, p. 370; BL Add. MSS 36916, fo. 233; PRO SP 104/176, fo. 299; Bod. Lib. Carte MSS 69, fos. 69, 164.

[48] For this suggestion see Lady Burghclere, *The Life of James, First Duke of Ormonde, 1610–1688* (2 vols., 1912), II, pp. 190–1.

his age and cheekily claimed that he had been engaged in a plot to kill Charles while the latter was bathing in the Thames but, 'his heart misgave him out of an awe of His Majesty'. Having also been asked what he would do if his life were spared Blood replied that he would endeavour to deserve it.[49] The interview over he was sent back to the Tower until the king and his ministers had decided what to do to him.[50] It soon became clear that he was a special catch for the regime and he was most fortunate in being captured in 1671.

The reason for Blood's good fortune must be sought in the wide political sphere of Restoration England, and specifically in the consequences of the secret treaty of Dover of May 1670. Part of the political preparation for the war against the Dutch was the move towards what was to become the Declaration of Indulgence of 15 March 1672. Faced with another major war against the Dutch it was entirely logical that the regime should seek some sort of compromise with those elements which had threatened to create such disturbances in the last war.[51] Thus the first obvious requirement was in-depth intelligence of the activities of the nonconformist sects and more militant elements, and in the spring of 1671 the regime had the great fortune to have a man whom Edmund Ludlow described as 'having been aquainted with most of the secret passages that have of late been transacted in order to ye reviving of the Lords witnesses'[52] fall into their hands. To a minister such as Arlington, we may be sure, Blood was not just someone to be immediately eliminated, but a man who could still be used for what the regime perceived as the greater ends. Moreover he was someone who may already have proved his worth in the mid-1660s.

It was thus that the way was cleared for Blood's public rehabilitation. Arlington was most assiduous in making Blood's peace with Ormonde and on 18 July 1671 dined at the Tower bringing with him the warrant for Blood's release.[53] On 29 August 1671 Blood received a full pardon for all of

[49] Carte, *Ormonde*, II, pp. 422–3; *CSPV*, 1671–2, p. 49; *HMC*, 4th Report, p. 370. The plot to shoot Charles was an unlikely scheme and was undoubtedly a fantasy on Blood's part. Greaves appears to accept the story at face value, which given Blood's character and the situation seems an odd thing to do.

[50] It is from this period that the forged document PRO SP 29/290, fo. 11 emerges. This led W. C. Abbott (*Colonel Thomas Blood: Crown Stealer* (1911)) amongst others astray. It is clearly not in Blood's hand and Williamson endorsed it 'a foolish letter'. Far from being the 'stunning document' R. L. Greaves claims it as, the letter was forged as part of the political in-fighting of the period. Greaves' long discourse upon this letter is therefore rather redundant as it is based upon a totally false premise. See Greaves, *Enemies Under His Feet*, pp. 212–13. See also Browning, *Danby*, I, pp. 84–7.

[51] *Miscellanea Aulica*, p. 66. [52] Ludlow, *Voyce*, p. 1265.

[53] *CSPD*, 1671, p. 385. Perrott was released while Blood junior remained in the Tower, perhaps as insurance against his father's activities. Blood wrote a token letter of apology

his previous crimes and a grant of Irish lands worth £500 per annum.[54] The turning of the former rebel appears to have been rather too public for some. It is a most curious event. Williamson was one of the first to complain, as in his eyes it devalued Blood.[55] No other agent was turned so publicly or in so spectacular a manner and what was behind it can now only be guessed. One possibility is that Blood was being used as an example to his still-outlawed friends of what benefits they could expect should they also come in. The other is that he was being justly rewarded for services rendered. Of course, it leads to speculation as to just how far back Blood's 'double agent' status went. This is especially interesting when we consider his possible Civil War royalist connections. He had undoubtedly come in this time, however, and almost immediately this began to have effects in the political underground.

It is clear from the available evidence that during this period Blood was no common informer, a breed with which later Stuart society was particularly infested. As might be expected, his work for the government was on a far grander scale. He was moving in the highest of circles. He was often seen in the royal apartments and openly frequented the court.[56] He was also assiduous in his attendance at the offices of the Secretary of State. Here his main contact was Joseph Williamson. The shrewd and indefatigable Williamson thought of Blood as a very valuable asset. According to him Blood was worth 'ten times ye value [of the] Crowne'. The 'Masters of Blood', as he put it, had clearly picked up someone quite extraordinary in the deep political games which Williamson played.[57] Williamson also clearly distrusted Blood. Nevertheless the meetings between the two were frequent and, as usual, minutely noted by the under-secretary.

The question of what exactly Blood was doing in the 1670s is therefore of some significance and because of the complex nature of his activities it is perhaps best to make some sort of functional definition of his work. In the main, the activities of the 1670s can be divided into four areas. The first of these was mentioned by Arlington to the Committee of Foreign Affairs on 22 October 1671. He told them that 'upon the pardoning of Blood he went away among his bretheren to bring in some of his friends on assurance of pardon'.[58] Soon afterwards many arrests were made of old ex-army officers and militants. Blood was naming names to the government in return for the favour shown to him. Other radicals also began to come in persuaded by

to Ormonde; Bod. Lib. Carte MSS 69, fo. 164. For Ormonde's opinion on the affair see Bod. Lib. Carte MSS 69, fo. 69.

54 *CSPD*, 1671, p. 421; Carte, *Ormonde*, II, p. 423; *HMC*, 7th Report, p. 464.

55 *CSPD*, 1671–2, p. 9.

56 Bod. Lib. Carte MSS 69, fo. 69; *HMC*, 6th Report, p. 370; Carte, *Ormonde*, II, p. 424.

57 Bod. Lib. MSS Eng. Letters, d.37, fo. 84.

58 PRO SP 104/176, fo. 315.

Blood that they would receive their pardons. Many in fact did so,[59] and the benefits to the government of the neutralisation of such notables was no doubt enormous. His second area of operations was as a domestic intelligencer who acted both as mediator for 'several parties, being well with the sectaries and enthusiasts';[60] this also enabled him to spy upon them. He provided Williamson with information upon the activities, habits and demands of the dissenters; information which was used to frame the Declaration of Indulgence. He intervened on behalf of sectaries who had fallen foul of the second Conventicle Act and also acted as a channel between the court and certain Presbyterian leaders. How effective he was in this is debatable. By December 1671 Williamson was suggesting that the government break with Blood for the 'phanaticks ... will not trust him any longer'.[61] Upon the publication of the Declaration of Indulgence Blood was regarded by many as the means through which the necessary licences could be obtained[62] and he was not above making a profit out of the system.[63] His third role was that of a counter-intelligence agent. This role emerged particularly after the outbreak of the Dutch War in March 1672. Blood was used to spy not only on the Dutch, but also upon those extremists who had refused to come in.[64]

Lastly, and most dangerously for himself, Blood had taken up an involvement in court politics. This was a dangerous game for anyone to play and there is little doubt that by doing so Blood increased his enemies. From his daily resort at White's coffee house near the Royal Exchange[65] he seems to have been free for hire by any enterprising minister. He not only kept up his connections with Arlington and Williamson, but was also reported to have 'gone off to Lauderdale'.[66] Other customers may have included Danby and James, Duke of York.[67] Blood's attitude to this aspect

59 *CSPD*, 1671, p. 565 is an example.

60 Evelyn, *Diary*, III, p. 576. Blood spied on Sir Robert Peyton and 'his gang'; *CSPD*, 1677–8, p. 388. See also *CSPD*, 1672–3, p. 595.

61 PRO SP 29/294, fo. 139.

62 For Blood's work see L. Echard, *History of England*, III, p. 286; G. Lyon-Turner, *Original Records of Early Non-Conformity Under Persecution and Indulgence* (3 vols., 1914); F. Bate, *The Declaration of Indulgence 1672: A Study in the Rise of Organized Dissent* (1908). Also W. Pope, *The Life of Seth, Lord Bishop of Salisbury* (Oxford, 1961), pp. 73–4. Also W. Veitch, *Memoirs* (2 vols., 1825), I, p. 15.

63 One correspondent noted the detention of the personal licences until Blood heard about his money, *CSPD*, 1671–2, p. 589.

64 For Blood's war work see A. Marshall, 'Opening Shots in the Third Dutch War' (unpublished paper); also PRO SP 84/188, fo. 125; PRO SP 84/195, fos. 24, 52; PRO SP 77/43, fo. 18. For his activities in England see PRO SP 29/317, fo. 94; PRO SP 29/332, fo. 68; PRO SP 29/333, fo. 181. For his pension as a spy PRO SP 29/366, fo. 25.

65 B. Lillywhite, *London Coffee Houses* (1963), p. 639.

66 *CSPD*, 1671–2, p. 46; also Edinburgh University Library, Mic. Dup., 653–6. Coltness Family Papers, reel 1, section 7, nos. 1, 2, 15.

67 For these connections see below.

of his career was, as it turned out, a dangerously flippant one. He is alleged to have said, 'It's no matter if one let[s] me fall, another takes me up. I'm the best tool they have.'[68]

III

M.R.D. Foot has wisely pointed out that 'One obstacle to the historian of any secret service is . . . inherent in his subject matter: the traces left for him to study are likely to be few.'[69] Moreover any attempt to trace the career of a man who lived and operated in the shadowy underground world of conspiracy, as Blood did, can be fraught with difficulties. While such difficulties can be exaggerated they should not be forgotten. It would therefore be valuable at this point to examine certain puzzling aspects of the evidence concerning Blood in the period between the collapse of the Dublin plot in May 1663 and his capture in 1671.

It may be stated at the outset that Blood himself left no memoirs as such. The circumstantial evidence suggests that his contemporary biographer of 1680 obtained some information from either Blood himself or someone close to him.[70] Some of the details in that life can be confirmed from other sources and it seems to be surprisingly accurate when compared with other examples of this genre. Blood did, of course, leave limited amounts of correspondence, but the majority of this has not survived due to the nature of his career. Conspiracies are in any case often things of word and deed rather than documentary evidence. Such correspondence as does exist therefore dates from the more settled and open period after 1671 when he was working for the government.

One particularly valuable and very personal document which does stem from the period in question should be noted. When Blood was captured in May 1671 it is said that upon being searched there was found upon him a small note book 'wherein he had set down ... signal deliverences from eminant [*sic*] dangers'.[71] The original of this book is now unfortunately lost, but a copy of its contents does exist, contained in a document in the Pepys manuscripts in the Bodleian Library. The notes therein, probably set down around 1671, throw new light upon Blood's own religious beliefs, character and his career. They consist of seventy 'deliverences since I was for ye Lord's cause', and a further twenty-two moral and religious precepts which Blood thought worthy of noting down.[72] They are a product of

[68] *CSPD*, 1671–2, p. 46. See also *Williamson Correspondence*, I, pp. 14–15; *Essex Papers*, I, pp. 90–1.
[69] M. R. D. Foot, *SOE in France* (1966), p. 449.
[70] The author was possibly Richard Halliwell as the pamphlet is initialled RH.
[71] *HMC*, 6th Report, p. 370. [72] Bod. Lib. Rawlinson MSS A, 185, fo. 473.

non-conformist reflection and a belief in divine providence as it affected his own life. On a basic level in the seventy single-line 'deliverences' we possess a basic framework for Blood's career during the period from 1663 to 1671. The entries themselves are undated, but they run in chronological order and certain entries can be positively dated to a specific year. These entries provide a key to the whole. Taken in conjunction with other available evidence we can begin to build up a picture of Blood's activities during the period in question.

The book is especially valuable for the events in Blood's life during the crucial year of 1666. All of Blood's previous modern biographers have noted the odd anomalies which exist in his fleeting appearance in the state papers for that year. We have already seen that in 1666 Blood went on a mission to Europe and eventually visited Edmund Ludlow. His part in the schemes and negotiations between the English exiles and the Franco-Dutch alliance appears to have begun in March 1666 when he undertook to travel to Europe with John Lockyer, a fellow conspirator, to persuade Ludlow to join Algernon Sidney on a trip to Paris to negotiate with the allies. The mission appears to have begun badly when the two men were taken prisoner in Zeeland by the Dutch authorities.[73] They possessed no passports and were held as English spies; there were possibly good grounds for Dutch suspicions of Blood at least. But Ludlow noted that the two men were eventually released with the aid of John Phelps.[74] It is possible to confirm that one of the two men picked up by the Dutch in Zeeland was Blood by entry 39 in the pocket book. This refers to his being a 'prizoner in Zealand'[75] and although undated falls between two entries which deal specifically with the plague in London and the Great Fire of September 1666.[76] Both of the documents thus provide independent confirmation of Blood's whereabouts.

Free to continue their journey Blood joined Phelps and both men undertook to visit Ludlow on Sidney's behalf.[77] During his travels at this time Blood was using the alias Morton and appears to have been introduced to Ludlow as such.[78] It was only at a later date that Ludlow seems to have discovered who his visitor had been and he or his amanuensis inserted the correct name above the line in the manuscript 'A Voyce From The Watch Tower'.[79] In the event the journey proved to be a fruitless one. Ludlow was

[73] *ibid.*, fo. 473v; and Ludlow, *Voyce*, p. 1111.
[74] Phelps was clerk to the High Court of Justice and a regicide in exile.
[75] Bod. Lib. Rawlinson MSS A, 185, fo. 473v, entry 39.
[76] *ibid.*, fo. 473v, entries 38, 44.
[77] Ludlow, *Voyce*, pp. 1111, 1114, 1265.
[78] *ibid.*, p. 1114. The choice of 'Morton' is unusual, his normal alias was a variation on Allen.
[79] *ibid.*, p. 1265.

content in writing his history and rejected the overtures made to him. He did not trust the Dutch, citing the case of the three regicides abducted by Downing as an example of their treacherous nature.[80]

There may also have been other reasons for Ludlow's reluctance to join the party. A piece of intercepted intelligence, which also provides independent confirmation of the visit, notes that Ludlow had intelligence that there were 'several persons sent out of England to destroy ye friends wheresoever they may be met with'.[81] The presence of government-inspired assassins in Europe at this time should have come as no surprise to Ludlow for some of them, as we shall see, had murdered the regicide John Lisle in Lausanne in August 1664. A further point to note perhaps is that the man who was to escort Ludlow to Paris was to be Blood, alias Morton.[82] Two questions are prompted by this case. Firstly why, aside from his natural caution, should Blood use an alias with those whom he regarded as friends and who were moreover the highest elements within the exile community, unless he had something to hide? Secondly, and to move into the realm of speculation, did Ludlow find something in Blood's manner which disconcerted him and made him even more wary of travelling to France, the grave of other notable exiles? Speculative questions these may be, but there exist other documents which appear to suggest that during the mid-1660s Blood had definite connections with the Stuart government. It is to these documents that we should perhaps turn for an answer to the mystery.

In his 1911 essay on Blood, W. C. Abbott noted two documents[83] in the state papers for this period which led him to speculate that Blood may have been 'playing a double part'[84] and providing information to the government. Abbott's essay, though sound in general, is seriously flawed by his apparent failure to examine any of the evidence in its original form. This led him in one instance to cite one document as genuine when it is an obvious forgery.[85] Maurice Petherick in his short popular essay claims that there is 'no definite record ... [that Blood was in the pay of the government] ... and his actions later make it improbable'.[86] Surprisingly, for his essay on Blood is also littered with errors, G. Lyon Turner, is correct in his suggestion that the two documents are misdated.[87] It is clear that the two

[80] See Worden's introduction to his edition of Ludlow, *Voyce*, pp. 12–13.
[81] PRO SP 84/180, fo. 62.
[82] Ludlow, *Voyce*, p. 1265.
[83] These documents are PRO SP 29/140, fo. 93, dated August 1665 on the document and December 1665 in the calendar; PRO SP 29/173, fo. 131, undated but placed in the calendar as September 1666. In fact both documents are from the post-1671 period.
[84] W. C. Abbot, *Colonel Thomas Blood, Crown Stealer* (1911), p. 123.
[85] It also misled Richard Greaves as we have seen above.
[86] Petherick, *Restoration Rogues*, p. 17.
[87] Lyon-Turner, *Original Records*, III, pp. 218–45.

letters in the state papers for 1666 must date from the period after 1671 when Blood was working in the aftermath of the Declaration of Indulgence. Internal and external evidence confirms this. Both these documents are genuine and are related by the inclusion of Jonathan Jennings who was committed to Aylesbury gaol in 1666. In December 1671 Blood was agitating to have Jennings' 'pardon perfected' and the man himself was given a licence under the Declaration of Indulgence in 1672. The general tenor of the documents therefore suggests that they should be placed in the post-1671 period and they can contribute nothing to this problem.[88]

There is, however, a document of more significance for Blood's real allegiance than either of these letters. This document is, of course, Williamson's own address book. It is not primarily an address book of intelligence agents, though it does include some interesting and significant names in that field. There are over 150 names in this document and from internal evidence it can be dated to the period 1663–7. Many of the names therein can only come from the mid-1660s.[89] The most significant entry for the present purposes concerns a 'Mr T. B.'[90] with his correspondence coming from Zeeland. Moreover he was to have been writing to either John Taylor at the Post House or Thomas Harris. If the entry is broken down it may immediately be noted that the name Thomas Harris is a code name for the office of the Secretary of State. There is evidence of this name being used in other documents.[91] A further point to be emphasised perhaps is that the entry is concerned solely with incoming mail from Zeeland and that the agent did not give Williamson an address for contacting him; obviously he was a very cautious man. Given that Thomas Blood is now known to have been in Zeeland in 1666 when he was captured by the Dutch authorities and imprisoned as a spy, what are the chances he is the person in question? It may be, of course, that the entry refers to another man and indeed there was in the 1670s an agent operating under the occasional use of the initials T. B. This was Thomas Barnes, but there are many problems in linking Barnes with this entry, as his first correspondence does not begin until 1675.[92] It has been suggested that Thomas Barnes is a pseudonym for Blood; however, a comparison of their correspondence shows the hands to be significantly different.

The conclusion which must be drawn therefore is that this entry does refer to Blood and relates to the period when he was in Europe. Though the

[88] See PRO SP 29/140, fo. 93; PRO SP 29/173, fo. 131 (see n. 83 for datings of these records). Also *CSPD*, 1672, p. 400; PRO SP 29/295, fo. 2.

[89] John Thurloe is one example of this. He died in 1668.

[90] PRO SP 9/32, fo. 213.

[91] It was also used by Colonel Bamfield when he wrote to Arlington; *CSPD*, 1663–4, pp. 392, 465.

[92] *CSPD*, 1675–6, p. 34.

general pattern of his career would seem to be at odds with such a theory, as we have already seen in the general context of intelligence activities at the time, such an idea is not altogether unique. Other agents before Blood had played this game. Indeed Joseph Bamfield had been at one point in his career simultaneously working for Arlington, de Witt and the exiles. There are many reasons why Blood should have been operating as a double agent, even if this proved to be a brief turn around in his career before going 'rogue' with the rescue of Mason. It would certainly provide a further explanation of how he was able to escape capture for so long, how he escaped punishment in May 1671 and why he was treated so generously at the same time; Arlington and Williamson would perhaps work a little bit harder for a former agent. The question remains unresolved, but if Blood was supplying information to the regime in 1666 then perhaps Ludlow was right to remain in Vervay. Otherwise he might well have found himself on board a ship back to England for his trial and execution.

The available evidence concerning Blood's actual religious beliefs is, on the surface, apparently slender. That he was a protestant and a nonconformist is certain; where he stood within the milieu of puritan faith is less clear. Contemporary evidence suggests that Blood found his way to God through Presbyterianism. Since denominational labels in the seventeenth-century England were not always used with any particular accuracy, this could mean any one of a number of things. However, there is some evidence for placing Blood, albeit very loosely, in this particular category.[93] At most, he can be seen as a Calvinist with strong leanings towards a providential faith. For a more detailed examination of Blood's spiritual life we must turn to the pocket book taken from him in May 1671.

It has already been noted how this document can be used on one level in detailing Blood's career, but it can also be used to outline something of his spiritual nature. With this document we can firmly fix Thomas Blood as adhering to the mainstream of nonconformist thought. Furthermore we can build up a picture of a hitherto unrevealed spiritual side of his character, tempered with the knowledge that we do not get the full picture of the man from notes of this kind alone, and they must be placed into context. Indeed, were we to know nothing of Blood's career at all, we would undoubtedly regard this document as the product of a deeply religious man, given to spiritual self-analysis. It is, of course, possible for a man of action to have a spiritual side to his nature, but it should be recalled perhaps that prior to an examination of this document, which seems to have lain undisturbed by any of the previous biographers of Blood, he had

[93] In 1676 he was attending a Presbyterian gathering in Westminster led by Mr Cotton. Thomas Blood junior was also labelled a Presbyterian by one of the witnesses after the attack on Ormonde. *HMC*, Duke of Leeds, p. 15; *HMC*, 8th Report, pt 1, p. 155.

not been regarded in anything other than one-dimensional terms. For the first time therefore we are able to perceive Thomas Blood as a more fully rounded and three-dimensional figure.

There is revealed for the first time, for example, Blood's intense belief in providence. This was a common-enough phenomenon amongst seventeenth-century nonconformists.[94] It stems from the 'conviction that God both ordained and spoke through life's events'.[95] Blood, as so many others of his time, looked for a pattern in his life. It may well be that he needed to find such a pattern in order to sustain himself while he was living at what were in effect the edges of society. The life of a rebel or spy was not an easy or an altogether romantic one, being filled with psychological tension as well as physical danger. To a great extent the person involved in such a world was living a lie. He was, to use one analogy, rather like an actor who could not leave the stage and resume his real identity. Moreover, as one modern authority has put it, 'The spy is always a stranger in a strange land.'[96] There were few indeed whom he could genuinely trust and there were many who would have betrayed him. Also exposure, whether as a rebel or a spy, meant almost certain death. Yet constantly we find men such as Blood placing their lives in danger for their cause. Whereas the modern rebel or agent would be sustained by an ideology (though we should remember that one motive seldom, if ever, makes a spy). Blood was partly sustained by a strong faith in God and himself. This was placed beside another motive with which we deal below.

Of course, such faith also turned to self-analysis and an attempt, as Samuel Jeake so aptly put it in 1647, to spy the 'finger of God in all these buffetings'.[97] Blood found God's intervention in most of his adventures and narrow escapes, whether from 'treppans' or being 'Taken by a Constable in Essex'.[98] In this case self-examination, or rather an examination of events in his past, had a positive end: it gave some reassurance that he should never, 'forsake ye cause of God for any difficu[lties]'.[99] Thus he not only saw the justice of his particular cause in general, in that as God's instrument he was assured his protection, but was given something to sustain him in his further exploits.

From this document and the general pattern of thought it reveals it is also possible to speculate that Blood may have at some point in his life

[94] Amongst the literature useful for discussions of providence in seventeenth-century thought see K. Thomas, *Religion and the Decline of Magic* (1971); B. Donogan, 'Providence, Chance and Explanation: Some Paradoxical Aspects of Puritan Views of Causation', *The Journal of Religious History*, 11, 1980–1, pp. 385–403.

[95] Donogan, 'Providence', p. 386.

[96] R. Seth, *Spies At Work* (1964), p. 37.

[97] Samuel Jeake quoted in A. Fletcher, *A County Committee in Peace and War Sussex, 1600–1660* (1975), p. 61.

[98] Bod. Lib. Rawlinson MSS A, 185, fo. 473v.

[99] *ibid.*

undergone the spiritual agonies of self-doubt and fears of eternal damnation that others of his generation are known to have endured. With this in mind we should perhaps note his first biographer's claim that Blood underwent a 'strict and sober education'[100] which had with others been sufficient to affect them and propel them into the throes of a personal agony. Perhaps this spiritual agony, if it took place, may have occurred at a later date. It is notable that the 'Deliverences since I was for ye Lord's cause'[101] begin in 1663 after the collapse of the Dublin Plot. It is a curious moment to begin such a self-examination for he was then forty-five years old. It might be thought that Blood might have sought the finger of God's providence in his life at an earlier period than this. Did the period 1660–3 see some sort of personal spiritual crisis for Blood? The question remains an open one.

Certainly it is clear from this document that there was a strong streak of morality in Blood's character. It was seen in his moral precepts to avoid strong wine and drink, 'recreations, or pomps or excess in apparale ... quibling or jokeing ... all obsene & scurulous talke'[102] and so on and so forth. Some of these precepts may, of course, have had a practical value for any man involved in clandestine activities. The idea is that the conspirator should not be noticed and should blend in with his surroundings; an argumentative, drunken and 'scurulous' Irishman is the last thing needed in a plot. In any case perhaps avoiding strong wine and drink was a necessity in Blood's life. Williamson later noted that Blood could easily have his head turned by 'wine and treats'.[103] They are therefore likely to have been legitimate moral precepts and a case of Blood being aware of his faults and attempting to correct them.

Blood's sense of morality is seen at its most striking in two of the 'deliverences' which concern his eldest son Thomas. They are worth quoting in full, '57: My sonn's wickedness ... 58: My Sonn's ... [being] ... Stop[ped] & ... [his] ... coming before Keeling'.[104] The two entries refer to Thomas Blood junior's brief career as a highwayman.[105] Blood junior, alias Hunt, as has been noted, had been set up as an apprentice around 1667 in an apothecary's shop run by 'one Holmes'. Hunt left after about six months to set up on his own in Romford as a grocer, druggist or mercer. In any case he soon fell into evil ways leading a 'debauched life' and was obviously a great disappointment to his father. His debt appears

[100] *Remarks*, p. 219.
[101] The document itself is a product of self-examination from the period 1669–70, Bod. Lib. Rawlinson MSS A, fo. 473v.
[102] *ibid*., fo. 474, entries 10, 15, 16.
[103] PRO SP 29/294, fo. 139.
[104] Bod. Lib. Rawlinson MSS A, 185, fo. 474.
[105] Thomas Blood junior's activities are detailed in *HMC*, 8th report, pt 1, pp. 154–6.

to have led him to crime, common assault and robbery as well as a conviction on 4 July 1670 and imprisonment, under his alias Hunt, in the Marshalsea gaol until August 1670. Then his father found two sureties for his release. Thomas Blood soon had his son involved in the assault of the Duke of Ormonde and the attempt on the Crown Jewels. It appears from his father's will that young Thomas was dead by 1680.[106] It is striking that Blood should condemn his son's activities as a 'knight of the post', while seeing his own as part of God's plan. Moreover the book from which the notes are taken was undoubtedly composed before he undertook the most daring criminal act of the reign. Obviously Blood regarded his own actions, conspiracy, treachery, kidnapping and more than likely murder, in a different light from mere highway robbery. Blood was working for the greater ends, for a 'cause', while his son was merely working for himself.

This of, course, leads to speculation about the motives behind the raid on the Crown Jewels. If we see the raid in the light of this document then it could be seen as the ultimate slight against the restored monarchy; stealing the king's crown thus becomes the worthy act of a true commonwealthman. Such apparently 'noble' ideals must of course be set against the more mundane view that Blood himself expressed, that he did it for financial gain. Certainly the attempt on the jewels puzzled Edmund Ludlow. He was not willing to condemn Blood outright, 'having not heard what he hath to say on his own behalfe', but clearly Ludlow was not satisfied and expressed his bewilderment in plain terms: 'I know not what advantage there would have bin to ye publique cause, should they have succeeded in their Enterprize.'[107] Clearly purely financial motives are unsatisfactory: if Blood condemned his son for robbery on the highway then what was the real distinction between that and robbery in the Tower, except the latter was a greater deed? The explanation obviously lies elsewhere and there are two possible answers which do not necessarily preclude each other.

The attempted murder of Ormonde had perplexed not just courtiers. It had also apparently alienated the bulk of the nonconformist community. There are tentative hints in the evidence that whereas it was generally agreed amongst the more radical elements in the nonconformist community that Blood had been most 'wonderfully owned' by God in his rescue of Mason, the attempt on Ormonde was not regarded in the same light. An informer's report after the attempt on Ormonde also notes that, 'those Congregations of Non-Conformists which they ... [Blood and his men] ... have formerly frequented abhor this fact, and would be glad to bring them to punishment if it were in their power'.[108] Such an attitude lends credence

[106] *ibid.*; for the will made on 21 August 1680, Perogative Court of Canterbury Wills, PROB/11/364, fo. 139.

[107] Ludlow, *Voyce*, p. 1265.

[108] *ibid.*; and *HMC*, 8th Report, pt 1, p. 159.

to the idea that Blood had been hired to perform the deed. Having lost credit with those whom he called 'god's people'[109] it may be that he thought to win it back by carrying off the Crown Jewels. He may have thought that by deliberately courting capture or merely with a most spectacular act of roguery he might appeal to Charles himself and with his court connections Blood would then be in a position to bargain for a relaxation of the penal laws against his co-religionists and thus win back their esteem. If this is thought to be too convoluted an answer to the problem one must only recall that if nothing else Blood was a man who undoubtedly thought on the grandest of scales.

There was also another element in Blood's character which must be considered, a slightly eccentric trait which contemporaries also recognised although they did not fully understand it. This was a delight in action or outrage purely for its own sake. The gambler's trait in Blood's career was very strong. One of the closest parallels to this is a comment which was made about Robert Harley that 'he loved tricks even when not necessary but for an inveterate need of applauding his own cunning'.[110] Something of a similar nature may be said of Blood. He also often seemed to delight in acting in such a way, hence the elaborate disguises, the frankly baroque plan to hang Ormonde at Tyburn and the plan to lure the guards out of Dublin Castle by using an overturned cart full of bread. There was within him 'a desire to make such a noise in the world'[111] and to escape from dangerous situations with all the skill of a good gambler. In many ways Blood can be seen as the 'pure' adventurer. The adventurer undertakes outrageous acts simply because they are there to be undertaken. He was motivated perhaps by the desire to 'live in story for the strangeness if not ... [for] ... the success of his attempts'.[112] But it is perhaps an epitaph which belies the complex nature of the man and, as we shall see, this gambler's instinct was eventually to play him false.

IV

By the late summer of 1678 the sixty-year-old Thomas Blood's life had moved away from his career as a rebel. Ensconced in White's coffee house and his other London haunts he had settled into a routine of what can best be described as 'useful roguery', working for a variety of masters on various matters. Blood was intent upon increasing his own as well as his family's fortune by such activities; he moved swiftly, for example, to gain

[109] Bod. Lib. Rawlinson MSS A, 185, fo. 475.
[110] Lord Cowper in M. Burn, *The Debatable Land: A Study of the Motives of Spies in Two Ages* (1970), p. 233.
[111] *Remarks*, p. 227. [112] *ibid.*

two ensigns' commissions for his sons when a war with France seemed imminent in 1678. Much was to change in the autumn and winter of 1678 when the political landscape altered under the impact of the revelations of Titus Oates. In due course Blood was to be swept into the ever more complex web of plots, counterplots and sham dealings until his ruin in 1680. The purveyors of the imaginary Popish and sham plots were invariably drawn from a sinister underclass in London about whom we still know relatively little. From the poverty-stricken environment of the city's slums emerged the discharged soldiers, crazed ex-ministers, beggars, footpads, thieves, pimps, vagrants and tricksters who were to further tarnish Whitehall and Westminster and who were to dominate the political scene with their lies and malice. It is often difficult to uncover the exact truth about such people in the dark and infernal world of London they inhabited. The doors through which we gain admittance to it are mainly via the newspapers and pamphlet literature of the period. They often lead into a maze of lies, counterfeits, sham plots and counter-plots, where reality was often tenuous to say the least. Often 'no sooner [was] one sham discover'd, but a new one [was] contrived to sham that'.[113] The informers themselves were a particularly disreputable set of people, willing to swear to anything, to 'swallow oaths with as nimble convenience as Hocus does ... and ready to spew them up again to murder the innocent'.[114] Samuel Bold, writing in 1682, noted that 'only the brutish and degenerate part of mankind ... men of desperate fortunes ... do commonly take up informing as a trade'.[115]

In spite of its significance the informer's actual motivation for participating in this trade has been too little explored in the past. It is too simplistic to claim that money and greed were the only motives in all cases, although both certainly played a part. The biographies and contemporary literature on such men and women, the logical place to uncover their motivation, unfortunately present something of a problem. Such literature is invariably either very hostile or gives the public image such men, and their sponsors, wished to project. Obviously such distortions have to be taken into account. Occasionally this type of literature does throw up a few grains of truth. In the end, however, as one contemporary put it, the informer's motivation remains the 'great riddle ... for here you have him and there you will have him ... and when you think you have him sure ... you do but hugg a Cloud and embrace a Shadow'.[116]

113 T. S. *The Horrid Sin of Man-Catching: The Second Part Or Further Discoveries and Arguments to Prove that there is no Protestant Plot* (1681), p. 1.
114 *The Character of a Sham-Plotter or Man-Catcher* (1681), p. 1.
115 S. Bold, *A Sermon Against Persecutions Preached March 26 1682* (1682), pp. 7–9.
116 *The Character of a Sham-Plotter or Man-Catcher*, p. 1.

The squalid and unstable world the informers inhabited also drew in Thomas Blood who soon became familiar with its byways and pitfalls. Although in many senses he had always been a part of this world, increasingly the men he associated with were drawn from it rather than from the dissenting community. This crew were the unsavoury down-at-heel thugs and weak-willed liars who haunted the capital's ginshops and taverns taking 'informations pick'd out of broken words in men's common talk which [they] with malitious misapplication hope ... will seem dangerous'.[117] There were also to be a number of his fellow countrymen involved in this trade. There was to be an influx of Irish informers in the period, often brought over by Shaftesbury in pursuit of the chimera of an Irish plot. Abandoned in London and left to their own devices these men were to add to the strong anti-Irish prejudice of the populace by their 'notorious adventures, their swearing and counter-swearing, quarrels amongst themselves, suborning and being suborn'd, endeavours to drop the Popish Plot and sham another upon protestants'.[118] These Irish witnesses we will return to, but what of the major English informers who emerged in London? How was Blood connected to them?

Of Thomas Blood's dealings with Titus Oates there is little surviving evidence. Having said this, there is no doubt that the names of the two men were often linked together in the period. One possible meeting place was Sir William Waller's 'Club at Westminster Market-Place'.[119] Waller, a corrupt justice of the peace of Westminster was a zealous hunter of priests and Catholics and a close friend of Titus Oates, who had a frenzied hatred of all things Catholic. Blood also patronised this political club, although his appearances there were infrequent and may have been for different motives.[120] Neither Blood nor Waller could claim to be friends and each regarded the other with contempt. Each also had a damaging effect upon the other's career. Naturally there were also signs of hostility between Oates and Blood. According to one pamphlet, Blood plotted to upset Oates' credibility as a witness by planting 'treasonable letters' in the informer's papers. These were to have proved Oates was a hireling of the Presbyterian faction. But Oates, coming across the documents, took them immediately to Sir Joseph Williamson, who allegedly brought them before the Privy

117 *The Women Hater* (1607), in F. Bowers, ed., *The Dramatic Works of the Beaumont and Fletcher Canon* (Cambridge, 1966), I, pp. 168–9.

118 *The Irish Evidence Convicted By Their Own Oaths Or Their Swearing and Counter-Swearing Plainly Demonstrated in Several of their Own Affidavits* (1682), p. 3.

119 There is mention of this club in E. Cellier, *Malice Defeated* (1680), p. 15. For Blood's attendance see *A Just Narrative of the Hellish New Counter-Plots of the Papists To Cast the Odium of their Horrid Treasons Upon the Presbyterians* (1679), p. 6.

120 For Waller, see *H of P* III, pp. 658–60; also below for more on his association with Blood.

Council.[121] Unfortunately this pamphlet is the only evidence we possess of this incident. Hostility between the two men, however, is not unlikely. Despite his sympathies for the Baptist sect, Oates was of an entirely different character to Blood. Nor would Blood have been sympathetic to Oates' erstwhile ally Israel Tonge. Almost everyone knew of Tonge's 'crazy reputation' and Tonge was prone to blaming the Great Fire of 1666 on the redoubtable colonel.[122]

Alternatively there was a man such as William Bedloe. Bedloe's unreliable character and his string of previous convictions were to make him a focus for numerous attempts to discredit him as a witness. Bedloe had been a fraud and confidence trickster long before his rise to fame in 1678. Invariably his technique was to masquerade as an aristocratic gentleman in order to gain cash. As the Baron of Newport in Flanders in 1677 and as Baron Cornwallis in Paris he had contrived to 'borrow' large sums of money and then abscond with the takings. He was a fraudster with a grand manner and Catholics in particular were susceptible to his wiles. Bedloe's opportune release as the first panic set in after Godfrey's death raised ample scope for the fraudster. Having never laid eyes on the late justice does not appear to have daunted him and the reward seemed too good to be true. One factor that stood in Bedloe's favour is that despite his rather brutal appearance he was a shrewd man who had 'oblidging winning [and] affable way with him'.[123] Thomas Dangerfield was another in the same mould and the last of this quartet with whom Blood had dealings. Almost every gaol in the country had enjoyed Dangerfield's presence. He was a subtle and dextrous liar as well as something of a charmer. In 1679 he was in Newgate with a string of convictions behind him when a Catholic midwife, Mrs Elizabeth Cellier, came upon him and took him, so to speak, under her wing. From this position Dangerfield was to have a major role in the variety of sham plots which emerged in 1679–80 and these plots also link him with the activities of Thomas Blood.

It is with such men that Blood began to associate. His part in the Popish and sham plots is, as one might expect with such an individual, an obscure one. Blood was adept at covering his tracks and the lies and malice which make up so much of the evidence in the period make his role rather enigmatic to say the least. In this arena each unscrupulous informer plied his

121 *The Horrid Sin of Man-Catching*, p. 20. 122 *HMC*, Ormonde, IV, p. 462.

123 On Bedloe, see *DNB*, William Bedloe; *The Life and Death of Captain William Bedloe* (1681); Cellier, *Malice Defeated*, pp. 2, 8–9; *A True Narrative of the Late Design of the Papists to Charge their Horrid Plot Upon the Protestants by Endeavouring to Corrupt Captain Bury and Alderman Brookes of Dublin* (1679); W. Smith, *Intrigues of the Popish Plot Laid Open* (1685); John Warner, *The History of the English Persecution of Catholics and the Presbyterian Plot*, ed., T. A. Birrell, Catholic Record Society, 47 (1953), pp. 214–15.

trade both for and against his fellows, alliances were formed, broken and reformed. We do know that Blood was at the centre, or on the periphery, of several of the sham plots. He had connections, as we have seen, with the major witnesses, as well as with the minor figures. In the same period he was also maintaining his connections with the court and the government. At any one time we can find him encouraged in his activities by the king himself, working for Sir Joseph Williamson and perhaps more significantly connected with James, Duke of York and Danby.

Nothing in Blood's varied career was ever what it seemed to be on the surface and there is evidence that his true role in the period was that of spy, or *agent provocateur*-cum-investigator, for the regime. In his own view he kept the 'Commonwealth party in awe'.[124] If this was so then it was to raise up a storm of jealousy and hatred in some quarters against him. Given his previously slippery loyalties, however, it must also be noted that Blood was intent upon staying on the winning side by playing the trimmer (switching from one side to another) and, if he could, increase his profits in the process. In the end his gambler's instinct was to play him false and lead him into conflict with a former patron, George Villiers, 2nd Duke of Buckingham, personal disaster, prison, illness and death.

The traditional view of the sham plots of 1679–80, and in particular the so-called Meal-Tub Plot, has been that the lead was taken by a small group of overzealous Roman Catholics bent upon deflecting the worst excesses of the anti-Catholic hysteria then in full flow. There were to be attempts to undermine the credibility of the Popish Plot witnesses and to turn the Popish Plot into an opposition or Presbyterian one. That is, they intended to claim that the Popish Plot was in fact devised by Shaftesbury and the Whigs. While this is a valid viewpoint it is also possible to argue that not enough emphasis has been laid upon the role of the informers in creating these schemes. In particular, as we shall see, Thomas Dangerfield was mainly responsible for the creation of the Meal-Tub Plot and seems to have given his naive victims, especially Mrs Cellier, exactly what they wished to hear.

The leaders of the Catholic faction who were involved in these schemes included Lady Powis, whose husband was incarcerated in the Tower, and Mrs Elizabeth Cellier, the celebrated Catholic midwife whose choice of tools to assist her in her schemes was singularly unfortunate. Also involved was a Catholic pamphleteer, Henry Nevil, and the apostate Whig MP Sir Robert Peyton, upon whom Blood had spied in 1676.[125] Many of the lesser figures who congregated around these people were also shifty in the extreme. According to one of the men involved there were at least eight

[124] PRO SP 29/414, fo. 23. [125] For Peyton see *H of P*, III, pp. 232–4.

others engaged in the attempts to suborn witnesses and spread rumours of sham plots.[126] One of the most prominent of them was an impecunious young rogue by the name of Thomas Dangerfield. In the initial stages of the game Dangerfield was perhaps a valuable asset to the Catholic game. But like others he was deeply untrustworthy and capable of turning what he had invented to his own advantage. Freed from prison with the assistance of Mrs Cellier, he soon busied himself enquiring as to where the main opposition factions met and in hunting out information on those who would be able to help him in his work.

The first of the plots in which Thomas Blood became involved was initiated by a Roman Catholic Irishman by the name of James Netterville. The main thrust of the plot was an attempt to undermine Bedloe's credibility as a witness and to spread rumours that the Popish Plot had originated with Shaftesbury and Buckingham.[127] Netterville had previously been a clerk in the Court of Claims in Dublin, who had been reported for seditious talk in St James's Park and was also connected with Danby as one of the Lord Treasurer's informers.[128] Brought before the Privy Council Netterville had compounded his crimes by getting into a fight outside the council chamber and then being impertinent to the king. He was sent to Newgate to cool his heels. Netterville was widely known as a troublesome man and ended up in the Marshalsea for debt. He also had links with Danby. Netterville may well have been a double agent working for the Lord Treasurer, who only remained in prison because his patron, Danby, was in the Tower.

In January 1679, another Dubliner, Captain Bury, who was also an intimate of Thomas Blood, received a note from Netterville. At a private meeting in the Marshalsea Netterville gave hints of a possible plot to 'turn the game ... the other way',[129] that is, to foist the plot on the opposition. Bedloe was to be undermined and in one version of the tale Blood was also to suffer the same fate. Bury, Netterville claimed, could be put in the way of four or five hundred pounds if he would assist in the scheme. Bury promptly took this information to Blood who urged him to continue the association and to try to discover who was supplying the funds. A different version of the story emerged in Netterville's confession to a Catholic priest. In this it was Blood himself who was to be bribed with £500 and the colonel promptly revealed the scheme to Williamson. As this version was not for public consumption it has its merits.[130] Nevertheless Netterville

126 *A Just Narrative of the Hellish New Counterplots*, p. 7.
127 *HMC*, Fitzherbert MSS, pp. 114–15.
128 See BL Add. MSS 28047, fos. 47–8.
129 See *A True Narrative of the Late Design of the Papists*; *CSPD*, 1679–80, pp. 46–7.
130 *HMC*, Fitzherbert MSS, pp. 114–15. Netterville was clearly convinced that the man he was talking to had stolen the crown. The possibility remains that Blood, using an alias, also paid a private visit to Netterville.

assured Bury of the genuine nature of the offer and it emerged the sponsor was a gentleman by the name of Russell. The latter was a servant to the French ambassador.[131] All the information was passed to Williamson. More was hoped from Netterville at this juncture, but Williamson and Blood were pre-empted by Oates, Bedloe and Waller. The King's Witnesses, as they were called, heard of the tale and paid Netterville a visit. They intimidated him into telling them everything and also left Bury as he put it 'in the lurch'.[132] Alderman Brookes, another Dubliner who was in London to collect a debt, was also contacted by Netterville. Brookes suspected that one of Netterville's Jesuit acquaintances was one of the four 'Irish ruffians' of ill fame. Under the direction of Williamson Brookes continued to encourage the attempt to suborn him, but little came of it.[133] The attempts against these two men merely heightened the suspicions against Catholics in general and allowed the regime to believe that there was a real threat. Other schemes soon followed on the heels of this plot. The role of Blood in the Netterville affair was clearly that of intermediary and *agent provocateur*. While Sir Joseph Williamson remained in office Blood was 'still at command' as the contemporary phrase had it. Such activities were usual fare in his later career, but they did put him in the public eye and according to some sources raised the jealousies of the Catholics. His name also became a focus for part of a greater sham plot created by Thomas Dangerfield.

The ideas which lay behind the scheme of the Meal-Tub Plot undoubtedly emerged from the fertile mind of Thomas Dangerfield. The exact nature of the relationship he had with Mrs Cellier remains obscure, but he certainly took the trouble to feed her fantasies that rebellion and civil war were coming again in the shape of an opposition plot. Sent out to find such a plot he naturally came back with one. The creation of the set of documents which both he and Cellier were to blame on each other was probably the result of Dangerfield's pen. Cellier emerges as a very naive woman who was often given to much wishful thinking and self-deception, traits which a rogue such as Dangerfield, with all his experience, was able to play upon. The documents themselves gave the names of the men involved in the 'plot' and they included Shaftesbury, Buckingham, Halifax and several others. They also gave a list of the rebel army in which both Waller and Thomas Blood figured as major-generals. Blood's inclusion in this list is not that surprising and he was not particularly singled out. He was known as a friend of the dissenters and, as has already been noted,

131 Coventry MSS, 11, fo. 363.

132 *A True Narrative of the Late Design of the Papists*, p. 5. The aggressive Waller threatened Netterville with irons and torture. See *CSPD*, 1679–80, pp. 46–7.

133 *ibid.*

attended Waller's club in Westminster Market, probably to spy on its affairs, given his links with the government. The idea that Blood was an associate of Dangerfield and assisted in the creation of the sham plot in order to be the second witness is unlikely, but at first sight not too improbable.[134] However, sources close to the colonel denied the tale in print and there is a lack of evidence to support such a close association with Dangerfield. Moreover such a move would have placed Thomas Blood on the wrong side, for from this point, if not earlier, Blood appears to have chosen the 'government' over the Whigs as the political crisis deepened. In itself this illustrates just how far he had travelled since his days as a political rebel in the 1660s.

With the production of his documents, Dangerfield was able to move into higher circles. He was introduced to the Earl of Peterborough who in turn took him to see the Duke of York. James encouraged Dangerfield, gave him some money and had him introduced to the king. Charles, by this stage no doubt heartily sick of the dregs of London turning up on his doorstep, nevertheless saw the young man and swiftly passed him into the hands of secretary Coventry. Before the somewhat dubious Secretary of State Dangerfield embellished his story and for good measure dropped in some letters he had stolen from Shaftesbury's desk to sustain his tale.[135] Although interested in the letters and especially how he had obtained them, Coventry was generally unimpressed and refused both Dangerfield's pleas for money as well as a warrant to raid the house of Colonel Roderick Mansell. The latter was a steward to the Duke of Buckingham whom Dangerfield tried to implicate and whose hands were not entirely clean of such matters. Having been thwarted, however, Dangerfield was forced to think again and what emerged was the Meal-Tub Plot.[136] In the meantime Thomas Blood had become involved in one of Dangerfield's subsidiary schemes.

Amongst his general rumour spreading and intelligence activities, and while still using his alias of Willoughby, Dangerfield had busied himself in spreading tales of commissions being issued for a rebel army made up of disbanded officers. These men were to be promised pay and told to 'linger about the Town'.[137] There were a variety of reasons for Dangerfield adopt-

134 See *A Just Narrative of the Hellish New Counter-Plots of the Papists*; also *The Narrative of the Design Lately Laid by Philip Le Mar And Several Others Against His Grace George, Duke of Buckingham*, (1680), pp. 30–1. Blood's name was also linked with that of Sir Robert Peyton see *HMC*, 7th Report, p. 477.

135 Coventry papers, 11, fos. 441–2.

136 For an account of the Meal-Tub Plot see R. Mansell, *An Exact and True Narrative of the Late Popish Intrigue to Form a Plot and Then to cast the Guilt and Odium Thereof Upon the Protestants* (1680); *A Just Narrative of the Hellish New Counter-Plots of The Papists*.

137 Cellier, *Malice Defeated*, p. 13.

ing this tactic. It was useful to sustain his credibility with Mrs Cellier; it also spread rumours and prepared the ground for later moves, bolstering the forgeries he had already created. It may also be that he was beginning to believe his own fantasies. Dangerfield was a man who thrived on fantasy, mainly about himself, hence the later pamphlets about the, more or less, fictitious adventures of the 'Don Thomazo' figure he believed himself to be.[138] The reality was somewhat different, but Dangerfield was a man who existed in a web of lies where reality and fantasy seldom crossed.

Thomas Curtis, a Lancashire man, former clerk to Henry Nevill as well as an MP, was also an erstwhile cloth worker of sorts, and far from a life of fantasy in 1679. For the most part he was drunk. Having taken to 'a debauch'd course of life'[139] he spent his days in the taverns and drinkshops of the city and sooner or later he was bound to encounter Thomas Dangerfield. In due course in October 1679 he made the acquaintance of one 'Thomas Willoughby' in the Hoop Tavern, Fish Street Hill. Drinking with his new friend, who praised him as an 'honest man', Dangerfield offered Curtis the chance of serving both his king and country, as well as some ready cash, and a free dinner at Mrs Cellier's house. After dinner and in private Dangerfield told Curtis that the rebels were forming an army and that commissions were being issued. He claimed that he had been at various meetings in Holborn and at Sir Thomas Player's and Shaftesbury's residences where such things were discussed. Dangerfield also said that if Curtis could get hold of some of these commissions then there would be a substantial reward for him. Curtis was dubious about the whole business, but he promised to make some enquiries.

Curtis then spent some of his time prying into various locations. He visited the political club at Westminster Market where he was introduced by a respectable member of the club. Unfortunately the sources do not give the man's name. The introduction proved useful to Curtis as he could then openly gather information upon the club's membership, scan their faces and 'certain innocent circumstances he might [then] be enabled to render

[138] See E. Cellier, *The Matchless Rogue or a Brief Account of the Life of Don Thomazo, the Unfortunate Son* (1680); T. Dangerfield, *Don Thomazo, Or the Juvenile Rambles Of Thomas Dangerfield* (1680); T. Dangerfield, *Particular Narrative of the late Popish Design to Charge those of the Presbyterian Party with a Pretended Conspiracy Against His Majesties Person and Government* (1679); T. Dangerfield, *More Shams Still or of Further Discovery of the Designs of the Papists to Impose Upon the Nation the Belief of their Feigned Protestant or Presbyterian Plot* (1681); Mansell, *An Exact and True Narrative.*

[139] *The New Plot of the Papists, by Which They Have Design'd to Have Laid Their Guilt of their Hellish Conspiracies Against His Majesty and Government Upon the Dissenting Protestants* (1679), pp. 4–5; T. Dangerfield, *Particular Narrative*, pp. 56, 72–3; Mansell, *An Exact and True Narrative*, pp. 66–7; *A Just Narrative of the Hellish New Counter-Plots*, pp. 4–10.

[as] falsehoods, that he should impose on them ... [and make them] plausible'.[140] Curtis then turned up in Blood's territory at the Heaven Tavern in Old Palace Yard, Westminster. There he talked freely to Jane Bradley who was the barmaid of the establishment. Perhaps by this stage he was again in his cups for he had a loose tongue and he told Bradley about the plot and that commissions were being issued for the rebel army, by Thomas Blood amongst others. He also told her if she could lay her hands upon one then he would be able to reward her. Unfortunately for Curtis, Bradley was one of Blood's informants. Although she claimed not to know the colonel very well she egged Curtis on and said she would try to obtain a commission for him. In the meantime she contacted Thomas Blood.

On his arrival Blood heard the tale and told Bradley ''twas very well done to tell him thereof'. He denied that there were in fact any commissions and encouraged Bradley by giving her a gold coin and telling her to continue to pump Curtis for information as he was keen to uncover the sponsors of the design. In the meantime he took pains to visit the Westminster club himself and to make some enquiries of his own. He sounded out the original sponsor of Curtis and took him to hear Bradley's tale. They both agreed that it was desirable to 'let the business ripen a little'. Blood then went directly to the king with his story. Charles encouraged Blood to discover more. With royal backing Blood proceeded to slowly draw in Curtis via Bradley. Curtis claimed that eight others were engaged in the scheme and promised more revelations.[141] At this point Dangerfield's other scheme concerning Roderick Mansell and the Meal-Tub broke into the public arena. Nevertheless Curtis was hauled before Edmund Warcup the justice of the peace who took his deposition and then committed him to the Gatehouse. He was also brought before the council to answer questions and was later given bail.[142] His involvement in such affairs was not over for Blood was to find the man useful at a later date in other ways. The scheme over the commissions, however, was stifled before it moved very far and remained a minor branch of Dangerfield's schemes. It does illustrate Blood's activities, his involvement in Whig clubs, and the use of a woman such as Bradley to alert him to dangerous schemes. It is also clear that Blood still had a direct line to the king himself. The affair also raises the interesting question of whether it was originally intended that Blood not Mansell should be the victim of Dangerfield's plan to plant evidence. If so, and it is not unlikely, then the colonel's own intelligence network foiled the design.

[140] *A Just Narrative of the Hellish New-Counterplots*, p. 4. [141] *ibid.*, pp. 4–10.
[142] 'The Journals of Edmund Warcup, 1676–84', *EHR*, 40, 1925, p. 247. Another observer of Curtis' interrogation noted he was also partly responsible for the distribution of pamphlets against Danby. *HMC*, Lindsay (Supplementary), pp. 34–5.

The events which led to the final collapse of Thomas Blood's fortunes in 1680 are often buried beneath the lies, malice and spite which made up the world of the informer in the 1680s. While Blood sanctioned his own version of the plot which led to his incarceration in the King's Bench prison in 1680, the resulting pamphlet was both self-serving and not entirely reliable. However, to understand what exactly happened to Blood in the final passages of his career it is necessary to plunge still further into the murky world of seventeenth-century London during the period of the sham plots. This is the dark undergrowth of political life in the period, a grey world of idle hands and idle talk bent upon making mischief, ministerial 'dirty tricks', squalid tavern settings and malicious gossip. For a while the focus of this world became the reputation of the Duke of Buckingham. This in itself is not surprising for Restoration politics was morally bankrupt at the best of times and became a particularly dirty game in the early 1680s. There was a willingness of 'greater persons' to sanction plots against their political rivals. The plot against Buckingham was only one of a number of such designs. Whig or Tory, minister or MP all were willing to undercut the other and use the dregs of the London underworld to do so.

Philemon Coddan and Samuel Ryther were two impecunious Irishmen of dubious reputation and shabby appearance. There were many of their kind in the London of the period and they were to plague the politics of the crisis of the 1680s. Coddan and Ryther had been on the fringes of the retinue of Buckingham and in that service they had accrued some debts from the duke which he had not paid. Naturally they resented this fact. It is also possible that they knew a few of Buckingham's secrets. The duke's lifestyle was lavish in its indiscretions and he attracted some particularly unsavoury company into his entourage. Most of these were 'useful rogues', hired thugs or bravos used for protection or for doing the unpleasant things other servants of Buckingham could not do; a beating here, minor unpleasantness elsewhere, it was all part of their daily routine. Thomas Blood himself had fallen into this class, but whether due to his independence of spirit or to Buckingham's penchant for quarrelling with everyone he came into contact with he was not part of that retinue in 1680.

In retrospect it is hardly surprising that Buckingham attracted malice. His reputation, both political and sexual, was notorious. He himself was aware of this, even to the extent of writing a defence of his private life. Therein he denied that he was of a 'cruel, insolent injurious carriage' (highly likely in reality), a poisoner, or a sodomite.[143] The latter accusation was something which dogged Buckingham's reputation throughout his

[143] A. Pritchard, 'A Defence of His Private Life by the Second Duke of Buckingham', *HLQ*, 44, 1980–1, pp. 157–71. His reputation as a poisoner might well have been merited; see above, Chapter 5.

political career. Of course, he denied it vociferously: 'God knows I have much to answer for in the plain way, but I never was so great a virtuoso in my lusts.'[144] It is not clear whether he was actually telling the truth in the matter, and whether he was or wasn't, sodomy was still a capital crime and the tales continued to circulate.[145] Moreover they were believed and could be used by his political enemies to damage both himself and the Whig cause which he favoured.

From his rooms in the Tower in late 1679 the ex-Lord Treasurer Danby's future looked bleak. Danby was far from being out of touch with events, however, and still continued to plan as well as attempting to exercise his considerable influence on matters outside the Tower. While still at liberty in the previous February his target had apparently been the Duke of Buckingham. Lord Ossory had a conversation with Danby in which the latter hinted that he was 'not out of hopes of procuring something very material' against Buckingham.[146] There were again whispered rumours of sodomy in the air. The design, whatever it was, fell through and Danby kept the actual details close to his chest. Once Danby was in the Tower things became a trifle more complicated, but what Danby had begun others could pick up, perhaps even with the earl's knowledge. The plan, whoever laid it, was to bring Buckingham's career crashing to the ground through an accusation of sodomy. What was necessary were the tools to do the job.

Edward Christian's part in the tangled plot which emerged against Buckingham was an obscure, but probably a crucial, one. While Christian was loudly to proclaim his innocence of the plot and that he had been trepanned, he did have a distinctly shady past. Christian had served the royalist cause in the Civil Wars[147] and from 1660 he had acted as a rent-collector on Buckingham's estates. Before long he had been promoted to become the duke's chamberlain and the chief financial figure in his affairs.[148] There is little doubt that Christian must have also come across Sir Thomas Osborne. In the early 1660s the future Earl of Danby was a client of Buckingham. What is certain is that Christian was corrupt above the ordinary sense of the word in the seventeenth century. He had stolen and embezzled large sums of money from Buckingham's estates before his dismissal in

144 *ibid.*

145 See *ibid.*; also 'The Litany of the Duke of Buckingham' (1680) in E. F. Mengel, ed., *Poems on Affairs of State* (7 vols., New Haven, 1965), II, p. 194, lines 18–20; Grey *Debates*, II, p. 246; Jones, *First Whigs*, p. 109. See also B. C. Yardley, 'The Political Career of George Villiers, Second Duke of Buckingham, 1628–1687', unpublished Ph.D thesis, University of Oxford, 1989.

146 *HMC*, Ormonde, IV, pp. 328–9.

147 See *The True Domestic Intelligence*, 20–7 April 1680.

148 See F. T. Melton, 'A Rake Refinanced: The Fortunes of George Villiers, Second Duke of Buckingham, 1671–1685', *HLQ*, 51, 1988, pp. 300–1.

1673.[149] Despite Christian's obvious guilt he may well have retained a grudge against the duke. By 1676 Christian had approached Danby for employment and despite the former chamberlain's reputation Danby made him his steward.[150] This trust was rewarded by Christian when he defended the Lord Treasurer and his own reputation at the height of the Popish Plot.[151] Christian's part in the plot against Buckingham, as far as it can be uncovered amidst all the lies, seems to have been to promote Danby's original design against the duke. Christian also seems to have provided the money and contacts to suborn witnesses to accuse the duke of sodomy. The plan had two parts: Coddan and Ryther were to swear that Buckingham had sodomised one Sarah Harwood and then sent her to France, while a further two witnesses were to emerge in the shapes of Philip Le Mar and his mother Frances Loveland. The former was a not very bright young man who fell into the hands of sponsors cruder and more dangerous than himself. He was joined by his mother in what seems to have been an unusual show of maternal affection. Le Mar was to claim that six years previously Buckingham had committed sodomy on him.[152] At his trial a variety of names were to emerge as Le Mar's sponsors. He was to be suborned himself by two of Buckingham's cronies who made him drunk, and possibly used drugs,[153] in order that he sign various confessions; some of the names revealed were undoubtedly unreliable. In such a case the mud flew in all directions as the parties attempted to score political points. One of the names mentioned was the Secretary of State, Sunderland. Eager to clear his name, Sunderland moved that Le Mar might be swiftly examined by the Attorney-General.[154] From this very 'severe and frequent [reflections] were made against the Earl and Countess of Danby'.[155] It was alleged that Lady Danby had offered Le Mar £300 to swear against Buck-

[149] *ibid.*

[150] BL Eg. MSS 3329, fo. 105; BL Add. MSS 28051, fo. 61; *The True Protestant Domestic Intelligence*, 3 February 1680; Yardley, 'Buckingham', pp. 309–10. F. T. Melton, 'Absentee Land Management in the Seventeenth Century', *Agricultural History*, 52, 1978, pp. 151–2.

[151] E. Christian, *Reflections upon a Paper Intitled Some Reflections Upon the Earl of Danby in Relation to the Murder of Sir Edmund Bury Godfrey* (1679); J. B., *Some Reflections upon the Earl of Danby in Relation to the Murder of Sir Edmund Bury Godfrey* (1679); *Timothy Touchstone, His Reply to Mr Christian's Letter Written in Vindication of the Great Worth and Innocence of the Earl of Danby* (1679).

[152] *The True Protestant Domestic Intelligence*, 11 May 1680; *HMC*, Ormonde, V, pp. 296–7, 324; *A Letter to a Friend in the Country Concerning His Grace the Duke of Buckingham* (1680); PRO 31/3/145, Barrillon to Louis XIV, 15 April 1680.

[153] This action cost Mr Barnsley, a justice of the peace from Southwark, his office. See PRO PC 2/68, fos. 395, 406, 465, 466. Also *London Gazette*, 1–5 April 1680; *HMC*, Ormonde, IV, pp. 296–7.

[154] PRO 31/3, fo. 145, Barrillon to Louis XIV, 15 April 1680; *London Gazette*, 1–5 April 1680; *HMC*, Ormonde, V, pp. 296–7.

[155] PRO 31 13/145, Barrillon to Louis XIV, 20 May 1680; *HMC*, Ormonde, V, pp. 296–7.

ingham. The investigation also implicated those tried and tested scapegoats, the Catholic lords in the Tower. The Duke of York's name also emerged in the investigation and York, as we will see, was connected with Thomas Blood. Having said this, beyond a certain point in the case the lies become so convoluted that they obscure the real truth of the matter.

While Le Mar and his mother formed one part of the design Coddan and Ryther formed the other. Coddan knew another Irishman by the name of Maurice Hickey, alias Higgins or Higges. According to Coddan both he and Hickey had come down to London with some others in late 1679. They had settled in Long Acre where they raised suspicions with their drinking, quarrelling and talk in Gaelic.[156] The focus of Hickey and Coddan's attention was Samuel Ryther. Ryther was the man whom they intended to use to swear against Buckingham in exchange for liberal supplies of money, and the protection of 'greater persons', or where these blandishments failed, a drugged confession was to be obtained.[157] As soon as Ryther signed a paper to the effect that he knew that Buckingham had sodomised Sarah Harwood and disposed of her, he was to be kept close in case he disappeared from the conspirators. As Ryther turned out to be an individual given to changing his mind this became increasingly likely. Coddan was to play the role of the second witness as he was a man willing to swear to anything he was asked if he was well paid. Hickey was the 'brains' in the group, although he was all too obviously being told what to do by the group's sponsors. At the very least the Irishmen must have hoped to obtain some money to keep their mouths shut; at most they could even have hoped to have emulated the careers of Dangerfield and Bedloe. The main problem with the scheme was the uncooperative nature of Ryther. As Hickey did not appear to be succeeding in his attempts to persuade Ryther to co-operate, another man entered the scheme. This was the rather bumptious figure of Thomas Curtis whom we last saw being dragged before the Privy Council and jailed. He had then been given bail and switched sides. Curtis' involvement leads to the man who originally dealt with him, the erstwhile government agent Thomas Blood.

Thomas Blood not only knew Curtis, whom we must now presume was working for the colonel, but he also knew Edward Christian. Blood had been in Buckingham's entourage, as had Christian. The two men disliked each other, Blood even to the point of grudging Christian the 'civility of drinking either publickly or privately' with him,[158] but the times made strange bedfellows and this public dislike should be taken with a pinch of

[156] BL Add. MSS 28047, fos. 66–7; *The Narrative of Thomas Blood Concerning the Design Reputed to be Lately Laid Against the Life and Honour of His Grace George, Duke of Buckingham* (1680), p. 18.

[157] BL Add. MSS 28047, fo. 67.

[158] *The Narrative of Thomas Blood*, p. 28.

salt. At this point in his career Blood was also linked with the Duke of York. James' name was to be bandied about by the plotter's, without his knowledge, as one of the 'great persons' who were sponsoring the scheme. Curtis indeed bragged of having been introduced to the Duke of York. Whether James knew of what was going on in his name is unclear.[159] Blood himself was keeping his distance from the plot by working through Curtis and perhaps Hickey. This in itself was suspicious; was he again playing a double game? If so, for whom was he really working? The short answer is that we do not know. By January 1680, however, a series of meetings had been taking place. The venues were varied but usually in the backrooms of squalid taverns such as the Crown in Ram Alley or the Bear near London Bridge.[160] Curtis bragged of his Yorkist connections to anyone who would listen and tried to bring Ryther round to the idea of taking on the role of a witness. Large sums of money were also promised as a bait, alongside the protection of 'great persons'. At one of these meetings Thomas Blood also appeared. In this company he was noted as being 'very busie' to know what exactly Coddan and Ryther would swear. Blood wanted particulars and pressed the pair for details. His persuasive manner and necessary caution in dealing with such men clearly emerges at this meeting. Persuading Coddan to swear took on all the attributes of a game of chess. Blood took his man aside from the group asked him what he would swear against Buckingham, and received the reply that he would swear anything they asked him to. But Blood pressed his man again before witnesses and seemed very pleased to get a positive reply.[161] Blood's persuasive manner was a useful trait in this sort of work. To be cautious and affable to all was something he deliberately cultivated.[162] One can easily see why: persuasion and guile would achieve far more with men such as Curtis, Coddan, Ryther and Hickey than outright violence. Despite appearances Blood seems not to have been a particularly violent or hot-tempered man, although there is no doubt he could use violence when he thought it necessary.[163] In his intelligence work it was more often the quiet word here, or the delicate bribe there, the drink or the drug rather than the poniard which would achieve more in the long run. With the two men apparently persuaded, Blood must have felt that the attack on Buckingham could proceed as planned. The men were unreliable, but then again so were most of the other witnesses at the time. At this point the plot began to go wrong.

[159] At this point it is as well to note that James was approached by Blood when the colonel was placed in the King's Bench prison and Blood's letter is very much that of a client to his patron. See PRO SP 29/414, fo. 23.

[160] BL Add. MSS 28047, fos. 67–71. The Crown and Ram Alley were notorious 'dives', for thieves and prostitutes. See Lordling Barry's drama, *Ram Alley, or Merry Tricks* (1611).

[161] BL Add. MSS 28047, fos. 67–71.

[162] Bod. Lib. Rawlinson MSS A, 185, fo. 475.

[163] As in the rescue of Mason.

Amongst such inherently untrustworthy individuals the chances of betrayal were high. The possibility that they could betray one another for profit was quite likely and so it proved. Coddan and Ryther appear to have decided to change sides. According to one alleged conversation between the pair Ryther was puzzled how they should proceed, but Coddan said 'we will do this rogue Blood's business for him and get enough to swear against him by [the] time Sir William Waller comes to town'.[164] At the next venue, a tavern in Bloomsbury, Hickey was supplied with a paper for both men to sign. It was alleged that he was to offer the pair £300 in gold and if they would not sign threaten to kill them.[165] As it turned out Ryther came to the venue on his own and asking to peruse the document promptly ran off with it. On discovering this Hickey grew panic-stricken, muttered something about 'he and his partners [being] undone' and fled. Ryther and Coddan meanwhile had gone off to Mr Whitaker, Buckingham's solicitor, with their evidence. Whitaker soon had an information out for Hickey with a £100 reward attached to it. Sir William Waller then took Coddan and Ryther under his wing.[166]

On 20 January 1680 Waller sent for Blood. Prior to this meeting neither man had liked the other very much. By the end of the meeting this had turned to mutual contempt. Waller's part in this affair was to cost him his commission as a justice: his over-zealous pursuit of this scheme, his tampering with witnesses, including keeping Hickey out all night drinking with him when the Irishman was supposed to be in gaol, which went a little too far even for a man of his reputation. Having latched onto the plot the evidence was stretched by Waller with some judicious bribery. At the meeting Blood was faced with a *fait accompli*; Coddan and Ryther had their story ready and were backed by the presence of Mr Whitaker and Francis Jenks, both old enemies of the colonel.[167] Blood attempted to brazen it all out, resisted arrest for a few days, but eventually ended up in the Gatehouse prison. Christian was next on the list. By this stage Waller had also arrested Hickey to use against Christian.[168] Nor did Christian's actions at his arrest look like those of the innocent man he claimed to be. He broke free from the constables and shouted out of the window that he was 'betray'd'.[169] He also claimed that he had been framed because he was Danby's servant. The rest of the plotters were soon mopped up. Le Mar

[164] *The Narrative of the Design Lately Laid by Philip Le Mar and Several Others Against His Grace George, Duke of Buckingham* (1680), p. 14.

[165] *The Narrative of Thomas Blood*, p. 16. [166] *ibid.*

[167] *ibid.*, Francis Jenks was a radical Whig and a client of Buckingham. See Haley, *Shaftesbury*, p. 409.

[168] PRO 31/3/144, Barrillon to Louis XIV, 26 February 1680; *The True Domestic Intelligence*, 6–9 April 1680, 9–13 April 1680.

[169] *The True Domestic Intelligence*, 3 February 1680.

became the subject of an attempt to suborn him with drink and other potions which made the young man desperately ill and he was to die in prison.[170] Christian carried on his complaints against Waller, while Blood carried on a campaign from gaol to proclaim his innocence.

In fairness a brief resumé of Blood's own published version of the events which led to his incarceration in the King's Bench prison should perhaps be given. He claimed that in January 1680 he'd been asked by Jane Bradley to call upon her. Bradley claimed that she had reason to believe that there was a major design in motion which would affect the government.[171] As Blood told the story, she had information from two men, Ryther and Coddan, who wished to reveal their story to a 'discreet person'. Blood agreed to meet the two men, but they fled when they learned of his identity. Having discovered their whereabouts he had them brought before Dr Chamberlain, a magistrate of his acquaintance to give their evidence and to protect himself from any charges of misprison of treason. Chamberlain examined the men separately; both denied any knowledge of the plot but they did claim that Buckingham owed them money. When pressed one of the pair said he was prepared to swear a crime of sodomy against the Duke of Buckingham. The magistrate was not prepared to believe the charges and the matter was dropped.[172] It was after this that he found Coddan and Ryther in Waller's company. Such was the public declaration of Thomas Blood on the affair. However, the reality, as we have seen, was somewhat different involving as it did a convoluted plot with very high connections indeed. Nor was Thomas Blood the innocent in the scheme he liked to proclaim.

After a series of engineered delays on both sides, disappearing witnesses and other events, the trial eventually took place at the King's Bench. Blood, Christian, Le Mar, Curtis, Hickey and three others were indicted on the counts of blasphemy, confederacy and subornation. All were found guilty, severely fined and imprisoned. According to Southwell who talked to the foreman of the jury, 'the proofs [against the plotters] are most evident and the whole contrivance most abominable'.[173] Moreover it was widely speculated that a noble 'Lord in the Tower' was behind the scheme. It was thought that Buckingham with this victory would then try to attack Danby, but the duke's prestige had been badly damaged and he was never to be the same force again. The fallout from the trial also affected others. The Attorney-General was clear that several 'undue practices' had taken

170 The *True Domestic Intelligence*, 9–13 April 1680; *CSPD*, 1679–80, pp. 488–9, 519.
171 *Remarks*, p. 229; *The Narrative of Thomas Blood*, p. 4. Bradley also stood trial as part of the conspiracy, but was found to be not guilty.
172 *ibid.*
173 *HMC*, Ormonde, IV, p. 579; *Smith's Current Intelligence*, 27 April–1 May 1680.

place. Waller in particular suffered because of this and his misdemeanours all provided the perfect excuse for the king to remove him from the commission of the peace. Waller subsequently fled to the Netherlands.[174] Blood, with his eye ever to the main chance, appeared to have finally overreached himself. He was all too quickly drawn into this murky world. If he was guilty of suborning witnesses then he suffered the consequences of these actions. What is clear in this episode is that the experienced conspirator and spy of the 1660s and 1670s appears to have been outflanked by those even more unscrupulous than himself. More significantly perhaps, there appears to have been no powerful patron willing to protect him from the consequences of his actions and Buckingham's revenge.

It was not until July 1680 that Blood was released from prison.[175] The whole affair appears to have crushed his spirit and to have made him mortally ill. He left prison a very sick man. By 22 August he had lapsed into a coma,[176] and on 24 August 1680, he died aged sixty-two. Even after his death rumours began to spread that some trickery was in progress. Finally to quash the rumours and lay the troublesome Colonel Blood to rest the authorities were forced to exhume his body.[177] This evidently settled the case and Colonel Thomas Blood, erstwhile adventurer, passed into history.

V

While we can examine Thomas Blood's life in some detail, that of John Scott remains something of an enigma. He was a man who made espionage part of his life and flitted in and out of various intelligence systems for some forty years. Scott was talented in many ways, he could be something of a gentleman as well as a wit, he was intelligent and wrote poetry – although the latter qualities do not always coincide. Nor was he above some classical learning. Scott even played the role of a lover. Yet at the same time there was a darker image to this man, a negative to the more positive elements in his character. In this we find the foul-mouthed, drunken misanthrope, the rogue and coward, a man whom few, if any, could trust and those who did so were often singularly disappointed.

[174] *London Gazette*, 1–5 April 1680; *The True Domestic Intelligence*, 6–9 April, 9–13 April 1680; J. Heading, *Sir William Waller His Vindication By A Friend That Understood His Life and Conversation* (1680); *Dagon's Fall Or the Knight* (1680); N. Lutterall, *A Brief Historical Relation of State Affairs from 1678 to April 1714* (6 vols., Oxford, 1857), I, p. 34. PRO 31/3/145, Barrillon to Louis XIV, 18 April 1680, 16 May 1680; PRO PC 2/68, fo. 471.

[175] The process can be traced in *CSPD*, 1679–80, pp. 560–8.

[176] He made his will on 21 August 1680; Perogative Court of Canterbury Will, PROB, 11, 364, fo. 139.

[177] *Remarks*, p. 234.

Scott's inner malaise cannot be laid totally at the door of his espionage activities, but they undoubtedly played a significant part in it. It is the consequences of these activities and the career of John Scott which is our concern here.[178]

One of Scott's major errors in his rather melodramatic life was the attempt he made in 1679 to destroy Samuel Pepys. The result was that Pepys took to collecting as much evidence as possible about his enemy's unsavoury past. Although this damned Scott's reputation in the eyes of history, the wealth of detail about his life it brought to light is a boon for the historian. Pepys and his agents uncovered the portrait of a particularly nasty individual. Not all of Scott's biographers would have it so. L. T. Mowrer's biography of Scott made an attempt to be rather too fair to her hero. In her account Scott is re-cast as the victim of Pepys' malice and as an early American patriot, a man more sinned against than sinning: someone who, had he been around at the time, would have readily embraced the spirit of 1776. Unfortunately such a view will simply not stand up to the evidence of Scott's life. While it is true that some of the evidence collected by Pepys was tainted against Scott – too many people had things to gain by disparaging him – he remains a ne'er-do-well and villain of the first order. At the same time this does not render him any less complex. He was a man of subtle character and there was a complexity in such men which belied their actions. There were no simple spies and Scott was not a simple man.

While Scott's activities as a spy assisted in the progressive degeneration of his character it might well be argued that he was morally handicapped from the beginning. His career began inauspiciously enough in the Americas where he had been transported by Emmanuel Downing, Sir George Downing's father.[179] Despite Scott's later protestations that America was the land of opportunity and a challenge, his presence there was more than likely to have been an involuntary one. In his adult life he acquired a bad reputation in the colonies, where amongst other things he deserted his wife, ended up in gaol and in general behaved no better than he might have done. In spite of this his reappearance on the English scene in 1660 occurred when he returned to the country on behalf of some respectable New Englanders. While in England Scott was also introduced by Thomas Chiffinch to Joseph Williamson.[180] Williamson took a keen

[178] For Scott see L. T. Mowrer, *The Indomitable John Scott: Citizen of Long Island 1632–1704* (New York, 1960); *Dictionary of American Biography*, XVI, pp. 494–5; *DNB*, John Scott; W. C. Abbott, *Colonel John Scott of Long Island, 1634–1696*, (1918); A. Bryant, *Samuel Pepys* (3 vols., 1933–8), II, Chapters 10–11; Haley, *Shaftesbury*, pp. 520–1; J. M. Sosin, *English America and the Restoration Monarchy of Charles II: Transatlantic Politics, Commerce and Kinship* (Lincoln, Nebr., 1980), p. 100.

[179] *Dictionary of American Biography*, XVI, p. 494.

[180] Sosin, *English America*, p. 100; *CSPCol*, 1661–8, p. 415.

interest in matters colonial, and aside from this, one of Scott's more legitimate talents was as a cartographer.[181] As one of Williamson's interests was in maps the two seem to have struck up a friendly rapport. The main business at hand was with New England and no espionage activities emerged from this first meeting. Scott was soon back in the Americas, but not before he had perpetrated a confidence trick on a Quaker couple and gained possession of their son, whom he rather imprudently sold to a New Haven innkeeper on his return to the colonies.

After various adventures, too numerous to relate here, Scott was forced to leave for the West Indies where he took a commission in Sir Thomas Bridge's regiment. There he saw some action against the French in the disastrous expedition against St Kitts. The result of Scott's participation in this fight was an accusation of cowardice, 'sculking' behind some rocks in the fight then fleeing to the ships, his accusers claimed, as well as a court martial. The image which his fellow soldiers had of him was not a positive one; he was thought to be a man 'generally known to be a notorious coward', who left his men in the lurch. All of this, of course, has to be regarded with more than a little scepticism, for the disaster at St Kitts led to many recriminations.[182] In the event Scott left the West Indies for England in 1667. Williamson at least seems to have thought something of him. In spite of his faults the under-secretary relied upon Scott for information on the situation in the West Indies. Scott's knowledge of the area was sufficient for Williamson to note in 1679 that he thought 'Scott the ablest man in England for a West Indies voyage, and it was a pity to lose him'.[183]

In 1667 on the strength of a volume on the coasts and islands of the Americas he was allegedly writing, Scott continued to cultivate his new patron, who also introduced him to Arlington. The result of this patronage was a title, Royal Geographer, of which Scott seems to have been inordinately proud.[184] However, nemesis, in the shape of his past, eventually caught up with him. He lost Williamson's friendship owing to some villainy committed in the under-secretary's lodgings by a man whom Scott had recommended.[185] Scott also spent some time in the Gatehouse in 1668.[186] By 1669 he had disappeared from the Whitehall scene only to re-emerge in the Low Countries in the company of some republican exiles. He claimed that he had fled the country after killing a page of the Duke of York, but this tale may well have been a cover story to conceal his new role

181 A. P. Thornton, *West-India Policy Under the Restoration* (Oxford, 1956), pp. 126–7.
182 For this campaign see A. Burns, *History of the West Indies* (2nd edn, 1965), pp. 305–13.
183 Williamson quoted in Grey, *Debates*, VII, p. 311; *CSPCol*, 1661–8, pp. 480–1.
184 Bod. Lib. Rawlinson MSS A, 175, fo. 1.
185 *CSPD*, 1667–8, p. 493. Scott himself was accused of stealing a petition from the office in 1666; *CSPCol*, 1661–8, p. 415.
186 *CSPD*, 1667–8, p. 189.

as a spy for the Stuart regime,[187] for whether he grew to dislike him or not, Williamson was never one to ignore unsavoury talents and would exploit them where he could. Scott also took the opportunity to join the Dutch army and apparently won over John de Witt with tales of his military skills. The life of a soldier led him to a colonelcy by 1672, which was a useful adjunct to his main business in these years, espionage. In spite of any unreliability in his character he was to be employed by the intelligence systems of three states, England, the United Provinces and France. While they were using Scott for their own particular ends, there is little doubt that he was returning the compliment tenfold.

War in the seventeenth century brought with it not only death and destruction, but many opportunities for the professional spy, if, that is, he survived long enough to enjoy them. For John Scott the Dutch War which began in March 1672, was an opportunity worth seizing. This war would require the gathering of secret intelligence and a large part of the responsibility for this would fall on the shoulders of Sir Joseph Williamson, his patron. And indeed Williamson began his war by preparing his correspondents in the coastal regions of England. He then fell to organising the gathering of covert information within the enemy's own territories and one of the men whom he engaged in this work was John Scott. On the eve of the war the Committee of Foreign Affairs finally initiated the planning for the gathering of covert intelligence in the Netherlands and Williamson noted that 'five or six persons [were] to be gather[ed] to goe into Holland to informe of their state'.[188] It is clear that prior to this meeting there was still little by way of English espionage taking place in the Low Countries aside from the usual diplomatic manoeuvrings and the perpetual interest the government had in the activities of the English and Scottish exiles. At the conclusion of the last war with the Dutch most of the agents engaged for intelligence in the Low Countries had been paid off or simply dropped by the regime. As we have seen, there were a number of reasons for this

[187] Bod. Lib. Rawlinson MSS A, 188, fo. 317.

[188] PRO SP 104/177, fo. 10. For a detailed study of the build-up to the war from a French perspective see the important work by P. Sonnino, *Louis XIV and the Origins of the Dutch War* (Cambridge, 1988) and the sources therein. No detailed modern history of the war exists in English, but there is the valuable, and relatively accurate, contemporary history by Swart, *Netherland-Historian*; also G. Edmondson, *History of Holland* (Cambridge, 1922), pp. 236–50; Hutton, *Charles II*, Chapters 10–11; C. F. M. Rouset, *Historie de Louvois et son Administration Politique et Militaire* (4 vols., Paris, 1873); D. J. Roorda, *Het Rampjaar 1672* (Bussum, 1871); Colenbrander, *Zeeoorlogen*, Rowen, *De Witt*, pp. 815–40; M. C. Trevelyan, *William the Third and the Defence of Holland 1672–1674* (1930); A. Hassell, *Louis XIV and the Zenith of the French Monarchy* (1910); Wolf, *Louis XIV*; S. B. Baxter, *William III and the Defence of European Liberty, 1650–1702* (1966); D. G. Schomette and R. D. Haslach, *The Raid on America: The Dutch Naval Campaign of 1672–1674* (Columbia, South Carolina, 1989).

disengagement. One of the most obvious was that of cost. The limited financial resources available to the regime for intelligence gathering could not be wasted. The notorious unpredictability of the diplomatic scene, where yesterday's enemies became today's friends, also dictated the employment of such people. Invariably in the realm of foreign intelligence such people were recruited and placed in strategic position as and when the situation demanded. The sort of intelligence they were gathering, mainly naval and military, was also of less use in peacetime than in time of war. A last point is that the move to hire, then fire, at the end of a conflict represents a familiar pattern in early modern English espionage at this time. It was something which occurred in 1674, as it had in 1667 and as it was to do again on the eve of what, to many, looked like a war with France in 1678. As has been noted above, such a policy led to a somewhat spasmodic intelligence system, at least in foreign affairs, and gave the whole a lack of permanence, as well as a fluctuating number of agents. With a monarch who tended to blow hot and cold in his foreign affairs this was perhaps inevitable.

After the meeting of 5 March 1672 Williamson's first move was to get hold of those who were willing to go into the United Provinces to spy out the posture of the Dutch fleet.[189] Initially his eye fell on Silas Taylor, the keeper of naval stores at Harwich since 1663.[190] An 'expresse' was sent to Taylor ordering him 'to passe into Holland with two persons to discover ye state of ye Dutch fleet'.[191] Taylor was an old, and reliable, correspondent of Williamson who had both military and naval experience. On the other hand his experience of the darker side of diplomacy, espionage, seems to have been rather limited and he could not speak Dutch. As he was chosen to observe and return, more of a 'pathfinder' than anything else, perhaps this did not really matter. Taylor was also well placed at Harwich to go directly to the Netherlands. Although he accepted the commission he was rather worried that the lack of an excuse for going might prove to be his undoing. He also recommended Captain Thomas Langley, master of the Harwich packet boat and former mayor of the town, as another who could be sent into enemy territory. In due course this advice was also acted upon by Williamson.[192]

While Langley and Taylor were trawling through the Dutch ports in search of intelligence Williamson was not idle. He turned to more experi-

[189] He did, of course, already possess correspondents in the ports and towns of the south and eastern coasts of England who could observe the movements of ships, the weather and wind direction. See *CSPD*, 1671–2, p. 462.

[190] *DNB*, Domville; Pepys, *Diary*, X, p. 429; J. R. Tanner, *The Further Correspondence of Samuel Pepys, 1662–1679* (1929); p. 85; J. Aubrey, *Brief Lives* (2 vols., Oxford, 1898), II, pp. 254–6.

[191] PRO SP 29/319A, fo. 7v.

[192] *CSPD*, 1671–2, p. 183.

enced hands to follow up the initial penetration of Dutch plans and preparations. On 12 March 1672 John Scott was seized by Williamson's minions and brought in for instruction and some gentle persuasion. Knowing that Scott was in the country and that he had an excuse to go into the Netherlands (he was after all still in the Dutch army), Williamson decided to use him as a spy. Scott's actual reasons for being in London in March 1672 are obscure. With his penchant for intrigue, they were unlikely to have been benign ones and may have been related to his work for de Witt. Scott was not personally requested to come to England by Williamson as Mower would have it.[193] Williamson's journal note is quite clear on this point: 'Major Scott *taken* & sent away to Holland for Intelligence',[194] the implication being that Scott was in London on his own, or on de Witt's behalf as a spy and arrested by the under-secretary's men.[195] As he was not a man to turn down the chance of money, favour or intrigue, the first and second of which were no doubt promised to him by Williamson and Arlington, they seem to have decided to put him to use for themselves in the United Provinces.[196] At the very least it would enable them to get the potentially troublesome Scott out of England on the eve of a new war and prevent him from spying for the Dutch. On the same day that Scott was taken up, another individual, John Lesh, who had also been recommended to Williamson by diplomats Edmund Custis and Benjamin Glanville, was given 'ample instructions to visite [the] State[s]' for a similar purpose.[197]

By this time there were other agents of Williamson in the United Provinces. Thomas Blood was contacted by Williamson at Amsterdam on 14 March. Blood soon made himself busy on the River Texel by observing the passage of Dutch ships.[198] While Williamson may have trusted Blood to act independently and in good faith (to some extent at least) Scott was another matter. It was decided that as Scott was unable to visit England James Vernon, a former clerk and protégé of the under-secretary and himself a future Secretary of State,[199] should go to Antwerp to talk to him and gather his information.[200] It is worth examining at this point the intelligence which Scott had uncovered in some detail.

By the time Vernon left on the packet boat, which was still running, the

193 Mowrer, *The Indomitable John Scott*, p. 219.
194 PRO SP 29/319A, p. 110. My emphasis.
195 Some information does exist about Scott at this time and may well relate to his presence in London in March 1672. If so, it implies that he might have been working for the Dutch government. See Bod. Lib. Rawlinson MSS A, 175, fos. 29, 29v; Bod. Lib. Rawlinson MSS A, 188, fo. 317.
196 PRO SP 29/319A, fo. 10. 197 *ibid.*, fo. 13v.
198 *ibid.*, fo. 13v; PRO SP 84/188, fo. 125.
199 Vernon was Secretary of State under William III. For more on his relations with Williamson, see PRO SP 78/135, fos. 4, 57, 76.
200 PRO SP 29/319A, fos. 11v, 19v.

two countries were at war. He left England on 16 March.[201] Vernon was to meet the colonel in neutral Antwerp. There Scott informed him that although he had been into The Hague and Amsterdam he had not 'procured [the] list of the Dutch fleet' which he had been asked to obtain.[202] However, Scott had gathered some general facts and figures about the fleet, as well as some information concerning the movement of Dutch vessels.[203] He also claimed to have obtained some interesting information concerning a Frenchman 'which he supposed to have some concerne under my Lord Arlington or in some way belongs to the office'.[204] According to Scott's tale this individual had been supplying information to de Witt for some time, using a surgeon named Brounstein as an intermediary.[205] Scott claimed that de Witt had 'received a letter on 6th March OS dated the 3rd giving him advice of the resolution the English had to seize the Smyrna fleet'. Forewarned of Sir Robert Holmes' attempt upon the Dutch Smyrna fleet, de Witt had been able to spoil that affair.[206]

Once this news had arrived back in England, suspicion fell on a Monsieur Morainville, a Frenchman who translated the *London Gazette*. Morainville fitted Scott's description and moreover he had been in trouble during the last war. His history is obscure but Williamson claimed that Morainville had been involved 'in the calamity of Monsr Fouquet . . . [and] . . . had been a considerable man' in France until that point.[207] Forced out of France he had gained the sympathy and patronage of Prince Rupert through service at sea. As a reward Rupert had recommended him to Arlington and arranged for him to receive the post of translating the *Gazette* into French for 20s. a week. Morainville soon lost this post because, as Williamson put it, 'When we had war with France his man was suspected to hold correspondence with the French, and was turned out.'[208]

201 *CSPD*, 1671–2, p. 210. The ferries from Dover to Calais, Dover to Nieuwpoort, and Harwich to Hellevoetsluis, ran three times weekly, at a fixed passenger charge. It is clear that by the beginning of the war the passengers on return runs of the packet boat from the United Provinces were being subjected to close scrutiny as well as questioning on their knowledge of events in the Low Countries when they arrived in England; for an example see *CSPD*, 1671–2, p. 474. For more on the packet boats see C. R. Boxer, 'Some Second Thoughts on the Third Anglo-Dutch War, 1672–74', *TRHS*, 5th Series, 19, 1969, pp. 75–6.

202 PRO SP 77/40, fo. 42.

203 The Dutch fleet, according to Scott, was to consist of '72 capitall ships of 84, 82, 80, 76, 66, 60, &c the least of 50 gunns which were sent out . . . 24 from Amsterdam 12 from North Holland 12 from Zealand 12 from Friezland & 12 from the Maes &c'. PRO SP 77/40, fo. 42.

204 PRO SP 77/40, fo. 42; PRO SP 29/319A, fo. 19v.

205 PRO SP 77/40, fo. 42.

206 *ibid*.

207 See Williamson's speech in the Commons, 6 November 1678, printed in Grey, *Debates*, VI, p. 158. Also Sainty, *Secretaries of State*, p. 45. For the fall of Fouquet see Wolf, *Louis XIV*, pp. 136–44.

208 Grey, *Debates*, pp. 158, 160–1.

Morainville only regained his position on the intercession of Rupert and he therefore appeared to be a very likely suspect for illicit espionage activities. In fact, Morainville was to be in trouble again in 1678. In that year he was accused by MPs in the House of Commons of deliberately mistranslating the *Gazette* so as to harm the 'protestant religion'. His, self-proclaimed, Roman Catholicism did not help matters as this accusation took place at the height of the Popish Plot scare and Williamson, for one, was quick to wash his hands of the hapless translator.[209] Morainville was called to the bar of the House of Commons to answer for his mistake. This resulted in his being placed in the custody of the sergeant at arms and his house was searched for incriminating evidence.[210]

In the light of the evidence which Scott put forward in 1672 Morainville's papers were seized, but they proved to be unrevealing.[211] The presence of a traitor, or a 'mole' in modern parlance, in the secretariat cannot have been a comforting thought at this stage of the war. However, there is little evidence, other than his previous and future problems, that Morainville was guilty. It might be thought that as these problems were to recur in 1678 he was very suspect indeed. In 1672 nothing seems to have come of the affair.[212] There is, however, evidence that the Dutch commanders of the Smyrna fleet had been warned of a possible attempt on the convoy. But this warning may have been due more to the obviousness of the convoy as a target with the clouds of war threatening than anything specific. Having said this, another warning was given to the commanders of the Dutch fleet when they were off the Portuguese coast as early as 14 February 1672.[213]

In 1672 at any rate Morainville, on the surface at least, must be considered to have fallen foul of Scott's malice, of which the latter had sufficient to worry most people. And it is invariably with Scott that the wheels within wheels begin to turn in this episode. What was his real part in this affair? It is possible, of course, that Morainville had been the victim of a Dutch counter-intelligence game via Scott himself. An alternative is that it was Scott himself who had knowledge of the attack on the Smyrna fleet and who had attempted to inform de Witt. Morainville was therefore useful to the colonel as someone with a 'past' who could have provided

[209] See Grey, *Debates*, VI, pp. 153–65 for the debate. Williamson's response was that Morainville 'has no more relation to my business than my Hatter or Glover'.

[210] *ibid*., p. 162. [211] *CSPD*, 1671–2, p. 269.

[212] The episode is illustrative, however, of the type of lesser functionaries which the secretariat was occasionally forced, through the patronage system, to employ. For a further example see *Williamson Correspondence*, II, p. 164 concerning the newsletter writer forced on Williamson.

[213] See R. C. Anderson, ed., *Journals and Narratives of the Third Dutch War*, Naval Records Society (1946), pp. 6–9; also Rowen, *De Witt*, p. 816; D. Hannay, *A Short History of the Royal Navy, 1217–1688* (1898), p. 413.

Scott with a scapegoat for covering his own tracks. Such a view has a certain plausibility given the nature of Scott's character and the fact that he was in London in March. The evidence is certainly obscure but amongst the documents collected by Pepys in his attempt to defend himself from Scott's lies is an attestation by John Beckman that 'att the time when the King of England did prepare a fleete to put out to sea, hee [Scott] went on the King's Fleet to looke how many shipps there were . . . and that afterwards hee made a rapport thereof to the State at Holland'. Beckman also claimed that Scott sent 'one Pots from the Hague to informe himself where the English fleet was and to endeavour to finde out the said Smirna fleet or shipps and bring a rapport off all this to Holland'.[214] In any case Scott's career shows that he was never a very trustworthy source of information and more than willing to turn his coat if it suited him to do so. He was to do just this in June 1672 when his luck finally ran out. Having been caught sketching the fortifications of Bruges he was forced to flee. He also managed to betray three British spies to the Dutch.[215] He may well have been playing a 'double' game for the rest of the year.[216] But Scott could possibly have been spreading disinformation on behalf of the States General shortly after his arrival in the country. Alternatively, taking the most favourable interpretation, he might just have been telling the truth, hoping that such information, provided to Vernon, would be something his political masters wanted to hear and for which they would reward him accordingly.

Vernon and Scott left Antwerp together in order that they could visit Zeeland and view the Dutch fleet there, in addition to gathering further intelligence. In Zeeland they were able to talk to a member of the States General whose own mouth outran any need for caution on their part. In Middelburg Scott uncovered the information that the Zeelanders had plans for an attempt to 'set upon My Lord Willoughby [in the Americas] and do what damage they could'.[217] Scott was in fact to pass on further information concerning the 'raid on America' in November 1672.[218] In this instance he was perhaps on safer ground than with Morainville.

The government of the province of Zeeland was indeed planning a commercial raid on the Americas. The real discussion about this, in strictest secrecy, began in the autumn of 1672. However, Scott's intelligence placed

[214] Bod. Lib. Rawlinson MSS A, 175, fos. 29–29v.

[215] Bod. Lib. Rawlinson MSS A, 175, fos. 50, 53, 68; *Williamson Correspondence*, I, p. 85.

[216] See also his letters to Williamson, who does not seem to have really encouraged Scott that much after his visit to England in June 1672. See PRO SP 29/319A, fo. 53. For his letters to Williamson 1672–3 see PRO SP 77/40, fos. 105, 110, 194, 202–202v, 225, 234, 276–276v, 289, 299, 301, 303, 306; PRO SP 77/41, fos. 4, 31, 37, 40, 52, 63, 65, 71, 87, 97, 107, 139, 152, 196; PRO SP 77/42, fos. 110, 152–3.

[217] PRO SP 77/40, fo. 42.

[218] PRO SP 104/177, fo. 106.

evidence for the raid at a much earlier date. His information came from the pensioner of Middelburg. This individual told him that they had '4 men of warr and 2 fire ships ... gone to the West Indyes'.[219] This was accurate intelligence as far as it went. The actual numbers of ships chosen for the raid, according to D. G. Schomette and R. D. Haslach, who have written an account of the expedition, was indeed six.[220] These were the vessels *Swaenburgh*, *Schaeckerloo*, *Suriname*, *Zeehond*, *Sint Joris* and *De Eendracht*. Vernon's relation of what Scott told him, for Scott had talked to the pensioner of Middelburg alone, was that these vessels were already departed for the West Indies.[221] However, Schomette and Haslach make it clear that the real expedition left on 30 November 1672.[222] Either Vernon or Scott had been misinformed or they had misinterpreted the information given to them.

Despite this the Zeelanders' secret plans appear to have been successfully penetrated very early on, a fact missed by Schomette and Haslach. Nor were the Zeelanders successful in slipping away secretly in November. For once again the agents of the government were on their mettle. Scott wrote to the secretariat from Bruges with the information of the designs of 'Holl[an]d & Zeeland against o[u]r foreign Plantacōns &c'.[223] This information was duly brought before the Committee of Foreign Affairs on 17 November 1672. It is true that his intelligence of March 1672 does not appear to have been acted upon by the regime and this obviously represents something of a missed opportunity. The various officials of the West Indies and American plantations were apparently not warned of a possibility of a raid by the Dutch until the information of November 1672 had emerged. Even then owing to the vast distances which were involved, as well as the vagaries of the wind and weather, the news did not reach Virginia until April 1673.[224] It was just too late for the colonists. By the time the information arrived the Dutch fleet was already on the way to raid Chesapeake Bay and attempt to capture or destroy the Maryland and Virginia tobacco fleet. But the lesson had been learned. In contrast to 1672, in 1678, when the possibility of a war with France loomed, there were plans to warn the colonies.[225]

Scott's career as a spy illustrates some general themes of the professional

[219] PRO SP 77/40, fo. 42.
[220] Schomette and Haslach, *Raid on America*, pp. 44–7.
[221] PRO SP 77/40, fo. 42.
[222] Schomette and Haslach, *Raid on America*, p. 52.
[223] PRO SP 104/177, fo. 106.
[224] For Virginia's warning see H. R. McIlwaine, ed., *Minutes of the Council and General Court of Colonial Virginia 1622–1632, 1670–1676, With Notes and Excerpts from the Original and General Court Records, Ante 1683* (Richmond, 1924) (22 April 1673), p. 334; also Schomette and Haslach, *Raid on America*, p. 132.
[225] Schomette and Haslach, *Raid on America*, pp. 132–51. For 1678 see BL Add. MSS 10115, fo. 21v.

espionage agent at work. The first point to note is that Scott usually gathered his information in person. Occasionally he was willing to use an intermediary. He was noted as having sent 'one Pots from the Hague to informe himself where the English fleet then was'.[226] On the whole, however, Scott seems to have thought of such 'sub-contracted' spies as 'mere tools'. They were occasionally useful, for 'if his tooles failed him he could not help it', and they provided a convenient excuse to his masters.[227] Scott seems to have felt confident enough of his own abilities to undertake the work himself on most occasions. Of course, with his character it could backfire. John Abbot's servant in Haarlem got into a fight with Scott after the latter had provoked a quarrel, whereupon Scott was soundly thrashed 'black and blew' and fled to the cellar of the house to escape the enraged servant. Later he complained to the burgomaster of Haarlem about the attack and was scoffed for his pains.[228] This physical cowardice sits strangely with the courage necessary to wander into the English fleet in the midst of the Third Dutch War, to go on board ship in order to count the numbers of vessels and question the 'people of the fleet' to gain further intelligence.[229] Scott also performed a similar operation against the Dutch, this time hiring a small boat to sail through the fleet earlier in the war when working for Williamson.[230] In 1678 when Scott was working for the French government he made daily reports of 'all proceedings of Court and Parliament'; he also made detailed lists of the English forces, 'numbers of men, officers and shypps ... and the present state of the severall Castles and Fortifications upon the sea coast of England perticularly [the] Isle of Wight, Portsmouth & Plymouth'.[231] Such activities must have involved some travelling around to the most vulnerable military and naval bases on the English south coast, which given the normal wariness of English local officers when faced with strangers, would have entailed considerable danger.[232] In any case Scott's life called for frequent disappearances from the scene 'privately and on a suddaine' as one witness put it.[233]

One means by which intelligence was gathered by Scott, and others, was

[226] Bod. Lib. Rawlinson MSS A, 175, fo. 29v.

[227] John Joyne, 'A Journal 1679', ed. R. E. Hughes in Greene, *Diaries of the Popish Plot*, p. 76. See also PRO SP 77/40, fo. 225.

[228] Bod. Lib. Rawlinson MSS A, 175, fo. 21. [229] *ibid.*, fo. 29.

[230] PRO SP 77/40, fo. 194.

[231] Bod. Lib. Rawlinson MSS A, 175, fos. 163–4.

[232] It seems Thomas Blood may have been involved in similar activities in England in 1666–7 see Bod. Lib. Rawlinson MSS A, 185, fo. 473v. The Dutch captured a countryman of Lakerwelt whom the French had 'made use of as Espy, to sound the Mote of the City of Gorcum'. A man such as this would have been of more use than one such as Scott. He would at least have had local knowledge. For this incident see Swart, *Netherland-Historian*, p. 233.

[233] Bod. Lib. Rawlinson MSS A,, 175, fo. 164.

to make the victim drunk. Writing to Williamson in July 1672 he noted that, in talking to some victims, 'I have had a great deal of discourse with them; I drank them into a Mellow and good talking strain.'[234] Possibly the difficulties of using this technique of gathering intelligence were something Williamson was to appreciate himself as he was to use it in Cologne in 1673 in the diplomatic world. One of the opposition plenipotentiaries, van Beverning, the Dutchman, he noted, 'seems harsh ... is franke, onely a little hott, especially upon wine'. When 'drinking ... high' he also got a little argumentative apparently. Thus Williamson noted to himself that van Beverning should 'ergo to be dealt with in the morning onely', presumably to catch his hangovers and gain some advantage over him. Williamson also noted that when 'a little fuddled, [he is] apt to talke and even drop his own senses [so] much may by this way he gott from him'.[235] As with the spy-master so with his spies.[236]

Of course, drinking one's victim under the table could lead to problems and even backfire. One of Lord Preston's spies noted that 'I took my opportunity to get the ould father in my company and gave him a supper, but never could put him in the humour as to get what I wished, for tho' I made him as drunk as anything, I was not myself much less.'[237] On other occasions Scott found that it was not even necessary to get his victims drunk for they had loose tongues and no sense of security whatsoever.[238] Scott's techniques may also be compared with another spy of the period, William Hill. Bent on insinuating himself with the ex-minister Edward Riggs he 'began exactly to fit Riggs with expressions suitable to his Tone'. After much of this type of religious talk, 'all of God's glory' Hill noted, Riggs had such a 'good opinion of me, that our souls were as David and Jonathan'.[239] Obviously if the victim was at ease and conversing with those he thought of as friends he could be made to share his thoughts with the spy.

Scott's talents as a cartographer would have also stood him in good stead in gathering information. He was a capable map-maker and always

234 PRO SP 77/40, fos. 202–202v.

235 PRO SP 105/229, fo. 20v. William Chiffinch also attempted to use alcohol to loosen his victims' tongues. See D. Allen, 'The Political Function of Charles II's Chiffinch', *HLQ*, 39, 1976, pp. 277–90.

236 See also PRO SP 105/229, fo. 153; an afternoon spent in conversation with the Bishop of Strasbourg who was a 'little merry' when he arrived and as Williamson put it 'we had hoped to have gott something materiall out of him, But he was presently aware of himselfe'.

237 *HMC*, 7th Report, Graham MSS, p. 392. For a drunken English ambassador from the 1690s and his problems see BL Add. MSS 34095, fo. 106.

238 See Scott's conversation with the *Pensionaris* of Middelburg; PRO SP 77/40, fo. 42.

239 W. Hill, *A Brief Narrative of that Stupendious Tragedie Late Intended to be Acted By the Satanical Saints* (1662), (p. 4).

had such useful items in his luggage. He frequently tried to sell charts and maps (sometimes stolen) to various governments.[240] The other side of such activities was that he was also not averse to betraying his fellow agents if it seemed prudent. Placed in Bruges in 1672 by the English regime he promptly betrayed some of his colleagues to the Dutch authorities. One spent a year and a half in prison before escaping, while the others went to ground or fled.[241] On one occasion Scott himself was discovered upon the walls of Bruges 'drawing a draught of ye Strength & Fortifications thereof'.[242] The local magistrates, who seem to have been rather lacking in initiative but with a penchant for the dramatic, gave him twenty-four hours to get out of the town or they 'would immediately call him in question'.[243] Naturally enough, Scott fled.

Another side to his work was the series of frauds and confidence tricks he perpetrated to gain money. There is little doubt that Scott, as with the others of his kind, had fluctuating financial circumstances. He was, noted one acquaintance, often 'very full of Guineys, while att other times he was very scarce of money'.[244] Occasionally his shabby dress and poverty seems to have left him bitter and resentful and turned him to his natural bent for fraud – a crime it might be noted which is of the least physically dangerous sort. At one small village in Flanders, for example, he claimed loudly and vociferously to have been robbed and demanded compensation from the parish officers. On other occasions he exaggerated his wealth and fortunes in order to survive. He claimed to have a sword 'whereof (to magnify its value) he pretended to have been Cromwell's'.[245]

Scott used a plethora of aliases and military titles to increase his social standing and to protect his real identity.[246] This was matched by the use of disguises when the need arose. John Joyne was with Scott on one occasion when he put on his disguise. It consisted of Scott blackening his eyebrows and beard with a little brush and then putting on a black periwig. This ensemble, Scott claimed, 'when he was so disguised ... noe boddy could know him in it'.[247] Joyne concurred about the disguise's effectiveness. He noted that 'though I was prepared about it yett he did see[m] very much disguised with it'.[248] To go with the disguise were some fine clothes, when Scott possessed them, including a 'rich Embroydered Coate and Belt' which the enterprising colonel had received in France for his services to that crown.[249]

[240] Bod. Lib. Rawlinson MSS A, 175, fo. 72. [241] *ibid.*, fos. 50, 53.
[242] *ibid.*, fos. 53, 68.
[243] *ibid.*, fos. 53, 68. [244] *ibid.*, fo. 163. [245] *ibid.*, fo. 68.
[246] *ibid.*, fos. 1, 10v.
[247] Joyne, 'Journal', p. 68. [248] *ibid.*
[249] Bod. Lib. Rawlinson MSS A, 175, fo. 163, and Joyne, 'Journal', p. 68.

The dauntless colonel also fancied himself as a ladies' man, or as he put it a 'Beau Garçon'.[250] He did not see this as a fault because he was arrogant enough to believe himself 'above ye Common [herd]'.[251] Moreover whatever 'it was that they [the ladies] liked in him if he hath a good fortune of prevailing upon them, more then other men so be it'.[252] Matched with this arrogant and confident approach to women was Scott's belief in his ability to impose his opinions and ideas on other men, by fair means or foul, for he was something of a bully. On one occasion he showed one of his techniques to Joyne, claiming that he would 'now ... set this man [his chosen victim] a talking & then make him cry when I please & make him think himselfe a greate man & talk of his former affaires', 'which', noted Joyne, 'he did'.[253]

Underlying this apparent confidence in his own abilities was a much darker individual. Scott was a man with a profound sense of insecurity and a suspicion of everyone he met or came into contact with. He hated his social superiors and had a great 'dislike to everybody that he obliged to, but that a man could do nothing out of nothing'.[254] Perhaps this 'Swiftian' dislike of his fellow man made it easier to betray them. But a dislike of their associates was common enough amongst such men. Someone who attempted to ensnare Thomas Blood shortly after his release from the Tower in 1671 is another example of this attitude. Blood asked Williamson how he should 'carry [myself] towards such creatures',[255] and throughout the letter the trepans remained 'creatures' to Blood, not human in any sense. The life of a spy could make even the most amiable man harsh in his approach to his fellows and few of the spies were amiable men.

Scott had a shifting 'mercurial' personality which moved from exuberance to depression as circumstances dictated. The ups and downs of Scott's character were shown clearly by Joyne's journal of the time they spent together.[256] The disguises, false names, arrogant attitudes to men and women and hatred of social superiors are all revealing. They show a personality under some distress. Scott also had a drink problem. He was prone to talking while in his cups and with an increasing violence in his language until he moved onto accosting serving maids and other women with kisses. He was also violent in his dislikes. As he drank Joyne noticed Scott 'grew

250 Joyne, 'Journal', p. 76. 251 *ibid.* 252 *ibid.*

253 *ibid.*, p. 60. Scott was also alleged to have cudgelled the Earl of Anglesey, perhaps on Buckingham's behalf, with whom he, as were many of these men, was also associated. See *HMC*, Various Collections, II, pp. 127–8; and Ashcraft, *Revolutionary Politics*, p. 132.

254 *ibid.*, p. 79. 255 PRO SP 29/293, fo. 12.

256 To follow his moods over a number of days it is necessary to read the whole journal. It is more reliable than Mowrer seems to suggest; see *The Indomitable John Scott*, pp. 202; 334–43. See also PRO SP 84/188, fos. 244, 289.

in his swearing and cursing till it came, to an excessive degree at last'.[257] His attitude is seen in a phrase which an acquaintance heard from his lips one day during such a drinking bout, 'God damn [all] creation', said Scott and there is no reason to doubt that he meant every word.[258]

Scott was also a braggart and a fantasist. He regaled one associate with the tale that he was a former English admiral who had been engaged to a noble lady. The king deciding that she should marry the Duke of Monmouth, Scott was ordered to sea. This farago of lies is representative of Scott's mental difficulties. The inability to hold onto the truth, the lying and bragging bully-like pose he put on was matched by physical cowardice. There is no doubt that he possessed valuable assets as a spy in his eloquence and ability to make instant friendships in order to garner information from his victims, but while he seems never to have trusted anyone, neither was he trusted in return. Was this the key to his ultimately self-destructive cycle of depression, arrogance and violence? Whatever the truth behind Scott's personality problems, and at this distance in time it is impossible to fully comprehend them, he provides a perfect example of what could happen to the spy on the ground level of the Restoration intelligence system.

Lack of encouragement in his work and what often seems to have been simple hostility from the Stuart regime at home led Scott to think of other ways of increasing his fortune. Spies were invariably poorly rewarded and basely used and a man with Scott's personality would have resented this basic fact of life in the world of early modern espionage. He had been on the fringes of the joint Arlington and Buckingham peace mission to Europe in June 1672. A French acquaintance, Denis d'Allais, saw him there 'very magnificent in his habit'.[259] Scott also dined at Buckingham's table and began an association with the duke which was to develop in later years. Arlington had provided Scott with an allowance to gather intelligence and placed him in Bruges for this purpose, but the colonel had soon been chased out of the city.[260] It is likely that Scott was still being encouraged by Williamson to gather intelligence, but how much faith was being placed in the results was another matter. There was also the question of Scott's betrayal of three British agents to consider.[261] He was soon in trouble all round. In 1673 Williamson, who had moved to Cologne for the congress there, heard that 'severall complaints have been made of Coll. Scott in Flanders [he] does the king all the ill service his capacity will give him leave'.[262] It would have come as no surprise to Williamson to find Scott

257 Joyne, 'Journal', pp. 57–83.
258 Bod. Lib. Rawlinson MSS A, 188, fo. 160.
259 *ibid*., fos. 262–3.
260 Bod. Lib. Rawlinson MSS A, 175, fos. 53, 68.
261 *ibid*., fo. 50.
262 *Williamson Correspondence*, I, p. 85.

had transferred his activities to Paris in the winter of 1673–4 in search of fresh pickings. He had wormed his way into the entourage of the Prince d'Condé, who passed Scott onto Jean-Baptiste Colbert. Scott was soon practising his old trade of touting maps and charts around the French government.[263] According to William Perwich, who was based in the English embassy there, Scott was full of himself and of a 'thousand chimericall projects'.[264] Over the next few years France was to provide a home of sorts for the Englishman. One of his 'chimericall projects' involved casting guns for the French king. This doubtful scheme, backed by the Secretary of State for the navy, the Marquis de Seigneley, floundered in mutual recrimination and bitterness. Despite engaging a number of Englishmen to assist him in the foundries at Nevers, the resulting cannons exploded on use, the makers quarrelled and Scott's hope of a fortune literally went up in smoke. The affair left him out on the streets, poverty stricken and, when d'Allais came across him in Paris, 'very shabby and much fallen from ... high splendour'.[265]

After the débâcle at Nevers there was little choice but to return to the old trade of espionage. He chose to enter French employ and he would have doubtless felt at home in the French service for the spies in the employ of France were an invariable mixture of rogues and adventurers, with the occasional loyal servant thrown in for good measure. It was not the occupation of a gentleman, but just occasionally useful information came in from the higher levels of society. The fact that land possession and titles cut across the many boundaries of the European states gave such people mixed loyalties. Many other spies in the employ of the Sun King were drawn, like Scott, from the professional coterie who haunted the staterooms and corridors of the ministries and palaces of Europe. Their actual value was often questionable, although the French crown had plenty of money, paid well and, perhaps more importantly, on time. On the other hand the risks were quite high if the spy were caught; there was the possibility of torture and execution if they were unlucky, a lengthy imprisonment if they were lucky. The spy who betrayed Louis XIV's government was also all too well aware of his fate if he were caught double dealing. The French regime had a long arm and a long memory and had little respect for international borders. The kidnapping of the guilty party in order to deal with him at leisure on French soil was always a distinct possibility.[266]

By 1678 Scott was back in the full flow of this world. He crossed back and forth over the Channel, haunting the entourage of Buckingham and

[263] PRO SP 78/138, fos. 145–145v, 177–9. [264] *ibid.*
[265] Bod. Lib. Rawlinson MSS A, fos. 262–3.
[266] See below, Chapter 7.

other opposition leaders to Danby. He spied for the French government and it was a profitable line of work. He could afford smarter clothes and show off his 'girdle ... full of guinneys'.[267] Giles Hancock made Scott's acquaintance in the summer of 1678. Hancock's association with Scott was deliberate for he was one of Williamson's spies.[268] The Secretary of State, as he now was, had set Hancock on to keep a wary eye on the affairs of his former employee. The possibility of a French war engaged Williamson's mind in the period before the outbreak of the Popish Plot and Scott had made himself such an ostentatious target that trailing him was the logical thing to do. In turn Scott rather stupidly engaged Hancock to write up some of the intelligence he was gathering. Considering the sort of material which passed before Hancock's eyes this might be seen as the height of folly. It included lists of English warships, with notes of crews and armaments, the numbers of English troops and garrisons on the south coast and the affairs of parliament. He was also intent on gaining knowledge of the deliberations of the Council of State on the apparently impending war with his masters in France. At this point he disappeared for six weeks, but was soon back, suitably attired and replenished with cash.

If anything Scott's character had deteriorated in the late 1670s. He was becoming even more foul-mouthed, unpleasant and, when drunk, prone to an active fantasy life as an English admiral.[269] Naval affairs were very much on his mind which may account for this fantasy. He was working for Monsieur de Pélissary, the Treasurer-General of the French navy. It is clear from the accusation later made against Pepys and Deane that it was Scott rather than the two Englishmen who supplied the French regime with naval and strategic intelligence.[270] The meetings with de Pélissary were useful items to store away for future use by the colonel and he was returning to England to continue his work there by developing an association with the opposition groups when the political and religious storm broke in England in the autumn of 1678. This time Scott would have hoped to have been well placed to exploit its opportunities.

Scott had already found a patron in the Duke of Buckingham and for a time remained in close orbit around the duke. As has already been noted, Buckingham's talents for attracting the sleazy and stranger elements of the Stuart underworld were considerable. They included the ex-Leveller and perennial plotter John Wildman, who worked for Buckingham in a variety of legal and illegal capacities. On Buckingham's orders Wildman paid off some of Scott's debts.[271] The enterprising French spy was also associating

[267] Bod. Lib. Rawlinson MSS A, 175, fo. 163.
[268] *CSPD*, 1680–1, pp. 584–5.
[269] Bod. Lib. Rawlinson MSS A, 188, fos. 182–3.
[270] Grey, *Debates*, VII, pp. 303–4.
[271] Bod. Lib. Rawlinson MSS A, 175, fo. 193; Haley, *Shaftesbury*, p. 521.

with other opposition groups now gathering under the auspices of Shaftesbury. Shaftesbury himself made use of Scott,[272] although the colonel was more closely associated with Buckingham and the Green Ribbon Club. Certainly as the crisis progressed Scott had his hopes raised of obtaining something lasting for once. He even planned to become an MP and would have probably been no worse than many of the real rogues who made it to the Commons. He also planned to marry Lady Vane whom he besieged in the manner befitting a soldier, much to her family's distress.[273] On a practical level he found himself being used as a messenger between the opposition and the French government. He was taking money from the French ambassador, but his own politics were entirely mercenary, consisting of Scott first and last.[274] There was also the question of Sir Edmund Godfrey.

Rumours that Scott had been involved in an assassination plot in this period emerged in late 1678. This intelligence had come from Thomas Blood, acting in his capacity as a government agent. One of Blood's sources was a tobacconist by the name of John Harrison, who was himself examined in 1683. According to Harrison, Scott had many associations with the men who were to be mixed up in the Rye House Plot. Indeed Scott himself later admitted that he knew something of the business. These men were radicals, Buckingham's minions and the extremists of the Whig party. Beyond the basics Blood had been unable to unravel much more of this possibly spurious design.[275] However, it may have also been linked with another scheme revealed to Williamson. This was a plot which combined three extreme groups, the Fifth Monarchists, the 'Atheists' and Sir Robert Peyton and his 'gang'.[276] Peyton and his so-called gang were an interesting factor for one of the men mentioned as a member of this group was none other than Sir Edmund Godfrey.

Godfrey, of course, was the justice of the peace to whom Oates and Tonge were advised by an unknown party to swear their depositions and whose mysterious death sparked off the Popish Plot hysteria. Godfrey remains a strangely mysterious figure for such a well-known London character.[277] Prior to his long afterlife as a martyr very little detail has survived of his actual life. He was a noted and occasionally rather ruthless man of

272 Haley, *Shaftesbury*, p. 521. 273 Joyne, 'Journal', p. 78.

274 See C. L. Grose, 'French Ambassadors' Reports on Financial Relations with Members of Parliament, 1677–81', *EHR*, 44, 1929, p. 627.

275 *CSPD*, 1677–8, p. 388.

276 *CSPD*, 1676–7, pp. 11–12; *CSPD*, 1660–85 Addendum, p. 466.

277 For Godfrey see BL Lansdowne MSS 235; BL Royal MSS 12A, 12,'Viola Martia', fo. 16; BL Add. MSS 33578, fo. 33; Greater London Record Office, Middlesex Record Accession 1376, nos. 205–212b; R. Tuke, *Memories of the Life and Death of Sir Edmund Bury Godfrey* (1682); W. Lloyd, *A Sermon at the Funeral of Sir Edmund Bury Godfrey* (1678); R. North, *Examen* (1740); R. L'Estrange, *A Brief History of the Times*, (1688), pt 3, pp. 168–9.

business, prominent in the world of his parish of St-Martin-in-the-Fields, known at court as a notable upholder of the law and relatively well off in financial terms. His politics and religion were apparently clear enough. On the surface he was a zealous Anglican and a patriot. Unfortunately, however, he presented a more contradictory picture. He moved in high circles, associating both with Danby and Gilbert Burnet. He was soft on nonconformity as well as Roman Catholicism and had a number of friends amongst the Catholic community, including Edward Coleman.[278] Godfrey had also been in trouble with the court at various times. With this in mind it seems odd to find him in the company of Sir Robert Peyton for Peyton was one of the more extreme opposition MPs, whose own actions may have concealed deeper motives. He was a staunch Green Ribbon Club member and for a time one of Shaftesbury's lieutenants. In 1680, however, he became something of a fallen angel amongst the Whigs after his attempts to come to terms with the Duke of York and his links, personal or sexual, with Mrs Cellier were made public. Peyton was unpleasant and occasionally quite violent.[279] Government informers had also been watching the activities of Peyton and his associates for he had been accused of seditious words and was thought to be quite a desperate character. It must be presumed that they were also interested in Godfrey.[280]

There has been speculation that Godfrey was murdered not by Catholics or others but at the instigation of the members of this group because of the secrets he knew, namely the connections between these men and the French.[281] The obvious candidate for organising the murder would have been a man such as Scott. There is unfortunately little beyond very circumstantial evidence to link Scott with the crime. Scott had met Godfrey before and the spy was associated with the more extreme members of the opposition.[282] He was also behaving oddly when Godfrey went missing – in fact Scott left London rather abruptly two days before the body was discovered. Beyond this there is little real evidence. If Scott had been involved in Godfrey's death there is little doubt that Samuel Pepys' extensive investigations would have uncovered the fact. Scott later claimed that he had fled the country, though in a roundabout way, because he had heard he was to be 'clapped up and starved', though there was no reason for him to believe

278 *HMC*, Ormonde, IV, p. 464. Burnet, *History*, II pp. 162–4.
279 *CSPD*, 1677–8, pp. 617–8.
280 *HMC*, Finch MSS, II, pp. 43–6; *CSPD*, 1676–7, pp. 11–12.
281 The speculation on the reasons for Godfrey's murder has been endless. As a starting point see Pollock, *Popish Plot*, pp. 83 *et passim*; A. Marks, *Who Killed Sir Edmund Berry Godfrey?* (1905); J. Dickson Carr, *The Murder of Sir Edmund Godfrey* (1936); the eccentric S. Knight, *The Killing of Justice Godfrey* (1986); J. G. Muddiman, 'The Mystery of Sir Edmund Bury Godfrey', *The National Review*, 1924, pp. 138–45.
282 For Scott and Godfrey see *CSPD*, 1667–8, p. 493.

this according to the public statements of secretary Coventry. However, we have already seen that Williamson was having Scott watched and Coventry was not being entirely honest with the House, for he also was interested in Scott's activities.[283] The secretary's statement to the House was thus rather misleading. Scott admitted he had been travelling the coasts of Sussex and Kent and had stayed with Sir Francis Rolle,[284] another radical MP who had taken money from the French. While there was reason enough for him to leave he eventually did so in a rather melodramatic fashion under the surprising alias of Godfrey. In the meantime Samuel Pepys became involved in the affair. He had been informed of Scott's flight and made attempts to stop him at the coast under the belief that Scott was a Jesuit priest.[285] This mistaken belief Scott greatly resented and revenge for this slur was very much on his mind from then on. At the least it gave him a sufficient reason to become involved in an attempt to destroy Pepys.

The plan to bring down Pepys and Sir Anthony Deane was certainly not the idea of Scott. Buckingham's associates and minions appear to have been behind it all. Colonel Roderick Mansell, William Harboard, Sir John Hotham and Thomas Papillon planned the scheme in conjunction with Scott. They also involved John James, the amorous ex-butler of Pepys who had been sacked for being caught in bed with Samuel's housekeeper, and who was destined for the role of second witness. The scheme was to destroy Pepys as well as have him removed from his post and through him attack his patron James, Duke of York. One failed attempt had already been made through the clerk William Hewer and another was sure to follow. Scott's part was to return to England. This led to his arrest,[286] but he soon deposed that he had seen charts, plans and other intelligence in the office of Monsieur de Pélissary, Louis XIV's Treasurer-General of the navy and his real master. Scott also claimed to have discovered that Pepys and Deane were responsible for passing on the information and were closet Catholics. James was used to back the accusation of catholicism with his inside information that Pepys was an aggressive papist, associated with one Morelli, a musician, and together they sang numerous psalms: in a time of such madness incriminating evidence indeed.

These allegations came out in an unsympathetic House of Commons in 1679 and both men were forced to fight hard to rebut them. Pepys denied the accusations and rightly claimed that John James' evidence was untrue and that in any case the ex-butler had a grudge against him over the housekeeper. Pepys also claimed that he had never heard of Scott except for the

[283] Coventry MSS, 2, fos. 303, 395–6, 506–7. [284] Grey, *Debates*, II, pp. 306–7.
[285] Bod. Lib. Rawlinson MSS A, 175, fos. 215–24; *CSPD*, 1683, pp. 390–1; *CSPD*, 1678, p. 509; R. Ollard, *Pepys: A Biography* (1974), p. 249; Coventry MSS, 2, fo. 303.
[286] Grey, *Debates*, VII, pp. 303–9.

incident in the previous year.[287] Deane was on much more insecure ground, for though he denied the charges he accidently revealed that he had been doing some intelligence work for the English crown. There was also the hint of double dealing. On a visit to France Deane claimed that he endeavoured to 'improve my time ... by information of their whole methods of government of their Navy'.[288] In due course he had passed his intelligence onto Williamson. The latter, who disliked such undercover activities appearing so publicly, reluctantly admitted to have 'borrowed great lights from Deane' and that Deane had been useful in other ways.[289] It made little difference; the House sent both men to the Tower.[290] After the initial shock, Pepys turned his formidable energies to undermining his enemies by gathering as much information about their unsavoury past as he could. In the long run Pepys managed to rebut the charges and save his life although he was temporarily out of office. Scott carried on much as before, attempting to make the most of his opportunities, but having little success overall. His violent temper eventually proved to be his undoing. In a drunken brawl in 1682 he murdered a coachman and was once again forced to flee the country.[291]

Scott's final years left him wandering the continent and saw his return to the Americas. With a murder to answer for, a return to England was out of the question and there was little improvement in his fortunes. John Gelson, a former agent of the regime, came across Scott in Sweden in 1683. In a talkative mood, perhaps he was drunk, Scott told Gelson that he knew numerous secrets about the Whigs and others and Gelson pumped him for information, but did not get very far.[292] After this Scott disappeared back into oblivion. He appears to have returned to the Americas. He did not reappear in Europe until 1695 when he promptly became involved in Jacobite intrigues, possibly as a spy for the regime of William III. He was in England in 1696 and claimed to have a pardon for the murder of the coachman in 1682. Little came of this except that it re-awakened the interest of Pepys in his former enemy's doings.[293] Scott was last heard of in the West Indies where he had a position in local government. His death in Bridgetown in 1704 finally put an end to his life of restless wandering.

[287] *ibid.* [288] *ibid.* [289] *ibid.* [290] Evelyn, *Diary*, IV, p. 169.
[291] *CSPD*, 1682, p. 211; *CSPD*, 1683, p. 184.
[292] *CSPD*, 1683, pp. 390, 437–8.
[293] J. R. Tanner, ed., *Private Correspondence and Miscellaneous Papers of Samuel Pepys, 1679–1703* (1926), pp. 129–30; *HMC*, Buccleuch MSS, pp. 291–6.

7

The foreign and diplomatic scene

I

In the later seventeenth century diplomacy was often merely seen as warfare by other means.[1] In such a world the cutting edge of diplomacy lay in its intelligence gathering and espionage activities. These 'secret services' were an essential part of the diplomatic arsenal of any state. They could, of course, cover a multitude of actions from subterfuge and chicanery, to bribery, corruption, simple news gathering and running spies, or even more complex operations such as kidnapping and murder. For the Stuart regime, as for others, the men who ran this seamy side of diplomatic life were located in two areas of government. The first of these, as we have seen, lay in the office of the Secretary of State in London. The secretaries divided European affairs between themselves, although not always equitably, and ran the second group of officials involved in foreign affairs, those ambassadors, agents, residents and consuls who made up the diplomatic corps. The diplomat stood in the front line of such activities. While the diplomat then, as now, was seen as the representative of his country abroad, more often than not he was also seen as a mere spy by another name; an 'honourable spy' as Abraham de Wicquefort put it, but still a spy. The concern here is less with the diplomat's role as a purveyor of his country's fluctuating foreign policy and more with his role in that area known as secret services. In general this can be divided into two main areas: intelligence gathering and espionage activities, or information and action. Nearly all English diplomats in the reign were involved in the first of these, invariably on behalf of the ubiquitous Williamson, and several of the most notable ones were involved in the second.

[1] For diplomacy in the period see Roosen, *The Age of Louis XIV*; D. P. Heatley, *Diplomacy and the Study of International Relations* (Oxford, 1919); P. Barber, *Diplomacy: The World of the Honest Spy* (BL, 1979); P. S. Lachs, *The Diplomatic Corps of Charles II and James II* (New Brunswick, 1965); G. Mattingly, *Renaissance Diplomacy* (Harmondsworth, 1973); V. Barbour 'Consular Service in the Reign of Charles II', *American Historical Review*, 33, 1928, pp. 553–78.

Diplomatic literature in the period apparently saw the diplomat as a vessel which should contain all the virtues of mankind. In reality none of the English diplomats of the reign of Charles II could claim to be such paragons. They were in fact a mixed bag of men, ranging from Williamson himself, to the irascible Denzil Holles,[2] and the austere and touchy Sir William Temple. There were also men such as the unscrupulous Sir George Downing, as well as that cool 'trimmer' Henry Saville, Marquess of Halifax. In its lower ranks the diplomatic corps of Charles II was ably served by men such as the ex-soldier Sir Richard Bulstrode or Jerome Nipho, who performed sterling service for some years in Antwerp.[3]

In comparison with the diplomatic corps of Louis XIV, that of the English crown does appear less professional, undermanned and under-financed. In its own way, however, it served the regime well, for although the English crown possessed diplomatic interests from Lisbon to Constantinople, it had only five permanent embassies of any real note. These were located in the capital cities of France, Spain, Portugal and the United Provinces, alongside the Hanse Towns, Hamburg, Bremen and Lübeck. Even at these embassies the rank of diplomat and the significance of the post itself varied according to the circumstances, policies and financial health of the English regime.[4] Of these embassies only two may be said to have been of real significance throughout the reign. The first of these was in Paris while the other was at the hub of European espionage in the later seventeenth century, that is to say in the United Provinces, at The Hague. For Charles II and his ministers Anglo-French relations were of course of primary significance. Inevitably, however, the presence of Louis XIV's own able ambassadors[5] at Charles II's court and the king's own private politics made the court in London more significant for Anglo-French relations than any English diplomat's dealings at Paris. Which is not to say that English espionage activities did not take place there.[6]

[2] See A. Marshall, 'Sir Joseph Williamson and the Congress of Cologne' (unpublished paper); and for Holles see P. Crawford, *Denzil Holles 1598–1680: A Study of His Political Career* (1979), pp. 199–208.

[3] For Bulstrode see *DNB*, Richard Bulstrode; BL Egerton MSS 3678, fos. 17, 19; PRO SP 77/44, fo. 62; PRO SP 84/91/2, fo. 295; *CSPD*, 1672–3, pp. xxx–xxxi; R. Bulstrode, *Memoirs and Reflections Upon the Reign and Government of King Charles the Ist and King Charles the IId* (1721); for Nipho and some of his work see PRO SP 29/87, fo. 65, PRO SP 84/180, fo. 10; PRO SP 77/40, fos. 102, 139, 274; *CSPD*, 1670, p. 12; *CSPD*, 1672–3, p. 87; *CSPD*, 1676–7, p. 486; W. Macdonald-Wigfield, *The Monmouth Rebellion A Social History* (Bradford, 1980), p. 94; E. Parry, *The Bloody Assize* (1929), p. 247.

[4] See Lachs, *Diplomatic Corps*, p. 10 *et passim*.

[5] On the French ambassadors in England see M. E. Houlbrooke, 'Paul Barrillon's Embassy in England 1677–1688: A Study in the Diplomacy of Louis XIV', unpublished B.Litt thesis, University of Oxford, 1971.

[6] See above, Chapter 4.

Second only to France in importance for English diplomacy was the Dutch Republic. A number of reasons lay behind this. Firstly there was the complex and usually acrimonious relationship between the English crown and the Dutch Republic which led the states into two wars. This latent hostility meant that Dutch territory was a hunting ground for the Stuart regime's spies of all sorts. There was also the presence in the Netherlands of the significantly large, as well as dangerous, exile community. These exiles drew in the government's spies to watch their activities and try to hold them in check. The importance of this task and the significance of Anglo-Dutch relations as a whole meant that the post of ambassador was filled by some of the most able English diplomats of the era. Two of the most experienced were Sir George Downing and Williamson's personal *bête noir*, Sir William Temple.[7]

During this period there was usually no specially constructed building designated as the embassy in such places.[8] The invariable pattern was for the diplomat to use the house where he lived with his diplomatic 'family' and transact his diplomatic business there. The diplomat's 'family' were the staff and servants which he took with him on his mission.[9] Their numbers depended on the importance of his post and in the first instance on his own wealth, for English diplomats' salaries were notoriously unforthcoming from the government. At the very least it was usual for the ambassador to have an official secretary and some clerks. These administrators worked in the embassy office, writing letters, transcribing or ciphering documents and translating, as well as digesting information obtained from the local press and manuscript newsletters for transmission to London.

François de Callières noted that the diplomat had to be careful in his choice of secretary and clerks. He argued that the diplomat should avoid employing 'light-headed, frivolous or indiscreet men'[10] for such people could cause him grave problems. To prove his point de Callières cited the case of a private secretary to a French ambassador who sold copies of the embassy's ciphers to rid himself of his debts.[11] A lapse, or an indiscretion, or just plain greed by one of these men could be seized upon and exploited by a clever man such as Joseph Williamson who would engage the victim

7 For Williamson and Temple see especially *CSPD*, 1678, pp. 360–1; Temple, *Works*, II, pp. 296–8.
8 D. B. Horn, *The British Diplomatic Service 1689–1789* (Oxford, 1961), p. 16.
9 See PRO SP 103/76, a loose bundle of papers one of which, headed 'Baron d' Wich', appears to be Williamson's list of some of those associated with his embassy to Cologne in 1673.
10 de Callières, *The Practice of Diplomacy*, pp. 97–8.
11 *ibid.* See also Rowen, *De Witt*, p. 256 on a Dutch spy on the French ambassador's staff.

to supply intelligence from within the embassy. In 1675 Williamson recruited Don Pardini, a clerk or secretary within the entourage of Don Pedro Ronquillo, the Spanish ambassador to London. Pardini was willing to supply Williamson with information from inside the embassy for the sum of £100 a year.[12] There could, of course, be added dangers for such people the more deeply they became involved in espionage. Petrus Cunaeus was secretary to Van Goch, the Dutch ambassador in London in 1665. Cunaeus was arrested for spying on the English fleet.[13] In retaliation the Dutch, with the assistance of the two exiles and erstwhile English spies, William Scot and Joseph Bamfield, arrested Downing's secretary Charles Gringand.[14] They also picked up Nicholas Oudart, who was in the service of the Prince of Orange and connected with Downing. The impecunious military historian, soldier and ex-spy of John Thurloe, Roger Manley, who had been in Dutch service and was at that point also assisting Downing, and the English merchant and spy Thomas Corney, were also arrested at the same time.[15]

Abraham de Wicquefort was another man who became involved in espionage as a minor diplomat. He came from a good Dutch Regent family and spent most of his life involved in diplomacy and in espionage.[16] He was a private 'gazetter' and part-time spy for a number of governments, amongst whom were the English. In the 1650s he was in Paris supplying information to de Witt, amongst others, until his news of the young Louis XIV's amatory adventures landed him in the Bastille.[17] By 1674, when Sir Joseph Williamson, then on his way back from Cologne, recruited de Wicquefort, the latter was an old hand at the game, with slippery loyalties. To Williamson, however, de Wicquefort was a potentially good source for intelligence as he was the Dutch secretary who 'translated the intelligence which came from England'.[18] Williamson took care to nurture de Wicquefort because the originals of this correspondence could occasionally be obtained by such a means. This enabled the Secretary of State to check the handwriting of such documents. At the time this was of more than usual significance as Williamson was engaged in uncovering the intelligence

[12] PRO SP 29/366, fo. 25; *CSPD*, 1675–6, pp. 143, 268, 476.

[13] Rowen, *De Witt*, p. 612.

[14] For Gringand see *CSPD*, 1667–8, p. 129.

[15] For Oudart see Rowen, *De Witt*, p. 612; Feiling, *Foreign Policy*, p. 88; *DNB*, Nicholas Oudart. For Manley's work for Thurloe under the alias of Jacques la Barre see BL Stowe MSS 185, fo. 183; also *CSPD*, 1664–5, p. 490. For Corney see PRO SP 29/236, fo. 100. For more on these events and individuals see R. R. Goodison, 'England and the Orangist Party 1665–1672', unpublished MA thesis, University of London, 1934.

[16] The best account of his life and work is in L. E. Lenting, ed., *Abraham de Wicquefort: Histoire des Provinces-Unies des Païs-Bas* (4 vols., 1861–74), I, pp. vii–lv.

[17] See Rowen, *De Witt*, fo. 276.

[18] Burnet, *History*, II, p. 62.

network of Pierre du Moulin.[19] Unfortunately de Wicquefort was arrested in March 1675 and sentenced to life imprisonment. This was partly Williamson's fault as de Wicquefort's masters suddenly decided to see some original documents and he was unable to produce them, having sent them off to the English Secretary of State. His letters from Williamson were also found when he was arrested, but the secretary could not be held responsible for that.[20] It took de Wicquefort nearly four years to engineer an escape. This he achieved in February 1679 when he gave up the dangerous life and retired into the territory of the Duke of Brunswick. He died at Zell in 1682.[21] In spite of such potential problems, to gain a place in a diplomat's 'family' was a useful step up the career ladder for a promising young man.[22]

Embassy routine itself mainly revolved around the post days when mail came into and went out of the embassy. The most important correspondence was with the secretaries' offices in London, although most ambassadors would also write to other ministers on an unofficial basis. However, the ambassador's instructions usually ordered him to 'keep a frequent & att least weekly correspondence with Our Principall S[ecretary] of State'.[23] In general the secretaries responded on similar lines. There were occasional complaints of neglect of course, William Wynne, for example, claimed that the Secretary of State never remembered 'one Day what had been done the Day before, or never cared what would be done the next' and that consequently they often left embassies 'without any instructions at all'.[24] There seems to be some 'sour grapes' in this view in light of all the work which went on in the office. However, Arlington, aware of the problems of distance and time, did note in 1668 that he thought it best to 'send a wise man on an errand and say nothing to him'.[25] Much seems to have depended on the posting itself and its importance to the government in London.

There were also occasional problems of jurisdiction for the secretaries

19 Williamson also wanted intelligence on the state of the Dutch government, as well as its navy and army.

20 M. Lane, 'A Relation of the Present State of Affairs in the United Provinces', *EHR*, 30, 1915, pp. 304–17.

21 For more on de Wicquefort see *CSPD*, 1673–4, pp. 263–4, 266, 274, 275–6, 277, 284, 288, 293, 299, 320, 325, 333, 356, 362, 378, 380, 399–400; *CSPV*, 1673–4, p. 382; Barber, *Diplomacy*, p. 80; Rowen, *De Witt*, pp. 256, 275–6; Haley, *William of Orange*, pp. 197–8.

22 Such as William Blathwayt for example, see BL Add. MSS 56240. Also *HMC*, Various MSS, II, pp. 140–1.

23 BL Stowe MSS 191, fo. 4v. For a diplomat receiving his instructions see *CSPD*, 1667, p. 503; *CSPD*, 1678, pp. 224, 226.

24 Wynne quoted in Lachs, *Diplomatic Corps*, p. 26. It may be that Wynne wished to defect criticism from Sir Leoline Jenkins who was notoriously indecisive as a diplomat.

25 *ibid.*, p. 26.

which provide some explanation for whatever neglect of ambassadors there was. The secretaries divided the countries of Europe between them, but at this stage in the office's history the division was not firmly fixed.[26] Of the two the southern office was undoubtedly the more important, containing, as it did, the regime's relations with France and Spain. To this Arlington added the regime's relations with the Low Countries and the United Provinces which theoretically should have been within the jurisdiction of the northern office. Williamson promptly took the United Provinces back into his province on becoming northern secretary in 1674, much to Temple's chagrin. In any case, whatever the province, Williamson tried to build up an extensive network of correspondents and newsletters with all sorts of diplomats and their servants in his time in Arlington's office. This benefited both sides. In return for their local news diplomats would be provided with domestic information. They were also obliged to keep up a correspondence between each other.[27] This obviously meant a lot of work for someone, usually the embassy's clerks. In Temple's office at The Hague William Blathwayt found himself spending much of his time translating foreign newsletters which came into the office. Their news could then be digested and forwarded to London. Much of the embassy office routine not unnaturally paralleled that of the work carried on in the Secretary of State's office in Whitehall. A life of drudgery was normal although ciphering and deciphering was all important, for there was 'little faire dealing' in the conveying of diplomatic letters.[28]

II

According to the Frenchman François de Callières there were certain recommended characteristics which went to make up the 'good' diplomat. The diplomat, he thought, should have an observant mind, and a spirit of application for work which was not distracted by pleasures or frivolities. Sound judgement was also necessary, alongside an ability to quietly uncover the thought of others. An agile and fertile mind was a bonus, as it enabled the diplomat to deal with a sudden crisis. He needed to have his wits about him and to be able to think on his feet, for the factors of time and distance from home dictated that he worked with a great degree of independence when it came to making decisions. One of the most important characteristics a diplomat had to have was the ability to hold his tongue and keep his own counsel. In effect the astute diplomat was able to use his situation to give out less information than he received. Henry

26 PRO SP 29/61, fos. 273, 275, 277.
27 See for example *HMC*, Various MSS, II, p. 131.
28 BL Stowe MSS 191, fo. 4v and Chapter 2.

Saville supported this view. Giving some advice on this matter to a prospective ambassador, he noted that 'At Court you will meet many open faces; let yours be so to, but your mouth [keep] shut'.[29]

The actual social rank of a diplomat was a point to some debate in the period. A man of birth and breeding would obviously fit well into the major courts of Europe and because of his rank, more easily gain the confidence of his fellow courtiers. However, the lower born but more practical man was usually more suited to the less gentlemanly activity of espionage. A man such as Sunderland, while he was very well suited to the court of Louis XIV, could not have hoped to have matched the more sleazy talents of a George Downing in this area. While a robust individual such as Denzil Holles, with his short temper, petty complaints and endless self-justifications when criticised, only caused trouble for himself and his country. Certainly one of the traits all diplomats needed to cultivate was that of being an apt listener. Information of all kinds came through the diplomat and to a great extent he acted as a filter, mentally sorting the significant from the trivial. Having said this, the late-seventeenth-century diplomat of whatever nation was never usually afraid of writing at length to his masters at home. Nor did the diplomats of the period attempt to be concise. A loquacious correspondence was part of their job and also reflected the diplomat's habit of talking without actually saying anything. Many of their letters, which often stretch to ten or twelve pages, could easily be condensed into half a side. Few ambassadors never had anything to write home about however dull life was at that particular moment.[30]

The different sorts of information which a diplomat would be required to obtain can be broken down into five main areas. The first was political information. This covered a variety of possibilities. News of possible treaties or alliances which the host government was making are one example, political news of the activities of the legislature, the alliances and cabals of ministers at court and in government are others.[31] A second area of information concerned personal intelligence about the head of state and his ministers. The diplomat would be expected to gather intelligence on the health, interests or current mistresses of the king; gossip at court on who was 'in' and who 'out' was also significant.[32]

A third area was that information concerned with military or naval intelligence. This information was particularly valuable in the build-up to

29 Savile quoted in R. Clark, *Sir William Trumbull in Paris* (Cambridge, 1938), p. 15.
30 For a very bored diplomat see BL Add. MSS 34332, fo. 88. This was Francis Parry who was writing from Lisbon.
31 Also the attitude of the local population to such things was useful; see *Arlington's Letters*, I, pp. 95–6.
32 See for example BL Add. MSS 4201, fo. 2.

a conflict.[33] Ambassadors were usually required to leave on the outbreak of hostilities between their nation and the host, but most attempted to delay their departure for as long as they could. George Downing was still at The Hague in June 1665, four months after the declaration of hostilities between England and the Dutch Republic. Downing was under great pressure to leave and facing hostility from the mob so he sought to barricade himself in his house with arms and powder rather than be forced out.[34] In any case, the outbreak of hostilities in the period was nearly always paralleled by diplomatic negotiations to end them almost as soon as they had begun. This provided an excuse for the diplomat to put off his departure and enabled him to carry on gathering intelligence. Such intelligence was mainly concerned with the movement of naval and military units, their make-up, numbers, leaders, arms, character and morale. It was also at such times that the diplomat would employ spies to go where he was unable to go himself. A fourth area of information was that which concerned itself with domestic rebels and exiles at large in the host country.[35] Lastly there was the question of miscellaneous information dealing with the weather, famine or plague and so on.

In diplomatic life there were both conventional, that is to say legal, and unconventional, or illegal, means of gathering such information. The conventional means of gathering information were basically through regular interviews with a variety of ministers, officials or the head of state. Most ambassadors would garner information through normal social intercourse. By being attentive and insinuating much valuable intelligence could be picked up in this manner. Another conventional means of gathering information was by trading it. An ambassador could trade news of his own country's affairs for that of the host country. It was thus, to coin a phrase, just as blessed to give as to receive in diplomatic life. Hence the essential nature of Williamson's manuscript newsletter system. Of course, the darker side of diplomatic life lay in the unconventional means of gathering intelligence. This consisted in a whole host of methods which may for the sake of convenience be labelled 'secret services'.

III

In general diplomatic conduct books and official advice for the aspiring diplomat took a practical view of secret activities in a very practical age. Most high-ranking ambassadors saw such activities as an essential part of their mission. Indeed it was often openly stated in their instructions that

[33] See *Arlington's Letters*, I, pp. 85–6, 90–1, 100–1, 102–3.
[34] Colenbrander, *Zeeoorlogen*, p. 198.
[35] See below for more on these exiles.

they were to 'carefully observe the motions of [the host country] and endeavour to penetrate into all their Councill[s and] designs'.[36] Abraham de Wicquefort, who had played the spy himself, was also quite blunt when he noted that one of the 'first things that the Embassador ought to do is succeed in the Profession of a Spy'.[37] De Callières, however, made the distinction between actively 'debauching' the subjects of a sovereign prince to ensnare them into a conspiracy and the more legitimate endeavour of using every opportunity to acquire information of use. The latter he saw as within the bounds of the diplomatic game, while the former lay outside it. Moreover such activities could lead to unforeseen consequences such as a change of regime, which might, in the end, be detrimental to the interest of the ambassador and his country. In real life, diplomats rarely seem to have made such distinctions, but in a period of international relations when religious fanaticism had cooled, few diplomats would actively have countenanced the overthrow of the host regime.

The practicalities of gaining useful information took the diplomat onto many levels, some of them quite sleazy. He was expected to undertake some unconventional intelligence work himself in the court or councils of government. Here there existed certain unwritten rules or methods of work. On the whole the most important rule was not to get caught and, if you did, deny it vociferously. In general the ambassador's first task was to gain the confidence of a man already closely involved in the councils of the host regime.[38] Of necessity this required caution. It was possible for the naive diplomat to light upon someone placed there by his hosts for that very purpose. The cleverest of these men would begin by feeding the diplomat true information so that he would more readily accept the false at a later date. Thus, as Sir William Keith was to say, the ambassador must not 'be too credulous [or] he will often be imposed upon'.[39]

The astute diplomat would be critical in his evaluation of intelligence by such a means. Ideally he would have taken care to examine both his source and the motives behind its appearance. If he were ingenious he might even be able to uncover the means by which his informant had gained his information and thus cut out the middle man. In any event the practical diplomat would test such information against other intelligence he received. It was here that the able diplomat's commonsense as well as discernment came into play. Of course, no rules could ever be laid down about such activities and much depended on the ability and personality of the diplomat himself.

[36] BL Stowe MSS 191, fo. 4.
[37] A. de Wicquefort, *The Embassador and His Function* (1716), pp. 296, 298.
[38] Arlington advised Temple to engage one of the Governor-General of the Spanish Netherland's secretaries for this purpose. *Arlington's Letters*, I, pp. 102–3.
[39] W. Keith, *An Essay on the Education of a Young British Nobleman* (1730), p. 52.

While at court it was also essential that the ambassador search out the company of ministers or others in the know. He might also attempt to bribe them or their servants to obtain information. A man such as Williamson, for example, would have been a prime catch for a diplomat to take on his books. However, as far as can be discovered, Williamson never accepted any bribes from any diplomats and was thought, unusually enough, incorruptible,[40] being more likely to turn such attempts to interrogate him in his own favour.[41] The indiscretions of servants, officials or ministers could also be exploited by the enterprising ambassador. The classic example of this occurred in 1658 when George Downing bought the indiscreet papers of Thomas Howard, brother of the Earl of Suffolk, who was close to the then exiled Charles II, from an intermediary. This nameless individual had purchased them from a 'whoor' of Howard's acquaintance. Downing then used the affair as a lever on Howard to get him to act the spy.[42] Thus the ambassador had to take his opportunities where they arose and by so doing he could personally send home reliable intelligence and further his own, as well as his country's fortunes.

The good diplomat would also inevitably take some time to set up a network of intelligence within the country in which he was stationed. One aspect of this would be the intelligencers whom he paid to inform him of news from around the country. They were usually situated in the major towns and cities, or in places where the diplomat himself would not or could not venture without raising questions. This intelligence might also emanate from the professional news supplier or via more private arrangements with merchants.

Covert intelligence activities – that is actual espionage – were accepted in practice, if not openly admitted. The only real rule in these uncharted waters was not to get caught. Such espionage networks operated on a variety of levels. As has already been noted, the diplomat himself would sometimes act the part of spy in his relationships with ministers or government officers. But his own work would be supplemented by that of others. Sir George Downing, for example, had 'friends' within the Dutch government at both the local and central level. The States General of the United Provinces provided a happy hunting ground for the unscrupulous Downing, much as the House of Commons did for his Dutch and French counterparts. Men such as William van Haven, a deputy to the States General for the province of Friesland, a body which leaked information

[40] C. L. Grose, 'Louis XIV's Financial Relations with Charles II and the English Parliament', *Journal of Modern History*, 1, 1929, p. 180.

[41] Magalotti, *Relazione*, pp. 44–5.

[42] For this action *Thurloe State Papers*, VII, pp. 347, 348, 426–9, 444–5. Downing was also to use this route to make his peace with the exiled king on the eve of the Restoration.

like a sieve in any case, fell into Downing's net and were on his payroll along with others.[43]

Another set of people with whom the ambassador could occasionally work were political or religious dissenters and opposition groups. The English worked with Roux de Marcilly in France for example, while Downing used his connections with the Orangists in the Dutch Republic. He exploited them for information as well as to put pressure on De Witt's government.[44] Such activities were more than matched by the Dutch, French and Spanish in England, who contacted the radicals and dissenters opposing the Stuart regime for much the same reasons. Opposition groups invariably lost out in such diplomatic games for the diplomats were unwilling to provide them with too much assistance for their plans in case they went too far.

Actual spies could be easily recruited or coerced into working for the diplomat. They were readily available either as professionals, adventurers, or disillusioned exiles. A man such as Johann Böeckell made a good living out of such work,[45] and there were others such as Don Lewis for example. He was an ex-Whig, who was willing to watch the activities and movements of the exiles for a price.[46] Temple paid out £22 to a person 'employ'd to watch the motions of Joice, Desborough and other Fanaticks'.[47] Such individuals could often be in contact with the secretary's office independent of any work carried out for the ambassador. Part of the problem was that, lacking loyalty, they could not be trusted too far. But as de Callières noted 'well chosen spies contribute more than any other agency to the success of great plans'.[48]

Of one point most diplomats and diplomatic authors were in agreement: such secret activities cost money. Downing bluntly told Clarendon that 'Men will not do things of this nature for nothing'.[49] In general, however, most ministers and diplomats would have said such money was money well spent. Better 'one regiment less', noted de Callières, 'than a poorly equipped system of espionage'.[50] The actual amounts spent by English diplomats on intelligence activities are, as with most of the financial dealings of this area of government in the period, often difficult to uncover. Frequently the

[43] Rowen, *De Witt*, p. 667.

[44] See R. R. Goodison, 'England and the Orangist Party, 1665–1672', unpublished MA dissertation, University of London, 1934, Chaper 1. For the States General see J. H. Grever, 'The Structure of Decision-Making in the States General of the Dutch Republic, 1660–1688', *Parliaments, Estates and Representatives*, 1–2, 1981, pp. 125–53.

[45] For Böeckell see below and above, Chapter 4; also PRO SP 29/232, fos. 211–12, 215–16, 217v–18.

[46] BL Add. MSS 41811, fo. 262. See below for the capture of Sir Thomas Armstrong.

[47] BL Add. MSS 22920, fo. 194.

[48] de Callières, *The Practice of Diplomacy*, p. 26.

[49] Lister, *Clarendon*, III, p. 182.

[50] de Callières, *The Practice of Diplomacy*, p. 26.

Bulstrode's submissions for intelligence

Dates	Amount for intelligence	Total
24 July 1674–24 July 1675	400 guilders	1,686 guilders
25 Dec. 1675–24 Sept. 1676	£120. 0s. 0d.	£572. 16s 0d.
25 Sept. 1676–28 Dec. 1677	£125. 0s. 0d.	£526. 14s. 6d.
28 Dec. 1677–24 June 1678	£50. 0s. 0d.	£365. 14s. 3d.
4 June 1678–24 July 1679	£100. 0s. 0d.	£759. 19s. 6d.
25 March 1680–25 March 1681	£100. 0s. 0d.	£680. 16s. 6d.
25 March 1681–25 March 1682	£100. 0s. 0d.	£534. 4s. 6d.

Note: In general it can be seen that Bulstrode spent an average of 18 per cent of his extraordinary expenditure on intelligence over the period 1674–82.
Source: PRO SP 104/237, fos. 6, 17, 24, 31, 37, 63–4, 84.

real figures are lumped in with other items upon the ambassador's extraordinary expenditure. Further it sometimes is not very clear what is meant by intelligence in these documents, for the word can cover a multitude of meanings and actions, from general news drawn from professionally produced newsletters to secret activities. The amounts for intelligence are also sometimes set down with those for postage of letters and expresses. Despite these difficulties there are a few documents remaining which illustrate the diplomat's expenditure in this area.

Sir William Temple, for example, gave some entries for specific amounts paid out for intelligence to spies when he was in the Netherlands. He paid out £60 to 'ye dutch intelligencer at ye Hague'. This was apparently a yearly sum paid out to the man on the orders of the Secretary of State. To further 'encourage' this individual, at one point another £26 was ordered to be paid out to him. An intelligencer at Brussels, however, only received £50, while Temple's intelligence 'from ye severall parts of Germany and maintaining ... several corespondencies there and in other parts ye whole time of his embassy' cost him £186. An individual spy employed to observe 'the motions of Joice, Desborough and other Fanaticks' received £22.[51] These figures may be compared with those submitted by Thomas Henshaw, envoy extraordinary to the King of Denmark. He paid £20 for his intelligence in 'Copenhagen, and to those who sent me Intelligence from Hamburgh, Amsterdam and other places'. This was out of a total extraordinary expenditure of £125.[52]

Sir Richard Bulstrode is one diplomat for whom a run of figures concerned with payments for 'intelligence' are available. This set of figures is

[51] BL Add. MSS 22920, fo. 194. [52] PRO SP 104/237, p. 11.

unfortunately incomplete but it does provide a useful guide as to what the agent and later resident at Brussels paid for his intelligence from around 1674 to 1682 (see table).

At the other end of the market was a professional spy such as Johann Böeckel. He submitted the following account of his expenditure after the close of the Second Anglo-Dutch War in which he had served the regime as a spy in the Netherlands (there were 10 Dutch florins to the pound sterling).

In primis Anno, 1664 in the beginning of the Month October by his Excellences the Lord Arlington was sent from London att the Hag[u]e to Sr George Downing concerning their correspondency in adviseing with one another how strong the Hollanders were in their ports of Men of Warr, pieces of Ordonnance and Souldiers an[d] when they would be ready and hath been att sea att their Rendevous without Letters and I have received from [the] Right Honorable the Lord Arlington		20£
And because they would knott . . . trust me, and that I could receive no letters from London I did not part again from the Hague for London anno 1665 ultimo die January. After *all* this I stayed in London above the 6 weeks and in ultimo Mensis Martÿ anno 1665 went for Antwerp to Meester Nipho, and from Antwerp the Hage with letters, and I have received for this voyage from his Excellences		20£
		40£
w[h]ich for a halfe yeare from October anno 1664 till March anno 1665 I doe reckon for my voyage and entertainment		
Follow nouw what from the Month march añ 1665 *till* the Month of August 1667 for 2 yeares and a half for his entertainement and Money for his Journeÿs that he hath emploied in His Majesty's Service which I have disboursed of mÿ owne Moneys One yeare hath 365 daies everyday for his Ordinary . . . because it was very deare that time in Holland for one yeare	florins 912	sols 10.
Extraordinary every daie because I was obliged to goe everyday in Severall Companies to inquire and informe myselfe for one years	365	–
For travelling most every Month to divers places Towns, Sea Ports, to Vriesland; Tessel in Nord Holland, to Meedenblick, Enckhuÿsen, Hoorn, to Amsterdam, upon de Meeze to Rotterdam; to Briel, Helvoetsluÿs and in Sealand att ter Veere, Rammekens and Vlussing where I went att great expenses for one yeare	200	–

For entertaining some Spyes to [send] from one place to another where I could not come myselfe, for one years	100	–
For my lodgeing att Amsterdam for one whole yeare and wood and coales	270	–
For a suite of Cloase Linning and Washing for a yeare	150	–
For postage and messages	30	–
In one yeare	2,027:	10.
For 2 yeares and a halfe	5,068:	15.
English money	506£	16 shilling.

Source: PRO SP 29/232, fos. 217v–218.

IV

With the return of the king in May 1660 many of those who feared for their lives under the monarchy of Charles II, fled the country into exile on the continent. They were the first of the numerous waves of exiles which were to continue throughout the reign. A mixture of dissenting ministers, regicides, republican conspirators and Whigs were to find their way into Europe over the years and there wander the streets of Dutch cities as well as further afield experiencing what another, earlier exile from his country, had described thus:

> Tu proverai sì come sa di sale
> lo pane altrui, e come é duro calle
> lo scendere è 'l salir per l'altrui scale.[53]

Their first, and more often than not last, point of call was the Low Countries. Escape for the refugee had always been easier into this area of Europe from England than elsewhere. Natural geography, plentiful transport facilities and moral, as well as physical assistance were available to the fleeing exile.[54] Throughout the period the Dutch Republic in particular proved to be a haven for numerous English, Scottish and Irish exiles of one kind or another. The Netherlands had distinct advantages for the exile. There he could enjoy religious and political as well as economic liberty.

[53] Dante, *Paradiso*, XVII, lines 58–60. Exile made some very disgruntled; see T. E. S. Clarke and H. C. Foxcroft, *A Life of Gilbert Burnet, Bishop of Salisbury* (Cambridge, 1907), p. 48.

[54] France was excluded for the obvious reason that it was a monarchy unsympathetic to rebels; the capture of Archibald Johnston of Warriston proved this to the exiles. For his capture see Ludlow, *Voyce*, pp. 944–5.

The state was geographically close enough to England to more easily acquire the latest news from that country. It was also a useful base for any enterprising conspirator planning a return to England by violent means.[55] As an economic entrepôt Dutch cities were also useful places to gather money and arms. The exile might even be able to squeeze some assistance from the Dutch authorities who had no great love for the new Stuart regime.[56] At the very least the Dutch Republic had a long tradition of welcoming exiles of all kinds and an equally strong reluctance to give up any refugees, despite pressure to do so from interested governments. Further, the baroque political structure of the Republic was something which the skilful exile could play to the full when faced with danger.[57]

English, Scottish and Irish exiles were to be found in most of the major towns and cities of the Netherlands but concentrations were particularly high in Rotterdam, Amsterdam, Leiden and Middelburg.[58] There were also large concentrations of English and Scottish merchants in these areas. They provided a useful cover for exile and government spy alike. Some were sympathetic to the plight of the exiles, providing financial assistance and places to live, while others were useful as sources of information for the intelligence work of the government, as well as cover addresses for illicit correspondence.[59] To give him spiritual comfort the exile could usually find a church to suit his beliefs in the major Dutch towns. Sir George Downing had noted with some disgust that in Rotterdam alone there were 'Independent, Anabaptist and Quaker Church[s who] doe hire the best houses and have great bills of exchange come over from England'.[60] Naturally both the ministers of these churches and their congregations attracted the interest of Williamson and the government in the shape of their spies.[61] All in all and despite certain problems the exile would have found many benefits in remaining within the bounds of the Dutch Republic.

Their safety depended upon the state of Anglo-Dutch relations. Usually these were poor and this proved of benefit to the exile. Even if the Dutch central government had been willing to assist in the banishment, capture or punishment of exiles, which it was usually reluctant to do, Dutch local government saw to it that any procedures could be lengthy; so lengthy in

[55] Military service in the forces of the Dutch Republic was also a possibility for ex-army men.

[56] The Republic's leaders had been unsympathetic to the exiled Charles II and were no more sympathetic when he came into power.

[57] See the case of Cornet Joyce; Temple, *Works*, II, pp. 138–50; *Arlington's Letters*, I, pp. 450–1; Feiling, *Foreign Policy*, p. 317.

[58] PRO SP 29/50, fos. 100–1.

[59] See above, Chapters 4 and 5 and the case of Edward Riggs.

[60] BL Egerton MSS 2537, fo. 349; also Lister, *Clarendon*, III, p. 139.

[61] See PRO SP 9/26, fos. 76, 147; also above, Chapter 6.

fact that by the time anything was achieved the individuals concerned had usually fled. Public opinion was surprisingly sympathetic to the exiles – perhaps as former rebels themselves this had become innate in the Dutch character. Thus while the public supported the exile, the local officers caused delays and the Dutch government connived at the exiles' presence, or at least gave them a fair warning of any trouble. Various treaties between England and the Republic did little to solve the problem.[62] Religious exiles were generally not affected by these treaties, and this allowed the exile another outlet by claiming religious persecution as a reason for being in the country.[63] There was also the possibility of extra insurance in the shape of Dutch citizenship.

Of course, such a heavy concentration of 'rebels' interested the Secretary of State's office intensely. Attempts were made, usually successfully, to penetrate these groups to find out what they were up to. Some government spies such as Edward Riggs, for example, give startling insights into the state of mind of the exile community in the 1660s.[64] But faced with the numerous political and religious exiles which its policies, if not its actual presence, had created the Stuart regime was left with two main options. It could, of course, choose to ignore the exiles. However, this would be politically impossible to justify as well as highly dangerous. Those members of the regimes of the 1650s who had not made their peace with the Stuarts, or had not already suffered execution, or imprisonment, were still regarded as a formidable threat. Moreover in the case of the regicides and other 'traitors' justice had to be seen to be done in England. The second alternative therefore was to take some form of action against the exile community – what might be thought of as a continuation of the battles of the English Civil Wars by other means.

In the first instance the regime needed to gather information on the exiles, their whereabouts, movements and activities. This was accomplished through a network of intelligence activities stretching from the crown's ambassadors and diplomats to their minions and spies; the penetration of exile groups by government agents posing as refugees was another significant thread to this. The result was that their plans, as well as state of mind, were often well known to the regime in London. Added to these activities was the general day-to-day news gathering which took place throughout the period. Once information had been received the regime then had to decide how to use it. The exiles could be kept under continued observation, and by so doing the regime could discover more

[62] See J. Walker, 'The English Exiles in Holland During the Reigns of Charles II and James II', *TRHS*, 1948, p. 114.
[63] BL Egerton MSS 2538, fo. 39.
[64] See above Chapter 5, for Riggs' work in this respect.

about their plans. The regime would thus allow their plots to mature sufficiently in order to break them at the right time. Psychologically this could be devastating for the hopes of the exiles; or it could frighten them sufficiently to keep them out of trouble. There was also the option of keeping them under pressure by attempting to negotiate with the host country for their return. A further possibility was to abduct them in order that they face punishment in England, or there could be an outright elimination of the problem through assassination. The benevolent attitude, of course, was to offer a pardon of some sort, but this was used sparingly and not where exiled regicides were involved.[65]

The kidnapping of the regime's political enemies from their exile on the continent of Europe was one means by which they could be eliminated as a problem for the government. In fact the technique of abducting and then executing, or otherwise disposing, of enemies was not all that rare in the early modern intelligence world. In this area much depended upon three main criteria. Firstly the vulnerability of the actual target, secondly the availability of reliable personnel who would be willing to undertake the actual operation, and thirdly the desirability of the effects which such actions, always controversial, would have both upon the opponents of the regime as well as the host country where they took place.

Certainly the abduction of opponents was a dramatic, if not melodramatic, means of proving a point, namely that the Stuart regime's arm was lengthy enough to mete out retribution where it thought fit. As with all such work, however, there could be complications. As the period progressed most of the vulnerable targets in whom the English regime was interested, such as the exiled regicides for instance, took reasonable precautions to protect themselves. This was particularly true after Sir George Downing's coup of 1662 in Delft.[66] In Switzerland the regicides took even greater care to retain the support of the political authorities of the Swiss cantons. In the case of the political exiles in the Netherlands a great many of them took out Dutch citizenship as extra insurance. In one sense while making the exile less vulnerable this additional precaution could still prove to be beneficial to the regime, for the fear which led many exiles into making such decisions also kept them out of conspiracies. A further problem in relation to abduction, however, was that it was very much a 'single-shot' weapon. A failure would mean that the potential targets would almost certainly scatter in the resulting uproar which invariably followed such occasions. Thomas Chudleigh, who pursued the exiled Whigs in the 1680s, was very cautious in his approach to taking Sir

[65] This was the tactic used by the regime with some success on the eve of the Third Dutch War.

[66] For this see below.

Thomas Armstrong, despite having had him closely watched. Chudleigh was loath to make 'a noyse to no purpose, which might occasion them to avoid ye place hereafter'. Even successful kidnappings brought problems in their wake. Chudleigh noted that when he caught Armstrong he had had 'success enough in what I was went about, but I doubt it will be allmost impossible to intrap anymore of them . . . because they will in all liklyhood keep ymselves more close'.[67]

There was also the question of the host nation's attitude to such activities to consider. Very few states were happy at having their territory and laws infringed by English diplomats. Exiles in France, or even the Spanish Netherlands were fair game, given the consent of the respective monarchs,[68] but those in the United Provinces were quite another matter. Downing, Temple, Chudleigh, as well as Bevil Skelton were all to experience the ambivalence of the Dutch authorities on the central as well as local level to their requests for assistance in bringing exiles to book. Nor was it merely a question of knowing whom to bribe. Even if the diplomat succeeded in persuading the authorities to help him the Dutch people themselves were adverse to having the 'Ancient rules and practices of their country' stamped upon by heavy-footed English diplomats. Both Downing and Chudleigh were eventually to receive warrants to seize rebels, but Chudleigh believed that they were given out 'only for a fine compliment to His Majestie and no more'.[69] The Dutch never thought that they would be used; hence Downing's unrestrained glee when he outfoxed the Dutch to capture the regicides John Barkstead, Miles Corbet and John Okey in 1662. In fact the whole question of the English diplomat's pursuit of exiles through semi-legal means raises an intriguing point. The insistence upon the legal niceties, however self-defeating they were, remains surprising. A more realistic, if less moral, position would have been to abduct first and then go to the law.[70] Certainly other governments of the period were not given to so many qualms. Neither the agents of Louis XIV nor the Emperor Leopold I ever felt the need to legalise their actions in this way. Louis XIV's government in particular had little scruple in kidnapping those individuals it believed dangerous to its security. Roux de Marcilly, for example, was hunted down by Captain Mazel and his men on the authority of Marshal Turenne, who had been asked by Louis to organise the operation personally. They caught up with Roux on a mountain road from Nyon and

[67] BL Add. MSS 41810, fo. 74v.

[68] Louis XIV was asked and gave his permission for the capture of Warriston. See Ludlow, *Voyce*, p. 945.

[69] BL Add. MSS 41810, fo. 97.

[70] Something which Downing did suggest to Clarendon that he should do, Lister, *Clarendon*, III, p. 152.

took him back to France to face torture and death. Despite previous failures the French had persisted until they got their man.[71] Debreuil, alias Samson, a native of Basle who had been a double agent, was another whom the Sun King's government ordered seized and smuggled over the border in 1676.[72] Leopold I broke diplomatic immunity and outraged public opinion by ordering the seizure of Wilhelm von Fürstenburg on the streets of Cologne in 1674, effectively killing off by this action the already dying congress being held there.[73] The English insistence on legal niceties can be put down to the previous decade's political traumas when, theoretically at least, all government action had been thought to be illegal until 1660. Thus the Restoration regime's agents had to be seen to be going through the motions even for something as quasi-legal as abduction. This view hardly makes them candidates for the servants of the absolutist state which so many historians are fond of claiming Stuart England was attempting to become.

A further problem faced by the potential kidnapper was that reliable personnel to carry out such operations were not always available. Downing was to suggest to Clarendon that if he might have 'my owne way I would ... employ three or fower resolved English officers' to carry out such operations.[74] When he finally moved against Barkstead, Corbet and Okey he used a Major Miles and some other English officers as well as his own servants.[75] But the ambassador might also come up against the military mentality which often looked askance at activities it considered beneath the dignity of a gentleman. Out of the 'good resolute Englishman' whom Downing had asked to assist him in his plans, 'some few started' at the very suggestion of it and would have nothing to do with such deeds.[76] Bevil Skelton may serve as an example of such a military mind in a

[71] For the capture and activities of Roux de Marcilly see M. M. Eug et E. M. Haag, eds., *La France Protestante ou Vies des Protestants Francais* (reprint, Geneva, 1966), IX, pp. 59–62; Aimé-Daniel Rabinel, *La Tragique Aventure de Roux de Marcilly* (Paris, 1969), Ludlow, *Memoirs*, II, pp. 409 *et passim*; J. Noone, *The Man Behind the Iron Mask* (1988), pp. 176–86.

[72] See Jung, *La Vérité sur le Masque de Fer*, p. 234, and above, Chapter 4.

[73] Fürstenburg was on his way back from visiting his mistress, the Countess de la Mark, when close by the church of St Maurice his coach was fallen on by nine or ten imperial soldiers and their officers. They held up the coach and claimed him as the emperor's prisoner. Fürstenburg's entourage notwithstanding this fired at the Imperialists and a fierce fire-fight broke out with wounded on both sides. Fürstenburg attempted to escape, but was forced back into his coach at swordpoint and taken out of the city. See Swart, *Netherland-Historian*, p. 387 for an account of this abduction.

[74] Lister, *Clarendon*, III, pp. 148–52.

[75] BL Egerton MSS 2538, fos. 37–37v. Downing had earlier made use of Colonel John Griffith a royalist officer whom Clarendon had recommended. See *CClSP*, IV, pp. 110, 150, 211, 224, 234, 422, 431, 449, 462; V, pp. 116, 134, 156, 163, 169, 172, 179, 193.

[76] Codrington Library All Souls College MSS, 240, fo. 411 (narrative of the capture of the three regicides at Delft).

quandry. As a diplomat he was faced with an offer to shoot to abduct the Duke of Monmouth 'upon the roade as he travelled from place to place'.[77] But Skelton, the honourable soldier, was horrified at such a mean action and refused to have anything to do with it. Having said this, there was always a man or two who for the right reward would prove suitable for the task.

V

By most standards George Downing sets fair to be one of the most disagreeable personalities of Restoration England.[78] Although the odious elements of his character have been exaggerated, Downing was never that popular in his lifetime and his reputation further declined after his death. He has been traditionally seen as a mean-minded, unsavoury sort of man, whose attributes, if he had any worth mentioning at all, relate to the founding of Downing Street. He could be petty, he was unscrupulous in his dealings, mean about money, guilty of greed and duplicity as well as arrogance. It is also only fair to point out that it was an age when these attributes were common enough and that his personality, as well as his actions make him no worse, if not much better, than many of his contemporaries. Downing's problem was that he was largely successful in what he set out to do. And what he set out to do was to survive in the turbulent world of later-seventeenth-century political and diplomatic life.

However, even this success brought forth condemnation. Downing was condemned for his all too successful transition from the service of Cromwell to that of Charles II – this is in spite of the fact that others who made this move largely escaped censure.[79] He has also been condemned for his anti-Dutch stance, again in spite of the fact that many of his views were shared by Englishmen in general in the period.[80] Downing was also villified for an action examined below, the capture of the three regicides Barkstead, Corbet and Okey. Again, this action was no worse than other, perhaps less-well-known, deeds in which the regime was involved. Downing was a vigorous as well as practical politician.[81] He certainly lacks the romantic

[77] BL Add. MSS 41812, fos. 20–1.

[78] The standard biography of Downing is J. Beresford, *The Godfather of Downing Street Sir George Downing 1623–1684: A Essay in Biography* (1925). More important has been the work of H. Roseveare, 'Prejudice and Policy: Sir George Downing as a Parliamentary Entrepreneur', in D. C. Coleman and P. Mathias, eds., *Enterprise and History: Essays in Honour of Charles Wilson* (Cambridge, 1984), pp. 135–50. Also *H of P*, II, pp. 224–9; *DNB*, George Downing; Burnet, *History*, I, p. 536.

[79] For example George Monck and Edward Montagu.

[80] See Schama, *The Embarrassment of Riches*, pp. 230–7.

[81] The anecdote related in *The Student or the Oxford Monthly Miscellany*, 3, March 1750, pp. 81–6, if true, shows the practical nature of the man.

aura which has clung to a man such as Sir William Temple, author, lover and patron of the arts. In fact because he lacked such attributes he was the ideal individual to operate in the murky world of seventeenth-century espionage where, while he might well have been just as odious, he was also extremely able.

Downing grew up in New England and was educated for the ministry at Harvard. He is thought to have served for a time as a chaplain in the regiment of his future victim John Okey. If the relish with which Downing wrote of the capture of his three victims is any guide, there may have been some personal animosity between Okey and himself which dated from this period. Downing also served as secretary to Sir Arthur Haselrige while his regiment was garrisoned at Newcastle in 1648–50.[82] It was at this point that Downing entered the world of espionage. From November 1649 he held the position of Scoutmaster-General in the army. The pay for this post was quite high, £4 per day, out of which the scoutmaster had to employ about twenty men.[83] Very little is known of Downing's actual work in the post. Originally the post had been used for the purely military function of sending out scouts to reconnoitre ahead of the army, but this expanded into general intelligence gathering. This work meant employing and dealing with spies and gathering other sorts of information, as well as assessing the information when it came in. The post was similar to an intelligence department in the army. In any event the position of scoutmaster would have undoubtedly provided Downing with a great deal of valuable experience which he was later to put to good use in diplomatic life.[84]

With the end of the Dutch War, and due to the natural growth of the secretary's office, the post of scoutmaster lost much of its significance. Indeed there is little trace of it after 1660. In the 1650s espionage activities passed into other hands, most notably those of John Thurloe.[85] Fortunately a new career opened up for Downing in diplomacy. As it would be difficult to discover a less diplomatic personality than George Downing, his merits for such work must have been more obvious to his masters than later writers. He was a supporter of the offer of the crown to Cromwell and widely regarded as a loyalist to the Protectorate, which in itself may have been sufficient for him to be shown the Protector's favour. In 1655 he was despatched to France to let the court there know of the Protector's displeasure over the treatment of the Vaudois. More important, however, was

[82] For this service see A. Laurence, *Parliamentary Army Chaplains 1642–1651* (1990), p. 122.

[83] Firth, *Cromwell's Army*, pp. 63–6.

[84] See Introduction and for a later history of the post (or rather the lack of one) see R. E. Scouller, *The Armies of Queen Anne* (Oxford, 1966), pp. 62, 65. It was widely known as the post for employing spies. See PRO SP 77/35, fo. 91v.

[85] See Introduction.

his next appointment as resident at The Hague which he took up in December 1657, at the princely sum of £1,000 per annum.[86]

It was during his time as a diplomat at The Hague that Downing was urged by John Thurloe to develop an intelligence network which would target both the exiled royalists[87] as well as the activities of foreign powers such as the Spanish. Thurloe was willing to pay highly for the intelligence such a network could bring in and to pay substantial amounts of money to the men who manned it. Thus various individuals were engaged by Downing as intelligencers. He again showed the energy and ability which were to be the hallmarks of his career. He could also be ruthless. He dismissed one man in July 1658 because he found in him 'extreame covertous and his service [was but] little'.[88] Others such as Colonel Palmer were more faithful, but Palmer was sensible enough not to trust the ambassador with letters written in his own hand. In any case, noted Downing, Palmer wrote 'so bad[ly], as nobody can read it and moreover he will not run the hazard'.[89] Naturally Downing's activities were resented both by the Dutch and, more especially by his royalist enemies. There were even, or so he himself claimed, one or two attempts on his life. A Major Whitefield took to lurking about Downing's dwelling with some of his friends. As Whitefield had allegedly been involved in the assassination of Isaac Dorislaus the elder, Downing took this threat seriously enough to inform the Dutch authorities.[90] Despite any threats to which he was subject it is during this period that the first glimpses of Downing's talents as a spymaster emerge. He was engaged in entrapment, hiring spies, harassing exiles as well as all the bribery and chicanery to which he appears to have been so well suited. He also showed a ruthlessness in his dealings which he continued into the Restoration period.[91] Of course, one or two refinements were to be added after 1660, such as more scope for assassination attempts, kidnapping and even suggestions of grave robbery, but in general the pattern of Downing's career in the shady side of diplomatic life was settled during these years.

The system and ideas which he built up during the late 1650s and the 1660s can unfortunately only be glimpsed in the evidence which remains. Downing appears to have been less open about such activities after the Restoration than he was before. There may have been many reasons for this. He was, to some extent, still on trial with the new regime. The turncoat of 1660, and more importantly the persecutor of 1658–9, had not been forgotten. Thus he had to be cautious in his dealings. Downing may

[86] *DNB*, George Downing.
[87] Downing College MSS, Sir George Downing's Letter Book 1658, fos. 76, 138, 141.
[88] *Thurloe State Papers*, VII, p. 272. [89] *ibid.* [90] *ibid.*, p. 334.
[91] Downing College MSS, Sir George Downing's Letter Book, 1658, fo. 141.

well have also felt more at ease in dealing with John Thurloe about such matters than he ever did with Clarendon, Nicholas or Arlington. Whatever the reason, some of the identities of Downing's 'friends' are now lost because of this natural caution. What can be discovered of Downing's work in the Netherlands in the period thus provides an interesting picture of a diplomatic spymaster at work. He built up a regular network of informants drawn from many different sectors of both Dutch and exile society. Correspondents were settled in the cities of Holland such as Amsterdam and Rotterdam to provide information from these parts.[92] In turn the intelligence was transmitted to his embassy at The Hague. In the main Downing was interested in the activities of the exiles and the possibilities of capturing them, almost as though by their blood he could win favour and trust for himself at court.[93] However, there were other areas which came under the ambassador's eye. He was able to draw upon his connections with the Orangist party.[94] During the first few months of the Second Anglo-Dutch War, while he was still at The Hague and reluctant to leave, he was able to send men out weekly to observe the Dutch fleet in the Texel and at Amsterdam. Occasionally he used his own servants for these missions. These men not only observed the motions of the ships but also took care to 'sound all yt come from their fleete'.[95] One useful place to gather information was from those who were on Downing's payroll in the States General. One of these informants wanted £400 per annum for his information, but he did promise to 'give certain notice of whatever passes in the States and will use his interest for the king'.[96] Such money was the basis for good intelligence, or as Thoms Corney the spy put it, more 'oyle for [the] lampe'.[97]

For the purposes of capturing exiles, Downing was able to draw from a pool of royalist officers and other 'resolute men' who were still in the Netherlands.[98] Attempts were made not just on Barkstead, Corbet and Okey but also upon other exiles such as Captain Edward Dendy,[99] Edward Wogan, George Joyce[100] and Dr Edward Richardson.[101] According to Gilbert Burnet, Downing was able to 'betray those who by their former

[92] Lister, *Clarendon*, III, p. 139.

[93] It was alleged that he had a unique chance to capture the exiled Charles Stuart in 1658, but managed to turn it to his own advantage. Downing College MSS, Sir George Downing's Letter Book, fos. 81–6.

[94] For this see P. Geyl, *Orange and Stuart, 1641–1672* (1969), pp. 169–74.

[95] Lister, *Clarendon*, III, p. 388; PRO SP 84/188, fo. 141.

[96] *CClSP*, V, pp. 121–2.

[97] PRO SP 77/35, fo. 91.

[98] *CClSP*, V, p. 354; also Lister, *Clarendon*, III, pp. 148–52.

[99] *BDBR*, III, p. 337.

[100] *ibid.* II, pp. 147–8.

[101] For Downing and Dendy see *CClSP*, V, p. 121; Lister, *Clarendon*, III, pp. 152–5; for Downing and Joyce see *ibid.*, p. 139; for Downing and Wogan see *ibid.*, p. 388; for Downing and Richardson see *CClSP*, V, p. 354; Lister, *Clarendon*, III, pp. 261–3.

friendship and services thought they might depend upon him'.[102] Burnet seems to imply that Downing was able to use his own republican past to draw exiles into his net. He played William Scot, the son of regicide and former spymaster Thomas Scot, out on a long line, only dealing with the adventurer and exile 'by a second hand' without Scot's knowledge of who was pulling the strings. Downing was, however, willing to 'throwe away some money to try w[ha]t this Scott can doe' for, he claimed, there were often difficulties to 'gett into the right trade'.[103] Abraham Kicke, the merchant and friend of the exiles, was treated with a mixture of brutality and generosity. Downing threatened to ruin him and then, perhaps playing on the man's greed, offered him £200 for each regicide he would betray.[104] In such a way Downing was to score some of his most notable espionage successes.

One of the first things Downing reported on his return to The Hague after the Restoration was that there appeared to be an excessive number of exiles and 'disaffected persons' coming daily out of England and into the Netherlands.[105] He began to set up correspondents and spies in all the likely places to keep an eye upon them. He also made suggestions to Clarendon, amongst others, as to how the problem could be solved. The major difficulty for the new royal ambassador lay with the Dutch government itself. Despite a formal request by the king in September 1660 for the regicides in the Netherlands, little had been done by the Dutch. Indeed they had been obstructive when, in the summer of 1661 Sir William Davidson, the Stuart government's agent in Amsterdam, had received word that some of the refugees were in Rotterdam.[106] Neither Davidson nor Downing had been able to seize them. Despite Downing's claim upon, as he saw them, dangerous refugees from his country, the government of the United Provinces resisted any attempts to apprehend errant regicides, a priority for Downing, and any other radicals in whom the Stuart government was interested. Moreover if the States did decide that there was a case to answer they felt honour bound to issue a proclamation before any action was taken and name the individuals concerned. This would naturally warn the fugitives of their danger. There was no treaty of extradition at this time. Moreover any surrender of a fugitive would be seen as a humiliation for the Dutch government with its long tradition of support for the exile. Whether Downing thought of this as a challenge is not clear, but he did, as he said, 'know the humour of these people' and took it upon himself to get round the problems by unconventional means.[107]

102 Burnet, *History*, I, p. 365.
103 Lister, *Clarendon*, III, pp. 388–9.
104 *CClSP*, V, p. 140.
105 BL Egerton MSS 2537, fo. 349.
106 *CClSP*, V, p. 119, 124; Rowen, *De Witt*, p. 453.
107 Lister, *Clarendon*, III, p. 148.

With the realisation that he would get little assistance in his task of rounding up regicides and others from the Dutch, Downing turned his thoughts to kidnapping the individuals he was interested in and then asking the Dutch authorities for permission to remove them. The Dutch government would be presented with a *fait accompli*. With this in mind he tried to gather some English officers for this purpose. One name in particular came up. This was Colonel John Griffith.[108] He was a staunchly royalist officer who had sent intelligence to Sir Edward Hyde in the 1650s and ironically enough had kept a wary eye upon the Protector's ambassador in the Netherlands, that is Downing himself. In any event Clarendon recommended the man and Griffith was hired to search the country and look for refugees. However, he does not seem to have got very far in his task. It was obvious that Downing would need assistance from someone inside the exile community and he found it in the shape of Abraham Kicke.

In May 1680 Sir George Downing had a visitor who encouraged him to relate the story of how he had captured the regicides Barkstead, Corbet and Okey at Delft some eighteen years previously.[109] The visitor claimed that he had dealt with the ex-ambassador with 'as much mercy as he used in carrying on the businesse' and the information which was gained was apparently for the use of the government, who may have had similar designs in mind.[110] In any case Downing's tale of the capture of the three regicides is fairly well known to historians of the period.[111] It does have some interesting aspects to it however, especially in light of the government's attitudes to kidnapping and abduction. Moreover if the 1680 document is used as evidence it is clear that the events of 1662 had set something of a standard for other attempts the regime was to make.

It was Abraham Kicke who had provided Downing with intelligence of the whereabouts of the various exiles.[112] Two of them, John Barkstead[113] and John Okey,[114] were living near Frankfurt[115] but came into Holland to visit Kicke at Delft. After their capture the regicides were to claim that one of the reasons they had come into Holland was that they were about to have 'laid out ten thousand pound sterling [in Delft] for ye setting up of

108 For Griffith, see *CClSP*, IV, pp. 110, 150, 211, 214, 224, 234, 422, 431, 449, 462; V, pp. 116, 134, 156, 163, 169, 172, 179, 193, 329.

109 Codrington Library All Souls College MSS, 240, fo. 411. There is no name on the document, so the interviewer is unknown. It is dated 6 May 1680.

110 This is a possibility in light of the government problems at the time.

111 See for example R. C. H. Catterall, 'Sir George Downing and the Regicides', *American Historical Review*, 17, 1912, pp. 268–89.

112 *CClSP*, V, pp. 140, 145, 153, 179, 193.

113 Ludlow, *Voyce*, pp. 300–1; *BDBR*, I, pp. 39–40.

114 Ludlow, *Voyce*, p. 301; *BDBR*, II, pp. 273–4.

115 *CClSP*, V, p. 153; although Ludlow claims they came from Hannau where they had been made burgesses of the town; Ludlow, *Voyce*, p. 297.

severall manufactures for ye imployment of ye poore'.[116] On hearing news of their journey into the province of Holland, Downing's first thought, naturally enough in light of his character, was to have them murdered. But this would have necessitated gaining royal approval. This was something which Clarendon thought was unlikely to be forthcoming.[117] This meant Downing's actions were somewhat restricted. However, the news that Barkstead and Okey were to visit Kicke at Delft so that the merchant could bring their wives over for a reunion[118] opened other options to the ambassador's fertile mind.

One of Downing's responses to the news Kicke brought was to encourage the visit of the two regicides, through Kicke. He also let it be generally known that he had no intention of harming them should they come within his grasp.[119] Thus reassured Barkstead and Okey turned up in the first weeks of March 1662 at Delft and stayed at Kicke's house in the town. Kicke brought Downing news on 14 March and the ambassador encouraged Kicke to invite Miles Corbet,[120] another regicide in Delft, to dine at the house. In such a way the ambassador might 'bag' three regicides instead of two. In the meantime the ambassador set to work to gain a warrant from the Dutch government without which all the preparations would be to no avail. By his persistence Downing managed to obtain a warrant from the States General via the very wary John de Witt. De Witt's motives for assisting the ambassador, whom he heartily disliked, are obscure. He had previously admitted to the ambassador that though he did not like the idea of seizing such people it seemed the logical thing to do and he had the wider international scene to consider. The current state of Anglo-Dutch relations weighed against the lives of three men must have been uppermost in his thought.[121] In any event Downing persisted and put de Witt under pressure. He refused to reveal the names of the regicides or their current residence, but still pressed 'hard upon de Witt, charging him with the miscarriage, if any should happen'.[122] By this he had de Witt carry the blank warrant to the States General. It was duly signed and given to the eager ambassador. It may be that the Dutch felt that any such scheme Downing had in mind could not be carried out in any haste and that by the time he was ready it would in any case have fallen through as had other schemes. Unfortunately for them Downing moved swiftly. He took a group of English soldiers and his own servants to Delft. There he lodged them in the churchyard while Major Miles and Downing went to talk to the *schout*

116 BL Egerton MSS 2538, fo. 39. 117 *CClSP*, V, pp. 155–6.
118 Ludlow, *Voyce*, p. 297.
119 *ibid.*, p. 297. 120 *ibid.*, pp. 299–300; *BDBR*, I, pp. 175–6.
121 Rowen, *De Witt*, pp. 454–5.
122 Codrington Library All Souls College MSS, 240, fo. 411.

of the town. The latter proved somewhat obstructive but was willing to be bribed and ordered his juniors to assist Downing. Having picked up Downing's men the group then proceeded to Kicke's house. It was growing dark as they arrived.[123] Miles knocked on the door and when it was opened the party burst into the room. There they found the three regicides sitting by the fireside with tobacco and a mug of beer, no doubt reminiscing over old times. The three men attempted to make for the back door but it was too late. Corbet, who had been just making ready to leave, apparently took his capture badly and 'fynding himself thus seized ... [fell] to purging upwards and downwards in ... a most strange manner'.[124] The trio were quickly hustled into the local gaol while Downing left to ensure their transfer into his custody.

Despite the success of the operation, Downing's main problem had only just begun. How was he to get the three men out of the country in the face of the growing Dutch hostility over his actions? Various rumours soon reached him that the gaol was to be raided in order to rescue the men, and that the local officials had been bribed to let the regicides go. The local officials themselves dragged the proceedings out to an extraordinary degree. In the meantime the prisoners were visited by various sympathetic people. The three men claimed that they were religious refugees who had only fought against 'Bishops and for ye Presbyterian Government'.[125] Downing, however, kept his head and his own men on the scene. He managed to persuade the States General to give him the authority to remove the men in spite of the lawyers who 'universally declared that it was against all right and reason'.[126] The men were subsequently removed at dead of night, Downing having again bribed the local officers. He spirited the three out of prison into a boat, along a canal and out of the town. They were then taken to an English ship the *Blackamore*, whereupon they were taken to England to suffer the agonies of a traitor's death.[127] There is little doubt that this was George Downing's finest hour and he relished his outwitting the Dutch. He also relished the praise which came his way and cared little about the scorn and abuse which some threw at him over the operation. To the ambassador this was a sweet hit against all of his enemies and more importantly it strengthened his hand at the court of Charles II.

VI

By the early 1680s the Stuart regime's intelligence and espionage work on the continent was turned against the various factions whom historians, for

123 BL Egerton MSS 2538, fo. 37. 124 *ibid.* 125 BL Egerton 2539, fo. 39.
126 *ibid.*, fo. 40.
127 Ludlow, *Voyce*, pp. 298–9, 302–3.

the sake of convenience, have labelled as Whigs. The regime attempted to combat the opposition on a number of levels, and entered into a clandestine form of political warfare which first took place in the taverns, alleys and streets of London and then spilled over into the territory of the Dutch Republic as the Restoration crisis deepened and numerous refugees fled the country. The exile community again became the focus for the attention of the regime's diplomats and spies. With everything in England in ruins many Whigs were forced to flee to the comparative safety of the Low Countries and the focus of the government's attention shifted to the cities of the Dutch Republic in particular. Here the diplomats of the Stuart regime were urged to curb the exile problem. In so doing they recruited spies to watch them and turncoat Whigs to inform the regime of the exiles' plans, and attempted to persuade the Dutch authorities to allow the seizure of troublemakers.

One of the exiles in whom the regime was interested was Sir Thomas Armstrong. He had been a close confident of James, Duke of Monmouth and he was seized by the regime in 1684. According to Burnet Armstrong 'was trusted in everything by the Duke'.[128] Armstrong had served alongside the duke in the French army and against the Covenanters in 1679. He also seems, all too readily on occasion, to have joined Monmouth's somewhat debauched lifestyle. Indeed some claimed that he had played evil genius to the naive Monmouth.[129] Whatever the truth of that matter, there is little doubt that in 1683 Armstrong was heavily involved in the series of events which came to be known as the Rye House Plot. When this was uncovered his arrest was ordered. As a consequence Armstrong fled to Europe and eventually turned up with other Whig exiles in the Netherlands. The king was particularly keen to see the seducer of his son's loyalty punished.

In 1684 the English ambassador extraordinary at The Hague was Thomas Chudleigh.[130] Chudleigh, a former protégé of Clifford, had been employed upon various diplomatic missions prior to his appointment. This had also included the Congress of Cologne in 1673–4 where, alongside Rene Petit, he had been a secretary to the plenipotentiaries.[131] Until his diplomatic mission to the Netherlands Chudleigh had been a moderately successful diplomat having 'all the accomplishments that can be desired in [such] a gentleman'.[132] His arrival in the Dutch Republic was to cause

[128] Burnet, *History*, II, p. 412; *DNB*, Thomas Armstrong; 'The Dictionary of National Biography', *Bulletin of the Institute of Historical Research*, 22, 1949, pp. 65–6.

[129] For more on their relationship see *H of P* I, pp. 544–45; J. N. P. Watson, *Captain-General and Rebel Chief: The Life of James, Duke of Monmouth* (1979), pp. 42, 75, *et passim*.

[130] For Chudleigh see *H of P*, II, pp. 67–8.

[131] See above for Petit.

[132] *H of P*, II, p. 67.

some problems. William of Orange soon grew to dislike the Englishman, and felt not only had Chudleigh been foisted upon him, but all too often he had the effrontery to argue back. This impertinence was made worse by Chudleigh's interference in Dutch affairs. William was eventually able to have Chudleigh recalled, but in the meantime had to put up with him.[133] In his later life Chudleigh was also to become a convert to the Roman Catholic faith and he left England after the Revolution, apparently to become a Carthusian monk in France.[134] By 1684 Chudleigh was making every effort to have the growing number of Whig exiles in the Netherlands watched. The ambassador was also keen to seize them should the opportunity arise.

To this end Chudleigh sought negotiations with the Dutch authorities for the return of certain exiles. He was later to claim that the Dutch had never really expected him to succeed in his attempts and had merely granted him permission 'designed solely for a fine complement to his Majest[y] & no more'.[135] It was supposed on the Dutch side that since no seizure could take place in any town without the consent of local magistrates, and as the latter were susceptible to public opinion, there would always be sufficient warning given to the victims to allow them to flee the scene before any action could take effect. Certainly Chudleigh claimed that Armstrong, for one, had relied upon this fact for his protection. However, Chudleigh was to prove all too apt at the game which he had begun. His first problem was to find the tools with which to perform the task at hand. Towards the end of April 1684 Chudleigh, through the auspices of a former customs officer and minor informer, Ezekiel Everest,[136] contacted James Hodgson. Hodgson was a consul at Rotterdam and Everest confided in him that Chudleigh had received permission from the States General to seize prominent Whigs. But the diplomat was unsure of the 'most proper wayes and means to bring that designe to a good effect'.[137] Chudleigh needed to discover the 'haunts' of the Whigs and had told Everest to ask Hodgson to pay him a visit to discuss the matter.

In the meeting which followed, Chudleigh explained his needs to the consul and Hodgson agreed to assist the diplomat in his task. Hodgson, or so he later claimed, disavowed any reward which might come to him for this service,[138] and claimed patriotic fervour as his motive for entering into such secret activities. Hodgson having the right connections in Rotterdam

133 For these arguments see Baxter, *William III*, pp. 197–8.

134 *H of P*, II, p. 67.

135 BL Add. MSS 41810, fo. 97v.

136 For Everest see Ashcraft, *Revolutionary Politics*, pp. 418–9; Chudleigh had been surveyor-general of customs from 1679 to 1682 and may have known Everest from his tenure of office.

137 BL Add. MSS 41811, fo. 262.

138 Which was just as well because he did not receive any; which did not prevent him complaining in a petition against Chudleigh; BL Add. MSS 41811, fo. 262.

brought up the name of one Don Lewis as someone who would be able to spy upon the Whig exiles and observe their movements.[139] Chudleigh was initially unconvinced, he thought Lewis an 'ill man', as indeed he could have been. Lewis was a former Whig and ex-friend of the protestant Joiner Stephen College. He had been a spy once before, acting as a double agent in the Exclusion crisis. Eventually Chudleigh was persuaded by Hodgson that, on the whole, the hiring of Lewis was the best means of proceeding. Accordingly on his return to Rotterdam Hodgson interviewed the man, Lewis' requirements for the use of his services are revealing of the sort of man the diplomats were forced to rely upon. He was willing to play the spy if Hodgson would only 'pay off his debts in Towne and furnish him with Cloathes and money'. This, he argued, would enable him to throw off his 'dependencies'. As with most of his breed the spy was short of money and greedy for whatever he could obtain. Hodgson agreed to his terms and having furnished Lewis with money, as well as some instructions, sent him off to Amsterdam around 2 May 1684. There Lewis was to watch, talk, and generally gather information from the exile community.

Hodgson's trust in Lewis was well founded. The spy performed his task well. He was in Amsterdam for five weeks or so spying on the exile community and staying close to his targets, even on occasion drinking with them in the local taverns. His life was often in danger and he feared discovery as the exiles did not really trust him.[140] At the end of this period, however, Lewis was able to inform Hodgson that Armstrong as well as the notorious plotter Robert Ferguson, were moving to Rotterdam. Almost immediately Hodgson ordered Lewis to shift to that city and uncover their haunts. At the same time he also wrote to Chudleigh informing him of the new developments. On receiving the news Chudleigh was keen to go to Rotterdam in person to co-ordinate events. He ordered that the two exiles be kept under observation while he went to the 'Grand Baliff' of the town and attempted to persuade the Dutch officials to assist him in seizing the exiles.[141] Although he succeeded in this there were many difficulties in the task of trailing the exiles in Rotterdam. Rotterdam was the second greatest city in the United Provinces and its numerous alleys and streets harboured many dangers for the regime's spies. The English community, however, lived mostly in the vicinity of Nieuwehaven and Haringvliet. Although this made things rather easier the exiles frequently moved around and had many places of shelter.[142] The ambassador was also hampered by his reluctance to make too much of a commotion over the matter in case the exiles

[139] *ibid.* [140] See Greaves, *Secrets of the Kingdom*, pp. 28; 254–5.
[141] BL Add. MSS 41810, fo. 74v.
[142] *ibid.*; Sprunger, *Dutch Puritanism*, p. 162.

heard of it and fled, or in case the Dutch themselves began to take umbrage at the situation he was pressing upon them.[143]

It was not until Armstrong moved to Leiden that Chudleigh and his men had a clear opportunity. Leiden had once been the home of the plotter Dr Edward Richardson who had died around 1677 and was notorious for its English as well as Scots radical community. The university town also had many English students in residence.[144] Working with as much secrecy as they could, Chudleigh's spies trailed Armstrong into the town. Their opportunity came just as he was about to board a boat. Faced with capture Armstrong put up a violent struggle and even attempted to fling himself overboard. He failed in this, but then tried to stab himself only to be overpowered.[145] Fortunately the Dutch authorities proved to be rather more co-operative than usual in this affair; a massive bribe of 5,000 guilders for the *schout* assisted Chudleigh's plans.[146] In the aftermath of the action the magistrates of the town were later 'troubled att this seizure' and heavily criticised by other local officials elsewhere in the province of Holland.[147] But by that time Armstrong was back in England.

Chudleigh saw no reason to take any chances with his prisoner now he had him, especially in light of rumours of a possible rescue attempt by the citizens of Rotterdam. He took care that the captive was heavily guarded and had him swiftly transferred to an English yacht, the *Catherine*, which lay in the middle of the river. Armstrong was also searched and Chudleigh 'eas'd him of a gold watch and gold snuff box' in case he endeavoured to bribe one of his guards. In fact Armstrong had already tried to do this on the road from Leiden.[148] Armstong was also tied up. Chudleigh's constant fear was that his prisoner might again try to commit suicide. The diplomat obviously thought that this was a possibility in light of what had occurred with the Earl of Essex.[149] Shortly afterwards Armstrong found himself committed to the Tower in London to await his fate.

Armstrong, no more than Barkstead, Corbet and Okey in 1662, did not long survive his return to England. Despite the fact that he had been born in Nijmegen, and was therefore, at least technically, a Dutch citizen, the government's main idea seems to have been to get him out of the way as soon as possible. He was allowed little by way of a trial. Armstrong was regarded as an outlaw, despite the fact that he had been brought back within a year. A statute dating from the time of Edward VI which would

143 BL Add. MSS 41810, fo. 74v.
144 Sprunger, *Dutch Puritanism*, pp. 415–16.
145 Burnet, *History*, II, p. 412.
146 A. Fea, *King Monmouth: Being A History of the Career of James Scott 'The Protestant Duke', 1649–1685* (1920), p. 189.
147 BL Add. MSS 41810, fo. 97.
148 BL Add. MSS 41810, fo. 93.
149 *ibid.*; for a discussion of the suicide, or murder, of Essex see Ashcraft, *Revolutionary Politics*, pp. 380–2.

have reversed his outlawry was merely ignored by an anxious government.[150] The judicial officer in charge of the case was George Jeffreys and, as usual, there were few quibbles from him over these 'legal technicalities'. Jeffreys was not one to let the law stand in the way of royal justice if it could be helped. Armstrong was swiftly sentenced and executed on the same day, 20 June 1684, producing a satisfactory result for all concerned, except presumably the prisoner and his followers.

Other English diplomats in the Low Countries also became involved in the clandestine war. Although he did not possess the sleazy talents of Sir George Downing, Bevil Skelton did have a dogged determination to counter the problems of the English exiles during his time in the Netherlands. Skelton was a former soldier and while he never showed much diplomatic skill, he did create a generally effective intelligence system to spy upon the exiles. He also tried to seize them where possible[151] and to deal with the collusion of the Dutch authorities in their activities. Skelton was sent to the Netherlands in March 1685 as successor to Henry Sidney. He soon busied himself in recruiting spies to work for him. Some of these recruits were highly placed. Dr Covel supplied Skelton with intelligence from inside the Prince of Orange's court.[152] Unfortunately Covel was soon exposed and was forced out of the country.[153] Skelton's main interest was in the burgeoning exile problem. He was fortunate to secure the services of a double agent in Utrecht. It may be that this was a Frenchman by the name of Massell, who also spied upon the exiled Sir William Waller and worked for Jenkins and Middleton.[154] The double agent was highly placed in the rebel's councils.[155] Fearing exposure, however, the agent passed his reports to Skelton through a husband and wife team of intermediaries. He was able to serve Skelton well prior to Monmouth's invasion and supplied intelligence about the duke's schemes, for the unsuspecting rebels often came to his house to stay.

Skelton initially encouraged the agent with small sums of money, but the demands from Utrecht grew while the intelligence faltered.[156] Eventually, however, the Utrecht spy overstepped the mark. A series of leaks at

[150] It was argued that he had not surrendered voluntarily of his own free will as required and therefore the statute could not apply. This would have reversed his outlawry and allowed him to stand trial. See *State Trials*, X, pp. 109–24; G. W. Keeton, *Lord Chancellor Jeffreys and the Stuart Cause* (1965), pp. 285–7.

[151] See BL Add. MSS 41814, fos. 46–7, 48, 54, 55–8.

[152] See also BL Add. MSS 22910, fo. 253.

[153] Ashcraft, *Revolutionary Politics*, p. 528.

[154] For this theory see P. Hoftijzer, '"Such Onely as are very honest, loyall, and active": English Spies in the Low Countries, 1660–1688', *Dutch Quarterly Review*, 19, 1989, pp. 174–5.

[155] BL Add. MSS 41812, fos. 70–72v; 85–6.

[156] BL Add. MSS 41812, fos. 230–3, 244–245v.

Whitehall filtered through to the rebels and on 22 August 1686 the agent was badly beaten by men associated with the exiled radicals Colonel Danvers and John Wildman.[157] He lost an eye and was 'in danger of being deprived of his sences through the many blows he received upon his head'.[158] The Dutch government proved reluctant to investigate the affair and Skelton's protest to the authorities merely led to the agent being fined 300 guilders for being a spy in the first place.[159] The other agent of note in Skelton's employ was the former court and Whig informer Edmund Everard, who had been involved in the destruction of Edmund Fitzharris in 1681.[160] By 1685 Everard was lurking in the Low Countries and associating with the exiles. He offered his services to Skelton in return for a pardon.[161] At first Skelton made a cautious use of him[162] for he thought Everard 'juggles with me ... [and] playes fast & loose of all sides'.[163] Later the spy grew fearful of his position, especially when the Utrecht spy was attacked by the exiles. Skelton was forced to take Everard with him when he left for his new post in France and advocated to Middleton that Everard be given an 'office in the Custome house or elsewhere that he may live upon [which] will be good worke and reward for him'.[164]

Despite the problems he experienced Skelton's intelligence work was much more able than some historians have claimed.[165] Excitable he may have been, as well as hampered by the passive resistance and letter-opening activities of the Dutch government,[166] but he did manage to inform the Stuart regime of most important happenings in the Dutch Republic. His move to Paris in July 1686, the result of Sunderland's interference, left a substantial gap in James II's armoury. His replacement was Sunderland's friend, the notorious ex-spy Ignatius White, Marquis of Albeville.[167]

After Skelton's departure it was left to Albeville to provide intelligence for the regime of James II. Albeville was not unfamiliar with this sort of work. Indeed Albeville and his brothers, Richard and Andrew, appear to have made espionage almost a family business at one time. From the 1650s onwards they were all professional spies, servants of a variety of masters. Their Limerick Irish Catholic background gave them a significant entrée

[157] BL Add. MSS 41813, fos. 247v, 249v–250; Ashcraft, *Revolutionary Politics*, p. 529.
[158] BL Add. MSS 41814, fos. 32–3. [159] *ibid.*
[160] For Everard see D. Ogg, *England in the Reign of Charles II* (reprint, Oxford, 1967), pp. 624–6; Kenyon, *Popish Plot*, p. 61.
[161] BL Add. MSS 41812, fos. 38, 171v. [162] *ibid.*, fos. 212–213v, 220v, 226–7.
[163] BL Add. MSS 41813, fo. 11.
[164] BL Add. MSS 41814, fo. 33.
[165] See P. Earle, *Monmouth's Rebels: The Road to Sedgemoor 1685* (1977), pp. 67–8.
[166] BL Add. MSS 41912, fo. 211.
[167] See Kenyon, *Sunderland*, p. 136. Sunderland wanted his own man on the ground in The Hague and Albeville was friendly to Sunderland's interests; see *HMC*, 7th Report, p. 423.

onto the European scene for there were a number of Irish mercenaries and shady individuals from Ireland in exile in Europe in the mid seventeenth century. Surplus Irish swordsmen, especially if they were Roman Catholic, had always been encouraged to leave the country for the continent, where they could fight in European wars and, so successive regimes hoped, die there.[168] Where such men could not live by the sword they were forced to live by their wits. These three particular 'wild geese' made their homes in various parts of Europe. On the whole they were as dishonest, self-serving and untrustworthy as most professional spies of that era. All three quickly sought Spanish connections. Andrew and Richard went on to serve Cardinal Mazarin in the French regime. As a result they ended up in the Bastille for their pains when Mazarin discovered that they had been serving two masters, the King of Spain, as well as the King of France. In a sense these men had only one real master of course, themselves. Incarcerated in the Bastille the two brothers formed a connection with Colonel Joseph Bamfield, at this point in his career working for John Thurloe.[169] Richard White was recruited to serve Thurloe and the English Republic, unreliably, in Madrid. Bamfield sent Andrew White to Italy. Both brothers had a penchant for attempting to bribe under-secretaries in various government offices to obtain information. In comparison with their brother Ignatius they were not very effective.[170]

Ignatius White came to prominence with the capture of Thomas Scot, the republican spymaster,[171] but he also had served his apprenticeship with the Spanish, the French and the English Republic as a spy. The hostility between European states offered ample opportunities for the professional spy and sometimes they paid well.[172] Ignatius had also served for a time on behalf of the States General of the United Provinces, but 'it was believed that he was corrupted by the French to give them intelligence'.[173] In 1660 White was in the Spanish Netherlands and as part-payment for his services to the Spanish crown picked up the title of Baron de Vicque. He was involved in anti-Stuart intrigues in the 1660s.[174] In spite of this Arlington engaged him as a spy during the Second Anglo-Dutch War for the hefty sum of £300 per annum.[175] How often he received the payment is another matter; most of the time he was 'on credit'.[176] Having refused a Spanish

[168] See R. D. Fitzsimon, 'Irish Swordsmen in the Imperial service in the 30 Years War', *Irish Sword*, 9, 1969, p. 23.

[169] Related in E. S. De Beer, 'The Marquess of Albeville and his Brothers', *EHR*, 45, 1930, pp. 397–408.

[170] *ibid.* [171] *ibid.*, p. 401–2. [172] See above, Chapter 4.

[173] De Beer, 'Marquess of Albeville', pp. 397–408.

[174] See R. A. Stradling, 'Spanish Conspiracy in England, 1661–1663', *History*, 87, 1972, pp. 269–86.

[175] BL Add. MSS 34342, fo. 91v. [176] *ibid.*

command in 1673 Ignatius found himself at the peace congress at Cologne and put himself in the way of Sir Joseph Williamson. Williamson, aware of White's background, used him cautiously.[177] By 1674 White had gained another title, this time from the Emperor Leopold I, the Marquisate of Albeville, which Gilbert Burnet believed had been a title awarded for White's services as a spy.[178] In due course Albeville had become trusted by James II and high in state affairs. In January 1687 James sent him as ambassador extraordinary to the Prince of Orange. If Chudleigh and Skelton had offended William, then Albeville's appointment was seen as a calculated insult. William had wished for someone who could assist in Anglo-Dutch relations, not a Catholic ex-spy with dubious titles. D'Avaux, the French ambassador, believed Albeville was an odd choice at best and 'un agent double' at the worst.[179] Moreover in spite of his previous espionage career Albeville proved a blunderer as a diplomat. While he cannot be held fully responsible for the Stuart disaster of November 1688 he was one of the contributing causes in the fall of James II. Having said this, it may finally be noted that spies had come a long way since the early days of the Restoration.

[177] De Beer, 'Marquess of Albeville', p. 404. [178] *ibid.*, p. 406. [179] *ibid.*, p. 405.

8

Assassination: 'an Italian trick, not used in England'

I

On Sunday 12 February 1682 three men were to be found sitting in the Black Bull, a tavern situated in Holborn. They were awaiting news of the movements of Thomas Thynne, the noted Whig MP and associate of the Duke of Monmouth. All three were foreigners, Captain Christopher Vratz, alias de Vallicks, a German soldier of fortune, Lieutenant John Stern, a forty-two-year old Swedish mercenary and Charles George Borsky, alias Boratzi, a not very bright Polish manservant. At around six in the evening news came to them that Thynne was out and about in his coach taking the air. On hearing this the three left the tavern and rode up the Strand in the direction of St James's heading for Pall Mall. Thomas Thynne had spent the afternoon talking with the Duke of Monmouth in his coach, and as the evening drew on he dropped the duke off at Hedge Lane, Thynne proposed to conclude his journey with a round of visits in the City.[1] As the coach headed up St James's Street towards the Countess of Northumberland's house it was gloomy enough for the vehicle to need a 'link man' with a torch in front to guide the way. At which point the three men on horseback rode up. Stern moved in front of the coach, while Vratz and Borosky came up to the coach itself. Vratz shouted 'Hold you dog!' to the driver and as the latter turned, Borosky fired his weapon through the window of the carriage. Five or six shots hit Thynne in the stomach and hip, mortally wounding him. The trio then fled into the darkness.[2]

The later seventeenth century, as is well known, was the age of plots and conspiracies in which ideas of political murder figured strongly. Actual assassinations which came to fruition however were much rarer. In this period political murder was rather like the dog which failed to bark in the

[1] J. N. P. Watson, *Captain-General and Rebel Chief* (London, 1979), p. 140, gives Monmouth's side of the story.

[2] The events themselves emerge through the evidence in *State Trials*, IX, pp. 3–124; Luttrell, *Historical Relation*, I, p. 164. See also A. Marshall, 'The Killing of Thomas Thynne' (unpublished paper).

Sherlock Holmes story.[3] There was much talk, but often very little action. The problem of political murder itself remains a little explored subtext in the period. The general question of political murder, in an English and more specifically late-seventeenth-century context, thus deserves some consideration here. This chapter attempts to deal with some of the arguments which revolved around this subject at the time. Within the general question there are two basic avenues of approach. The first of these is concerned with those assassination plots directed against the government of Charles II. The second deals with political murder used by this government against its opponents and raises the question, as it did at the time, of whether that most extreme of all actions in the world of 'dirty politics', assassination, can be used legitimately against the enemies of the state. It is a debate which, in our own age of terrorism and counter-terrorism, remains with us.[4]

It is clear that contrary to what was proclaimed at the trials of Vratz, Stern, Borosky (for the three men were soon caught and executed), assassination was far from being solely an 'Italian Trick', something only practised by foreigners and others, but that the Stuart regime was also involved in this world. It both countenanced the assassination of some of its political opponents, as we shall see, and it was also subject to the more general fear of the assassination of its monarch and statesmen by the radical community. Assassination can be defined as the sudden and treacherous killing of a public figure who has, or did have, responsibilities in public life, by someone who kills in the belief that he is acting in the public interest. On the whole little has been done to delineate the typology of political murders, but we can say that there are different types and that the rationale for one assassination is not necessarily the same as for another. Such deaths range from the quasi-moral justification of state action to the murder carried out for personal motives which is given a political overtone. The murder of an enemy for political ends has in fact a long history behind it. Biblical precedents for assassination abound, from the story of Judith and Holfernes onwards, in spite of equally strong biblical strictures against murder in general.[5] There is little doubt that some of these influenced early modern philosophy and politics.[6] The philosophical debate on political

3 Sir Arthur Conan Doyle, 'Silver Blaze', in *The Complete Sherlock Holmes Short Stories*, (1976).

4 See M. Urban, *Big Boys' Rules: The SAS and the Secret Struggle Against the IRA* (1992).

5 The story of Judith and Holfernes is in Judith, XIII, vv. 1–20 in *The Apocrypha* (Oxford, 1939), pp. 146–7.

6 As well as art and literature, Judith and Holfernes was a popular subject for artists of the time; by Caravaggio for example, *Judith Beheading Holfernes* (c. 1598), in Galleria Nazionale dell'Arte Antica, Rome. In philosophical terms the theme was classically examined in

murder in this period reveals a complex web of ideas and opinions. Generally philosophical ideas on this subject revolved around two main areas. Firstly there were the ideas of tyrannicide, and secondly questions concerned with reason of state. The flow of ideas and opinions on both of these matters was extensive in the sixteenth and seventeenth centuries. They set the context for any actual assassinations. The classical English text on this matter was Edward Sexby's pamphlet *Killing Noe Murder*.[7] Sexby with his practical views on the problem of tyranny set standards in the traditional view of such matters. He outlined the majority of arguments which faced those who wished to take up the tool of assassination. But the state itself had problems on this front and sought to justify the removal of its enemies by political murder.

The discussions which took place over the use of reason of state as the justification of political murder were classically exposed by Machiavelli, but other theorists also had their say and influenced the seventeenth-century perspective. Justus Lipsius, in his *Six Books of Politics or Civil Doctrine* generally noted that 'It [can] be sometimes lawful and reasonable to trace out indirect courses in this tempestuous sea of the affairs of the world'.[8] Machiavelli, however, was able to be more direct. Taking as his text the tale of Romulus and the foundation of Rome through political murder, he noted that in such cases it was the common good which counted and 'reprehensible actions may be justified by their effects ... when the effect is good, as it was in the case of Romulus, it always justifies the action'.[9] If this seemed morally reprehensible, then he went on to note that it was only the men who used 'violence to spoil things, not [those] who use[d] it to mend [that were really] blameworthy'.[10] Here then was the justification for political murder by the state in stark terms: if the ends could be justified, so could the means used to achieve them and, to coin a phrase, the ends of government took priority over the literal ends of citizens. Moreover, Domhall O Colmáin, an Irish writer of the later Stuart

the works of Machiavelli, but see also H. F. Brown, *Studies in the History of Venice* (2 vols., 1907), I, pp. 216–54.

[7] For Sexby see *DNB*, Edward Sexby; *BDBR*, III, p. 161–3; also relevant in this context was the *Vindiciae contra tyrannos* (1577); see J. H. Burns and M. Goldie, *The Cambridge History of Political Thought 1450–1700* (Cambridge, 1991), pp. 211–14. Also M. Dzelzainis, ed., *John Milton, Political Writings* (Cambridge, 1991), p. xxv. The most readily available modern edition of Sexby's work is in D. Wootton, ed., *Divine Right and Democracy: An Anthology of Political Writing in Stuart England* (Harmondsworth, 1988), pp. 360–88. See also *Harleian Miscellany*, IX, pp. 284–307; and Firth, *Last Years of the Protectorate*, I, pp. 223–32; and C. H. Firth, 'Killing No Murder', *EHR*, 18, 1902, pp. 308–11; O. Lutaud, *Des Révolutions d'Angleterre á la Révolution Française: Le Tyrannicide et Killing No Murder (Cromwell, Athalie, Bonaparte)* (The Hague, 1973), p. 47.

[8] J. Lipsius, *Six Books of Politickes or Civil Doctrine* (1589, translated 1594) p. 114.

[9] Machiavelli, *Discourses*, p. 132.

[10] *ibid.*

period noted that in his eyes it was never 'right to say or think it murder or [even] a misdemeanour to kill a proclaimed traitor ... [if there was] a special order from the king'.[11] Little survives directly of the Stuart government's policy other than its actions in this area, but we can uncover some individual opinions on the matter.

At the highest levels of government most seventeenth-century English statesmen tended to regard the possibility of their own assassination as both an occupational hazard and, as Oliver Cromwell expressed it 'little fiddling things', only worthy of their contempt.[12] But there is no doubt that an underlying anxiety and concern over the possibility remained whether one was a monarch or minister. In Europe a number of politicians, not to mention some monarchs, had fallen to the assassin's bullet or knife during the course of the century. Thus rumours of plots against the lives of statesmen had to be regarded with some seriousness. However, within royalist circles in the period, there had always been something of a double standard operating with regard to the question of political murder. While it was considered most reprehensible to murder the divinely ordained monarch, the same men were often perfectly willing to countenance, where they did not actively encourage, the murder of others. We can trace the beginnings of this double standard to at least 1648, if not earlier, with the murder of the Leveller leader Thomas Rainsborough by Captain Paulden and his men.[13] It is entirely possible that the Civil Wars had accustomed many men on both sides to casual brutality in order to achieve their aims. The murder of prisoners and political opponents in the context of the Civil War, which Charles Carlton has recently outlined, must have led to a certain cynicism in respect to violent political action.[14] The men who took power in 1660 also had the experience of the 1650s to look back on. While in exile they had occasionally countenanced the murder of their political opponents. Indeed from the establishment of the English Republic that state's envoys and politicians at home and abroad had been subject to the threat of assassination; the royalists had even been successful on occasion.

They were able to justify this sort of action because it was argued by many royalists that those who had rebelled against royal authority, and even more reprehensibly had executed their king, had in fact placed them-

[11] Ó. Colmáin quoted in B. Ó Cuív, 'James Cotter: A Seventeenth Century Agent of the Crown', *Journal of the Royal Society of Antiquaries of Ireland*, 89, 1959, p. 144.

[12] See Firth, *Last Years of the Protectorate*, I, pp. 235–6, for more on Cromwell's attitude which belies the later royalist propaganda.

[13] For this murder which began as a botched kidnapping see *DNB*, Paulden, Thomas Rainsborough. Contrary to his first biographer's view Thomas Blood was not involved in this killing. See *Remarks*, p. 220.

[14] C. Carlton, *Going to the Wars: The Experience of the British Civil Wars, 1638–1651* (1992).

selves outside of the normal rules of political life. In such a situation it was necessary to resort to unorthodox methods of exercising 'justice' against them. It is this type of view which readily explains the murders of Isaac Dorislaus, Anthony Ascham and the various attempts made upon Oliver Cromwell.[15] It was a view which survived the Restoration and also goes some way to explaining the attempts to murder the exiled regicides and other leading exiled statesmen in the 1660s, one case of which we shall shortly examine. The regicides in particular were often pursued with a fanaticism which sometimes even went beyond the grave.[16] Conversely the numerous plots against the Stuart regime, real or spurious, after the Restoration invariably had the murder of someone in the government as a central element, whether it was Albermarle, widely regarded as a traitor by most radicals, Clarendon, or the royal brothers themselves. In an era when government clearly rested on the strength, as well as the personality of a handful of men, the mere threat of assassination was sufficient to worry most regimes. The right bullet at the right time could, if it was unable to bring the whole structure tumbling down, certainly cause chaos.

Charles II's attitude towards assassination, as with so much else about that monarch, is often difficult to discern. Of his own possible murder he seems to have shared with Cromwell a contempt for both the deed and the possible assassin. It was an occupational hazard which, in the unsteady times in which he lived, monarchy must endure. Having said this, he seems to have been well aware of the various attempts on Cromwell's life as well as the later attempts upon the regicides. In general he gave very little encouragement to such schemes. Clarendon told the wily Sir George Downing, who was a constant advocate of such 'dirty tricks', that he did not believe Charles would ever give a direct order to have the regicides in the Netherlands murdered.[17] While the republicans had set a price on the exiled king's head, and he retaliated in kind, it seems that he thought it prudent not to encourage assassination as a wholesale policy. Once begun there was no knowing where such things might end. A spiral of political violence might engender reciprocal assassination. The most that may be said is that while Charles would not have objected to the results of such deeds, he would have regarded the methods used as beneath his dignity as a

[15] For these murders see Gardiner, *Commonwealth and Protectorate*, I, pp. 73, 309–12. For the various attempts on Cromwell see Firth, *Last Years of the Protectorate*, I, p. 35 *et passim*, and below. Also 'The Process and Pleadings in the Court of Spain upon the death of Anthony Ascham (1651)', *Harleian Miscellany*, VI, pp. 236–47; E. Scott, *The King in Exile* (1905), pp. 96–7, 290.

[16] See for example the idea put to Downing concerning the removal of Colonel Hewson's body from his grave in order that it could be sent back to England; *CCl.SP*, IV, p. 138.

[17] See the discussion in E. Scot, *The Travels of the King* (1907), pp. 124–5.

king and gentleman.[18] According to one historian Charles was genuinely shocked, when the Rye House Plot was uncovered in 1683, that anyone would wish to kill him, although it is difficult to believe this of the cynical and worldly wise monarch, especially with his experience over the previous twenty-three years.

The king's ministers often viewed the technique of political murder with a little more equanimity. The loyal Secretary of State, Sir Edward Nicholas, had relished the thought of Cromwell's death by such a means.[19] Ormonde had also favoured the use of the method in the 1650s, although it is unclear whether he changed his mind after his own brush with assassination in December 1670.[20] Arlington was ever the subtle courtier in such matters. Clarendon had also consented to such schemes. Although he may have protested otherwise in public, he had discussed assassination with Sir George Downing. Of Buckingham's views it may be said that very little of this sort was beneath the duke's dignity, which is all the more surprising as his own father had been assassinated. Buckingham indeed often went out of his way to associate with such men.[21] James, Duke of York appears to have held an ambivalent view. In May 1655 he was willing to entertain the offer of four Catholic officers to kill the Protector, yet when he was king, one of his diplomats thought that a proposed scheme to murder Monmouth in 1685 would have been rejected with horror.[22] In 1696, with the assassination of William III in the air, James again seems to have disliked the idea, but did little enough to prevent it going forward.[23] Of Shaftesbury, that most able politician, it may be said that he was willing to countenance assassination when all else failed.[24]

In the murkier world of espionage where the light only occasionally penetrated, there was a much more casual attitude to such brutality. The knife in the back and the premeditated elimination of enemies was far more common. Spies who played false, or were uncovered by their enemies, or were just plain unlucky, could, of course, be murdered, often without any reference to the legal process. A few examples may suffice to illustrate what we mean. Seigneur de Tellières, a Huguenot soldier working for the French

18 See *CCl.SP*, V, p. 156; Hutton, *Charles II*, p. 421.

19 See Firth, *Last Years of the Protectorate*, I, p. 39.

20 See Marshall, 'Blood', pp. 565–6.

21 His father had been murdered by John Felton in 1628; see R. Lockyer, *Buckingham The Life and Political Career of George Villiers, First Duke of Buckingham 1592–1628* (1984), p. 453. For his son's attitude see Marshall, 'Blood', pp. 565–6.

22 BL Add. MSS 41812, fos. 20–1 for the threat to Monmouth, Scott, *The Travels of the King*, pp. 124–5 for James' earlier thoughts.

23 J. Garrett, *The Triumphs of Providence: The Assassination Plot 1696* (Cambridge, 1980), p. 62.

24 For a discussion, perhaps more favourable to the earl than it should be, see Haley, *Shaftesbury*, pp. 708 *et passim*.

to infiltrate the conspiracy against James II, was probably murdered by agents of William of Orange in August 1688.[25] Henry Manning, supplying information to John Thurloe about royalist plans, was uncovered in 1655, interrogated at Cologne and then taken to a nearby wood and shot out of hand:[26] rough justice for Manning, but all too typical of what could happen to the spy who was discovered.

There was then a background atmosphere of violence in the period which made such acts as assassination and murder, if not totally acceptable in moral terms, at least accepted as a risk in political life. There were also numerous private vendettas settled in Restoration England with violence. Attacks were even made on men such as John Dryden. Thomas Thynne, as we have seen, was murdered in his coach and the Dukes of Buckingham and Monmouth's brawls, beatings and killings were the scandal of the court.[27] Whether in a back alley in Amsterdam or in a procession to parliament in London, political murder apparently had its place in the scheme of things.

It is perhaps pertinent at this point to account for the reason why, given such a background, so many schemes failed to come to fruition. To fully succeed assassination had to fulfil certain criteria. Firstly the actual target itself had to be vulnerable. All potential targets were by their very definition as public figures vulnerable to some extent to the assassin. The 'trick', as the Rye House plotters styled it,[28] was to discover at what point the killing could take place. It was in the planning rather than the execution that the successful assassin showed his skills. The assassin, while he may have found his task of killing not particularly difficult, invariably found it rather more difficult to be certain of escape afterwards. Once this problem began to bear upon the assassin's mind then the actual chances of success began to decline rapidly. Miles Sindercombe, John Cecil and the mysterious Mr Boyes came up with a variety of schemes to murder the Lord Protector in 1657. These schemes showed enterprise and some ingenuity. That they did not succeed can only be explained by a failure of nerve at the final hurdle. After various failed attempts to catch Cromwell as he rode in his coach to Hampton Court the assassins thought to kill him as he was taking the air in Hyde Park. They had broken the hinges of the park gates so that a quick escape was possible. Cecil was on the fringes of the

25 For de Telliéres see W. A. Speck, 'The Orangist Conspiracy Against James II', *HJ*, 30, 1987, p. 459.

26 Manning was murdered by Sir Nicholas Armorer and James Hamilton. See Scot, *The Travels of the King*, pp. 140–52. See also William Leving above, p. 168.

27 Duelling was rife in Restoration London and noblemen of any pretention usually had some hired thugs in their entourage. See V. G. Kiernan, *The Duel in European History: Honour and the Reign of the Aristocracy* (Oxford, 1989), pp. 7, 100, 118.

28 Sprat, *A True Account*, p. 51.

Protector's retinue at one point, but Sindercombe was still outside the park. Oliver, with his eye for good horseflesh, noticed Cecil's horse and called him over to enquire about the animal. Faced with the great man himself Cecil lost his nerve and claimed later he would have killed Cromwell, but the horse Oliver was admiring so much was in fact ill. With this somewhat feeble excuse Oliver went on his way unmolested by Cecil.[29]

In the next scheme Sindercombe, using the alias of John Fish, took a lease on a house near to Westminster Abbey which proved very convenient for another assassination attempt. He, Cecil and Boyes resolved to shoot Oliver as he proceeded from the abbey to parliament. The backyard next to the street was apt for their design and they began to erect scaffolding for building work in order to cover their real business. The day of the parliament dawned and Cecil, Sindercombe and Boyes went to the yard. Cecil stood on the wall with his pistol at the ready, while Sindercombe paced nervously below, as if building himself up for the deed. Unfortunately at that point some people came into the yard, Boyes immediately decamped into the crowded street and the scheme had to be abandoned.[30] The killing was only one part of the whole; what came after rarely seems to have been considered in the conspiracies of the period.

A second criterion necessary for a successful assassination was that the assassins themselves had to be fairly competent and capable of committing the deed. The most dangerous type of assassin was without doubt the single individual with a private grudge who was bent on achieving his purpose. The deaths of such men as the 1st Duke of Buckingham, William the Silent and Henri IV prove this.[31] The most common assassins appear to have been military or ex-military men who needed to make their fortunes, or bore a grudge. They also usually had little by way of moral scruple to hamper them in committing the deed. Certainly they were usually aware of the dangers if they were caught, but the rewards could be great enough to outweigh these. The former Leveller Miles Sindercombe was a man of violent passions who fought hard when his captors came for him. He beat off the guard and only submitted after one of them had cut off his nose.[32] Even then he was not a man to submit quietly. He used 'violent and threatening speeches', tried to bribe his prison guards and in true Roman fashion committed suicide in the Tower, much to the dismay of the regime and the cheers of Edward Sexby. Lieutenant John Stern was another who fitted the pattern for the professional assassin. The Swedish soldier claimed to be the illegitimate son of a Swedish baron and was a mercenary who, having

[29] *State Trials*, V, pp. 869–70. [30] *ibid*.

[31] For the killing of William see C. V. Wedgewood, *William the Silent* (1960); for the death of Henri IV see R. Mousnier, *The Assassination of Henry IV* (1973).

[32] *State Trials*, V, pp. 842–72.

begun his career in the forces of the Elector of Brandenburg, during the next twenty-three years or so went wherever his sword took him. The brutality of the soldier's life would have innured him to bloodshed. For twelve years he had been a Roman Catholic, more it seemed because, as he put it, 'I was commonly all the time in Popish territories' than out of any sincere religious convictions. Indeed in 1681, whilst residing in Holstein, Stern had returned to the Lutheran religion of his youth. He was a mercenary in the spiritual as well as the military sense. Europe held many such men as Stern, willing and able, if paid well, to turn their hands to most things including murder. Christopher Vratz was another. A German of a good family he became a tough professional soldier; 'hard as flint' as one contemporary put it.[33] Vratz had served in various armies in Europe and had been something of a hero at the siege of Mons. But he also had a darker side to his career, having been a highwayman in Poland and on the wrong side of the law in other countries. He was a brutal but brave man who went to his death on the scaffold with great aplomb. The mysterious Mr Boyes was involved with Miles Sindercombe. His fellow conspirators knew very little about him and he disappeared after the plot was uncovered. He moved a great deal between England and Flanders and was apparently an expert in explosives, for it was he who made the device which was to fire Whitehall. There seems little doubt that Boyes had royalist connections and that he was using an alias.[34]

Assassination, first emerging as it did in Renaissance Italy,[35] was very familiar to the English public through numerous Jacobean revenge dramas, as well as through the thought, albeit usually in a popular form, of Niccolò Machiavelli.[36] The dramatic and literary use of Italy and Italians in such a way helped to set the tone, and indeed the standard, in the English mind for such deeds. Despite being based largely on fear and ignorance the 'Italy' they created became 'a mode of human experience rather than . . . a [real] country'.[37] The myth of Italians as the best assassins available in the market entered the English consciousness, where it mingled with those

33 *State Trials*, IX, p. 95. 34 *CSPD*, 1656–7, pp. 258–9.

35 D. Hay and J. Law, *Italy in the Age of the Renaissance, 1380–1530* (1898), pp. 163–4. For the contemporary anonymous tract, 'Of the Right that Princes have to compass the Lives of their Enemies', which deals with the subject see H. F. Brown, *Studies in the History of Venice* (2 vols., 1907), I, p. 225.

36 As an instance of this see the prologue to Christopher Marlowe's *The Jew of Malta* in *The Complete Plays* (Harmondsworth, 1975), pp. 347–8; also G, K. Hunter, '"English Folly and Italian Vice": The Moral Landscape of John Marston', in *Dramatic Identities and Cultural Tradition: Studies in Shakespeare and his Contemporaries Critical Essays* (Liverpool, 1978), pp. 103–32.

37 G. K. Hunter quoted in John Webster, *Three Plays* (Harmondsworth, 1980), p. 26. See also M. Wiggins, *Journeyman in Murder: The Assassin in the English Renaissance Drama* (Oxford, 1991).

other favourite villains, the evil papists, and the cunning Jesuit, to provide a potent brew. There was in fact some truth in these rumours about Italy. The Republic of Venice for example, kept a professional poisoner in its employ and was willing to receive tenders for the assassination of its enemies.[38] The English grew to possess a great belief in the ingenuity of the Italian assassin which went far beyond the actual reality. In this respect they remained a credulous nation. This may be easily perceived by the case of the Italian diplomat Passerini. He was sent by the Swedish Queen Christina with letters to the court of the Lord Protector, Oliver Cromwell. He asked to see the Lord Protector alone and this raised fears amongst the Protector's entourage that, as he was an Italian, he might be carrying letters impregnated with poison, the Italians being noted inventors of such ingenious devices. True to form Cromwell laughed at such nonsense and saw the diplomat anyway.[39]

The English belief in the cunning of the Jesuit order, as well as its penchant for using the tool of assassination in its work, matched the belief in the Italian assassin.[40] The Jesuits were regarded as a particularly dangerous movement as it was thought that they possessed the philosophical justification for regicide in the ideas of the Jesuit Juan de Mariana. Mariana's view that 'anyone who [was] inclined to heed the prayers of the people may attempt to destroy a tyrant' was regarded as evidence of the immorality of the order.[41] The last group strongly identified in the English mind as being prone to use, or be involved in, assassinations, were those familiar English bugbears, the Irish. During the Popish Plot there emerged, assisted by the fantasies of Titus Oates, a plethora of images of Irish assassins – incompetent ones at that, as one might expect from Oates – dropping flints from their muskets behind bushes.[42] No-one appears to have questioned the fact that if the Catholic church *had* wished to kill Charles it could have hired far more competent hands than Oates' fantasticks for, as we have seen,

[38] Which duly surfaced in the period of the Popish Plot. For a scale of the poisoners' prices (the more valuable the life the higher the price), see Brown, *History of Venice*, I, pp. 236–7.

[39] For this story see Firth, *Last Years of the Protectorate*, I, pp. 234–5.

[40] See for example *Jesuits Assassins or the Popish Plot Further Declared and Demonstrated in their Murderous Practices and Principles, All Extracted out of Dr Tong's Papers* (1680). See also T. Harris, *London Crowds in the Reign of Charles II: Propaganda and Politics from the Restoration Until the Exclusion Crisis* (Cambridge, 1987), pp. 140–44; Jonathan Scott, *Algernon Sidney and the Restoration Crisis, 1677–1683* (Cambridge, 1991), p. 280.

[41] Mariana quoted in Q. Skinner, *The Foundations of Modern Political Thought* (2 vols., Cambridge, 1978), II, pp. 346–7; also Burns and Goldie, *Cambridge History of Political Thought*, pp. 240–1.

[42] Lane, *Titus Oates*, p. 34.

there were professional assassins, Irish and otherwise, available for hire if one knew where to look.[43]

One of the problems of an assassination conspiracy was the possibility of discovery in a variety of ways. Individuals might lose their nerve and inform the authorities of what was going on; alternatively the conspirators might accidently include a spy in their numbers. Planning an assassination in the period was obviously a difficult undertaking: the more men involved, and they needed to be sounded out as well as taken into confidence, the greater the chance of the plot collapsing.[44] Hence the discussions for the alleged Rye House conspiracy, at least on the lower and perhaps, more genuine level, brought in a man such as Josiah Keeling, who then betrayed the plotters. This 'plot' is in fact an interesting example of an assassination plot. While some elements of its genuineness can be doubted (there was much talk and little action), some of the details of the designs and tactics which emerged from the interrogations and trials were remarkably practical in nature. This is to be expected with the involvement of men such as Richard Rumbold. And if it had gone forward there is little doubt that it could have been successful in its immediate aims, although the resultant chaos might well have brought another civil war in its wake.[45]

What then were the best weapons and tactics to use in a political murder? One of the most favoured weapons used in assassination in the period seems to have been the musquetoon. This was a cavalry weapon of relatively short range, but capable of delivering many bullets at the same time. Its merits were that it had a short barrel and a flintlock and so it could be concealed under a cloak. In enclosed spaces such as a carriage or in an alleyway its effects could be devastating.[46] Moreover the fact that it fired several balls at once meant that even the most clumsy assassin was liable to hit something. Another favoured weapon was the blunderbuss – pocket or otherwise – which could be effective at close quarters.[47] Another means of making sure of the victim was to use a knife or a poniard, a short

[43] Only the lack of language appears to have prevented the killers of Thomas Thynne from realising this.

[44] Something which Machiavelli had discussed in some detail. See Machiavelli, *Discourses*, pp. 398–424.

[45] For the Rye House Plot see Sprat, *A True Account*; Ford, Lord Grey, *The Secret History of the Rye House Plot and of Monmouth's Rebellion* (1754). A useful discussion is also given in Ashcraft, *Revolutionary Politics*, Chapter 8. For more upon the actual designs see below.

[46] See, for example, the wounds inflicted on Thomas Thynne; *State Trials*, IX, pp. 20–2.

[47] For the musquetoon see D. G. Chandler, *The Art of Warfare in the Age of Marlborough* (1976), pp. 33, 35, 77; C. H. Firth, *Cromwell's Army* (1967), pp. 120–1; Garrett, *The Triumphs of Providence*, Plate 7; although she mistakes the weapon for an early 'revolver', which it most certainly was not. For a pocket blunderbuss see Sprat, *A True Account*, p. 51.

stabbing dagger. This had the advantage that if it struck home the wound could be fatal, but the disadvantage that at such a close range the chances of escape for the assassin were limited.

Where best to kill the victim depended on the circumstances. A lonely road, late at night, was possibly the most promising tactic, as long as the assassin did not attempt anything too elaborate,[48] but a crowded room also had advantages.[49] One possibility raised by the Rye House conspirators was the theatre. According to some sources Rumbold and Colonel John Rumzey had plans to shoot Charles by planting armed men in the pit of the playhouse. There was a further, less subtle, suggestion that the conspirators should merely blow up the whole theatre. Robert Ferguson is said to have relished this, claiming that 'they would [then] die in their own calling'.[50] The fact that the innocent would have died alongside the 'guilty' did not appear to be of much concern to him, for as he put it, 'What did the Jack-Daws do amongst the Rooks.'[51]

The victim might be in a carriage, in which case the chances of his death were raised by a shot through the window into a confined space. Sindercombe, Cecil and Boyes had planned to shoot Cromwell as the Protector was on the road to Hampton Court.[52] Interestingly this was to be paralleled by a similar design against Charles II in 1683, although the Lord Protector's killers later thought to unleash more violence. Sindercombe and Cecil had hired a house in Hammersmith which possessed a banqueting room. This room's outer wall formed part of a 'narrow dirty ... passage' in which the passing coaches were forced to slow down. The killers meant to blow up both wall and passage as Cromwell's coach went slowly down the alleyway.[53] The Rye House plotters planned to kill Charles II as he returned from the horse racing at Newmarket.[54] There was in fact a variety of ingenious schemes by which the king was to be despatched during the reign. These included while Charles was hunting, riding, walking, swimming (the idea of the ever-enterprising Thomas Blood) or while the king was boating on the Thames.[55] He was also to be despatched by being stabbed or poisoned. The lack of security surrounding the king at Whitehall and elsewhere meant that some of these were at least possibilities, where they were not complete fantasies.

A further design which emerged from the Rye House schemes was the

[48] As did Thomas Blood when he tried to kill Ormonde. See Marshall, 'Blood', pp. 565–6.
[49] Witness the murder of Buckingham on 23 August 1628. Lockyer, *Buckingham*, p. 453.
[50] Sprat, *A True Account*, p. 54. [51] *ibid.*
[52] *A True Narrative of the Late Trayterous Plot Against the Lord Protector, 23 January 1657*. Also Firth, *Last Years of the Protectorate*, I, p. 38.
[53] *A True Narrative*, p. 5. [54] See *State Trials*, IX, pp. 3465–6.
[55] Marshall, 'Blood', p. 568. Charles' boating 'accident' was one of the Rye House plotters' schemes. See Sprat, *A True Account*, p. 51.

fairly complex plan of killing the king as he passed through Covent Garden. Men were to be infiltrated in the Piazza and places alongside it. At a suitable point they would 'issue forth ... to compass the coaches and dispatch the business'.[56] The plan which the plotters eventually decided upon, however, was the ambush at the Rye House. The good points about the scheme were that it was to be undertaken in a relatively isolated spot and there was good cover for the assassins. The numbers involved were to be kept relatively low and the weapons were to be muskets or carbines. The Rye House itself was also near a staging post where the coach horses would have normally been changed, so by the time the horses had reached the ambush point they would be exhausted. With the coach in a narrow passage and blocked by a cart, the horses would have been shot, bringing the coach to a halt, then a general firefight was to have seen off the guards, postillion and coachmen. A group led by 'Hannibal' Rumbold would then have opened their fire against the coach itself killing the occupants.[57]

It is also clear that the methods used could well have been interpreted by some of the men involved as more soldierly than a mere murder. Rumbold later declared that he regarded the very idea of assassination with horror, making the distinction that the chosen ambush would have given the monarch at least a fighting chance, if Charles had had the opportunity to take it. Murder would therefore turn into an act of war. A similar distinction seems to have been made by the Jacobites who planned to kill William III.[58]

II

John Lisle was a well-connected parliamentarian of an 'independent' religious persuasion. He had been one of the most active members of the High Court of Justice which had tried Charles I and had gone on to serve the various regimes of the English Republic. At the Restoration in 1660 Lisle had been forced to flee the country and thus he became fair game for royalist killers. Eventually he came to settle in Switzerland in the company of Edmund Ludlow and some of the other regicides.[59] In general the Swiss political authorities were sympathetic to the exiled regicides, allowing them to remain within their borders. However, official and unofficial royalist policy was that all the regicides who had not surrendered themselves to royal justice in London had forfeited their lives.[60] Nor was the regime

[56] Sprat, *A True Account*, p. 51. [57] *ibid.*, p. 53.
[58] See T. B. Macaulay, *The History of England* (2 vols., 1889), I, p. 277.
[59] For Lisle see *DNB*, John Lisle.
[60] See Ludlow, *Voyce*, p. 12; also *Proclamation to Summon the Regicides*, Somers Tracts (2nd edn, 1812), VII, p. 437.

content to let their death rest on mere chance or old age. While nothing apparently survives of an official policy statement within the circles of government it was clear that the regime would look favourably on anyone who took on the task of abducting or murdering these men. The regime certainly wished to trace the links between the exiles and the radicals in England.[61] Moreover as Edmund Ludlow noted the 'kings bloodhounds [also began to] hunt . . . after the [lives] of the pretious servants of God'.[62]

One of these 'bloodhounds' was an obscure Irish mercenary by the name of Germaine Riordane. His real name, according to Edmund Ludlow, who took a personal interest in his history, was MacCarty and he was an impecunious Catholic soldier who had served for a time as a major in the Duke of York's regiment of horse while it was on the continent. By 1663 he was unemployed, having lost his position in the regiment while undertaking obscure services for the king in Europe. Little else is known of Riordane's life. He had a brother named Denis or Dermod, who had also served in the royal army using the name of Riordane and was apparently as poverty-stricken as he was himself.[63] An opportunity to make some money, as well as earn some favour at court and thereby raise his fortunes, would naturally have been seized upon by the Irish major. He was a violent man, not weighed down by any particular moral scruples, brutalised by his various continental experiences and ever ready to resort to the knife or the pistol in arguments. He was one of the many Irishmen who found themselves in the semi-criminal espionage world.[64] What little is known of Riordane/MacCarty is mainly known through Edmund Ludlow and is thus tainted by Ludlow's obvious dislike of the man who was, as we shall see, out to kill him, but even Ludlow could not disguise Riordane's real nature.

Since Riordane was to correspond with Arlington's office throughout his operations of 1663–4 and was to make a brief appearance in Williamson's correspondence in 1673 it must be presumed that to some extent Riordane's activities were under the control of the secretary's office. This would

[61] See PRO SP 29/86, fos. 32–3.

[62] Ludlow, *Voyce*, p. 192. See also A. Sidney, *Works* (1813), pp. 3, 33–4.

[63] *CSPD*, 1663–4, pp. 425, 426; *CSPD*, 1664–5, pp. 351, 579; *CSPD*, 1666–7, p. 125; There is a Denis Macarthy also mentioned in C. Dalton, *English Army Lists and Commission Registers, 1661–1714* (6 vols., 1892), I, p. 209. See also B. Ó. Cuív, 'James Cotter: A Seventeenth Century Agent of the Crown', *Journal of the Royal Society of Antiquaries of Ireland*, 89, 1959, pp. 135–59. He claims that Cotter rather than Riordane was the leader of the assassins. But it was Riordane, not Cotter, who was in contact with the secretary's office, as will be seen. A further claim that Riordane was killed at the crossing of the Rhine while in French service, via a source dating from 1715, is plausible, but Riordane was in contact with Williamson in 1673. See *CSPD*, 1673, p. 566.

[64] For some Irish sources see Ó. Cuív, 'James Cotter', pp. 134–59. But Ó. Cuív had not seen the Voyce manuscript and some of his sources are rather distant from the events they purport to describe.

not be improbable. Joseph Williamson, the *de facto* head of espionage under Arlington, possessed a contact address for Riordane in his address book and both he and Arlington were well aware of Riordane's work.[65] It is likely that Riordane was encouraged by the pair, but beyond this they would not have officially moved. Clarendon had already pointed out to Sir George Downing that royal approval was necessary to sanction such actions and he thought that such approval would be very reluctant. If Downing, whose talents for such work were already notorious, could not have a killing sanctioned then Arlington, the suave courtier, and his ever-discreet right-hand man Williamson would not have tried to seek it. Nothing would have been committed to paper, but Riordane would have possibly been given a mild verbal encouragement, unattributable and thus safe for all concerned.[66] Care had to be taken to choose the right sort of man. The actors in such activities might well come up against the military mentality which often looked askance at things it considered beneath the dignity of a gentleman to do. Bevil Skelton in 1685 was faced with an offer to shoot or abduct the Duke of Monmouth 'upon the roade as he travelled from place to place' in the Netherlands.[67] But Skelton, as an honourable soldier was horrified at such a mean action and refused to have anything to do with it. Even the unscrupulous George Downing had difficulties in hiring men to do his dirty work, which as an ambassador he found necessary and relished. The 'good resolute Englishmen' whom Downing asked to help him in the capture of the three regicides at Delft in 1662 were horrified at his request.[68] Other members of the court, such as James Halsall, for example,[69] had experience of such operations, so the choice of Riordane may have been the result of having friends in high places. Alternatively he was obscure enough to be disowned should things go wrong.

Edmund Ludlow's information was that the Queen Mother was on friendly terms with Riordane after Lisle's killing and the resourceful Irishman may have been known to her before this. She was to obtain a pardon for Riordane after he had murdered a fellow countryman, one Colonel Dillon, in Paris. She certainly had no love for the men who killed her husband and her involvement in hiring Riordane is a possibility.[70] However, Ludlow believed that a more likely candidate was Henriette, Duchess of Orléans. She was to give Riordane £300 for his work and Riordane was to claim that he was still £150 out of pocket despite this

65 See PRO SP 9/32, fo. 220.
66 For Clarendon and Downing see *CCl.SP*, V, pp. 155–6.
67 BL Add. MSS 41812, fos. 20–1.
68 For Downing see Codrington Library, All Souls College MSS, 240, fo. 411.
69 For James Halsall's experience see Scott, *Travels of the King*, pp. 125–30, 136–7.
70 Ludlow, *Voyce*, fo. 1010.

reward.[71] Henriette's involvement, or so Edmund Ludlow claimed, was a front for her brother Charles in the business, but Charles' involvement was, as we have already seen, unlikely. Moreover Henriette was a strong-willed young woman who was perfectly capable of undertaking this and other tasks herself, as the negotiations concerning the Secret Treaty of Dover prove.[72] Nor was Riordane on his own in such affairs. There were other royalist assassins also working in Europe at this time. Andrew White and his men had tried to kill Algernon Sidney in 1663.[73] Sidney had also claimed that attempts were to be made to murder him in 1665 in Augsburg. The main target of Riordane, however, was to be the much-feared Edmund Ludlow.

For all of his faults, and they were many, Edmund Ludlow was regarded by the Stuart regime as the main danger on the continent amongst the exile community. His name, if not the man himself, continually emerged in the 1660s as the one most likely to stir the radicals in England into rebellion. He certainly played the part of the elusive 'pimpernel', although the fact is that he never left Switzerland and was rendered incapable of action by his belief in religious providentialism. Thomas Blood met Ludlow in 1666 and garnered a poor impression of the erstwhile general, which he may have eventually passed on to the government. Blood found him 'very unable for [any] such ... employment' as leading a rebellion and more content in 'writing a history as he called it'.[74] Despite this, in 1663 at least, Ludlow was regarded as a threat to the stability of the English state. His elimination would have been welcomed by the regime and any other regicides who fell with Ludlow would have been regarded as an added bonus. Certainly this was something which Ludlow, never one to underestimate his own value, also thought.[75]

Riordane's first task was to gather around himself a variety of military men, some Frenchmen, some Savoyards and a couple of Irish compatriots. Unlike Aphra Behn's romantic royalist characters, Willmore and Belville, who were mainly interested in affairs of the heart, these men were mercenaries from the lower end of the European market. They made their living by the sword, or more commonly by the knife in the back. They were also often involved in the world of espionage for a variety of masters. For the Irishmen, since commissions in Charles II's army were scarce, hard service abroad had been their lot in life.[76] They were 'ruffian like ... des-

71 *ibid.*, fo. 1160.

72 See Ludlow, *Voyce*, fo. 1010 and fo. 945 for the king's involvement in the kidnapping of Warriston.

73 For these attempts see Sidney, *Works*, pp. 3, 33–4.

74 See Marshall, 'Blood', p. 564. A reading of Ludlow's manuscript 'A Voyce From the Watchtower' makes it clear that Ludlow had become a very indecisive man after 1662.

75 Ludlow, *Voyce*, p. 1020.

76 See Childs, *Army of Charles II*, p. 21.

peradoes', 'Grim fellows', which is why Riordane had chosen them.[77] What is known of the careers of the group tends to confirm this view.[78] Two of the men Riordane hired were fellow countrymen. One was a soldier by the name of O'Croli who also appears to have worked under the alias Thomas MacDonnell. The other was one Sémus mac Emoinn Mhic Choitir, or in English James Fitz Edmund Cotter, who went by the name of James Cotter. Both were involved in the killing of John Lisle.

On Saturday 14 November 1663 Riordane and eight others, with two 'lackeys', hired boats and crossed Lake Geneva from Savoy.[79] They were bound for the town of Vevay on the other side of the lake where Edmund Ludlow and some of his colleagues were then living. The boats landed after dark at around six in the evening. The men then scattered into two local inns in the town where they gave out the story that they were pilgrims on their way to a Catholic shrine at a local church. To that end they ordered horses to be made ready. They then spent the rest of the night waiting for the reports of a spy who was already in the town noting the movements of the regicides.

The next day, Sunday, found them scattered about the approaches to and behind the house of the regicides. Their plan was to fall upon their victims while they made their usual journey to church on a Sunday morning. What was to happen then would have depended on the victims. There is every reason to believe that they were to be taken alive across Lake Geneva. However, if they had put up any resistance Riordane and his men, who were armed with carbines, would undoubtedly have shot them out of hand. As a prelude to their own escape, and to prevent a chase across the lake, the assassins had sabotaged the other boats in the area. Fortunately for the regicides their landlord, Monsieur Dubois, went out earlier than usual to church. On his way he came across 'two unknowne persons, ruffian like fellows, desperadoes with long Cloakes and Carbines under them'.[80] He immediately deduced that the men were up to no good, especially on seeing others guarding the way to the church. He thus returned to the house and informed Ludlow and his colleagues of what he had seen. Nothing daunted, Ludlow and the exiles decided to go to the

77 PRO SP 29/86, fos. 225–6.

78 Ludlow, *Memoirs*, II, pp. 374–6. One man recruited by Riordane, a Monsieur Du Pre of Savoy was particularly brutal. He eventually murdered his brother-in-law, de la Fleischere, after quarrel. Du Pre shot him and then despatched his victim with a stilleto. He then attempted to cover the crime by dumping the body outside a bawdy house. He even had the gall to attend the funeral as the innocent husband comforting his wife for the loss of her brother. After this the authorities grew suspicious and he fled.

79 For the first attempts of Riordane and his reports thereafter see PRO SP 96/6, fo. 141, 267; PRO SP 92/24, fo. 76; PRO SP 29/86 fos. 225–6; and compare with Ludlow, *Voyce*, p. 1020; Ludlow, *Memoirs*, II, pp. 361–3; also *CSPD*, 1663–4, pp. 380, 661–2.

80 PRO SP 29/86, fos. 225–6.

church by a more secretive route, but first he and John Phelps, with some bravado, had a brief and furtive look at these 'grim fellows'.

Puzzled by the non-appearance of the regicides the assassins retired to an inn, somewhat 'disconsolate' at this state of affairs, while one of their number went to the church to see whether their intended victims were there. The church services being over, the local people of Vevay began to appear on the streets and discovered the damaged boats. At this some of them began to accuse the Savoyard boatmen in charge of Riordane's vessels with the crime. Word was quickly passed to the visitors that if they wanted to leave they had best do so now, while there was still the opportunity. The latter, deciding the scheme had collapsed and that discretion was the better part of valour, hastened to the vessels and fled over the lake. As they fled they were overheard to say 'Le Bouger ne viendras pas.'[81]

Naturally the invasion raised a storm of protest amongst the local authorities who sent out an order that in future all innkeepers were to give an account of all furtive-looking visitors. Further precautions were taken to protect the regicides,[82] but the episode had unnerved John Lisle. Having debated with the exiles he decided to move to the town of Lausanne which he believed would be safer, this despite the intelligence the exiles had received that there was safety in numbers. In any case Lisle was expecting a visit from his wife and did not wish to endanger her by remaining in Vevay.[83] Ludlow believed that Lisle thought he would be safer elsewhere and especially out of Ludlow's company. Ludlow claimed to have heard that Lisle had said that Ludlow, 'was his bulwarke, and that till ye enemy had despatched me, they would not attempt the taking away of his life'.[84]

Over the next few months, however, groups of strangers were regularly spotted lurking in the area of Vevay and on the road to Lausanne. They were usually frightened off by the locals. Riordane appears to have changed his tactics and hoped that smaller parties would succeed where the larger one had failed. With this in mind on 11 August 1664 MacDonnell and Cotter found themselves in the streets of Lausanne. They had spent a week scouting out the chances to 'snap' Ludlow but these being too few they had come to Lausanne to see what the chances were against John Lisle.[85]

[81] Ludlow, *Voyce*, p. 1028.
[82] See J. Y. Akerman, 'The Farewell Address of General Ludlow to the Authorities of Vevay', *Archaeologia*, 35, pp. 114–15.
[83] Ludlow, *Voyce*, pp. 1020, 1030; also Ludlow, *Memoirs*, II, p. 367.
[84] Ludlow, *Voyce*, p. 1030.
[85] The sources are not clear about Riordane's actual presence at the scene of the crime. Ludlow does not mention him being there. See *The Newes*, 8 September 1664 and *The Intelligencer*, 14 September 1664, in Ludlow, *Memoirs*, II, pp. 487–9. There are various accounts of what happened that day in Lausanne. Some of them, especially those of the

The attack took place on a Thursday. The two Irishmen had spent the previous evening encamped outside the town. To while away the time the killers had thrown lots to see who would kill Lisle. Lisle was on his way to a church near the town gate when he was shot. He had been aware that the assassins were on his trail as they had been lurking in and around the town for some days. Various friends and acquaintances had tried to dissuade him from going to divine service that day, but Lisle had put himself in the hands of God.[86] MacDonnell was waiting in a barber's shop on the pretext of getting something for his teeth. Cotter stood nearby waiting with the horses. On seeing Lisle approach, MacDonnell left the shop. According to one source Lisle was guarded and had armed himself.[87] MacDonnell hailed and saluted Lisle by name as the regicide went past. He then followed Lisle into the churchyard, where he drew the musquetoon from under his cloak and shot him in the back. The official royalist version, not wishing to have their heroes seen as cowardly backshooters, claimed that Lisle and his guards, when MacDonnell called out his name and told him to surrender or he was a 'Dead man', had drawn their pistols. Seeing their guns MacDonnell shot Lisle dead.

The first version is undoubtedly more plausible. The men may well have wanted to take Lisle alive, but under the circumstances they were willing to kill him there and then. Nor were they the type of men to be over fussy about whether Lisle had a fair chance to defend himself. Moreover MacDonnell was so close to Lisle that the regicide's clothes had powder burns upon them and all three bullets passed through his body. As MacDonnell fired the recoil of the gun, which he had probably overcharged in his nervousness, knocked him over. He lost his hat, fell over a piece of timber and ran for his horse. Mounted, the Irishmen rode off, some versions claim through the gathering crowd and over Lisle's body, shouting 'Vive le roi' as they rode away.[88] As Lisle lay dying Ludlow painted the fantastic picture of a 'poore woman [who] being neere him ... put ye nipple of her breast into his mouth to give him of her milke but after his fall he never spake[,] but immediately departed'.[89] In the meantime the assassins made off towards Gex, a town not far from Geneva, and although pursued by

royalist press, were tainted by royalist prejudice. Ludlow's version has more plausibility about it than most, Ó. Cuív's Irish sources, a mixture of late oral memories and Gaelic manuscripts, must be treated with caution.

[86] Ludlow, *Voyce*, p. 1030.

[87] *The Intelligencer*, 14 September 1664; Ludlow, *Voyce*, pp. 1030–1; Ludlow, *Memoirs*, II, pp. 371. Irish folk memory also had Lisle armed and guarded. Ó. Cuív, 'James Cotter', pp. 142–3.

[88] *The Newes*, 8 September 1664; *The Intelligencer*, 14 September 1664; Ludlow, *Voyce*, pp. 1030–1; Ludlow, *Memoirs*, II, pp. 370–1.

[89] Ludlow, *Voyce*, p. 1031, surely taking the milk of human kindness a little too far!

horsemen made their escape. After that it only remained for them to inform the authorities in England and collect their reward.

There was naturally great pleasure at the news of Lisle's murder in the English court and in the press, where it was believed that justice had finally caught up with another of the late king's unrepentant judges. Riordane and his assistants duly collected various rewards. Carried away with his success Riordane appears to have promised further attempts on the lives of the other regicides. For the present, however, he was content to relish what glory came his way, despite being financially out of pocket. After the first flurries of reward and congratulation, however, the men seem to have quietly disappeared from the scene. As a Catholic Riordane lost his post in the army in September 1667,[90] but he had already moved to France. In Europe he was again to attempt to take up his trade in murder, but he soon disappeared from view.[91] Around 1670 he made a move to ingratiate himself with the friends of Ludlow, possibly under orders from England. Riordane claimed that he had had a change of heart and that he had quitted the service of the king, because of Charles' ingratitude, and now wanted Ludlow's good opinion. He also claimed to have been in the company of Richard Cromwell and had been convinced thereby that he should serve the 'honest party', all of which Ludlow dismissed as a charade.[92] One of the last traces of the assassin is in October 1673 in a letter to Joseph Williamson while the latter was in Cologne. Nothing more is known of Riordane for certain after this.[93]

Of the others involved in the murder of Lisle, O'Croli or MacDonnell's history is equally sparse. Little can be recovered of his life beyond the fact that he had served, alongside Cotter, in Riordane's regiment. His reward for the murder of John Lisle was a commission in the English army.[94] Ludlow claimed that he did not live very long after receiving his reward as he died in late 1665 or early 1666, of the 'French pox' and in great poverty.[95] On the other hand another source from 1715 identifies him as

[90] For this purge of Irish officers see Childs, *Army of Charles II*, p. 26.

[91] Ludlow, *Voyce*, fo. 1262.

[92] Ludlow, *Memoirs*, II, p. 425. See *CSPD*, 1673, p. 566.

[93] See Ó. Cuív, 'James Cotter', p. 146 for the view that the MacCarty who is significant was Viscount Muskerry and Riordane was one of his followers; thus Riordane was known as Maccarthy (MacCarty) Riordane, that is, a follower or dependant of Muskerry.

[94] Dalton, *English Army Lists*, I, p. 52; he was given a lieutenancy in the Guards, 4 May 1665. See Ó. Cuív, 'James Cotter', pp. 145–6.

[95] Ludlow, *Voyce*, p. 1262 for O'Croli's death by the 'pox'. See also *CSPD*, 1665–6, p. 143 for the petition of James Cotter and Thomas MacDonnell (O'Croli). The *DNB*, lost amongst the welter of aliases, confuses MacDonnell and Cotter. See *DNB*, William MacCartain. For a confirmation of MacDonnell's death see the petition of Captain Thomas Thornton who wanted his place; *CSPD*, 1665–6, p. 421. See also Ludlow, *Voyce*, p. 1262; and Ludlow, *Memoirs*, II, pp. 427–8.

one Miles Crowly who served in France, was ennobled and naturalised there in 1694. It is entirely possible that Crowly was the surviving O'Croli and Ludlow merely invented a suitable end for someone he saw as a murdering villain. Of Cotter's fate a little more is known. Cotter also requested a commission from the government for his part in the murder and eventually received a captaincy in the Holland regiment.[96] Unfortunately for him he soon found himself transferred out to the West Indies.[97] While hardly the most popular spot for the average soldier with its heat and disease, Cotter decreased his chances of life still further by leading a forlorn hope of fellow Irishmen in the disastrous attack on the Caribbean island of St Christopher in June 1667.[98] It was bloodily repulsed when, in the midst of the action, the English and Irish officers fell out with each other. Cotter's Irishmen refused to follow their local guide in the attack and instead ended up in a gully where they suffered a few casualties, amongst them Cotter, and then promptly surrendered; rather too promptly for English tastes.[99] The notorious rogue John Scott was also involved in this attack. Cotter and he disliked each other heartily and Scott was to be accused of cowardice by the Irishmen under his command and was courtmartialled as a result. Cotter on the other hand spent the next eight months in captivity.[100]

On his release Cotter's fortunes slid further, as the government had no money to pay the troops and kept them suffering in the West Indies.[101] He had made his way back to England by 1676 where he resumed his old career under the auspices of Sir Joseph Williamson. Cotter was sent to spy on the activities of Edmund Ludlow and the exiles in Switzerland. A visit to Vevay proved that Ludlow was in retirement and not the threat he had been.[102] As a reward for this and other services Cotter was given a pension of £200 per annum from the Irish revenue as well as enjoying the sinecure of secretary and marshal of the Leeward Islands.[103] He eventually retired to Ireland around 1682, where at some point he received a knighthood. He subsequently made a few appearances in the historical record when investigating a 'plot' in Ireland in 1683–4 and in 1686 he was made a lieutenant-colonel of an Irish regiment.[104] Apparently he also lived on his reputation

[96] Dalton, *English Army Lists*, I, p. 68.
[97] In the Barbados Regiment of Foot; see *ibid.*, I, pp. 75, 115.
[98] For earlier references see *CSPD*, 1665–6, pp. 143, 499. For his time in the West Indies and the attack on St Christopher, see *CSPCol.*, 1661–8, pp. 480–1. For the attack on St Christopher, Childs, *Army of Charles II*, pp. 155–7.
[99] *CSPCol.*, 1661–8, p. 480–1.
[100] *CSPD*, 1670, pp. 615, 736.
[101] Childs, *Army of Charles II*, pp. 156–7. Although Cotter paid a few visits to England see Ó. Cuív, 'James Cotter', pp. 148–9.
[102] See *CSPD*, 1676–7, pp. 287, 577. Also Ó. Cuív, 'James Cotter', pp. 149–50.
[103] *CSPD*, 1680–1, p. 568; *CSPD*, 1682, pp. 334–5.
[104] *CSPD*, 1683–4, pp. 306–7; *CSPD*, 1685–6, p. 391; *CSPD*, 1686–7, p. 309. He was also in James II's army in 1689, see D'Alton, *Illustrations Historical and Genealogical of King*

as one of the killers of John Lisle and was well respected for the deed, being the subject of some laudatory verse by the Gaelic poet William MacCartain,[105] and ending his days as a staunch Jacobite.[106]

James's Irish Army List (1689) (Dublin, 1855), pp. 33, 374–5, 489. Ó. Cuív, 'James Cotter', pp. 151–8.

105 BL Egerton MSS 154; *DNB*, William MacCartain.

106 A revenge of sorts for Lisle's murder was taken on Cotter's son, Sir James Cotter, who was hanged for rape in Ireland in 1720. The Lord-Lieutenant's wife just happened to be Lisle's grand-daughter. See S. J. Connolly, *Religion, Law and Power: The Making of Protestant Ireland, 1660–1760* (Oxford, 1992), pp. 229–30. I am indebted to Dr D. W. Hayton for this reference.

Conclusion

In November 1688 the Secretary of State, Charles Middleton, was concerned to note that despite the fact that Dutch troops were on English soil his intelligence from the West Country was extremely poor. The reason 'we have so little intelligence' he noted, was that 'none of the gentry of this or adjacent counties come [anywhere] near the court and the common [folk] are spies to the enemy'.[1] Even the Stuart regime's professional spies proved to be unreliable during the invasion; they took the king's money only to join William's forces at the first opportunity.[2] As the regime finally collapsed King James and his ministers were left virtually blind in intelligence matters, forced to rely upon the exaggerated common reports for their assessment of invaders' intentions. This lack of intelligence was undoubtedly one of the contributing factors in the final collapse of the regime in 1688 and confirmed Sir Samuel Morland's view that 'for want of this art [espionage] & intelligence a Prince may lose his crown'.[3] Having said this, however much poor or faulty intelligence contributed to the disasters of 1688, it was never the only, or even perhaps a major, cause of the fall of James Stuart. While the history of intelligence work in the Restoration period was often one of casual betrayal, brutality and error in its political life, clearly some final assessment of the real impact such activities had upon the state as well as the nation at large should be made.

Assessing the ultimate value and the contribution of intelligence work to the success, as well as the eventual failure, of the Stuart regime is clearly important. It revolves around a number of significant issues. The primary function of such work was, as we have seen, to obtain by covert means information not readily available by more conventional methods, as well as to ensure the regime's security in the face of domestic dissent and foreign interference. It used a number of means to do this from the nightly abuse of the Post Office by intercepting correspondence to the encouragement of local officers to create local intelligence networks, the employment of spies

[1] *CSPD*, James II, June 1687–February 1689, p. 360.
[2] Burnet, *History of My Own Time* (6 vols., Oxford, 1833) III, p. 333.
[3] BL Add. MSS 47133, fos. 8–13.

and informers to break plots and gather intelligence, the use of the diplomatic corps to collect foreign intelligence in peace and war, or even, as a final resort, eliminating problems by assassination. In most cases it has been argued the regime's intelligence system, when strongly led, performed fairly efficiently on all these fronts. Certainly if the life of the Caroline government was not made any easier by the employment of such arts, then it was not quite as hard as it would have been had they been neglected. A government which eschewed such work was effectively blind and defenceless. Daniel Defoe, himself an old hand at the game of intelligence for Robert Harley, was to point out that in many senses 'Intelligence is the soul of government and directs all its actions ... without it you consult in the dark and execute blindfold.'[4] None of the European powers in the late seventeenth century could afford to neglect intelligence and the English were no exception to this general trend. They as much as their neighbours were content to exploit whatever advantages they could gain by working in the covert world. In a number of ways the international dimension of the intelligence system also reflected the foreign policy of Charles II as it was centred around short-term advantages and objectives without much continuity being seen from one to the other.

I have already made an attempt to assess the second issue around which the intelligence system emerged, that of the problem of domestic dissent and conspiracy. That there was a threat from this quarter there is little doubt. The vast majority of dissenters might well have wished for an opportunity to worship in peace and without government interference, but a country which emerged from the political chaos of the 1640s and 1650s with a background of civil war, violent politics, anti-Catholic rhetoric and domestic problems, could not help but be suspicious of them. There were also those to whom the Restoration was never going to be a final settlement and who resented the return of the king, suffering persecution and even exile because of it. This problem at least suggests that the regime was right to take measures to protect itself. We have seen that there was also a debate at the time, as well as subsequently, over the true significance of the plots which the regime claimed to have uncovered. Whether they were real, sham, or a mixture of both, there were sceptics enough to doubt the genuine nature of such affairs, believing them the result of either misguided individuals or an abuse of power by the government for its own ends. While some of the schemes were genuine there is also little doubt that abuses by the regime also occurred. Given the background of the men who led the Restoration government they proved all too human in their willing-

[4] D. Defoe, *A Dialogue Betwixt Whig and Tory, alias Williamite and Jacobite* (1693), p. xi. See also Monck, *Observations*, p. 61.

ness to take whatever political advantage was offered to them by their enemies. On the other hand the threat from a hard core of activists, millennarians and even some radical intellectuals, was not something to be handled lightly; it at least remained genuine. Revolutions or rebellions do not have to be led by the masses, indeed they rarely were in the seventeenth century. The murder of the king by such men could undoubtedly have led to chaos, even if this was only short-term and if the rebels had been able to seize the opportunity offered by such an event. Thus the regime, as far as its own survival was concerned, was right not to neglect the opportunity to deal with such men as best it could. It might well have been an immoral and bloody business on occasion, but as Clarendon pointed out 'it was not wisdome [for any government] to neglect small beginnings'.[5] Occasionally the dangers were exaggerated by the government, to whom another rebellion always seemed just around the corner, and there is evidence that the innocent suffered alongside the guilty. But if hindsight is eschewed and the conspiracies are seen in a contemporary light then the government's actions become more understandable. They must be seen within the context of a state with a troubled past, where numbers of former soldiers, often with a grievance, were unemployed and scattered throughout the country, but particularly prone to live in London. They formed a potentially dangerous military strength. Their grievances were further fostered by the harsh treatment of their co-religionists. They were capable of militant action and this in itself can help to justify the regime's harsh attitude to them. On the government side this legacy of the past had to be contained in order that it was not to become the reality of the present.

Ultimately while the development of an intelligence system could contribute to the containment and even the elimination of some of the people who troubled the regime these merely represented the tip of the real problems which faced the English state in the later seventeenth century. These lay within the body politic itself: the mistrust engendered between government and governed, the dislike of a diversity of religious and political opinion, the inability to see criticism in anything other than malevolent terms. These were problems which no intelligence system, however efficient, could resolve for, as Sir Francis Bacon had once noted, 'the surest way to prevent sedition . . . is to take away the matter' of it.[6] If the development of an intelligence system could not ultimately resolve such matters it could aggravate them. The use of spies, ministerial 'dirty tricks' and so on, inevitably led to some resentment. More than once the Caroline regime was likened to the notorious reign of the Emperor Tiberius.[7] Algernon

[5] Clarendon quoted in Ludlow, *Voyce*, p. 276.
[6] Francis Bacon, *Essays* (1986), p. 44.
[7] See PRO SP 29/85, fo. 25.

Sidney complained about the men such a rule brought to power. He saw their rise as the result of an essentially malign political philosophy and noted that the 'old Arts of begging, stealing and bawding' were now joined by 'the new ones of informing, and trepanning'.[8]

Joseph Williamson, whose rise Sidney would have almost certainly regarded as a result of such policies had, as we have seen, a major role to play in this world. Opportunities were given to him in government which were eagerly seized upon by the enterprising under-secretary. Williamson also showed that he regarded it as the state's business to protect itself and that it should be well informed at all times. As he was later to put it, it was necessary 'to secure the government against all ill-affected persons'.[9] In general this could be achieved by order in government and religion, centralisation and a monopoly of information, as well as the use of spies and informers, for such methods gave power in what was essentially a 'Hobbesian' world. Of course, his schemes were never entirely successful. Williamson was never to fully realise all of his aims for he never possessed enough power or influence to do so. Even so he achieved much in this field, although the lack of continuity in English intelligence affairs is a distinctive trait which neither Williamson nor his successors managed to resolve. Progress from reign to reign or even from minister to minister was always fitful; a series of stops and starts was the norm. However, intelligence and espionage did become increasingly acceptable, at least in government circles if nowhere else, as part of the state's business as well as its responsibility throughout the later seventeenth century, as successive regimes faced the problems of sedition. Joseph Williamson played a significant part in this process. He certainly deserves to rank, alongside Francis Walsingham and John Thurloe, as one of the forefathers of espionage and intelligence gathering in England or even, had he been given a free hand, as one of the originators of the 'secret state'.

In short it is clear that the intelligence system in the Restoration period developed both from the urgencies of the international situation as well as the belief within the government that there was a basic and genuine threat to the regime from a relatively small, but committed, group of individuals. While the government was able to play its hand sufficiently well to stifle the threats it faced the fear was that in the case of conspiracies they were merely the tip of a larger 'fanatick' problem. Some of the evidence we have of conspiracy in Restoration England was undoubtedly alarmist, some of the evidence was undoubtedly exaggerated, and in the murky world of spies and plotters the evidence of genuine conspiracy was not only difficult

[8] A. Sidney, *Discourses Concerning Government* (1698, reprint 1979), p. 153.

[9] Williamson quoted by S. N. Handley, 'Sir Joseph Williamson', History of Parliament (unpublished paper). I am grateful to Dr Handley for the loan of his draft article.

to obtain, it was often even more difficult to prove. Moreover even where it seems likely that something genuinely disturbing was going on, the historian is still often left asking the question, as was the government at the time, whether this was something really dangerous or yet another crack-brained scheme from a small group of deluded men. Thus it may be seen that ultimately the value of the intelligence system which came into being lay as much in its use to allay fears and end ignorance as to counter genuine threats, or to put it another way, to extract certainty from uncertainty in the turbulent world of Restoration politics.

BIBLIOGRAPHY

MANUSCRIPT SOURCES

Bodleian Library

Bod. Lib. MSS Eng. Hist. c.487, 'Edmund Ludlow, A Voyce From the Watch-tower'

Carte MSS
31 Correspondence and Papers of the First Duke of Ormonde, 1660–2
30 Miscellaneous Correspondence and Papers
32 Correspondence and Papers of the First Duke of Ormonde, 1662–3
33 Correspondence and Papers of the First Duke of Ormonde, 1661–4
34 Correspondence and Papers of the First Duke of Ormonde, 1664–6
35 Correspondence and Papers of the First Duke of Ormonde, 1666–7
36 Correspondence and Papers of the First Duke of Ormonde, 1667–8
37 Correspondence and Papers of the First Duke of Ormonde, 1668–72
38 Correspondence and Papers of the First Duke of Ormonde, 1672–9
39 Correspondence and Papers of the First Duke of Ormonde, 1679–82
46 Letters from Arlington to Ormonde, 1660–71
69 Miscellaneous Irish Papers, 1660–88
81 Correspondence, 1660–94

Rawlinson A 173 Pepys MSS 4
Rawlinson A 174 Pepys MSS 5
Rawlinson A 175 Pepys MSS 6
Rawlinson A 183 Pepys MSS 14
Rawlinson A 185 Pepys MSS 16
Rawlinson A 188 Pepys MSS 19
Rawlinson D 916 Tangier Papers
Rawlinson D 974 'A Merry Alarum for Melancholike Spirits', c.1654

British Library

Additional MSS
4201 Montagu Embassy Documents
10115 Collection of Papers Relative to the Projected War with France in 1677
15643 Original Minutes of the Privy Council, 1679–81
22919–22920 Downing Correspondence
25117–25125 H. Coventry Correspondence, 1672–80

27872	Correspondence and Papers of George Villiers, 2nd Duke of Buckingham
28054	Danby Correspondence
28945	Miscellaneous Papers
28953	Journal of the conference at Nijmegen by John Ellis
28954	Note Book of John Ellis
32499	Letter Book of John Wallis
33578	Hale Papers
33770	Collection Chiefly Relating to Leeds (Farnley Wood Plot Documents)
34095	Official Letters of Sir William Dutton Colt
34329–34335	State Papers, Portugal and Spain (Southwell MSS)
38015	Southwell Papers
38861	Privy Council Memoranda, 1540–1718
40677	A Collection of Late Seventeenth Century English Diplomatic Cipher Keys
41803–41846	Middleton Papers
47133	Egmont Papers
56239–56247	Blathwayt Papers

Egerton MSS

154	A Collection of Irish Poems
2533–2562	Nicholas Correspondence
3678	Bulstrode Papers

Harleian MSS

6859	Memoirs and Narratives by Sir Gilbert Talbot
7365	'A General Survey of the Post Office with Several Useful Remarks' by H. Gardiner

Lansdowne MSS

235	Domestic chronicle of Thomas Godfrey

Royal MSS

12A, 12	'Viola Martia'

Sloane MSS

505	'The Present State of Morocco & Fez with Somewhat of Gaylan's Original Rise'
2448	Tangier Papers

Stowe MSS

185	Miscellaneous Historical Papers
191	Historical Papers (Instructions to Ambassadors, 1651–80)
203–217	Essex Papers (Williamson Correspondence)
549	Warrants and Other Papers

Codrington Library, All Souls College, Oxford

All Souls College MSS

120	Various Manuscripts

233	Office Book of the Secretary of State (2 vols.)
237	Register of Appointments, Warrants &c 1664–88
240	Miscellaneous Papers of Sir Leoline Jenkins
241	Collection of Various Papers
253	Large Collection of State Papers Passing Through the Office of the Secretary of State 1675–84
272	Collection of Passes, Passports Granted To and By the English Ambassadors at Cologne in 1673 and Nijmegen 1676–8

Cumbria Record Office (Carlisle)

Lowther MSS D/Lons L1/10–11
Musgrave MSS D Mus Letters Bundles 5–6

Cumbria Record Office (Kendal)

Fleming MSS WD/Ry 34 Fleming Papers

Downing College Manuscripts, Downing College Library, Cambridge

Sir George Downing's Letter Book, 1658

Durham University Archives

Cosin Letter Books, 1–5, 1660–70
Mickelton and Spearman MSS, 31, Letters Relating to the County of Durham, 1663–7

Edinburgh University Library

Mic. Dup. 653–6, Coltness Family Papers, reel 1, section 7, nos. 1, 2, 15

Greater London Record Office

Middlesex Records Association 1376/205–12

House of Lords Record Office

Main Papers HL, years 1660–85

Institute of Historical Research

Longleat MSS, Marquess of Bath/Coventry Papers, vols. i–xciv (microfilm)

Kent Record Office

Darnley MSS (Cobham Hall Estate Documents)

U565/F1/1–41	Family Papers, 1737–1800
U565/T83/1–11	Title Deeds, 1537–1885

U565/L7/4–9	Legal Papers, 1647–1701
U565 addnl./T212–13	Title Deeds, c.1250–1538
U601 E201–215	Estate Papers

Public Records Office London

CO 279/1–33	Original Correspondence (Tangier)
PC 2/55–59	Privy Council Registers
PCC Wills	PROB/11/359/46, fos. 357–9
	PROB/11/364, fo. 139
PRO Adm 77	Greenwich Newsletters
PRO ASSI/45/6/3	North-Eastern Circuit Assize Records (the Northern Rising of 1663)
PRO 30/24	(Shaftesbury Papers)
PRO 31/3	Transcripts of French Diplomatic Correspondence
SP 9	State Papers Miscellaneous: Sir Joseph Williamson's Collection
SP 18	State Papers Interregnum
SP 29	State Papers Charles II
SP 44	State Papers Entry Books
SP 77	State Papers Flanders
SP 78	State Papers France
SP 80	State Papers Germany (Empire) and Hungary
SP 81	State Papers German States
SP 82	State Papers Hamburg and Hanse Towns
SP 84	State Papers Holland
SP 92	State Papers Savoy
SP 94	State Papers Spain
SP 95	State Papers Sweden
SP 96	State Papers Switzerland
SP 101	Newsletters
SP 102	Royal Letters
SP 103	Treaty Papers
SP 104	Foreign Entry Books
SP 105	Archives of British Legations
SP 106	Ciphers
SP 109	Various

Queen's College, Oxford

Queen's College MSS 42, 'A Catalogue of Sir Joseph Williamson's Library'

PRINTED PRIMARY SOURCES

Aglionby, W., *The Present State of the United Provinces of the Low Countries* (1669)

Akerman, J. Y., *Moneys Received and Paid for Secret Services of Charles II and James II from 30th March 1679 to 25th December 1688*, Camden Society, 52 (1851)

Allen, W., *Killing No Murder* (1689), Harleian Miscellany, 9, pp. 284–307

Aubrey, J., *Brief Lives* (2 vols., Oxford, 1898)
J. B., *Some Reflections Upon the Earl of Danby in Relation to the Murder of Sir Edmund Bury Godfrey* (1679)
Bamfield, J., *Colonel Joseph Bamfield's Apologie Written by Himselfe and Printed at His Desire* (1685)
Barnes, A., *Memoirs of the Life of Ambrose Barnes*, Surtees Society, 50 (Durham, 1867)
Barry, L., *Ram Alley: Or Merry Tricks* (1611)
Barwick, P., *The Life of John Barwick* (1728)
Bedloe, W., *A Narrative and Impartial Discovery of the Horrid Popish Plot* (1679)
Bold, S., *A Sermon Against Persecution Preached March 26 1682* (1682)
Boyer, A., *Memoirs of the Life and Negotiations of Sir William Temple* (1714)
Brown, T., *Miscellaena Aulica: Or, a Collection of State Treaties, Never Before Publish'd* (1702)
Brockbank, T., *The Diary and Letterbooks of Rev. Thomas Brockbank, 1671–1709*, edited by R. Trappes-Lomas, Chetham Society, NS, 81 (1930)
Bulstrode, R., *Memoirs and Reflections Upon the Reigns and Court of King Charles the 1st and King Charles the IId* (1721)
Bradstreet, D., *The Life and Uncommon Adventures of Captain Dudley Bradstreet*, edited by G. S. Taylor (no date)
Calamy, E., *The Nonconformists Memorial* (3 vols., 2nd edn, 1802)
de Callières, F., *The Practice of Diplomacy*, translated by A. F. White (1919)
Carr, W., *Travels Through Flanders, Holland, Germany, Sweden and Denmark* (1725)
Carte, T., *A History of the Life of James, Duke of Ormonde* (3 vols., 1736)
Cellier, E., *Malice Defeated* (1680)
The Matchless Rogue: Or a Brief Account of the Life and Many Exploits of Don Thomazo, The Unfortunate Son (1680)
Chamberlayne, E., *Angliae Notitia: Or the Present State of England* (1669)
The Character of an Informer Wherein His Mischievous Nature and Low Practices are Detected (1675)
The Character of a Sham-Plotter or Man-Catcher (1681)
Christian, E., *Reflections Upon A Paper Intitled Some Reflections Upon the Earl of Danby in Relation to the Murder of Sir Edmund Bury Godfrey* (1679)
Clarke, J. S., ed., *The Life of James II, King of England, etc. Collected out of Memoirs Writ of His Own Hand* (2 vols., 1816)
Colenbrander, H. T., *Zeeoorlogen: Bescheiden uit vreemde archieven omtrent de Groote Nederlandsche Zeeoorlogen, 1652–1676* (2 vols., Rijks Geschiedkundigne Publication, The Hague, 1919)
Cosin, J., *The Correspondence of John Cosin DD, Lord Bishop of Durham*, edited by G. Ormsby, Surtees Society, 52 (2 vols., Durham, 1869–72)
Dagon's Fall: Or The Knight (1680)
Dangerfield, T., *Don Thomazo: Or the Juvenile Rambles of Thomas Dangerfield* (1680)
Particular Narrative of the later Popish Design to Charge those of the Presbyterian Party with a Presented Conspiracy Against His Majesties Person and Government (1679)
More Shams Still: Or A Further Discovery of the Designs of the Papists to Impose Upon the Nation the Belief of Their Feigned Protestant or Presbyterian Plot (1681)

Defoe, D., *A Dialogue Betwixt Whig and Tory, alias Williamite and Jacobite* (1693)
Depositions From the Castle of York Relating to Offences Committed in the Northern Counties in the Seventeenth Century, edited by J. Raine, Surtees Society, 40 (Durham, 1861)
A Description of Tangier the Country and People Adjoyning with an Account of the Person and Government of Gayland (1664)
Echard, L., *The History of England* (3 vols., 1718)
An Exact and True Narrative of the Late Popish Intrigue to Form a Plot and Then to Cast the Guilt and Odium Thereof Upon the Protestants (1680)
Fanshawe, R., *Original Letters* (1701)
Firth, C. H., 'Secretary Thurloe on the Relations of England and Holland', *English Historical Review*, 21, 1906, pp. 319–27
'Thomas Scot's Account of His Actions as Intelligencer During the Commonwealth', *English Historical Review*, 12, 1897, pp. 116–26
'Thurloe and the Post Office', *English Historical Review*, 13, 1898, pp. 527–33
Fleming, D., *Description of Cumberland 1671*, edited by E. Hughes, Fleming–Senhouse Papers. Cumbrian Record Society, 2 (Newcastle, 1961)
Fox, G., *Journal*, edited by J. A. Nickalls (revised edn, Cambridge, 1986)
Greene, D. G., *Diaries of the Popish Plot* (New York, 1977)
Ford, Lord Grey, *The Secret History of the Rye House Plot and of Monmouth's Rebellion* (1754)
Greatrakes, V., *A Brief Account of Mr Valentine Greatrak's and Dives of the Strange Cures by him Lately Performed* (1666)
R. H., *Remarks on the Life and Death of the Famed Mr Blood* (1680)
Halket, A., *The Autobiography of Lady Anne Halket*, edited by J. G. Nichols, Camden Society (1875)
The Memoirs of Lady Anne Halket and Anne, Lady Fanshaw, edited by J. Lofts (Oxford, 1979)
Heading, J., *Sir William Waller His Vindication By A Friend That Understood His Life and Conversation* (1680)
Herbert, H., *Captain Henry Herbert's Narrative of His Journey Through France with his Regiment 1671–3*, edited by J. Childs, Camden Society, 4th Series, 39 (1990), pp. 271–370
Hill, W., *A Brief Narrative of that Stupendious Tragedie late Intended to be Acted by the Satanical Saints* (1662)
Hodgson, J. C., 'Papers Relative to the Plot in the North in 1663 Extracted from the 31st Volume of the Mickleton and Spearman MSS', *Archaeologia Aeliana*, 1st series, 1822, 1, pp. 143–8
Hooke, R., *The Diary of Robert Hooke*, edited by H. W. Robinson (1935)
Hume, D., *The History of Great Britain* (2 vols., 1754–7)
Hyde, H., *Correspondence of Henry Hyde. Earl of Clarendon and his Brother Lawrence Hyde. Earl of Rochester* (2 vols., 1828)
The Impartial Narrative of the Indictment, Arraignment, Tryal and Sentence of Thomas Tonge, December 11 1662 (1662)
The Informer's Lecture to His Sons, Instructing them in the Mysteries of that Religion (1682)
The Intelligencer (1664)
The Irish Evidence Convicted by their own Oaths or Their Swearing and Counter-Swearing Plainly Demonstrated In Several of Their Own Affidavits (1682)

Jones, R., *Mene Tekel: Or the Downfall of Tyranny* (1663)

Jesuits Assassins or the Popish Plot Further Declared and Described in their Murderous Practices and Principles, All Extracted out of Dr Tong's Papers (1680)

A Just Narrative of the Hellish New Counter-Plots of the Papists to Cast the Odium of their Horrid Treasons Upon the Presbyterians (1679)

L'Estrange, R., *A Brief History of the Times* (1688)

A Letter To A Friend in the Country Concerning His Grace the Duke of Buckingham (1680)

The Life and Death of Captain William Bedloe (1681)

Lipsius, J., *Six Bookes of Politickes or Civil Doctrine* (1589)

A List of Officers Claiming to the Sixty Thousand Pounds Granted by His Sacred Majesty for the Relief of the Truly Loyal and Indigent Party (1663)

Lloyd, J., *Wonders No Miracle: Or Mr Valentine Greatrakes Gift of Healing Examined upon Occasion of a Sad Effect of his Stroaking, March the 7 1665 at one Mr Cressets House in Charter-House Yard* (1666)

Lloyd, W., *A Sermon at the Funeral of Sir Edmund Bury Godfrey* (1678)

London Gazette, 1665–85

Luke, S., *The Journal of Sir Samuel Luke*, edited by I. G. Philip, Oxfordshire Record Society, 29 (1947)

The Letter Book of Sir Samuel Luke, 1644–5, Bedfordshire Record Society, 42 (1963)

Luttrell, N., *A Brief Historical Relation of State Affairs from 1678 to April 1714* (6 vols., Oxford, 1857)

Machiavelli, N., *The Prince* (Oxford, 1984)

Magrath, J. R., *The Flemings in Oxford: Being the Documents selected from the Rydal Papers in illustration of the Lives and Ways of Oxford Men, 1650–1700* (3 vols., Oxford, 1904–24)

Mansell, R., *An Exact and True Narrative of the Popish Intrigue to Form a Plot and then to Cast the Guilt and Odium Thereof Upon the Protestants* (1680)

A Modest Vindication of Oliver Cromwell from the Unjust Accusation of Lieut-Gen. Ludlow (1698)

Monck, G., *Observations on Military and Political Affairs* (1796)

The Narrative of the Design lately Laid By Philip le Mar and Several Others Against His Grace George, Duke of Buckingham (1680)

The Narrative of Thomas Blood Concerning the Design Reputed to be Lately Laid Against the Life and Honour of His Grace George, Duke of Buckingham (1680)

Nedham, M., *Certain Considerations Tendered in all Humility to An Honourable Member of the Council of State, August 1649* (1649)

The Newes (1664)

Nicholson, W., *The London Diaries of William Nicholson, Bishop of Carlisle, 1702–1718*, edited by C. Jones and G. S. Holmes (Oxford, 1985)

North, R., *Examen* (1740)

Oldenburg, H., *The Correspondence of Henry Oldenburg*, edited by A. R. Hall and M. B. Hall (13 vols., Madison, Wisconsin/London, 1965–86)

Original Memoirs Written During the Great Civil War: Being the Life of Sir Henry Slingsby and the Memoirs of Captain Hodgson (Edinburgh, 1806)

Otway, T., *Venice Preserved* (1682)

Bishop Parker's History: Or the Tories Chronicle, from the Restauration of King Charles II 1660, to the Year 1680 (1730)

Peacock, E., *The Army Lists of the Roundheads and Cavaliers* (2nd edn, 1874)
Pepys, S., *The Further Correspondence of Samuel Pepys*, edited by J. R. Tanner (1929)
Private Correspondence and Miscellaneous Papers of Samuel Pepys, 1679–1703, edited by J. R. Tanner (1926)
Perwich, W., *The Despatches of William Perwich, English Agent in Paris, 1669–1677*, edited by M. B. Curran, Camden Society, (1903)
Pritchard, A., 'A Defence of His Private Life by the Second Duke of Buckingham', *Huntingdon Library Quarterly*, 44, 1980–1, pp. 157–77
The Process and Pleadings in the Court of Spain upon the Death of Anthony Ascham 1651, Harleian Miscellany, 6 (10 vols., 1808–13), pp. 236–47
Ralph, J., *History of England* (2 vols., 1744)
Records of a Church of Christ in Bristol 1640–1687 edited by R. Hayden, Bristol Record Society (Bristol, 1974)
Report from the Secret Committee on the Post Office 5 August 1844, Parliamentary Papers Report Committee, 14, 1844
Reresby, J., *The Memoirs of Sir John Reresby*, edited by A. Browning (Glasgow, 1936)
The Registers of Bridekirk, 1584–1812, transcribed by J. F. Haswell (Penrith, 1927)
The Rupert and Monck Letter Book, 1666, edited by J. R. Powell and F. G. Tinning, Naval Record Society, 112 (1969)
T. S., *The Horrid Sin of Man-Catching: The Second Part or Further Discoveries and Arguments to Prove that there is no Protestant Plot* (1681)
Sanderson, C., 'Selections from the Diary of Christopher Sanderson of Barnard Castle', in *Six North Country Diaries*, Surtees Society, 118 (1910), pp. 34–63
Scriba, C. J., 'The Autobiography of John Wallis FRS', *Notes and Records of the Royal Society*, 25, 1970, pp. 34–40
Sidney, A., *The Works* (1813)
Smith, W., *Intrigues of the Popish Plot Laid Open* (1685)
Smith's Current Intelligence (1680)
Sobiere, S., *A Voyage to England* (1709)
Sprat, T., *The History of the Royal Society*, edited by J. I. Cope and H. W. Jones (St Louis, 1958)
A True Account of the Horrid Conspiracy Against the Late King, His Present Majesty and the Government (1685)
Stubbe, H., *The Miraculous Conformist: Or An Account of Several Marvailous Cures Performed by the Stroaking of Physicall Discourse Thereupon* (Oxford, 1666)
Swedish Diplomats at Cromwell's Court 1655–1656: The Missions of Peter Julius Coyet and Christer Bonde, Camden Society, 36 (1988)
Temple, W., *The Works* (4 vols., 1757)
Thickesse, P., *A Treatise on Deciphering and Of Writing in Cipher* (1772)
Rapin de Thoyras, T., *The History of England Written in French by M. Rapin de Thoyras* (2 vols., 1732–3)
Timothy Touchstone: His Reply to Mr Christian's Letter Written in Vindication of the Great Worth and Innocence of the Earl of Danby (1679)
The True Domestic Intelligence (1680)
A True Narrative of the Late Trayterous Plot Against the Lord Protector, 23 January 1657 (1657)

A True Narrative of the Late Design of the Papists to Charge Their Horrid Plot Upon the Protestants by Endeavouring to Corrupt Captain Bury and Alderman Brookes of Dublin (1679)
The True Protestant Domestic Intelligence (1680)
Tuke, R., *Memoires of the Life and Death of Sir Edmund Bury Godfrey* (1682)
Veitch, W., *Memoirs* (2 vols., 1825)
Vindiciae Contra Tyrannos (1577)
Wallis, J., *Grammer of the English Language with an Introductory Grammitico-physical Treaties on Speech or on the Formulation of Speech Sounds*, edited by J. A. Kemp (1972)
de Wicquefort, A., *The Embassador and His Functions* (1716)
'A Relation of the Present State of Affairs in the United Provinces, 1675', *English Historical Review*, 30, 1915, pp. 304–17
Wilkins, J., *Mercury or the Secret and Swift Messenger Shewing How a Man May With Privacy and Speed Communicate His Thoughts to a Friend at Any Distance* (1641)
Wilson, J., *The Cheats*, edited by M. C. Nahm (Oxford, 1935)
Wood, A. A., *Athenae Oxonienses* (4 vols., 1969 reprint)
The Life and Times of Anthony Wood, Antiquary, of Oxford, 1632–95, Described by Himself, edited by A. Clark (6 vols., Oxford, 1891–1900)
Wynne, W., *The Life of Sir Leoline Jenkins* (2 vols., 1724)

SELECTED SECONDARY SOURCES

Abbott, W. C., *Colonel John Scott of Long Island, 1634–1696* (1918)
Conflicts With Oblivion (Harvard, 1935).
'The Origin Of Titus Oates' Story', *English Historical Review*, 25, 1910, pp. 126–9
Allen, D., 'Political Clubs in Restoration London', *Historical Journal*, 19, 1976, pp. 561–80
'The Political Function of Charles II's Chiffinch', *Huntingdon Library Quarterly*, 39, 1976, pp. 277–90
Andrew, C., *Secret Service: The Making of the British Intelligence Community* (1986)
Andrew, C. and Dilks, D., eds., *The Missing Dimension: Governments and Intelligence Communities in the Twentieth Century* (1985)
Ashcraft, R., 'Revolutionary Politics and Locke's "Two Treatises Of Government": Radicalism and Lockean Political Thought', *Political Theory*, 8, 1980, pp. 428–86
Ashley, M., *John Wildman: Plotter and Postmaster. A Study of the English Republican Movement in the Seventeenth Century* (1947)
Aubrey, P., *Mr Secretary Thurloe: Cromwell's Secretary of State 1652–1660* (1990)
Austen, B., *English Provincial Posts, 1633–1840: A Study Based on Kent Examples* (1978)
Aylmer, G. E., *The King's Servants: The Civil Service of Charles I* (1961)
The State's Servants: The Civil Service of the English Republic, 1649–1660 (1973)
Baker, E., 'John Thurloe Secretary of State, 1652–1660', *History Today*, 8, 1958, pp. 548–55
Ball, B. W., *A Great Expectation: Eschatological Thought in English Protestantism to 1660*, Studies in the History of Christian Thought, 12 (Leiden, 1975)

Barber, P., *Diplomacy: The World of the Honest Spy* (British Library, 1979)
Barnes, T. G., *Somerset 1625–1640: A County's Government During the 'Personal Rule'* (Oxford, 1961)
Bate, F., *The Declaration of Indulgence: A Study in the Rise of Organised Dissent* (1908)
Baxter, S. B., *The Development of the Treasury, 1660–1702* (1957)
William III and the Defence of European Liberty, 1650–1702 (1966)
Bell, W. G., *The Great Fire of London in 1666* (1920)
Unknown London (1919)
Beresford, J., *The Godfather of Downing Street Sir George Downing 1623–1684: An Essay in Biography* (1925)
Beresford, M. M., 'The Common Informer, the Penal Statutes and Economic Regulation', *Economic History Review*, 2nd series, 10, 1957–8, pp. 221–37
Bots, J. A. H., *The Peace of Nijmegen 1676–1678/9* (Amsterdam, 1980)
Boyle, A., *The Climate of Treason* (revised edn, 1980)
Braithwaite, A. W., 'Early Friends And Informers', *Journal of the Friends Historical Society*, 51, 1965–7, pp. 107–14
Braithwaite, W. C., *The Second Period of Quakerism* (Cambridge, 1961)
Braubach, M., *Kurköln Gestalten und Eneignisse aus zwei Jahrhunderten rheinischer Geschichte* (Münster/Westfalen, 1949)
Brewer, J., *The Sinews of Power, War, Money and the English State 1688–1783* (1989)
Brown, H. F., *Studies in the History of Venice* (2 vols., 1907)
Browning, A., 'Parties and Party Organization in the Reign of Charles II', *Transactions of the Royal Historical Society*, 4th series, 30, 1948, pp. 21–36
Buckroyd, J., *Church and State in Scotland, 1660–1681* (Edinburgh, 1980)
Burghclere, Lady, *George Villiers, 2nd Duke of Buckingham 1628–1687: A Study in the History of the Restoration* (1903)
The Life of James, First Duke of Ormonde, 1610–1688 (2 vols., 1912)
Burn, M., *The Debatable Land: A Study of the Motives of Spies in Two Ages* (1970)
Burns, J. H. and Goldie, M., *The Cambridge History of Political Thought, 1450–1700* (Cambridge, 1991)
Burrage, C., 'The Fifth Monarchy Insurrections', *English Historical Review*, 25, 1910, pp. 722–47
Burton, G., *The Life of Sir Philip Musgrave, Bart.* (Carlisle, 1840)
Cameron, W. J., *New Light on Aphra Behn* (1961)
Campbell, G. A., *Imposter at the Bar: William Fuller, 1670–1733* (1961)
Capp, B. S., *Cromwell's Navy: The Fleet and the English Revolution, 1640–1660* (Oxford, 1989)
The Fifth Monarchy Men: A Study in Seventeenth Century English Millenarianism (1972)
Carlton, C., *Going to the Wars: The Experience of the British Civil Wars, 1638–1652* (1992)
Carr, J. D., *The Murder of Sir Edmund Berry Godfrey* (1936)
Carter, C. H., *The Secret Diplomacy of the Hapsburgs, 1598–1625* (1964)
Catterall, R. C. H., 'Sir George Downing and the Regicides', *American Historical Review*, 17, 1912, pp. 268–89
Chadwick, S., *The Farnley Wood Plot*, Thoresby Society, 15 (1909), pp. 122–6
Chandaman, C. D., *The English Public Revenue, 1660–1688* (Oxford, 1975)
Childs, J., *The Army of Charles II* (1976)

Nobles, Gentlemen and the Profession of Arms in Restoration Britain, 1660–1688: A Biographical Dictionary of British Army Officers on Foreign Service, Society for Army Historical Research Special Publications, 13, 1987
Clark, R., *Sir William Trumbull in Paris, 1685–1686* (Cambridge, 1938)
Coate, M., 'William Morice and the Restoration of Charles II', *English Historical Review*, 30, 1918, pp. 367–77
Coleby, A., *Central Government and the Localities: Hampshire 1649–1689* (Cambridge, 1987)
Coox, A. D., 'The Dutch Invasion of England 1667', *Military Affairs*, Winter 1949, pp. 223–33
Corbett, J. S., *England in The Mediterranean, 1603–1713* (2 vols., 1904)
Cowan, I. B., *The Scottish Covenanters, 1660–1688* (Edinburgh, 1976)
Cragg, G. R., *Puritanism in the Period of the Great Persecution, 1660–1688* (Cambridge, 1957)
Craik, H., *The Life Of Edward, Earl of Clarendon* (2 vols., 1911)
Cranston, M., *John Locke: A Biography* (Oxford, 1985)
Cruickshanks, E., *Ideology and Conspiracy: Aspects of Jacobitism, 1689–1759* (Edinburgh, 1982)
Cust, E., *Some Account of the Stuarts of Aubigny in France (1422–1672)* (1891)
Davies, J. D., *Gentlemen and Tarpaulins: The Officers and Men of the Restoration Navy* (Oxford, 1991)
De Beer, E. S., 'The Marquess of Albeville and His Brothers', *English Historical Review*, 45, 1930, pp. 397–408
Del Court, W., 'Sir William Davidson in Nederland', *Bijdragen voor Vaderlandsche Geshiedenis en Oudheidkurde*, 4th series, 1906, pp. 375–425
Dickinson, H. W., *Sir Samuel Morland Diplomat and Inventor 1625–1695*, The Newcomen Society Extra Publication, 6 (Cambridge, 1970)
Duffy, M., *The Passionate Shepherdess: Aphra Behn, 1649–89* (1989)
Earle, P., *Monmouth's Rebels: The Road to Sedgemoor 1685* (1977)
Ekberg, C. J., *The Failure of Louis XIV's Dutch War* (Chapel Hill, 1979)
Ellis, K., *The Post Office in the Eighteenth Century: A Study in Administrative History* (Oxford, 1958)
Elton, G. R., 'Informing for Profit', *Cambridge Historical Journal*, 1954, 11, pp. 149–67
Policy and Police: The Enforcement of the Reformation in the Age of Thomas Cromwell (Cambridge, 1972)
Evans, F. M. G., 'Emoluments of the Principal Secretaries of State in the Seventeenth Century', *English Historical Review*, 35, 1920, pp. 513–28
Ewald, A. C., *The Life and Times of the Hon. Algernon Sidney, 1622–1683* (2 vols., 1873)
Feiling, K., *British Foreign Policy, 1660–1672* (1968)
A History of the Tory Party, 1640–1714 (Oxford, 1965)
Ferguson, J., *Robert Ferguson the Plotter or The Secret History of the Rye-House Conspiracy and the Story of a Strange Career* (Edinburgh, 1887)
Field, F. J., *An Armorial for Cumberland* (Kendal, 1937)
Firth, C. H., *The Last Years of the Protectorate 1656–1658* (2 vols., 1909)
Foster, W., 'Venner's Rebellion 1661', *London Topographical Record*, 18, 1952, pp. 27–33
Frank, J., *The Beginnings of the English Newspaper, 1620–1660* (Cambridge, Mass., 1961)

Fraser, P. M., *The Intelligence of the Secretaries of State 1660–1688 and Their Monopoly of the Licenced News* (Cambridge, 1956)
Fritz, P. S., 'The Anti-Jacobite Intelligence System of the English Ministers, 1715–45', *Historical Journal*, 16, 1973, pp. 265–89
Gardiner, S. R., *History of the Commonwealth and Protectorate* (4 vols., 1989)
What the Gunpowder Plot Was (1897)
Garrett, J., *The Triumphs of Providence: The Assassination Plot, 1696* (Cambridge, 1980)
Geddes, J., *History of the Administration of John de Witt, Grand Pensionary of Holland* (1879)
Gee, H., 'A Durham and Newcastle Plot in 1663', *Archeologia Aeliana*, 3rd series, 14, 1917, pp. 145–56
'The Derwentdale Plot', *Transactions of the Royal Historical Society*, 3rd series, 11, 1917, pp. 127–40
Geyl, P., *Orange and Stuart 1641–1672* (1969)
Goldie, M., 'The Roots of True Whiggism, 1688–94', *History of Political Thought*, 1, 1980, pp. 195–236
Goreau, A., *Reconstructing Aphra: A Social Biography of Aphra Behn* (1980)
Greaves, R. L., *Saints and Rebels* (1985)
'The Tangled Careers of Two Stuart Radicals: Henry and Robert Danvers', *Baptist Quarterly*, 29, 1981, pp. 32–43
Greaves, R. L., and Zaller, R., *A Biographical Dictionary of British Radicals in the Seventeenth Century* (3 vols., 1982–4)
Grose, C. L., 'The Anglo-Dutch Alliance of 1678', *English Historical Review*, 39, 1924, pp. 349–72, 526–71
'Louis XIV's Financial Relations with Charles II and the English Parliament', *Journal of Modern History*, 1, 1929, pp. 177–204
Haley, K. H. D., *An English Diplomat in the Low Countries: Sir William Temple and John de Witt, 1665–1672* (Oxford, 1986)
Hall, M. B., 'Oldenburg and the Art of Scientific Communication', *The British Journal for the History of Science*, 2, 1964–5, pp. 277–90
Handover, P. M., *A History of the London Gazette, 1665–1965* (HMSO, 1965)
Hardacre, P. H., 'The English Contingent in Portugal 1662–1668', *Journal of the Society for Army Historical Research*, 38, 1960, pp. 112–25
'The Royalists in Exile During the Puritan Revolution, 1642–1660', *Huntington Library Quarterly*, 16, 1952–3, pp. 353–70
Hardwich, J. C., 'The Thynne Affair', *Cambridge Journal*, 4, 1951, pp. 599–610
Harris, T., *London Crowds in the Reign of Charles II: Propaganda and Politics from the Restoration until the Exclusion Crisis* (Cambridge, 1987)
Politics Under the Later Stuarts, Party Conflict in a Divided Society 1660–1715 (1993)
Harrison, J. F. C., *The Second Coming: Popular Millennarianism 1750–1850* (1979)
Hartmann, C. H., *Clifford of the Cabal, 1630–1673* (1937)
Heath, J., *Torture and English Law: An Administrative and Legal History from the Plantagenets to the Stuarts* (Westport, 1982)
Hemmon, J. C., *The History of the British Post Office* (Cambridge, Mass., 1912)
Hill, C., *The Experience of Defeat: Milton and Some Contemporaries* (1984)
A Turbulent, Seditious and Factious People: John Bunyan and his Church (Oxford, 1989)

The World Turned Upside Down: Radical Ideas During the English Revolution (Harmondsworth, 1980)
Hobman, D. L., *Cromwell's Master Spy: A Study of John Thurloe* (1961)
Hodgson, J. C., 'Papers Relative to the Plot in the North in 1663 Extracted from the 31st Volume of the Mickleton and Spearman MSS', *Archeologia Aeliana*, 1st series, 1, Newcastle, 1816–22, pp. 143–8
Hollings, M., 'Thomas Barret: A Study in the Secret History of the Interregnum', *English Historical Review*, 43, 1928, pp. 33–65
Holmes, G., *Augustan England: Professions: State and Society 1680–1730* (1982)
Hooper, W. E., *History of Newgate and the Old Bailey* (1935)
Hopkins, P., *Glencoe and the End of the Highland War* (Edinburgh, 1986)
Horn, D. B., *The British Diplomatic Service, 1689–1789* (Oxford, 1961)
Hutchinson, W., *The History of Cumberland* (2 vols., 1794–7, reprint, Wakefield, 1974)
Hyde, J. W., *The Early History of the Post In Grant and Farm* (1894)
Jabez-Smith, A. R., 'Joseph Williamson and Thomas Lamplugh', *Transactions of the Cumberland and Westmorland Antiquarian and Archeological Society*, 86, 1986, pp. 145–62
Jacobsen, G. A., *William Blathwayt: A Late Seventeenth Century English Administrator* (New Haven, 1932)
Jarvis, R. C., 'The Lieutenancy in Cumberland and Westmorland, 1660–1760', *Transactions of the Cumberland and Westmorland Antiquarian and Archeological Society*, 64, 1964, pp. 219–39
Jenkins, P., '"The Old Leaven": The Welsh Roundheads after 1660', *Historical Journal*, 24, 1981, pp. 807–23
Jones, G. H., *Charles Middleton: The Life and Times of a Restoration Politician* (Chicago, 1968)
Jones, I., 'Captain Nathaniel Desborough: A Post-Restoration Sidelight', *History*, 42, 1957, pp. 45–56
Jones, J. R., *Charles II: Royal Politician* (1987)
The First Whigs: The Politics of the Exclusion Crisis 1678–1683 (Oxford, 1961)
Jung, H. F. T., *La Vérité sur le Masque le Fer (Les Empoisonneurs) d'apres des Documents Inédits ... (1664–1703)* (Paris, 1873)
Kaplan, B. B., 'Greatrakes the Stroker: The Interpretations of His Contemporaries', *Isis*, 73, 1982, pp. 178–85
Keeton, G. W., *Lord Chancellor Jeffreys and the Stuart Cause* (1965)
Kent, J. R., 'The English Village Constable 1580–1642: The Nature and Dilemmas of the Office', *Journal of British Studies*, 20, 1981, pp. 26–49
Kenyon, J. P., *Robert Spencer, Earl of Sunderland* (1958)
The Popish Plot (Harmondsworth, 1974)
Khan, D., *The Codebreakers: The Story of Secret Writing* (1963)
King, J. E., *Science and Rationalism in the Government of Louis XIV 1661–1683* (Baltimore, 1949)
Kitchen, G., *Sir Roger L'Estrange: A Contribution to the History of the Press in the Seventeenth Century* (1978)
Kynaston, D., *The Secretary of State* (Lavenham, 1978)
Lachs, P. S., *The Diplomatic Corps Under Charles II and James II* (New Brunswick, 1965)
Lane, J., *Titus Oates* (2nd edn, Westport, 1971)

Lane, M., 'The Diplomatic Service Under William III', *Transactions of the Royal Historical Society*, 4th Series, 10, 1927, pp. 87–109
Lapsley, G. T., *The County Palatine of Durham: A Study in Constitutional History* (New York, 1900)
Lee, M., *The Cabal* (Urbana, 1965)
'The Earl of Arlington and the Treaty of Dover', *Journal of British Studies*, 1, 1969, pp. 58–70
Lutaud, O., *Des Révolutions d'Angleterre á la Révolution Française: Le Tyrannicide et Killing No Murder (Cromwell, Athalie, Bonaparte)* (The Hague, 1973)
Mackenzie, E., and Ross, M., *An Historical and Descriptive View of the County Palatine of Durham* (Newcastle, 1834)
Mackenzie, W. C., *The Life and Times of John Maitland, Duke of Lauderdale 1616–1682* (1923)
McKie, A., 'The Arrest and Imprisonment of Henry Oldenburg', *Notes and Records of the Royal Society*, 6, 1928, pp. 28–47
Magrath, J. R., *The Queen's College*, (2 vols., Oxford, 1921)
Mallett, C. E., *A History of the University of Oxford* (3 vols., Oxford, 1924)
Miller, J., *James II: A Study in Kingship* (1978)
Popery and Politics In England 1660–1688 (Cambridge, 1973)
Monod, P., *Jacobitism and the English People 1688–1788* (Cambridge, 1993)
Morley, I., *A Thousand Lives: An Account of the English Revolutionary Movement 1660–1685* (1954)
Morrill, J., *Oliver Cromwell and the English Revolution* (1990)
Mowrer, L. T., *The Indomitable John Scott: Citizen of Long Island 1632–1704* (New York, 1960)
Muddiman, J. G., *The King's Journalist 1659–1689: Studies in the Reign of Charles II* (1923, 1971 reprint, New York)
'The Mystery of Sir Edmund Bury Godfrey', *The National Review*, 1924, pp. 138–45
Nicholas, D., *Mr Secretary Nicholas, 1593–1664: His Life and Letters* (1955)
Nicholson, F., 'The Kaber Rigg Plot', *Transactions of the Cumberland and Westmorland Antiquarian Society*, 11, 1911, pp. 212–82
Nicholson, J., and Burn, R., *The History and Antiquities of the Counties of Westmorland and Cumberland* (2 vols., 1776)
Noble, M., *The Lives of the English Regicides* (2 vols., 1798)
Noone, J., *The Man Behind the Iron Mask* (1988)
Norrey, P. J., 'The Restoration Regime in Action: The Relationship Between Central and Local Government in Dorset, Somerset and Wiltshire, 1660–1678', *Historical Journal*, 31, 1988, pp. 789–812
Nuttall, G. F., 'English Dissenters in the Netherlands 1640–1689', *Nederlands Archieff voor Kerkeschiedenis*, NS, 59, 1978, pp. 37–54
O'Connor, J. T., *Negotiator Out of Season: The Career of Wilhelm Egon von Fürstenburg, 1629–1704* (1978)
Ó Cuív, B., 'James Cotter: A Seventeenth Century Irish Agent of the Crown', *Journal of the Royal Society of Antiquaries of Ireland*, 89, 1959, pp. 135–59
Petherick, M., *Restoration Rogues* (1951)
Pollock, J., *The Popish Plot: A Study in the History of the Reign of Charles II* (Cambridge, 1903)
Porter, B., *Plots and Paranoia: A History of Political Espionage in Britain 1790–1988* (1989)

Rabinel, A. D., *La Tragique Adventure de Roux de Marcilly* (Paris, 1969)
Raine, J., *History of North Durham* (1852)
Read, C., *Mr Secretary Walsingham and the Policy of Queen Elizabeth* (3 vols., 1967)
Robinson, H., *The British Post Office: A History* (Princeton, 1948)
Rogers, P. G., *The Dutch in the Medway* (Oxford, 1970)
Romanes, C. S., *The Calls of Norfolk and Suffolk: Their Paston Connections and descendants* (privately printed, 1920)
Roosen, W. J., *The Age of Louis XIV: The Rise of Modern Diplomacy* (Cambridge, Mass., 1976)
Roseveare, H., 'Prejudice and Policy: Sir George Downing as a Parliamentary Entrepreneur', in D. C. Coleman and P. Matthais, eds., *Enterprise and History: Essays in Honour of Charles Wilson* (Cambridge, 1984)
The Treasury: The Evolution of a British Institution (1968)
Roth, C., *Essays in Jewish History* (1934)
Routh, E. M. G., *Tangier: England's Lost Atlantic Outpost, 1661–1684* (1912)
Sargeaunt, J., *Annals of Westminster School* (1898)
Schomette D. G., and Haslach, R. D., *The Raid on America: The Dutch Naval Campaign of 1672–1674* (South Carolina, 1988)
Scott, J., *Algernon Sidney and the English Republic 1623–1677* (Cambridge, 1988)
Algernon Sidney and the Restoration Crisis, 1677–1683 (Cambridge, 1991)
Scott Robinson, W., 'Six Wills Relating to Cobham Hall', *Archaeologia Cantiana*, 11, 1877, pp. 199–304
Seaward, P., *The Cavalier Parliament and the Reconstruction of the Old Regime, 1661–1667* (Cambridge, 1989)
Sharp, B., 'Popular Public Opinion in England 1660–1685', *History of European Ideas*, 10, 1989, pp. 13–29
Shelley, R. J. A., 'The Division of the English Fleet in 1666', *Mariner's Mirror*, 25, 1939, pp. 178–96
Smith, D. E., 'John Wallis as a Cryptographer', *Bulletin of the American Mathematical Society*, 24, 1917, pp. 82–96
Smith, G. R., 'Royalist Secret Agents at Dover During the Commonwealth', *Historical Studies of Australia and New Zealand*, 12, 1967, pp. 477–90
Sonnino, P., *Louis XIV and the Origins of the Dutch War* (Cambridge, 1988)
Speck, W. A., 'The Orangist Conspiracy against James II', *Historical Journal*, 30, 1987, pp. 453–62
Spurr, J., *The Restoration Church of England 1646–1689* (New Haven, 1991)
Stoye, J. W., *English Travellers Abroad 1604–1667: Their Influence in English Society and Politics* (revised edn, 1989)
Stradling, R. A., 'Spanish Conspiracy in England, 1661–1663', *History*, 87, 1972, pp. 269–86
Surtees, R., *The History and Antiquities of the County Palatine of Durham* (4 vols., 1920)
Sutherland, J., *The Restoration Newspaper and Its Development* (Cambridge, 1986)
Ternois, R., 'Saint-Evremond et la Politique Anglaise 1665–1674', *XVIIe Siècle*, 57, 1962, pp. 3–33
Thomson, G. S., 'The Bishop of Durham and the Office of Lord Lieutenant in the Seventeenth Century', *English Historical Review*, 40, 1925, pp. 351–74

Thomson, M. A., *The Secretaries of State, 1681–1782* (Oxford, 1932; 1968)
Trevelyan, M. C., *William the Third and the Defence of Holland 1672–4* (1930)
Turner, E. R., 'The Secrecy of the Post', *English Historical Review*, 33, 1918, pp. 320–7
Underdown, D., 'Sir Richard Willys and Secretary Thurloe', *English Historical Review*, 69, 1954, pp. 373–87
Walker, J., 'The English Exiles in Holland During the Reigns of Charles II and James II', *Transactions of the Royal Historical Society*, 30, 1948, pp. 111–25
'The Secret Service Under Charles II and James II', *Transactions of the Royal Historical Society*, 15, 1932, pp. 210–24
'The Yorkshire Plot', *The Yorkshire Archaeological Journal*, 31, 1935, pp. 348–59
Whitaker, J. D., *Loidis and Elmete* (1816)
Whiting, C. T., 'The Great Plot of 1663', *Durham University Journal*, 22, 1920, pp. 195–7
Whitley, W., 'Militant Baptists, 1660–1672', *Transactions of the Baptist Historical Society*, 1, 1908–9, pp. 148–55
Willcock, J., *A Scots Earl in Coventing Times, Being the Life and Times of Archibald 9th Earl of Argyll 1629–1685* (Edinburgh, 1907)
Williamson, G. C., *Lady Anne Clifford, Countess of Dorset: Her Life, Letters and Works* (2nd edn, Kendal, 1922, reprinted Wakefield 1967)
Wilson-Hyde, J., *The Early History of the Post in Grant and Farm* (1894)
Wingfield Stratford, E., *The Lords of Cobham Hall* (1959)

UNPUBLISHED WORKS

Goodison, R. R., 'England and the Orangist Party, 1665–1672', MA thesis, University of London, 1934
Harris, T. J. G., 'Politics of the London Crowd in the Reign of Charles II', PhD thesis, University of Cambridge, 1985
Hopkins, P. A., 'Aspects of Jacobite Conspiracy in England in the Reign of William III', Ph.D thesis, University of Cambridge, 1981
Houlbrooke, M. E., 'Paul Barrillon's Embassy in England, 1677–1688: A Study in the Diplomacy of Louis XIV', B Litt. thesis, University of Oxford, 1971
Johnson, W. G., 'Post-Restoration Nonconformity and Plotting', MA dissertation, University of Manchester, 1967
Marshall, J. A., 'Sir Joseph Williamson and the Development of the Government Intelligence System in Restoration England, 1660–1680', Ph.D thesis, University of Lancaster, 1991
Scott, J. H., 'The Early Life and Writings of Algernon Sidney', Ph.D thesis, University of Cambridge, 1986
Stradling, R. A., 'Anglo-Spanish Relations From the Restoration to the Peace of Aix-la-Chappelle, 1660–1668', Ph.D thesis, University College, Cardiff, 1968
Taylor, D. F., 'Sir Leoline Jenkins, 1625–1685', M Phil. thesis, University of London, 1974
Walker, J., 'The Republican Party in England From the Restoration to the Revolution (1660–1688)', Ph.D thesis, University of Manchester, 1930–1
Yardley, B. C., 'The Political Career of George Villiers, Second Duke of Buckingham 1628–1687', Ph.D thesis, University of Oxford, 1989

Index

Cambridge Studies in Early Modern British History

Titles in the series

*The Common Peace: Participation and the Criminal Law in Seventeenth-Century England**
CYNTHIA B. HERRUP

Politics, Society and Civil War in Warwickshire, 1620–1660
ANN HUGHES

*London Crowds in the Reign of Charles II: Propaganda and Politics from the Restoration to the Exclusion Crisis**
TIM HARRIS

*Criticism and Compliment: The Politics of Literature in the England of Charles I**
KEVIN SHARPE

Central Government and the Localities: Hampshire, 1649–1689
ANDREW COLEBY

John Skelton and the Politics of the 1520s
GREG WALKER

Algernon Sidney and the English Republic, 1623–1677
JONATHAN SCOTT

Thomas Starkey and the Commonwealth: Humanist Politics and Religion in the Reign of Henry VIII
THOMAS F. MAYER

*The Blind Devotion of the People: Popular Religion and the English Reformation**
ROBERT WHITING

The Cavalier Parliament and the Reconstruction of the Old Regime, 1661–1667
PAUL SEAWARD

The Blessed Revolution: English Politics and the Coming of War, 1621–1624
THOMAS COGSWELL

Charles I and the Road to Personal Rule
L. J. REEVE

George Lawson's 'Politica' and the English Restoration
CONAL CONDREN

Puritans and Roundheads: The Harleys of Brampton Bryan and the Outbreak of the English Civil War
JACQUELINE EALES

An Uncounselled King: Charles I and the Scottish Troubles, 1637–1641
PETER DONALD

*Cheap Print and Popular Piety, 1550–1640**
TESSA WATT

The Pursuit of Stability: Social Relations in Elizabethan London
IAN W. ARCHER

Prosecution and Punishment: Petty Crime and the Law in London and Rural Middlesex c.1600–1725
ROBERT B. SHOEMAKER

Algernon Sidney and the Restoration Crisis, 1677–1683
JONATHAN SCOTT

Exile and Kingdom: History and Apocalypse in the Puritan Migration to America
AVIHU ZAKAI

The Pillars of Priestcraft Shaken: The Church of England and its Enemies, 1660–1730
J. A. I. CHAMPION

Stewards, Lords and People: The Estate Steward and his World in Later Stuart England
D. R. HAINSWORTH

Civil War and Restoration in the Three Stuart Kingdoms: The Career of Randal MacDonnell, Marquis of Antrim, 1609–1683
JANE H. OHLMEYER

The Family of Love in English Society, 1550–1630
CHRISTOPHER W. MARSH

*The Bishops' Wars: Charles I's Campaigns against Scotland, 1638–1649**
MARK CHARLES FISSEL

*John Locke: Resistance, Religion and Responsibility**
JOHN MARSHALL

Constitutional Royalism and the Search for Settlement, c. 1640–1649
DAVID L. SMITH

Intelligence and Espionage in the Reign of Charles II, 1660–1685
ALAN MARSHALL

The Chief Governors: The Rise and Fall of Reform Government in Tudor Ireland
CIARAN BRADY

Politics and Opinion in Crisis, 1678–1681
MARK KNIGHTS

Catholic and Reformed: The Roman and Protestant Churches in English Protestant Thought, 1604–1640
ANTHONY MILTON

Sir Matthew Hale, 1609–1676: Law, Religion and Natural Philosophy
ALAN CROMARTIE

* *Also published as a paperback*